MARQUIS JAMES

was born in Springfield, Missouri, in 1891. He was raised at Enid, Oklahoma, where at the age of fourteen he became a full-fledged re-porter for the weekly Enid Events. *At twenty he took to the road as a tramp reporter, and in a year got to be assistant city editor of the Chicago* Evening Journal. *A year later he went to work for the New York* Tribune. *From there he went to the* American Legion Monthly *and later to the* New Yorker. *He then quit to begin a biography of Sam Houston which took him four years to write. It was pub-lished in 1929, became a tremendous success, and won him the Pulitzer Prize. This encour-aged him to tackle still another of his boyhood heroes: Andrew Jackson. This developed into two books of which this is the first and took seven years to write. For this great achieve-ment he was again awarded a Pulitzer Prize in 1938.*

In 1952 Mr. James embarked on the largest undertaking of his career, a biography of Booker T. Washington. It was still unfinished when he died in 1955. Mr. James was a mem-ber of the National Institute of Arts and Letters.

ANDREW JACKSON

THE BORDER CAPTAIN

By MARQUIS JAMES, *1891-*

GLOUCESTER, MASS.

PETER SMITH

1977

To the Memory of My Mother
RACHEL MARQUIS JAMES

CONTENTS

ANDREW JACKSON
The Border Captain

BOOK ONE

THE ORPHAN

Make friends by being honest, keep
them by being steadfast.

ELIZABETH JACKSON to her son.

ANDREW JACKSON

CHAPTER I

THE GARDEN OF THE WAXHAWS

I

THE allure of a graceful name had something to do with the fact that nineteen families made up their minds to sail with the Andrew Jacksons from Larne, in Ireland, for the "Garden of the Waxhaws." But these tenant farmers from County Antrim were not adventurers to the manner born, and on second thoughts soberer counsel prevailed. In the end just two households accompanied the Jacksons, and it required only the North Atlantic crossing in April and May of 1765 to modify their impulse to rise in the world.

At what appears to have been the settlements along Conowingo Creek in Lancaster County, Pennsylvania,[1] peopled by Scotch-Irish of earlier transplantings, the little party rested from the sea-leg of the journey. Frankly homesick and discouraged, Mr. Jackson's neighbors said they would remain in Pennsylvania among people who spoke their own burry brogue, rather than lay out for wagons and like costly gear requisite to a farther excursion of nearly five hundred miles to the Waxhaws.

It was not in the power of Mr. Jackson, or of any one, to contend successfully that the route to the Waxhaws bore an especially friendly reputation. True, "The Great Waggon Road" from Philadelphia thrust itself confidently enough as far as York, but once across the Potomac and beyond the comforting shelter of the Blue Ridge, this air of assurance diminished until the Carolina highlands were attained under the less sophisticated title of Catawba Traders' Path. The neighbors lacked the heart to undertake the Path, and, indeed, two years more found them back in

3

Ireland.[2] But Andrew Jackson was for the Waxhaws and would not be dissuaded.

2

There seems to have been more to this young man than met the eye or has descended in tangible form to posterity. Son of a comfortably well-off linen weaver and merchant of Carrick-fergus, he had forsaken an apprenticeship in that calling to take a small farm from which he maintained a vicarious contact with the world. His brother Sam was a sailor who rolled on his tongue the names of exotic ports and places. The voyage just completed had been on board a vessel in which Sam served before the mast, an association that probably elevated Andrew Jackson among the passengers to something of a lay authority on navigation.

Another circumstance of import was the knowledge of America that Andrew had derived from a second brother, Hugh Jackson. Late of His Majesty's Forty-Ninth Regiment of Foot, Hugh had accompanied Braddock in Virginia, Wolfe at Quebec and Amherst at the surrender of Montreal. He had fought Cherokees in the Waxhaws and hunted with the docile Catawbas. Indeed, the present expedition was of Hugh's inspiration, and would have tackled the New World under his experienced leadership except for an insuperable domestic obstacle. Home from the wars, Hugh had taken a wife, and, smiling at her remonstrances, extolled America in such large terms that twenty families placed themselves at his disposal for emigration. Belongings were made ready, passage money got in hand, but Mrs. Hugh Jackson simply declined to leave Ireland and nothing could budge her. The crestfallen grenadier hauled down his flag, which all but ended the project, seventeen of the families refusing to embark.[3]

Andrew Jackson's mate was of different goods. In the snapping blue eyes and brisk little body of red-haired Elizabeth Hutchinson burned a zeal for accomplishment that made handicaps seem to resolve themselves in her favor. A five-months-old baby boy at the breast and one of two years by her side only sharpened the desire of this mother for the land of spacious opportunity. Moreover, four of Betty Jackson's sisters already had traversed the Catawba Path and were in the Waxhaws, married, settled and, from all accounts, doing well. Three of these enterprising Hutchinson girls appear to have crossed the ocean unmarried, and, finding North-of-Ireland husbands in Pennsylvania or Virginia, accompanied them into the southwestern wilderness. The fourth and eldest, Margaret, had sailed to join her husband, George McKemey, who had come out alone and established himself in the Waxhaws.[4]

The family of Andrew Jackson followed the trace of these pioneers. With the breadth of Virginia behind them, they crossed the uplands of North Carolina—not a lonely journey, for the newcomers found themselves a part of a great tide of emigration spilling southwestward over the Catawba Path. Residents of Hillsboro, North Carolina, counted a thousand wagons going through in this same year of 1765. But the tide had thinned by the time the Jacksons forded the stony-bedded Yadkin and rested their blown horses by the impressive log court-house which dominated the cluster of cabins calling itself Salisbury. This was the last town they saw. Salisbury distinguished itself by a greater degree of primitiveness and by the vocabulary of the tavern-talk, which was not so much of Philadelphia and the north as of Charles Town and the Low-Country.

At Salisbury the Catawba Path veered toward the mountains of the West and the true unknown. But the Jacksons changed roads. Salisbury also marked the wilderness end of the trail over which appeared at intervals the post-rider, a weather-stained and cosmopolitan personage, with the royal mail from Charles Town and all the word-of-mouth gossip of the country intervening. The post route saw Mr. Jackson into the Garden of the Waxhaws, which at first sight may have struck him as having been rather enthusiastically named.

3

But after weeks of sleeping under a wagon it was something

for a man to have his wife and two young ones out of the weather In point of fact he was lucky, and must have known it, for few of the transient acquaintances met on shipboard or during the long overland trek looked forward to the prospect of starting life in the New World under the sponsorship of so large a colony of kinfolk and connections as received the Andrew Jacksons into the Waxhaws.

Mrs. Jackson's sister Jennet,[5] called Jane, was the wife of James Crawford, a well-to-do man by frontier reckoning. Five years before they had come from Cumberland County, Pennsylvania.[6] Now slaves tilled their bottom-land fields on Crawford's Branch of Waxhaw Creek, and their residence had a pleasing situation on a knoll commanding the post road. It was roomy enough to accommodate Mr. Crawford's large family and still offer hospitality to the passing traveler. Margaret Hutchinson and her husband, George McKemey, bought a farm of their own the following year[7] and built a cabin with a stone chimney on the post road two and a half miles from the Crawfords'. Mary and Sarah Hutchinson who were married to John and Samuel Lessley[8] lived—shortly afterward, at any rate—within two or three miles of their sisters.

The streams of immigration from the north by way of the Catawba Path and from the south over the Charles Town-Salisbury Road, merged on this rim of civilized life called by the Indian name of Waxhaw. The more desirable lands had been preempted by 1765, and older residents had acquired a sufficiently colonial point of view to damn the Stamp Tax. The land that Andrew Jackson took seems to have represented choice tempered by expediency. It was on Ligget's Branch near the headwaters of Twelve Mile Creek and the most isolated of any of the lands belonging to husbands of the Hutchinson sisters—being about four miles from the post road, eight miles from McKemey's and ten from the plantation of James Crawford, the most substantial of the in-laws. The red soil was washed and thin. The stand of pine and hickory and oak was drubbed and scrubby-looking. After traveling three and a half thousand miles for a new home had Andrew Jackson gone twenty miles farther he might have found land more inviting to the plow-iron. But he would not have been so near his wife's relations.

Even the Ligget's Branch tract was not vacant. Thomas Ewing was on it, though by what authority no surviving record discloses.[9] He may have filed with the Governor the officially requisite form of "entry," or rested content for the time being with "tomahawk rights,"—his blaze on trees roughly bounding his claim,—tranquil in the knowledge that they would be respected by community sentiment regardless of how a remote Royal Governor might feel about it. Probably he had thrown up a shack and cleared a field.

Neither entry paper, tomahawk rights nor clearing invested Mr. Ewing with anything he could legally convey, but frontiersmen were not hair-splitting constructionists in that particular. Therefore, Thomas Ewing and Andrew Jackson made a private dicker by which the latter occupied this portion of the public domain. The following spring a busy provincial surveyor and two chain bearers appeared in the Waxhaws. They ran a line around the Jackson place "Beginning at a White Oak South side of the creek by a small Branch & thence N 10 E 180 Poles"—a pole being sixteen and a half feet—"to a Red Oak" and so on, enclosing "200 acres being in . . . the county of Mecklenburgh Province of North Carolina."[10]

The rule-bound surveyor entered the homestead in the books as that of Thomas "Yewing."

4

With no sense of insecurity on this account, Andrew Jackson made a late crop and entered into the expanding life of the Waxhaws. New settlers appeared from north and south, falling upon the woods with axes and mauls. New fields were brought to the plow, new cabins dotted the red creeks that snaked westward toward the tumbling Catawba River. Henry Eustace McCulloh gave the land, and other bigwigs, like the Alexanders, the Polks and the Phifers (who had a crest on their silver), combined to promote a court-house for Mecklenburg County which they insisted should be more pretentious than the court-house at Salisbury. The first story was built of brick, the second of logs, and, however roundly they might extirpate her husband's Stamp Tax, these sentimental Irishmen named their work of beauty Charlotte, for George III's yellow-haired girl queen.

Yet for some time Sugar Creek Church was to rival the court-house and taverns of Charlotte as the fixed center about which affairs of the locality revolved. This was due to the importance that Scotch-Irish Presbyterians attached to their faith and to the robust personality of the Sugar Creek pastor, Reverend Alexander Craighead, whose wine-glasses were regarded as the finest in the county. Something for those wine-glasses or, failing in that, simply rye whisky, would have been acceptable to many clergymen and to most schoolmasters in part payment for their services. Salisbury and Camden, in South Carolina, the market towns of the Waxhaws, were each a wagon journey of three or four days, and it paid a farmer to refine his grain into liquor at home, thus reducing the bulk of the produce he carried away to sell. James Crawford owned a still and made whisky of his neighbors' grain for sixpence a gallon in toll.

Although they lived within the orbit of its influence, the Andrew Jacksons did not attend the Sugar Creek Church, but drove some twelve miles southwest to Waxhaw Church to worship with Mrs. Jackson's relations.

Waxhaw Church was on the road to recovery from an unfortunate incident. A pioneer of the region, Robert Miller, had built the meeting-house on his farm and begun to hold services. He proved "a man of popular talents and lively," but these very qualities contributed to his downfall in "little more than a year [when] . . . too much familiarity with a young woman . . . laid [him] under a sentence of excommunication for violating the seventh commandment."[11] The disgraced preacher deeded to the community the church house with four sloping acres for a burial ground and departed. The countryside never saw Mr. Miller again, though it was years before he was forgotten; and a wayfarer was the more welcome to the warmth of a Waxhaw fireside when he brought news of the proscribed wanderer who lived by odd jobs, teaching school or preaching under trees, as he dared not enter a house of God.

The congregation had been on the point of discouragement in its quest for a preacher to succeed Mr. Miller when there descended from the Cherokee country over the mountains a slender, quiet-spoken young man on horseback, distressed by his failure to win the Indians from the creed of their fathers. William Richardson was an English-born patrician and a Master of Arts of the University of Glasgow. The missionary accepted the beclouded pulpit, and, by virtue of his ecclesiastical standing, Waxhaw Church became the only pastorate in the Back-Country enjoying full Gospel ordinances. If anything more were needed to complete the recrudescence of Waxhaw Church, it seemed to be supplied when Doctor Richardson rode to Sugar Creek and brought back a wife from the household of the celebrated Reverend Alexander Craighead.

This particular addition to the luster of the Waxhaws was presently viewed in different lights, however. The vivacity of Virginia-born Nancy Craighead smacked a trifle too much of the liberal ways of the Low-Country aristocracy. Although the new minister continued to be perfection, a sentiment developed that some of Mrs. Richardson's fine qualities were unsuited to her husband's station. But these insinuations failed to impress Betty Jackson. The new parishioner from Twelve Mile Creek liked the high-spirited Nancy and they became friends.

5

Elizabeth Jackson was soon in need of the consolation that friendship could offer. In February of the second year, when she was about to bear her third child, Andrew strained himself lifting a log, it was said, and took to bed in great pain. While a heavy snow fell in the southerly Waxhaws Andrew Jackson died.

Neighbors sat beside the body in Old-Country fashion to guard it from hostile tenants of the invisible world, handing around the whisky gourd to fortify their spirits against the responsibilities of the occasion. The provision of such cheer formed an admissible charge against a deceased's estate, and a few months later when another Mecklenburg County pioneer passed to his reward a record was deposited at the new court-house, along with his will, to show that seven gallons of rye were on hand to enable those left behind to submerge their grief. On the morning after the wake Mr. Jackson's coffin was put on a sled drawn by a mule. Mrs. Jackson and her two boys, Hugh, four, and Robert, two, were bundled into a wagon and the procession started for Waxhaw Church.

It was hard work getting the sled over the broken ice of the creeks and "branches" that intersected the curving road, as James Findley, who assisted, recalled to the end of his days. But Mr. Findley also remembered that they had "liquor along & would stop at the branches . . . & take a drink."[12] At the McKemey cabin the procession received reenforcements and doubtless more refreshment. James Crawford's would have been the next stop and perhaps it was there that an especially appreciated jug of brandy was introduced among the pall-bearers who had made the cold march from Twelve Mile Creek. "The brandy was good and the host was kind and before they knew it night was upon them."[13]

Wagons carrying the mourners splashed over the Waxhaw Creek ford, vague in the winter twilight, while the sled escort left the road to cross the ice. The company was huddled in the dark at the graveside when the pall-bearers arrived with the sled— but not the body.[14] This painful disclosure sent them scurrying back, fortunately to recover the corpse of Mr. Jackson where it had caught in the brush after slipping off of the sled while they were negotiating the steep south bank of the creek. The classical diction of that strangely environed scholar, William Richardson, pronounced its promise of life everlasting, and the dust of the novitiate backwoodsman became one with the red earth of the Waxhaws.[15]

6

Elizabeth and her boys slept that night at the home of one of Mrs. Jackson's sisters, one would think Jane Crawford, whose house was nearest by two miles and the best provided for the reception of guests. Before sunrise a few mornings later "at the plantation whereon James Crawford lived . . . on the 15 of march in the year 1767,"[16] Elizabeth Jackson's third son was born. Such is General Jackson's own statement as to the place of his birth. In the opinion of the present reviewer it is the best evidence available bearing on the issue, though several of his biographers have accepted an elaborate and interesting tradition that he was born at George McKemey's.[17] In any event, Elizabeth named the baby Andrew, carried him to be baptized in Waxhaw Church and took up her permanent abode under the Crawford roof.

7

But not as a poor relation. Elizabeth Jackson maintained her inherited equity in the two hundred acres on Ligget's Branch, and in 1770 when a clear title could be conveyed, paid "fourteen Pounds Current Money of North Carolina" to Thomas Ewing who deeded the property to "Hugh, Robt and Andrew Jackson,"[18] by which instrument the youngest of the brothers became a landed proprietor at the age of three. Moreover, there was need for an active woman in a household teeming with eight Crawford offspring besides the three little Jacksons, for Mrs. Crawford was an invalid. Elizabeth Jackson's competent hand must have been especially useful at this time when the master of the home was preoccupied by a turmoil that had seized the Waxhaws, turning neighbor against neighbor. The controversy was over the location of the boundary between North and South Carolina and threatened the validity of every land title in the community. A band of armed "South Men" roamed the countryside, asserting the claim of the southern province to the greater part of the Waxhaws. They drove off a surveying party running lines for grants under authority of North Carolina, defied a sheriff's posse, and dispersed only after a company of militia stacked arms on the post road. When the militia departed the South Men reassembled, this time with Thomas Polk, one of the personages of the region, on their side.

James Crawford and George McKemey were North Men, their titles bearing the emblems of North Carolina authority. As a matter of fact this authority had not the force of law, their holdings, as well as many other North Carolina land grants in the Waxhaws, being well within the precincts of South Carolina. Thus it is to no purpose to debate, as has been done interminably, in which house Andrew Jackson was born, in expectation of determining thereby in which province he was born. As the boundary was ultimately fixed by a compromise, the McKemey house stood four hundred and seven yards in North Carolina territory, while the Crawford house remained in South Carolina. In 1767, however, when Andrew Jackson was born, both houses were on the soil of South Carolina, over which North Carolina exercised a vigorously contested jurisdiction.

The contest had begun in 1764 when surveying commissioners representing both provinces discovered that, owing to an earlier surveyor's error, a guesswork line then in use was more than eleven miles south of the thirty-fifth parallel of latitude which actually separated the respective provinces. The controversy flared and simmered until 1772 when by a compromise the North Men carried the day in the Waxhaws. North Carolina was awarded most of the eleven-mile strip east of the Catawba River in exchange for a strip about equal in area west of the Catawba.[19] Even this arrangement failed to shift James Crawford's place from South Carolina to North Carolina, but Mr. Crawford was able to obtain at Charles Town a new grant confirming him in possession. The two hundred acres of the Jackson minors, having always been in North Carolina proper, were outside of the zone of contention.

8

The settlement of the boundary issue, when Andrew was five years old, enabled his elders to focus their concern on other topics, such as the deportment of the minister's wife. Nancy Craighead's husband had made a name for himself. He organized an "academy" at Waxhaw Church and imparted instruction in Greek and Latin. He went on long wilderness journeys, building churches and rejuvenating congregations. These enterprises were profitable to Doctor Richardson as well as to the Lord. The clergyman acquired a plantation that prospered under the toil of ten slaves. His two-story "manse" was one of the sights of the Waxhaws, his library its pride. His "literary evenings" were mentioned with awe on a frontier where the social tone was otherwise fixed by cock-fights, log-rolling and funerals. As no children blessed his union with Nancy Craighead, the pastor brought from England a nephew, William Richardson Davie, whom he reared as his son and sent to college at Princeton, New Jersey. Such magnificence captivated the Celtic imagination of Elizabeth Jackson who determined that one of her own sons should wear the cloth. Her "fresh-looking," eager face glowed at the prospect toward which she bent all her bustling energy. "Betty Jackson . . . [was] very conversive," wrote a woman who knew her, "[and] could not be idle. She spun flax beautiful"—being, indeed, a spinner's daughter. "She spun us heddie-yarn for weaving and the best and finest I ever saw."[20]

Alack, neither success nor Elizabeth Jackson's tribute encompassed happiness for Doctor Richardson. His solitary rides became longer, his silences deeper.

On the evening of July 20, 1771, William Boyd rode up from Rocky Creek, on the other side of the Catawba, the emissary of a new settlement from Ireland, to solicit the guidance of Reverend Richardson. At the same time the minister's wife, who had been to a quilting party, arrived at the house. She showed Mr. Boyd to her husband's study where Doctor Richardson was found in an attitude of prayer, but dead with a bridle twisted about his throat.

After a feverish consultation, the Waxhaw Church trustees announced that the minister had died during his devotions, but said nothing of the bridle. Every one attended the funeral and Mrs. Richardson ordered the finest tombstone that was to be seen in the Waxhaws for many years. The coat of arms of her husband's family was on it, with a bust in low relief and seventeen lines of carving to recount his virtues. The widow celebrated the arrival of this monument from Charles Town by marrying George Dunlap, a member of a large and wealthy local family whose sires had done almost as much as the Hutchinson sisters to populate the Waxhaws.

The news about the bridle leaked and the swift consolation Nancy Craighead found in the arms of Mr. Dunlap gave wings to conjecture. In vain the trustees—two of them Dunlaps—insisted that their deletion of the story of the tragedy was designed to shield the good name of the church from the stain of suicide. Among a faction of the congregation, all too ready to believe ill of Nancy, passed the whispered sentiment that other hands than his had buckled the fatal bridle about the neck of William Richardson. Rumors multiplied, passions mounted and a year after the interment the population of the Waxhaws met at the church to determine according to the ancient wisdom of the Scottish clans the innocence or guilt of Elizabeth Jackson's friend.

The grave was opened, the coffin exhumed, the skeleton of the late M.A. of Glasgow bared to view. Nancy Craighead was sternly directed to touch her finger to the forehead of the skull. If the finger bled she had murdered her husband.

Nancy touched but the finger did not bleed.

Then and there she would have stood acquitted, but for her brother-in-law, Archibald Davie. Mr. Davie had practically lived on the bounty of the late Reverend Richardson and regarded the future with concern. He seized Nancy's fingers and thrust them cruelly against the skull. She sobbed hysterically, then raised her hand—triumphant. There was no blood.[21]

9

Mr. William Humphries reopened the school at Waxhaw Church. Andrew Jackson attended this select institution while his brothers made out at a school of fewer pretensions. Andy was the bright one in the matter of letters. He could read when he was five. At eight he wrote "a neat, legible hand" and had a passion for maps.[22] Mrs. Jackson decided that her youngest was to be the preacher of the family, but Andrew, the man, remembered more clearly the winter evenings when his mother's tart rapid speech recounted "the sufferings of their grandfather at the seige of Carrickargus [Carrickfergus] & the oppression by the nobility of Ireland over the labouring poor."[23]

It was a time for splendid plans. The Waxhaws flourished. An active market for indigo, corn and barley transformed cabins into houses. Slave-traders from the Coast paraded their wares up the post road and auctioned them off at Charlotte. They were mostly "new niggers," raw from holds that plied the Middle Passage, South Carolina having abandoned its extensive attempt to enslave the non-warlike Indians[24] who only curled up and died for all the white man's pains. Virginia and Low-Country thoroughbreds began to replace the "grass ponies" of an earlier decade. Pastures were fenced and filled with cattle. "Cow-pens" became a fixture, where beef was fattened for the market. To accompany a "drive" to the seaboard was the zenith to which a Back-Country boy's ambition might aspire. The red dust rising from the heels of the herd twinkled like gold in the sunshine: a foretaste of fabulous Charles Town.

Andrew's uncle, James Crawford, better than kept abreast of these changes. His lands increased eightfold and ran to the Catawba River four miles away where he built a grist mill. There was more room in the large house now since the three eldest Crawford girls were married and had houses of their own. A son, Thomas, also married and his father deeded him a hundred and fifty acres. Then Aunt Jane died and Andrew's mother became the actual head of woman's domain on the busy farm.

But for all his lands and goods Uncle James played second fiddle to his brother, Robert Crawford, who owned the place adjoining on the south and was called "Esquire" because of his participation in public affairs. Squire Robert's residence, which Andy passed every day on his way to school, was the most elaborate of the countryside and the boy was proud of a connection so important.

10

Just now the Squire had his hands full. Following the Tea Party, of which a lengthy account reached the distant Waxhaws, the Crown had closed the port of Boston thinking a slender menu would coax his subjects there into a more amenable frame of mind. But it was not so. Boston appealed to her sister colonists against this indignity and nowhere was the response prompter or more substantial than in South Carolina. The Waxhaws sent corn, barley and cattle to vary the diet of rice that went from the Low-Country. Thus waist-bands in Boston did not shrink, and Charlotte's better-half blundered again. Musketry rattled on Lexington green and at Concord bridge. Its afterclap prompted his Excellency the Governor of South Carolina, a seafaring man by profession, to remove his official seat aboard a vessel in Charles Town harbor, where the Governor of North Carolina presently arrived to bear him company.

Home-made governments popped up in the places of these departing worthies, and express riders ranged the farthest trails with proclamations calling for measures of defense. South Carolina's answer was immediate. "Every man turned himself into a soldier; even the children . . . drilling with sticks."[25] The Waxhaw militia company elected Robert Crawford its captain.

In June of 1776 Captain Crawford's command took the field to help repel the invader. In July it returned, covered, if not with glory, at any rate with mosquito welts, and the Captain out of pocket eleven pounds, five shillings "South Currency," for "English flour" and pork to sustain his troops on the march to

Charles Town.[26] But the Waxhaw men had been present during the astonishing defense of that port which confounded British plans for a comprehensive land-and-water subjugation of the southern rebels. They had lain in Lynch's pasture on the Neck ready to salute with their long rifles a British landing force in case the fleet should best the log fort on Sullivan's Island, thus clearing the way for a descent on the city. The fort bested the fleet, however, and, as the landing force mired in the mud, Captain Crawford's company had only to slap gnats and listen to the cannonade six miles down the harbor.

The Philadelphia newspapers which came by post from Charles Town were more than ever an event. Neighbors came miles to Captain Crawford's house to hear them read aloud, column by column. The post of "public reader," always important, acquired new dignity. Nine-year-old Andy Jackson was, to use his own language, "selected as often as any grown man in the settlement." His voice was "shrill," but he "could read a paper clear through without getting hoarse ... [or] stopping to spell out the words."[27] This was achievement in an environment where some of the men and nearly all of the women signed their names "X." The Hutchinson sisters could write, but George McKemey could not. James Crawford may have spelled and evidently pronounced his name "Crafford,"[28] as deed drawers and clerks frequently entered it that way in the records.

The papers that came in August after Captain Crawford's return contained momentous news. "Thirty or forty" citizens came to his house to hear it. Andy had prepared for his audience and read "right off," long words and all:

"In Congress, July 4, 1776. The Unanimous Declaration of the Thirteen United States of America. When, in the course of human events ..."[29]

CHAPTER II

AN OFFICER'S BOOTS

I

Andy's precocity in the unorthodox use of biblical names might have disturbed his mother's pious ambition to see her son an ornament of the pulpit had he been less considerate about swearing around the house. Thus Elizabeth Jackson's aspiration remained a bright hope extinguished only by her courageous death. Sixty years after that event an old man looking wistfully toward the sunset embraced the faith. Then, remembering the boy fidgeting through the long sermons at the Waxhaw meeting-house who had noticed on his mother's lap a Bible covered with checked cloth, Andrew Jackson covered his own Bible in the same way.

The repulse of the British at Charles Town in 1776 brought three years of comparative peace to the Carolinas, while the northern Colonies carried on the war. Andy entered his thirteenth year, a tall, lean, remarkably agile, freckle-faced boy with bright blue eyes, a shock of tousled hair that was almost red and a temper in keeping. He would fight at the drop of a hat, by that means mitigating a misfortune that would have ruined the prestige of an ordinary boy. Andy had a habit of "slobbering" which he was unable to control until almost grown, but a jest at this circumstance spelled combat, whatever the odds. George McWhorter, a schoolmate at Mr. Humphries's, tried it often, with the same result, "& . . . said that Jackson never would give up, although he was always beaten, as he, McWhorter, was much the stronger of the two."[1]

Andy was a reckless horseman and few could best him in a foot-race or jumping match, but he was too light to wrestle. "I could throw him three times out of four," another classmate said, "but he would never *stay throwed*. He was dead game and never would give up."[2] Like all frontier boys, Andy had used a musket from the time he could lift one. Some of his friends gave him a gun to fire that had been loaded to the muzzle. The recoil sent Andy sprawling. He sprang to his feet with eyes blazing.

"By God, if one of you laughs, I'll kill him!"[3]

South Carolina filled wagons with grain and long trains creaked up the slope from Waxhaw Creek where Captain Crawford had built a bridge. They passed Andy's house on their northward trek to General Washington's encampments. In 1778, when he was eleven, Andy himself participated in the great adventure of a cattle drive to Charles Town. There were profits from these undertakings, and in pursuit of the goal she held for her youngest son, Mrs. Jackson sent him to Francis Cummins's "classical" boarding school in the New Acquisition. This was the name given the territory across the Catawba which South Carolina had received from North Carolina to settle the Waxhaw boundary.

Nothing survives to indicate the progress Andrew Jackson made in the classics, but the oldest document to be found among his personal papers bears the date, "March the 22d 79," and lifts a corner of the curtain on the extracurricular activities of the new pupil. "A Memorandum," it is entitled, "How to feed a Cock before you him fight Take and give him some Pickle Beaf Cut fine. . . ."[4]

2

While Andy was experimenting with Latin declensions of which he remembered nothing, and cock-fighting on which he became an authority, Captain Crawford's militia company received its second summons to oppose a British thrust at South Carolina. Savannah had fallen, Georgia was overrun, and a King's army advanced upon Charles Town. Andrew Jackson's brother Hugh, aged sixteen, joined his "uncle's" company. James Crawford sent two of his sons and a valuable wagon, with a hired driver, to haul the troops' provender. A mounted company also marched under Lieutenant William Richardson Davie, godson of the late Waxhaw Church pastor.

They returned victorious but at a price. Several had fallen in the action at Stono Ferry which helped to roll the British back into Georgia. Davie was badly wounded and left behind. James Crawford's wagon was lost. Hugh Jackson, ill and ordered not to fight, had fought anyhow, and after the battle died of "the excessive heat . . . and fatigue of the day."[5]

Another British army sailed for the South, and again the Waxhaws went to the defense of Charles Town, this time unsuccessfully. On the twelfth of May, 1780, South Carolina's capital fell and General Lincoln and his army became prisoners. Robert Crawford—a major now, with a silver-mounted sword—also was captured, but released on parole.[6] Colonel Thomas Sumter with a few bands of unparoled militia escaped toward the Back-Country to reorganize and resist. He was opposed by two of the most energetic officers who served their royal master in America, the Earl of Cornwallis and Lieutenant-Colonel Banastre Tarleton.

Chaos imperiled the Revolutionary cause. Outspoken Tories who had fled the Province after the American victory of '76 returned in the wake of the invaders. Soft-spoken Tories who had stayed showed their true colors, and the weak-kneed everywhere begged the King's protection. Sumter not only had to elude British regulars but also Tory militia that sprang up in his path. Major Crawford took the perilous step of breaking his parole. He reformed his shattered command as mounted militia. Sumter himself appeared in the Waxhaws—a giant over six feet tall and weighing two hundred pounds, cool, unharassed and afraid of nothing. The distracted community rallied about him.

The classical school having disbanded, Andrew Jackson hung about the Major's camp, all boyish usefulness, and, as one born to it, picked up the manual of arms and "some idea of the different evolutions of the field."[7] But Major Crawford left his youthful connection behind when he joined Colonel Buford, whose small regiment, in retreat toward Virginia, was resting in a creek bottom some ten miles to the eastward. A day or so later, on May

29, 1780, came shocking news, confirmed in a few hours by wagons
filled with wounded. Marching his cavalry one hundred and
fifty-four miles in fifty-four hours, Tarleton had obliterated
Buford's force, leaving one hundred and thirteen dead. Waxhaw
Church was filled with the wounded, where Andy and Robert
Jackson helped their mother minister to the sufferers on the straw-
covered floor. From three members of their own household who
had been there—Joseph, William and James Crawford, junior—
they heard the story of the "massacre" that made the name of
Tarleton a byword in the Waxhaws.

A large British force moved up to Crockett's plantation, a few
miles south of the Crawfords', and Tory marauders began to
drive off horses and other live stock. Nor were the English themselves as considerate as inhabitants thought they might have been.
Had he fallen into the hands of the enemy Major Crawford's
neck would have been a grave embarrassment to him. But the
Major managed to avoid the Redcoats, being more fortunate in
that respect than "Mr. Adam Cusack . . . [whom] Major Weymss,
of the sixty-second regiment deliberately hung . . . though charged
with no other crime than . . . shooting at some British officers
across the river."[8] This intensified the resentment of the patriots
who felt that some allowance should have been made for Mr.
Cusack's poor marksmanship, as he had not hit any of the officers.
Yet the British commander meant to be just and promised security
to all who would sue for the King's mercy. Elizabeth Jackson,
her boys, and such Crawfords as were not already fugitives, declined to sue. Driving their live stock before them, they retired
into near-by North Carolina where Sumter stood guard.

3

This exile was of very short duration. The British were obliged
to withdraw and the émigrés came back, followed by Sumter at
the head of six hundred men of whom Major Davie's "dragoons"
were the corps d'élite. Major Crawford, "on a three quarters
Blooded gelding 15 hands high,"[9] his two sons and three nephews

rode with the dragoons. Andrew Jackson, aged thirteen years and four months, could keep out of it no longer. With his sixteen-year-old brother Robert, he presented himself at the encampment, and, in one of his few allusions to his military service in the Revolution, which were always brief and modest, relates that the dragoon commander made him "a mounted orderly or messenger, for which I was well fitted, being a good rider and knowing all the roads."[10] Major Davie gave his boy adherent a pistol, and remained to the end of Andrew Jackson's life his absolute ideal of an officer and a gentleman.

Three weeks thereafter, on August 6, 1780, the mounted orderly "witnessed," as he said, the notable assault on the fortified British post at Hanging Rock where the dragoons dismounted under fire and with the infantry stormed the works. But for the disorganiz-ing effect of plundering the enemy's camp which contained an excellent store of rum, Sumter would have captured the whole British force. It was a victory, nevertheless, and brought re-cruits to Sumter who pushed south to cooperate with Horatio Gates, lying near Camden with four thousand men ready to at-tack Cornwallis and confident of victory. Andy and his brother returned, however, to Waxhaw Church with the wounded, among whom was their cousin, James Crawford, junior.

Ten nights later the Jackson boys may have heard hoofs on the post road in front of their home and seen a cluster of hard-riding men stream by in the moonlight. It was General Gates and staff fleeing in advance of the wreck of their army which Cornwallis had annihilated in the most smashing victory British arms have gained on American soil. But Sumter, having captured one of Cornwallis's supply trains, fell back to defend the Waxhaws, halt-ing at Fishing Creek to rest his command. There Tarleton surprised him completely. Sumter escaped to Charlotte on an unsaddled horse and without a hat, accompanied by a naked drummer boy who was taking a bath in the creek when the British cavalry struck. Major Crawford escaped on foot, leaving behind the fancy gelding and his silver mounted sword.[11] Wil-liam and Joseph Crawford were captured.[12]

4

The Smart family lived on the post road five miles below Charlotte. Father and sons were in a North Carolina militia regiment that had been with Gates at Camden. The countryside knew of the disaster through the wild tales of fugitives who had strewn the roads, but the Smarts had no word of their men-folk. A vigil was kept upon the highway and every traveler from the south beset for news. Fourteen-year-old Susan perceived the approach of a figure on horseback in a cloud of sultry September dust. She hailed him and a boy reined up, dirty and tired looking, with a battered broad-brimmed hat that flopped over his face. His long legs almost met under the belly of the worn little grass pony he bestrode. Susan wanted to smile, and perhaps something in her appraising eyes told the rider that he was not regarded precisely in the light of a cavalier.

"Where are you from?" asked Susan Smart.

"From below," the boy replied briefly.

"Where are you going?"

"Above."

"Who are you for?"

The boy answered the delicate question without equivocation: "The Congress."

Susan indicated that they were rebels together and asked for news from "below."

"Oh, we are popping them still," said the boy.

Susan thought the "we" assumed a good deal. "What's your name?" she asked.

"Andrew Jackson."[13]

Susan told her story and Andy related what he knew of the fate of Gates's army, which was far from reassuring. The army was no more. The population of the uplands was in panic-stricken flight before the invasion, and the roving bands of outlaws who cloaked their depredations with whichever standard was ascendant. The British commander-in-chief had moved into the Waxhaws, quartering himself in Robert Crawford's house and penning this proclamation.

"WHEREAS, notwithstanding ... His Majesty's unparalleled clemency ... [certain] deluded subjects ... either in the service of the rebel Congress ... or by abandoning their plantations ... [oppose] His Majesty's just and lawful authority ... I have ordered the estates ... belonging to traitors above described to be sequestered. ... GIVEN under my hand ... in the Wacsaw ... the sixth day of September one thousand seven hundred and eighty. CORNWALLIS."[14]

Tarleton's cavalry raked the countryside, harrying the fugitives. But the late mounted orderly could have informed Miss Smart that his recent commanding officer, the splendid Davie, and his "uncle," Major Crawford, had rallied a remnant of Sumter's command and kept the field. "Farming utensils were wrought into rude arms ... pewter dishes moulded into bullets," Andrew Jackson recalled in later years.[15] Tarleton replied to this impertinence by seizing the plantation of James Wauchope,[16] a captain under Davie. By a swift march and a dashing assault Davie surprised him there. A fierce fight swirled about the homestead, which, catching fire, drove the family out-of-doors—and into the arms of Captain Wauchope. The Captain had only time to embrace his wife and children, when Davie gave the signal to retire, richer by a herd of fine horses and a large stand of captured arms. He left sixty British dead in the Wauchope yard.

Five days later, on the morning of September twenty-sixth, Andrew Jackson, his mother and brother Robert, approached Charlotte from the south. The houses were there but the villagers had taken to the woods. Behind the stone wall of the courthouse square lay Davie with twenty men. Across the road behind a garden fence were two companies of North Carolina militia. Their rifles commanded the southern road. They were expecting Cornwallis and had orders to delay his advance at any hazard. The Jacksons passed through the waiting battle line three hours before Davie took the British columns unaware and made Cornwallis lose a day.

Mother and Robert found refuge with the McCollochs in Guilford County, but Andrew dropped off with the Wilsons, six miles east of Charlotte and closer to the scene of action. Mrs. Wilson was a sister of George McKemey. She had a son named John who was about Andy's age, but of different temperament. John grew up to become a locally distinguished preacher who never forgot Andy's robust language or the way he flourished weapons. Once John found him in an absolute fury mowing weeds on the assumption that they were British soldiers. John was not sorry when his playmate left, and forty-four years later declined to vote for him for President.[17]

5

Some of the victims of the débâcle of 1780 did not stop until they reached the steep green valleys "up west" beyond the mountains, where dwelt a buckskin-clad race of men who had taken little more than an academic interest in the war, but regarded hospitality as a duty. Nolichucky Jack Sevier passed the sign— and a thousand followers, white by blood, half-Indian in appearance and technique of war, carried their Deschert rifles and tomahawks to the Sycamore Shoals. In five days they were across the divide at Roan Knob with eighty miles behind them. At King's Mountain, assisted by Virginians and South Carolinians, they wiped out a formidable British force. Dropping back over the Blue Ridge by a wind-gap and through the Big Smokies by a water-gap they overcame a horde of Cherokees that had hung like a cloud on their rear. Under these circumstances Andrew Jackson, annihilating weeds at the Wilsons', heard for the first time in his life the name of John Sevier.

This neighborly turn broke the precedent of defeat, and Nathanael Greene arrived to help restore the fortunes of the Revolution in the South. The Back-Country word "cow-pens" was glorified by a victory and the hamlet of Guilford Court House gave its name to a battle that revised Cornwallis's plans entirely.

Waxhaw refugees began to filter back to their desolated farms.
Major Robert Crawford was on hand to receive them, his house
still a military post, but American, with sentinels mounting guard
and officers tramping in and out. He bought of William Wrenn,
a neighbor, sixty-six bushels of corn "for the Use of the Destressed
Inhabitants . . . January ye 16th 1781."[18] The redeemed countryside became an armed camp, every man sleeping within reach
of a weapon, and the houses of the principal Revolutionary
partizans guarded by Crawford's mounted militia. Andrew and
Robert Jackson reentered the ranks and were assigned to the
domicile of Captain Land across the Catawba River. One night
the picket was asleep, except one of their number, a British deserter, who was dozing when he heard a noise.

"The Tories are on us!" he yelled, seizing Andy by the hair.

Jackson slung a short-barreled musket, loaded with nine buckshot, into the fork of an apple tree. He saw figures crouching in
the shadows. He cocked his gun and challenged. When a second
hail was ignored Trooper Jackson fired. A volley from the
shadows killed the deserter. Jackson dived into the house and
with his six companions began to shoot from windows. A second
defender dropped, dying by Jackson's side. Andy's uncle, James
Crawford, was hit. With only four rifles to answer them the
assailants were pressing the fight when, in their rear, a bugle
sounded the cavalry charge. The Tories dashed for their horses.
The defenders were mystified until a solitary neighbor, Mr. Isbel,
appeared with a bugle.[19]

At other times the Tories were more successful. Young Martin
McGary had married Betty Crawford and settled on some of the
Crawford land where Waxhaw Creek enters the Catawba. Returning on a furlough from Major Robert's command, he found
his house ransacked and his wife dead of fright from a Tory
raid. His first-born babe survived its mother by only a day. This
unhinged the mind of Mr. McGary who became a one-man army
in quest of Tories, prowling the roadside thickets with a two-
shooting rifle, one barrel loaded with ball for long range, the other
with buckshot for close quarters.

A body of British dragoons moved on the Waxhaws to help the Tories, and Major Crawford gathered his squadron to resist. One of the points of assembly was the church. On April 9, 1781, the Jackson brothers and forty others were there when a group of mounted men in country dress was seen approaching by the road. A reenforcement under Captain Nesbit, thought the party at the church. When a few hundred yards away the screen of men without uniform, who were Tories, turned aside and a company of dragoons with sabers drawn charged the meeting-house.

Eleven of the forty men were captured and the church was set on fire. Springing on his horse, Andy dashed away by the side of his cousin, Lieutenant Thomas Crawford, with a dragoon at their heels. They sought to shake pursuit in the swampy "bottom" of Cain Creek. Andrew got across but Crawford's horse mired and the dragoon, after wounding his quarry with a saber, made him a prisoner. Jackson found his brother and the two spent a chilly night in the brush. In the morning they crept to the house of Lieutenant Crawford to convey the news to his family. But a Tory named Johnson had seen them and the boys were surprised at their breakfast by a file of dragoons. While his men wrecked the furnishings of the house, the officer in command "in a very imperious tone," directed Andy to clean his boots.

"This order he very promptly & positively refused, alleging that he expected such treatment as a prisoner of war had a right to look for."[20]

The officer lifted his sword and aimed a violent blow. The boy threw up his left hand. It was cut to the bone, and a gash on his head left a white scar that Andrew Jackson carried through a long life that profited little to England or any Englishman.

The wounded boy was ordered to mount a horse and guide the English party to the house of a noted Whig named Thompson. Threatened with death if he misled them, Andrew started off in the proper direction. He knew that Thompson, if at home, would be on lookout and prepared for flight. By road the party could have approached very near to the house without being seen. But Andrew took a path through a field which brought the British within sight of the house while half a mile away. Thompson saw them, and, leaping on a horse, escaped by swimming a swollen creek.[21]

6

Andy paid for his audacity by marching forty miles to Camden without a morsel of food or a drop to drink. When he tried to slake his aching throat by scooping up a little water from streams they forded, the soldiers would hustle their fourteen-year-old prisoner on.

The British military prison at Camden was the District jail house with a stockade around it. Andrew was confined on the second floor of the house where the only food was a scanty issue of stale bread once a day. His youthful appearance attracted the notice of an English officer, however, who engaged him in conversation. When Jackson complained of the lack of food, the officer made an investigation which disclosed that the rations contractor, a Tory, was taking too short a cut to financial independence. Another Tory had taken Andy's coat and shoes. His wounds had not been dressed and he was ignorant of the fate of his brother and his cousin, for as soon as their relationship was discovered the three had been separated. Robert Jackson also had reached Camden ill as a result of a saber cut from the British subaltern with muddy boots. A few days after the boys' arrival smallpox, the panic-spreading scourge that killed a tenth and marked a fifth of mankind, invaded the crowded prison.

But deliverance seemed near when General Greene encamped just beyond the British works upon Hobkirk's Hill, clearly visible from the north window of the jail. One evening, as he afterward related, Andy saw "an american soldier . . . supposed to be a deserter . . . coming in from the american lines to the [British] redoubt." The activity that followed raised a hope among the prisoners that the British were preparing to retreat. But this ended "about sunset [when] a carpenter . . . came into our room

with a plank, and nailed up the windows" while the guard of
Tory soldiers "told us Green was on their lines without artillery,
and they intended to make a second Gates of him, and hang us
all. . . .

"Being anxious to see the Battle . . . [and] having only a razor
blade which was allowed us to divide our rations with, I fell
to work to cut out a pine Knot, out of the plank . . . obstructing
the view of Greens encampment, and with the aid of a fellow
prisoner compleated my object before day, making an aperture
about an inch and a half in diameter which gave a full view of
Genl Greens situation." The morning of April 25, 1781, found
Andy with his eye to the peep-hole, describing events to his
comrades. "The British army was . . . drawn up in column, under
cover of the stockade and Col. Kershaws houses." Silently it
moved out, circling under the cover of woods to surprise the
American flank. It reached a road at the foot of Hobkirk's Hill
when suddenly "it recd. a severe fire from the american piquet,
and was seen to halt."

The check was momentary, however. The picket retired,
"keeping up a brisk fire of musquetry" while the British deployed
and advanced "in order of Battle up the Hill." On the heights
Andrew saw the American camp spring to life. "The British
supposing Green had no artillery," advanced boldly, "the officers
in front . . . [of] their men, when Greens battery opened!" This
was a surprise to the prisoners as well as the British, and they
cheered as Andy relayed the news: the enemy in confusion; "many
wounded;" others "running helter skelter." But the red line
steadied and engaged the American infantry, "when the american
squadron of horse . . . charge [d] them on their left and rear, and
cut off the retreat. . . . Never were hearts more elated than ours
at the glitter of americans swords . . . which promised immediate
release to us. . . .

"How short was our Joy. . . . The *roar* of our cannon ceased
and the sound of our small arms appeared retiring."[22] The
Americans' last hope was the cavalry, which the British attacked
with such vigor that it barely was able to join the main body,

already in retreat. The failure of a single American company had lost a battle half won. A day or so later Andrew was stricken with smallpox.

At this moment Lord Rawdon, the British commander, was receiving a caller, a brisk, blue-eyed little Irishwoman whose country attire showed the stains of travel. Elizabeth Jackson had ridden all the way from the Waxhaws to second the request of an American militia captain for an exchange of prisoners, and to ask that her two wounded boys be among the number. His lordship was a kindly man, and probably he admired the rebel mother's pluck. In any event the Jackson brothers and three neighbors were liberated.

Robert was so weak from smallpox and an infection of his wound that he had to be held on a horse. Mrs. Jackson rode another pony. Andrew walked, barefooted, bareheaded and without a coat. A beating rain drenched the little cavalcade. They put Robert to bed raving. In two days he was dead and Andrew was delirious. For several weeks little more tangible than hope sustained Elizabeth Jackson in her fight to save her remaining son.

7

Though Cornwallis, now fortifying Yorktown, had virtually taken the war out of the Carolinas, the British held Charles Town where two of James Crawford's sons lay with "ship fever" in the floating British prison. As soon as Andrew was out of danger Elizabeth Jackson, Mrs. George Dunlap (Nancy Craighead), and a lady named Boyd set out to nurse the boys from home.

Andy's mother understood the risk of the undertaking. "Kissing at meetings and partings was not so common as now," Jackson said of that leave-taking. Simply "wiping her eyes with her apron," Elizabeth stammered some words of "a mother's advice." She told her son to make friends by being honest and to keep them by being steadfast. "Andy . . . never tell a lie, nor take what is not your own, nor sue . . . for slander. . . . *Settle them cases yourself.*"[23]

They found Joseph Crawford beyond help. William was saved but it cost the life of his nurse. On an unrecorded day in November, 1781, Elizabeth Jackson was hastily buried with other victims of the plague in an unmarked grave on the gloomy flat of Charles Town Neck, a mile from Governor's Gate. With this news Andrew received a small bundle containing his mother's spare clothes.[24] "I felt utterly alone," the orphan said, "and tried to recall her last words to me."[25]

CHAPTER III

DICE AND BEAR'S OIL

I

THE war was over, except to sign the papers, but it was not paid for. Accordingly, on December 12, 1782, Major Robert Crawford and Andrew Jackson, "being Duly Sworn . . . appraise[d] for the use of the publick . . . for William Crawford Owner viz one Bay Horse Brands unknown to the appraisers— Value £150."[1] This animal, which young Mr. Crawford had lost at the time of his capture at Sumter's Surprise, formed only a part of his bill against the state. There was a "Waggon, Gears and hand screw taken in Beauforts defeat," "one horse lost at hanging Rock," pay as "centinel," as "adjutant," "as Issuing Commissary" and many other items footing up to sixteen hundred and twenty-five pounds. Mr. Crawford's claim reached the state auditor in rather good order, but this eagle-eyed servant of South Carolina's gaunt Treasury whittled it down to thirteen hundred and thirty pounds, paper currency, for which the petitioner accepted one hundred and ninety pounds[2] in sterling money to restore his farm and contemplate the blessings of liberty. Yet in this liquidation William Crawford had fared better than most.

The blessings of liberty seemed somehow illusory. Major Robert Crawford had served seven years and in six campaigns, the staunch comrade of one whom another generation would mention with the great light-horse leaders of the war. But in 1783 Colonel William R. Davie was simply a pleasant young gentleman of English birth and no occupation who had spent his inheritance in his adopted country's service. He went off to North Carolina to undertake the practise of law, leaving the Major to his muddled accounts.

Major Crawford had neglected until 1783 to file a claim for the money laid out for flour and pork on the march to Charles Town in '76. The seller's receipt for the money? queried the meticulous auditor. Fortunately the Major had kept it. Proving a claim for services and losses in maintaining a "station" on his property and for timber and fences destroyed was a more difficult matter. A piece had become torn from the appraiser's certificate. The Major's copy of the missing part was not accepted without a great deal of quibbling.[3] And auditors had other ways of diminishing their popularity. "James Craford Certifies to Wm Craford's acc^t & the latter the former's by which means the publick are liable to Great Impositions."[4] Impositions, indeed! More than one harassed veteran washed his hands of it and impulsively set his face toward the gray roof of the Big Smokies. "Up West" was liberty from auditors, from debtors' jails and taxes.

Martin McGary left in quest of peace in heart. He had killed twenty Tories but it was no use.

2

Andrew Jackson, aged fifteen and publicly certified as a competent judge of horse-flesh in a region where every one knew something of horses, made his home at George McKemey's for a while and then with Major Crawford, where a Captain Galbraith also was sojourning. Andy mimicked the rich Highland brogue of Captain Galbraith who lost his head, and, seizing a horsewhip, announced his intention of imparting a lesson in deportment. Andy coolly suggested that before lifting his hand the Captain would do well to prepare to meet his Maker.[5] Whereupon the Major stepped in, and shortly afterward apprenticed his youthful connection to a saddler. This lasted for six months, after which Andy turned up at a school, or several schools, if all claims advanced in behalf of casual educational institutions of that frontier are valid. More probable is the essence of tradition involving the juvenile Jackson in an exhilarating cycle of personal encounters, horse-racing, cock-fighting and gambling.

This was the state of affairs when Hugh Jackson, a weaver and merchant of Carrickfergus, Ireland, passed to his reward, leaving his American grandson a legacy which Jackson later valued at "three or four hundred pounds sterling."[6] Andy set out to claim his money at Charles Town—or Charleston since the war, unless one would contradict the General Assembly to whom the royal name, standing apart, seemed inconsistent with the triumph of freedom's cause.

Thus it was that the Revolutionary orphan found himself on a March day of 1783[7] leaving the Quarter House Tavern possessed of a fortune sufficient to begin his life auspiciously—which Andrew Jackson, according to his lights, meant to do. Three or four hundred pounds sterling would have worked wonders with the acres on Twelve Mile Creek of which the death of his brothers had put Andrew in sole possession. Half of the sum would have seen him through college. But it was not toward the Garden of the Waxhaws or the classroom that thrifty Hugh Jackson's heir turned his horse's head.

From the Quarter House it was four miles by the Broad Path to Charleston's battered military wall, a native work of masonry contrived of oyster shells and lime. On either side of this road rice-fields alternated with a jungle of moss-curtained live-oak, palmetto, myrtle and fine-leafed little cassina trees with their bright red Christmas berries. Vine-covered gate-posts framed a prospect of white-and-brick plantation seats—Belmont, the ruined home of the Pinckneys; Accabee, the Dart place—a stimulating overture to the richest and gayest of American cities.

The long occupation of Charleston by the British army had made refugees of all the great families who had turned their backs on the King. A few had gone to the Waxhaws[8] where Andy had made acquaintances among the boys of his age. This was natural. Andrew Jackson belonged to all the aristocracy there was in the Back-Country, and think you him not oblivious to this fact. The Low-Country émigrés had pressed courteous invitations to which Andrew could hardly have anticipated an opportunity to comply so soon.

Beyond the fortifications the Broad Path became Meeting Street paved with English cobblestones transported as ballast. The town was a little shabby, though not to Andrew's eyes, but lively with the stir of reclamation. In great houses windows long dark gleamed again, neglected gardens took form and fragrance and gave up silver buried at the roots of magnolia trees. "There is courtesy here, without stiffness or formality," wrote a German traveler. Neither "domestic circumstances" nor "religious principles" stood in the way of "pleasures of every kind." A French dancing master was sponsored by the "first minister of the town" who knew how to retain the favor of his parishioners. "Milliners and hair dressers . . . grow rich."[9] And of course there were the races, for which "courts of justice" closed, "all the schools were regularly let out," and merchants put up their shutters. "Clergymen and judges" joined the procession to the track, and the stones of Meeting Street rang as "Splendid equippages" rolled by, displaying "liveried outriders—gentlemen in fashionably London made clothes."[10]

Horses, horses. In the talk at McCrady's Tavern and the paddock at New Market, the late fight for freedom loomed merely as a vexatious interruption to the historical progress of affairs on the Charleston turf. "Not only were horses thrown out of training" by the hostilities, "but on the appearance of Lord Cornwallis' army they were . . . hid in the swamps." In no Colony or Province did a larger proportion of the gentry espouse the rebel cause, George III "being neither a sportsman nor a horseman."[11] They bore their parts well, these Low-Country dandies, and now they were back to exchange reminiscences—of their horses.

Twice Captain James, "surest scout of Marion," had made escapes impossible to explain, except by the fact that he rode Roebuck. And imagine Mr. Ravenel's indignation upon finding his Lucy ("out of Rose by imported Friar") ridden by a *servant* of the American Colonel Maham. Mr. Ravenel presented himself to General Marion. He had decided to join the Army. That was good, said Marion. But there was only one horse in the corps that Mr. Ravenel desired to ride. Yes? said General Marion.

Yes, replied Mr. Ravenel, Colonel Maham's servant's horse. It was arranged. . . . And Red Doe was at the post again, but a couple of years before she had carried a British officer at the head of a firing squad to execute an American soldier named Hunter. The condemned man asked the officer to dismount as he had something of importance to communicate. Thinking the prisoner meant to reveal military information the officer complied. No sooner did his foot leave the stirrup than a single bound landed Hunter in the saddle, and Red Doe flashed into a thicket before the astonished soldiery could close their mouths.[12]

Andrew Jackson had the qualities his late sovereign lacked. He was both a sportsman and a horseman but, alack, his luck was bad. The legacy dwindled and disappeared. The young adventurer was in debt to his landlord, and, one evening wondering how he could pay it, strolled into a place where dice clicked across a tap-room table in a high-stake game of rattle and snap. A player offered two hundred dollars against Andrew's horse. Andy thought for a while and then requested the dice. He cast and won. The landlord was paid and Andy left for home with "new spirits infused into me."[13]

3

After that Andrew was not long for the Waxhaws, where one occupation seemed as unstable as the next. He went to school at Queen's Museum in Charlotte. He taught a school near home. Girls as well as horses swam within his ken. Susan Smart thought "Ande" a "lank, leaning-forward fellow." She also remembered his eyes, and that there was "something very agreeable about him."[14] Mary Massey is said to have entertained a less favorable opinion,[15] but Mary Crawford received Andrew's ardent addresses with a sense of satisfaction not shared by her father, the Major. On December 4, 1784, Andrew Jackson acted as an appraiser of "a Bay horse of James Crawford Lost in the Service of the State,"[16] and a few days thereafter was gone for ever from the scenes of his boyhood. Some have said it was to be shut of

reproaches over his squandered inheritance. Local tradition adds
a complication over Mary Crawford and a tender parting "on the
bank of the Catawba." In any event, of that farewell Jackson
carried away a memory to be recalled at strange hours and places
as when, across the débris of fifty years, a silver snuff-box found
its way from the hands of a lonely widower in the White House
to Mary Crawford Dunlap in the Waxhaws.[17]

Andy spent Christmas of 1784 at the lively Rowan House in
Salisbury, North Carolina, where refreshment for man and beast
cost four shillings a day. The spirit of Yuletide may have favored
the wayfarer for he persuaded Spruce Macay, who already had
two young scapegraces in charge, to let him read law in his office.

The new protégé of Mr. Macay—pronounced Macoy—was soon
known and long remembered by the inhabitants. "Andrew Jackson was the most roaring, rollicking, game-cocking, horse-racing,
card-playing, mischievous fellow, that ever lived in Salisbury . . .
the head of the rowdies hereabouts . . . more in the stable than in
the office."[18] But there was something instantly attractive about
this tall young Celt, not eighteen when he came to Salisbury, with
intense blue eyes and a long, fair, pock-marked, apperceptive face
interestingly seamed by a scar that lost itself in his ruddy hair.
An acute imagination animated that face—an imagination of
action, fierce in its loyalties and its hatreds, projecting through dim
generations of Scottish rains and Irish mists to strike confusion in
the breast of this plunging orphan on a savage hinterland across
the ocean.

Not that Salisbury would have fancied being called a part of
a savage hinterland. The Waxhaws—yes; but in Salisbury a
native of the Waxhaws could feel that he had accomplished a steep
social climb. Salisbury was an old town at the beginning of the
Revolution. It was not large—some fifty families—but no
southern towns were large. Several of those families, including
that of Spruce Macay, were wealthy and maintained mansions
with a Low-Country flavor. What of it? Andrew Jackson who
had been to Charleston declined to be terrified by Salisbury. He
dressed as well as, or better than, he could afford. Debts or not,

he rode a good horse; and no horse was ridden better. If liquor, cards and mulatto mistresses filled the rôles that legend assigns to them in the history of the student's residence in Salisbury, these diversions were enjoyed in a company that enabled Andrew to attain a position of leadership among the socially eligible bloods of the countryside.

Nor were the young ladies of quality indifferent. Nancy Jarret "often met him at parties, balls and . . . at the house of my relative, Mr. McKay. I knew him as well as I did any other young man when I was a single girl . . . for his ways and manners . . . were most captivating. . . . We all knew that he was wild . . . that he gambled some and was by no means a Christian young man. . . . When he was calm he talked slowly and with good selected language. But . . . animated . . . he would talk fast with a very marked North-Irish brogue. . . . Either calm or animated there was something about him I cannot describe except to say that it was *a presence.* . . . This I and all the other girls in Salisbury . . . talked about among ourselves."[19]

Their mothers also talked. Two hundred Waxhaw acres did not support Andrew Jackson's scale of living. They feared that he gambled not always as a sportsman who can afford to lose, but as an adventurer who has to win. They would have been glad to hear that salutary progress in his legal studies promised a swift removal of the captivating "presence" from Salisbury.

They heard the contrary. Judges rode the circuit, trailed by a curious following of lawyers and sharpsters. Courts came and went, filling the sprawling Rowan House with patrons and the town with news: Ordered, that "Susannah Hartman, Orphan, 13 years old, be bound to Paul Rodsmith to serve till she shall attain the age of 18." . . . Recommended, that James Hughes be "exempt from Taxes being poor, aged & infirm and having a large family." . . . Ordered, that John Fraize "keep the County free from all Costs respecting a Bastard child begot on the Body of Dorotha Goose." . . . Ordered, that tavern proprietors serve, on request, "small Beer or Grog" with dinners at no extra charge.[20]

John McNairy completed his preparation in the office of Mr. Macay and was admitted to the bar, but the conclusion of Andrew Jackson's second year in Salisbury found him engrossed principally by his duties as a manager of the Christmas ball. It was the ambition of the gilded youth of Salisbury that this affair should eclipse all precedent.

It did so. Every one came—never the girls more beautiful, the young men more gallant: no flaw anywhere until a flurry at the door stopped the music, stopped the dancing. There stood Molly and Rachel Wood, mother and daughter, the only white prostitutes in Salisbury. Moreover, their cards of invitation were in order. Speechless chaperons shooed their charges into a buzzing group at the far side of the hall.

Andrew Jackson approached them. He "humbly apologized." He alone had sent the cards to Molly and Rachel Wood, as "a piece of fun," not thinking for an instant they could misunderstand. One story is that Jackson was half-forgiven, another that he had no choice but to follow Molly and Rachel into the night.[21]

4

Not long after the Christmas ball Andrew parted company from Spruce Macay and attached himself to Colonel John Stokes, one of the most brilliant figures in the annals of the North Carolina bar. If Colonel Stokes's convivial habits cost him a conspicuous place in history, they also sponsored a sympathetic view of the contiguous problems of youth and wild oats. Moreover, the Colonel had lost a hand at Buford's Defeat and may have been nursed at Waxhaw Church by Andy and his mother. In place of the missing hand he wore a silver knob, and, whether pleading a cause in court or leading a tap-room chorus, dramatized his points by bringing the knob down on a table so that it rang like a bell.

After six months of John Stokes's guidance, the pupil joined the itinerant court at Wadesborough. On September 26, 1787, Judges Samuel Ashe and John F. Williams, after examination, directed that "Andrew Jackson . . . a person of unblemished moral character, and . . . competent . . . knowledge of the law," be admitted to "practice . . . in the said several courts of pleas and quarter sessions . . . with all and singular the privileges and emoluments which . . . appertain to attorneys."[22]

In November the court arrived at Salisbury. "The girls had a habit," wrote Nancy Jarret, "of going to the court-house when any friend or acquaintance . . . was to be licensed." They saw Andrew in "a new suit, with broad-cloth coat [and] ruffled shirt . . . his abundant suit of dark red hair combed carefully back . . . and, I suspect, made to lay down smooth with bear's oil. He was full six feet tall and very slender, but . . . graceful. . . . His eyes *were* handsome . . . a kind of steel-blue. I have talked with him a great many times and never saw him avert his eyes from me for an instant."[23]

One of the judges advised Jackson to try his fortunes "up West" and he left Salisbury with the court. The end of the short North Carolina winter found Lawyer Jackson a fairly seasoned circuit campaigner for a boy not old enough to vote. But it was all on the side of experience rather than the more negotiable emoluments which appertain to attorneys. At Richmond he is supposed to have defended a thief on a guarantee of acquittal or no fee. The defendant got the whipping post and his counsel left town owing a board bill. At Martinsville he loafed with two friends who kept a store, and visited at the pleasant home of his schoolmate, John McNairy. At Johnsonville Colonel William Moore rode his horse into the court-room and was fined fifty pounds after a posse had dismounted him. There, in his first case of record, Barrister Jackson was successful in an action against the Coroner growing out of a family dispute among the county officers.[24]

Brighter prospects spread before him. Andrew had made himself agreeable as a guest of the influential McNairys whose neighbor was Governor Martin, of North Carolina. Indeed, he had organized the first known celebration of the anniversary of the Battle of Guilford Court House, with speeches, horse-races and a cock-fight.[25] North Carolina extended to the Mississippi. The westernmost reach of this domain was hardly explored, but one hundred and eighty miles beyond the regular outposts of civilization, astride a vague stream named Cumberland, a band of settlers had made an island for themselves which they called the Western District of the state. Jackson's eye was on the Western District, and the most plausible explanation of what followed seems to be that, to smooth his own path, he communicated this interest to John McNairy,[26] by no means a timid young man, but also by no means an adventurer, probably because his future was provided for at home, while Jackson had his way in the world to win. In December of 1787 the Legislature dignified the Western District with a Superior Court and elected John McNairy to its bench.[27] No legislative provision was made for an attorney-general, as the public prosecutor was called. This appears to have been a disappointment to Jackson,[28] until it occurred to him and McNairy that this officer could be appointed by court, thus providing the sought-for means of financing a reconnaissance of the West.

5

It was a triumph of enterprise as well as luck, for with all his impetuosity there was a shrewd streak in the composition of this superficially irresponsible young Back-Country dandy. Andrew Jackson had got what he was after, a pioneering trip de luxe with the prospect of comfortable fees to pad the prickly edges of life in the new land of promise, where thousands of unhappy countrymen would have sold their shirts for a chance to swing an ax.

Jackson had watched the western fever mount as the trickle of disillusioned soldiers swelled to a bold stream of restless men from Georgia to New Hampshire, who converged upon the mountain passes as the best escape from the fruits of a revolution that seemed to have soured on the vine. The national government of the American "Confederation," a frail enough reed in war-time, had declined to a simulacrum of bankrupt authority, unable to meet interest on its debts, to command respect abroad or obedience at home. Reflective men who had borne arms in support of the flaming watchwords of independence brooded over the failure of the democratic experiment. Nathaniel Gorham, presiding officer of Congress and weary of the humiliation, caused a brother of Frederick the Great to be approached with a view of establishing a monarchial government to avert retrocession to England, who, believing her moment near, complacently retained troops on our soil. Nor could the states keep peace within their several households. Massachusetts had contended against armed rebellion, while others forestalled it by mixed displays of courage and cowardice.

North Carolina's problems arose chiefly from the isolated character of her ultramontane settlements which had little in common socially, economically or politically with the eastern part of the state. These settlements comprised two geographically distinct groups the most remote of which was the Western District athwart the Cumberland, accessible only by traversing nearly two hundred miles of Indian country. As the keen Jackson probably knew, the Western District was speculating already on the advantages of an independent political future. The other transmountain settlements filling the narrow Holston, Nolichucky and Watauga Valleys just beyond the crest of the Blue Ridge, were past the speculating stage. They had seceded from the parent commonwealth under the title of the State of Franklin. This circumstance gave a lively cast to the proposed journey of Messrs. McNairy and Jackson who must pass through Franklin, where other North Carolina officials riding in on horseback had ridden out on rails, and held themselves fortunate for the privilege.

Franklin stood by republican institutions. Its legislators traveled to their meetings with rifles under their arms which sustained the spirits by a chance shot at an Indian or North Carolina partizan, democratically equal in their eyes; sustained the body by adding to the mound of game outside the log house in Jonesborough where the lawmakers conducted their deliberations. Otter skins were legal tender which might have placed the fiduciary system of Franklin on a sounder basis than some of the paper-stuffed treasuries nearer the seaboard but for the under-mining influence of counterfeiters. Bales of what had passed for otter pelts were found to be raccoon with otter tails sewed on. But as the Legislature had also monetized a number of other articles, including "good" whisky, a collapse of the state's credit was averted. The personality of their Executive remained, how-ever, the greatest resource of the over-mountain men.

The Governor of Franklin was John Sevier—pronounced Seveer. Without him it is hard to see how the state could have lasted three months. With him it had lasted three years. The history of Nolichucky Jack was a legend among the people who had known him most of his life. He could shoot the straightest, ride the hardest, and dance the best. He was tall, handsome, a soldier and a cavalier. The belle of the valleys was Catherine Sherrill. An attack on Watauga Fort caught her outside the walls. Under a "hail" of arrows, she tried to climb the stockade, slipped and was snatched to safety by John Sevier. This enabled Bonny Kate to choose among a shoal of suitors. Just before he started for King's Mountain, she married Nolichucky Jack. His military record surpassed Cæsar's—at any rate, in the eyes of the border legion he had led in twenty-six battles against the Indians and one against the British without defeat.

But when Andrew Jackson arrived at Morganton in the foot-hills to prepare for his journey West he learned, to his great satisfaction, that victory had incredibly deserted the banner of John Sevier. North Carolina had moved against him with the sinister weapon of tact. There was no arrow in the quiver of Nolichucky Jack to contend with such womanish artifices. His right-hand man, John Tipton, had gone over to the foe, and, cocking a rifle, declared himself a court sitting by North Carolina authority ten miles from Sevier's capital at Jonesborough. Sevier raided this tribunal and was ready for civil war. So was Tipton, and the poison of conciliation had had its affect. Nolichucky Jack's force melted at the first encounter. Two of the Governor's sons were captured. Tipton ordered them hanged, but cursing himself for his weakness, signed a reprieve. Sevier, senior,

plunged into the wilderness and began an Indian campaign—
a stratagem ever calculated to burnish the fortunes of a frontier
captain.

The Spanish Minister to the United States continued to address him as Governor and the nebulous rumors of western intrigue with Madrid glowed anew. Louisiana was on every lip.
Explanations of this circumstance ranged from a comprehensive
frontier conspiracy to open the Mississippi to western commerce
by the capture of New Orleans, to the creation of a separate republic beyond the mountains under protection of Spain as a
buffer to hostile encroachment by the seaboard Confederation.

Irrespective of this complication, the absence of Sevier gave
North Carolina an opportunity she did not neglect. A "loyal"
court was established in Jonesborough. In April of 1788, Mc-
Nairy joined Jackson at Morganton where a red road rolled
away toward the high blue mist. No time could be lost if they
were to open court on the Cumberland for the session of the
second quarter of the year. With two pistols slung from his
saddle, a beautiful rifle lashed to the pack of his stout "bat"
mare and trailed by a troop of hunting dogs Andrew Jackson
departed, adequately prepared to defend the dignity of the Old
North State while in transit through the seduced domain of
Nolichucky Jack.

In quiet Salisbury Nancy Jarret sighed. Her graceful friend
"would get himself killed" the next thing she knew.

BOOK TWO

THE ROBE

"Do what is *right* between these parties. That is what the law always *means*."

JUDGE JACKSON to a jury.

CHAPTER IV

The Mero District

I

ANDREW JACKSON stated with pride that the stout mare carried "half a dozen books" over the windy summits of the Blue Ridge. Of these Matthew Bacon's *Abridgement of the Law* was the sheet anchor of the journeyman solicitor. Or so it seemed to Waightstill Avery who found himself opposed to young Mr. Jackson in a suit before the Superior Court at Jonesborough, where Jackson and McNairy had decided to tarry, finding it impossible to get through to Nashville in time to open court before the autumn session. Waightstill Avery, of Morganton, was a personage in North Carolina, a wise and scholarly old lawyer mellowed by the experiences of life. He liked Jackson and had gone out of his way to be helpful to him, but this did not deter him, in an address to the court, from twitting his adversary upon the liberal doses of Bacon that spiced his arguments.

Andrew squirmed in his seat, and, when Colonel Avery concluded, he blurted out, probably forgetting to suppress his Irish accent:

"I may not know as much law as there is in Bacon but I know enough not to take illegal fees!"

Silence in the log court-room. Colonel Avery arose to ask if Mr. Jackson meant to imply that he had taken illegal fees.

"I do, sir," replied Andrew Jackson.

"It's false as hell!" shouted Waightstill Avery.[1]

Mr. Jackson was writing rapidly on a fly-leaf of his Bacon. He tore out the page and bowing—"Your obedient servant, sir"— presented it to Colonel Avery.

The promptitude with which the unknown stripling had invoked the Code of Honor against one of the most popular men in that part of the country rather captured the fancy of Jonesborough. The yea and nay and tergiversation that forms the half-concealed background of most duels dims their glamour. A word and a challenge was the Code in its purest ray.

Some of the most respectable gentlemen of the place civilly approached Andrew Jackson with the inquiries and offers of mediation that etiquette required. Jackson admitted that he did not impute dishonesty to Colonel Avery, but ignorance of the statute governing fees in a certain instance. Avery's remark, however, had ended the discussion as an explanation now might be construed as an act of cowardice. Avery had no desire at all to fight. He had charged an unwarranted fee, but had returned it, and so declined to take the first step toward an amicable adjustment with Jackson, thinking the armor of his reputation sufficient against the cause of this quick-tempered young man.

Colonel Avery entered the court-room the next morning without taking notice of Mr. Jackson's challenge. Near the end of a tense day, the ignored one took up his quill again.

"August 12th 1788

"Sir

"You rec^d a few lines from me yesterday & undoubtedly you understand me My charactor you have injured; and further you have Insulted me in the presence of a court and a large audianc I therefore call upon you as a gentleman to give me satisfaction . . . & further . . . an answer immediately without Equivocation and I hope you can do without dinner untill the business is done . y^r obt S^t

"AN^{DW} JACKSON[2]

"Coll^o Avery"

The Colonel could sustain his attitude of indifference no longer. His second, John Adair, called on the challenger. Details were arranged and the two met on a hill south of town at sunset.

But conciliators had accomplished their end. Both parties fired in the air and shook hands.

"Mr. Jackson," said Colonel Avery producing a parcel, "I feared that in event of my wounding you mortally you would be inconsolable in your last moments without your beloved Bacon."

Jackson undid the wrappings and exposed a side of smoked pork. The laugh that went up died on the lips of the company assembled. Jackson was not laughing and two of the gentlemen stepped anxiously to his side. It took Andrew Jackson thirty years to perceive the humor of Colonel Avery's bold little pleasantry.[3]

2

In September of 1788 the Cumberland Road was opened across the Cumberland range and one hundred and eighty miles of Cherokee country, linking the former State of Franklin with the ultima thule on the shores of Cumberland River. Andrew Jackson, accompanied by a negro girl he had bought of Micajah Crews for two hundred dollars,[4] joined the first immigrant train to use the new trail. The state furnished a guard of sixteen men under Martin McGary, late of the Waxhaws, who, deprived of his occupation of eliminating Tories, had found Indians the best substitute available. Aside from the pursuit of his hobby, Mr. McGary was one of the gentlest of men, and could stop a baby from crying as quickly as its mother. But it was Jackson's alertness one night that put the train in so bristling a state of defense that a Cherokee war-party forebore to attack. Four hunters were scalped on the spot, however, a few hours after the caravan had left. On another night Jackson shot a panther and tomahawked its cub when they tried to kill a colt. On Sunday, October twenty-sixth, the wagons climbed to the crest of a bluff overlooking the Cumberland. Inside a shambling fence built to keep the browsing buffalo at a distance, stood, in order of importance, two taverns, two stores, one distillery, one court-house and a fringe of cabins, bark tents and "wagon camps." Andrew Jackson had reached the theater of his labors.

Nashville's court-house was a hewn-log structure eighteen feet square with a porch on the south side. Its interior was filthy. Doors askew and sagging window-shutters leered the community's contempt for authority. The courts of the Western District had sunk in the slough of disrespect that marked the decline of the old Confederation. Horses were hitched to the stocks and whipping-post. Twenty-six-year-old John McNairy took the bench on November third[5] and quickly changed all this, in so far as the jurisdiction of the Superior Court was concerned. If the sheriff could not sustain him, he knew his twenty-one-year-old prosecutor would. Debtors, defying the law's machinery, had banded together to run the town. Andrew Jackson espoused the cause of the creditors. In thirty days he had enforced seventy writs of execution[6] and changed the attitude of Nashville toward its wheels of justice. This was the kind of lawyer the property owners of Nashville wanted and the prosecutor got all the private business he could handle. Money was scarce but land was illimitable, inasmuch as it belonged to no one except the Indians. Mr. Jackson became a land holder almost before he knew it.

Of Nashville's two taverns, the young prosecutor probably would have preferred "King" Boyd's "notorious" Red Heifer had not his official course placed him in opposition to the interests of so many of Mr. Boyd's patrons. Boyd also owned the distillery whose prosperity was founded on the new and far-reaching discovery that whisky could be manufactured from corn. Therefore, one finds Mr. Jackson gracing the table of the Widow Donelson's blockhouse, which, on first thought, strikes an observer as an out-of-the-way abode for one so actively employed at Nashville. To reach Mrs. Donelson's it was necessary to ferry the river and take the Kentucky Road northward for six or seven miles, then branch off on a poor trail for three or four miles more. A man as eager for advancement as Jackson would not have undertaken this ride twice daily without good reasons, and good reasons Jackson had.

Residence at the Donelsons' established him with a family first in numbers and second or third in influence along the Cumberland. Moreover the landlady's youngest and most beautiful daughter, Rachel, had lately arrived at the blockhouse after an absence of four years.

The return of Rachel Donelson Robards to her mother's house had provided the Cumberland with a mildly stimulating topic of conversation. Her deep dark eyes and full flexible lips had inadvertently spelled trouble for men before, and when, early in 1789, her husband suddenly appeared in Nashville the apprehension grew that this might happen again. For those dark eyes had met the level glance of Andrew Jackson—and found it quite undisturbed by the proximity of jealous Captain Robards.

3

Restless and energetic John Donelson was born in Somerset County, Maryland, April 7, 1725. His father was an importer, his maternal grandfather an Episcopal clergyman, a great-uncle the first president of the college of Princeton, New Jersey. John Donelson removed to Virginia where his star ascended. He was vestryman for two parishes, surveyor for two counties and thrice elected to the House of Burgesses. He was a lieutenant-colonel of militia and a friend of Colonel George Washington. As a Cherokee treaty-maker, his services were extolled to the Home Government. He married Rachel Stockley of Accomac County, Virginia, born in "a mansion, an old Hanoverian hip-roofed house" built by her great-grandfather who had represented that county in the House of Burgesses.[7] Eleven children had been born to John and Rachel when, in 1778, a speculation in an iron-works in Pittsylvania County swept away the accumulations of thirty prosperous years.

Under the stress of ill-fortune the close-knit family threatened to disintegrate. The eldest daughter Mary and her husband, John Caffery,[8] succumbed to the lure of Louisiana and made preparations for the immense journey. The second son, John, junior, who was engaged to be married, prepared to accompany the Cafferys as far as the Kentucky District, as western Virginia was

called, to locate a new home in the blue-grass. Colonel Donelson's travels had taken him into over-mountain North Carolina
where he knew John Sevier, James Robertson and other principals
of that semi-independent domain. Colonel Donelson had about
decided to go along with his son to Kentucky, when Robertson
urged him to enter into partnership to plant a settlement in the
valley of the Cumberland, of which the "long hunters"
brought such enticing stories. The Colonel consented and
the family agreed to begin their several westward journeys
together.[9]

Robertson went overland with a party of men to find the best
place to settle and to put in a crop of corn. Donelson was to
bring the families by water—a project as audacious as any of its
kind in our history—down the Holston to the Tennessee, down
the Tennessee to the Ohio, up the Ohio to the Cumberland and up
the Cumberland until he should meet Robertson. Donelson's
sketchy charts could only approximate the distance, which was
nine hundred and eighty-five miles. One hundred and twenty
women and children, with forty men to handle the boats and
fight Indians, presented themselves at the rendezvous, Fort Patrick Henry. Colonel Donelson's flag-ship, the flatboat *Adventure,*
carried his wife and eleven children, several slaves and the household silver, engraved "JD^e." John, junior, made a flying trip
back to Virginia for his bride and dubbed the trip their wedding
journey. This light-hearted view found echo in the ringing laugh
of the Colonel's youngest, his little minx of a Rachel, tanned as
an Indian and agile as a boy. She was thirteen.

"December 22, 1779.—Took our departure and fell down to
the mouth of Reedy Creek," wrote a Colonel Donelson in his
"Journal of a Voyage intended by God's Permission, in the good
boat Adventure." For the first five weeks all went well except
that the coldest weather in years filled the river with ice.

"Sunday, the 27th [of February] Struck the Poor-valley. . . .
In much distress.

"Monday, February 28th, 1780—Got off the shoal after landing thirty persons to lighten our boat. . . . Lost sundry articles. . . .

"March 2d—Rain and . . . Mr. Henry's boat being driven on a point of an island . . . was sunk. . . . Reuben Harrison went out a hunting and did not return. . . .

"Tuesday 7th—Very windy. . . . Smaller crafts in danger. . . . Wife of Ephraim Peyton delivered of a child."

Indians in war-paint stalked the boats.

"Wednesday 8th—Must regret the unfortunate death of young Mr. Payne [killed by an Indian] . . . and the more tragical misfortune of poor Stuart, his family and friends to the number of twenty-eight. . . . Being diseased with the small-pox, it was agreed that he should keep [his boat] some distance to the rear; and he was warned each night when the encampment should take place by the sound of a horn. The Indians . . . killed and took prisoners the whole crew: their cries were distinctly heard.

"We are now arrived at the Whirl or Suck. . . . John Cotton['s] . . . canoe was overturned and the little cargo lost. . . . The company concluded to assist him in recovering his property . . . when the Indians . . . firing down . . . occasioned a precipitate retreat to the boats. . . . We have now passed through the Whirl . . . except the family of Johnathan Jennings, whose boat ran on a large rock . . . where we were compelled to leave them, perhaps to be slaughtered."

With the Jennings party was Mrs. Peyton, whose husband had gone overland with Robertson, and day-old babe. They met the Indian onslaught with rifle-fire. The baby was killed first. A man drowned. Two were captured. The rest saved the boat and joined the fleet. Running the Muscle Shoals was another "dreadful" experience. More Indian ambuscades. Food ran low. On the Ohio famished men struggled at the sweeps to force the boats up-stream. The Cumberland River was picked by lucky guesswork. Food ran out. "Killed a swan, which was very delicious."

"Monday Ap^l 24th 1780 This day we arrived at our journey's end . . . where we have the pleasure of finding Capt. Robertson & his Company . . . [and] a few log Cabbins on a Cedar Bluff."[16]

Such was the odyssey of Rachel Donelson terminating on the day a sandy-haired boy a few months older than she peered through a knot-hole in Camden jail to announce the battle of Hobkirk's Hill.

4

The Cafferys had parted from the family at the Ohio to float on toward Louisiana. John, junior, and his bride had stopped off in Kentucky. On a rich level stretch, later called Clover Bottom, six or seven miles up the Cumberland from the bluff, the Colonel encamped his family and put in crops. But sixty days later the water rose and flooded him out, the family taking refuge at the block-house of Casper Mansker, a retired long hunter who had settled his family about ten miles distant the year before. There the Donelsons remained until the end of summer when the river had receded and some corn and cotton was found to have survived. While gathering this in, the Colonel was attacked by Indians and lost a slave or two. The Indians were within their treaty rights in expelling him from this land, and the consequent inability of Donelson to perfect his title led him to abandon the Cumberland and join John, junior, in Kentucky in the autumn of 1780.

Father and sons entered homesteads in Mercer County, the boys buckling down to work, two of them becoming deputy county surveyors, while their impatient sire sought a shorter road to the redemption of his fortunes. He made three hazardous trips to the region of Muscle Shoals upon whose contiguous lands the old speculator had cast an approving eye from the deck of the *Adventure*. For four years the Colonel was gone most of the time. His children were growing up and marrying, and the light of childhood faded from the "lustrous dark eyes" of Rachel, to be succeeded by something that stirred men with desire. "She was irresistible to men," recorded a female relation. "Medium heighth, beautifully moulded form, full red lips," a glowing, olive, oval face "rippling with smiles and dimples."[11] Suitors came from leagues away. In 1785 Rachel married Lewis Robards before she was eighteen.

About the same time the Indians drove Colonel Donelson from Muscle Shoals, ending his hopes in that direction. Whereupon he turned his attention again to the Robertson settlement on the Cumberland, and, such was the hold of this veteran pioneer on his large family, that despite his failures, all followed him thither, excepting Rachel and her husband.[12] But even Robards wavered, going so far as to "enter" six hundred and forty acres which apparently had been recommended by his father-in-law.[13]

Although Rachel was said to be her father's favorite, it is easy to understand why she stayed in Kentucky. She had married extremely well, her husband's family being one of the most prominent in Mercer County. The young couple lived with Robards's mother, a well-connected and proud old Virginia lady, whose stone residence was called the finest in the vicinity of Harrodsburgh. Perhaps Mrs. Robards dipped snuff instead of smoking a pipe as her border-bred daughter-in-law did, but she liked Rachel. Three years went by and Peyton Short, a young attorney, came to board at the house. He liked her, too. Then John Overton, a law student and remote connection by marriage, joined the family circle.[14] He had not been there "many weeks before I understood that Captain Robards and his wife lived very unhappily on account of his being jealous of Mr. Short,"[15] who showed the irresistible Rachel "perhaps a little more than ordinary politeness." The Captain, "surprising them chatting together on his mother's porch,"[16] placed a grave construction on the tête-a-tête. Although the elder Mrs. Robards took the side of her son's wife and Short "swore" to the innocence of their relations, Robards "ordered his wife . . . never to show her face in his house again,"[17] and wrote the Donelsons to send for her.

As the old Colonel had been killed by Indians—or white outlaws, the family insisting that no Indian could kill their father—

Samuel Donelson took his sister away. A subdued Rachel re-appeared at her mother's blockhouse ten miles from Nashville, "withdrawing herself from all places of pleasure, such as balls, parties, etc."[18] A few weeks thereafter Andrew Jackson became one of the household. The somber light in eyes that were made for laughter did not elude the notice of the border cavalier. "Always polite, [he] was particularly so to the beautiful Mrs. Robards," observed a boy who was doing chores about the place.[19]

John Donelson's widow did not have to keep boarders, but she welcomed a man of Jackson's stamp as a protection against Indians. Besides the boy, George Davidson, the only other white man about the house was John Overton, who had taken up residence at the blockhouse about the same time as Jackson with whom he divided a bed in a cabin apart from the main house. Overton had come to practise law in the new settlement and also as an emissary of Lewis Robards, who, finding himself more unhappy away from his wife, asked forgiveness. As a friend of both parties and a connection of the Robards family, Overton conveyed this overture, and discussed the whole matter freely with Jackson.

Some progress must have been made for, in the early spring of 1789, Robards himself appeared on the Cumberland, began improving his land and pressing his importunities for a reconciliation. Rachel gave in, and there is a local tradition that she lived for a while on her husband's river farm,[20] but both seem to have spent most of their time at the blockhouse. In any event coming upon Rachel and her mother in tears one day, Overton learned that Robards had made a scene over Andrew Jackson.

All, except Robards, seemed to understand the gravity of a careless use of this man's name. Overton promised the women he would do what he could, and pleaded with Robards "that his suspicions were groundless."[21] The husband, however, was determined to see it otherwise, and a suppressed "commotion" clutched the household. Overton felt that he should acquaint

Jackson with "the unpleasant situation," but shrank from so delicate a duty.[22]

5

The departure of the court brought a measure of composure
to the blockhouse. John McNairy's jurisdiction formed a community fifty miles long and twenty miles wide straddling the
winding Cumberland. Judge and prosecutor rode up the river
to Gallatin and down it to Ashland holding court. A scene of
vibrant activity met their eyes. The Cumberland Road was proving a great thing for the Western District. "Movers" filed in
to enlarge the frontiers of this island of elementary civilization.
White men stood together against the Indians who saw their
hunting-grounds depleted, and against the forces of Nature. "Did
a neighbor wish to erect a cabin, or roll his logs, or gather his
harvest each man was a willing hand and in return received aid
from others. . . . Did a man want a bushel of salt he received
it in exchange for a cow and a calf . . . and the force of moral
sense sustained by public sentiment was a stronger guarantee than
all forms of law."[23]

John McNairy superseded "Judge Lynch" and "Chief Justice
Birch." Court and retinue reined their horses at the habitation
nearest to where night found them, ate bog and hominy with
the family, drank burnt-barley "coffee" and spread their saddle
blankets on the floor. At Gallatin Mr. Jackson encountered an
echo of the resentment of the Nashville debtors. While he was
speaking with a gentleman in the street, a local bully shouldered
up and deliberately trod on Jackson's boots. Without a word
the slender prosecutor picked up a slab of wood and knocked
the man down.[24]

Mr. Jackson returned from the tour with a larger comprehension
of the remote forces molding the fortunes of the salubrious valley.
Candles burned late in the cabin which he used as an office as
well as sleeping quarters; and this preoccupation helped to guard
the secret of the blockhouse. On February 13, 1789, the "dull
and heavy" weather being an encouragement to correspondence,

Mr. Jackson wrote to Brigadier-General Daniel Smith, an officer of the Revolution, now commanding the militia of the Western District.

"I had the pleasure of seeing Capt Fargo yesterday who put me under obligations of seeing you this day but as the weather . . . prevents my coming up . . . I comit to you in this small piece of paper the business he wants with you." This officer was a person of importance, continued Mr. Jackson, "the commission of Capt. under the King of Spain . . . being an honorable title in that country," where military prefixes were bestowed more frugally than on an American frontier. "He is related to his Excellency"—his Excellency being identification enough in Nashville for Don Estéban Miró, the Governor of Louisiana. Moreover the visit of Captain Fargo did not appear to be without the knowledge of this personage. "He [Fargo] expresses a great friendship for the welfare and harmony of this country; . . . he wishes you to write to the governor informing him the desire of a commercial treaty with that country; he then will importune the Governor for a permit to trade to this country which he is sure to obtain; . . . then he will show the propriety of having peace with the Indians for . . . the benefit of the trade . . . and also show the governor the respect this country honors him with." Mr. Jackson begged General Smith to do Captain Fargo the honor of seeing him "before he sets out for Orleans."[25]

Andrew Jackson's solicitations in favor of the Spanish officer formed a part of an interesting arrangement of Western affairs. The Cumberland settlers' compliment to Estéban Miró, to which Jackson alluded, was at the moment a topic of spirited discussion on both sides of the mountains. They had changed the name of their community from Western District to "District of Mero," as it was written in the nonchalant orthography of the frontier. "It seemed strange [to the East]," wrote a local historian who lived through the events he described, "that the name of an officer of a foreign government . . . should be given to a great political section of the country which might perhaps sustain that name for many ages. . . . Why select a Spaniard . . . at the very time when that nation unjustly withheld from us the free navigation of the Mississippi, and when this very officer was the one chosen by the Spanish courts to see that exclusion executed?" Did the people of the Cumberland see "more congeniality between their circumstances and Spanish connections · than . . . the prostrated . . . Atlantic confederacy?" Were they concerned with the dark maneuvers of "certain political characters in Kentucky . . . accused of intriguing with Spanish agents to detach the western country from the Union?"[26]

In brief, they were. The winter he left Salisbury, Mr. Jackson had seen the "prostrated Confederacy" throw its dying energies into the convocation of a convention to write a new constitution as a last cast to sustain independence by federal union. This Constitution had now been adopted by enough states to make it binding on the adopters. Electors were being chosen to designate General Washington the head of the new government, and the authority of his name stirred many hearts to hope. But North Carolina had no share in this. The Western delegates voting aggressively for rejection, she had declined the Constitution and was not a part of the Republic. Isolated Mero found more interest in the man at New Orleans whose name it had taken than in the retired soldier of Mount Vernon.

Thanks to the respectably placed gentlemen in Kentucky who had paved the way to a private understanding with Señor Miró, Cumberland tobacco found an enormously profitable market in New Orleans, a port legally closed to American products. Two things the West must have to prosper: peace with the Indians and the New Orleans market. The East could give it neither. Spain, controlling the powerful Creeks, could give it much of one and all of the other.

To this add the feeling in the West that the new experiment at union would fail and the West be left to fend for itself. Should that come to pass, over-mountain men would need an ally to resist the confidently contemplated British attempt at reconquest.

6

Brigadier-General Daniel Smith must have been amused by
Mr. Jackson's solicitations in behalf of the man he called Fargo,
in the flesh, Captain André Fagot, a Frenchman in His Catholic
Majesty's service. They revealed Nashville's new lawyer as a
man of enterprise—such enterprise, indeed, as to triumph un-
consciously over the formality of fact in the present premises.

Finding Jackson a newcomer, Monsieur Fagot had drawn a
long bow. It being a cold wet evening and something to dispel
the chill in order, the visitor's estimate of himself seems to have
expanded until a veritable kinsman of Estéban Miró evolved.
But surely Fagot had not charged Jackson to carry this tale to
Smith. That could only have been Jackson's own idea of a way
to impart a more enticing cast to the visitor's speculations.

Actually Smith and Fagot were old acquaintances. As far
back as 1785, the American militia officer and trader on the Cum-
berland had transacted official and private business with the
Spanish militia officer and trader on the Illinois. Smith knew
Fagot to be no relative of Miró. He knew Fagot had never seen
Miró. But there is no indication that Smith chided Jackson for
his excess of zeal, which, after a talk with Fagot, the Brigadier-
General decided had been in a good cause.

On the other hand Smith wrote a letter to Miró introducing
"Mr. Fagot" in whom the Cumberland people "have very great
confidence . . . and beg leave to refer your excellency to him
for a particular intelligence. We have honored our district with
your Excellency's name . . . and I should look upon myself as
much honored by a Correspondence from you."[27] James Robertson, the first citizen of the Cumberland, also wrote: "Every
thinking person in this Country" wished "to be on good terms"
with the government "in possession of the mouth of the Mississippi. Nature seems to have designed the whole Western
Country to be one people." Robertson's letter was carried to New
Orleans by "Cap^{tn} John Bosley my son in law who is desirous

of seeing" Louisiana "with a view of settling there."[28] Smith's letter was carried by André Fagot. The "particular intelligence" to which Smith referred, was communicated verbally, however. Miró relayed it to Madrid in these terms:

"The inhabitants of the Cumberland . . . would in September send delegates to North Carolina . . . to solicit from the legislature . . . an act of separation, and . . . other delegates . . . to New Orleans with the object of placing the territory under the dominion of his Majesty."[29]

To this important intelligence, Estéban Miró replied by letter in the polished but restrained idiom of intrigue. "His Excellency Danl Smith Brig.[r] gral & Commander of Miró District &ca, &ca, &ca. I have had the greatest satisfaction in the honour I received in being acquainted that the Inhabitants of your District have distinguished[ed] my name . . . for the denomination of that country, which impels me" to any number of good wishes for their "prosperity. . . . I anxiously expect the consequences of the operation you are to transact in September."[30]

As a matter of fact the Cumberland already had a representative in New Orleans, and an exceptional spokesman he was. Born in Philadelphia and educated by the Jesuits in France, Dr. James White had been a delegate from North Carolina to the Congress of the defunct Confederacy. At his ease in salon or cabin, and no stranger to the conventions of Latin diplomacy, this sophisticated surgeon had not inspired a feeling of unreserved trust in the breast of Don Estéban. Nevertheless, the Governor asked him to carry to the Cumberland his letter to General Smith and to communicate certain additional reflections which were not committed to paper.

7

Governor Miró's Creek allies lent an effective stimulus to the negotiations. "On the 20th of January [1789] the Indians killed Capt. Hunter and dangerously wounded Hugh F. Bell," wrote a local chronicler. "A party of white men collected and pursued the Indians . . . [who] fired upon the pursuers, killed Maj. Kirkpatrick, and wounded J. Foster and William Brown. . . . In the spring of this year, at Dunham's Station, the Indians killed a man of the name of Mills; in May they killed Dunham, and in the summer Joseph Norrington and another Dunham. They kept up hostilities during the whole summer and killed a number of persons whose names are not remembered. . . . Near the mouth of Sulphur Fork of Red River, the Indians fell upon two moving families by the name of Titsworth and killed their wives and children. Killed Evan Shelby and Abednego Lewellen as they were hunting in the woods. . . . Came to Buchanon's Station and scalped John Blackburn near the spring on the bank of the creek, and left a spear sticking in his body."[31] On an average of once in ten days throughout 1789 some one was killed within a few miles of Nashville.

Andrew Jackson continued his travels. In March he saved the lives of three companions by a perilous crossing of the Emery River on a raft. In June he joined a militia company in the relief of beleaguered Robertson's Station where Nashville's founder had been wounded. The Indians fled. With nineteen others Jackson pursued for ten miles and surprised them at dawn,[32] breaking the dismal sequence of defeats.

In September Don Estéban Miró penned a proclamation offering peace and liberal bounties of land to American emigrants, which had "the obvious tendency" to "draw off the [Cumberland] settlers," and "make them desirous of a Spanish alliance."[33] Jackson was among the first to be drawn off.[34] At Natchez, second in importance only to New Orleans and the focal point of most of the American emigration, he was entertained at the homes of the most influential Americans of the district, including Abner Green and Thomas Marston Green, junior, brothers from Virginia. Abner had prospered sufficiently to purchase the summer home of Manuel Gayoso de Lemos, the Spanish commandant. Thomas had constructed in that far world a white pillared replica of a Virginia plantation manse. There were not two such homes in North Carolina west of the mountains. Mr. Jackson was

impressed. Acquiring a tract of excellent land where Bayou
Pierre meets the Mississippi thirty miles above Natchez, he ordered
one hundred and ninety dollars' worth of supplies, including white
wine, from a Natchez merchant,[35] built a log house and projected
the construction of a race-track and other improvements. He
arranged to sell slaves to the Greens,[36] to be delivered at Bayou
Pierre, and posted home in time for the April, 1790, term
of court at Nashville where, in one hundred and ninety-two
cases on the dockets, Andrew Jackson was employed in
forty-two.

The solicitor was getting on—"a restless and enterprising man,"
as a son-in-law of Abner Green, who was a friendly critic, described him, "embarking in many schemes for the accumulation
of fortune, not usually resorted to by professional men."[37] The
revenue from his law business regularly went into deals in land and
sometimes in slaves. "List of Negroes for A Jackson," reads an
accounting, "One fellow Daniel about 28 years old sawyer 250
One Wench Kate [aged] 32 150" and three young ones making
the sum of seven hundred and ten pounds.[38] Rachel's brother,
Stockley Donelson, needed a loan. Jackson advanced the money
taking Donelson's promise to repay with "one likely Country
born Negro boy or girl . . . on or before the 1st day of December
next ensuing."[39]

In May of 1790 Jackson was preparing to return to Natchez
when a party of Kentuckians arrived from there with "a Negro
Fellow named Tom or Peter" who called himself a freedman, but
turned out to be "a Run away slave of M[r]. Petit of New Orleans."
Here was another chance for the Cumberlanders to show their
good will. "I have requested M[r]. Andrew Jackson, a Gentleman
of Character & Consideration, very much respected in this Country,
& generally esteemed, to take Charge of the Negro, & deliver
him to your Excellency"—James Robertson to Commandant
Gayoso.[40]

8

If Mr. Jackson made this trip,[41] he was back by July. But a
great deal happened before he went.

Forty-two cases at the April term, and plans for a three-hundred-mile ride to Natchez had failed to occupy Jackson sufficiently to subjugate the jealous emotions of Lewis Robards. Accordingly, upon John Overton devolved the long-deferred task of telling his friend how matters stood. Mr. Overton did this with suitable tact, suggesting that the sensibilities of all the ladies of the household would be spared if he and Jackson sought other lodgings.

Jackson agreed, but, before he took his departure, accidentally encountered Robards "near the orchard fence." In the circumspect language of Overton, Jackson "began mildly to remonstrate" with Robards "respecting the injustice he had done his wife." Robards offered a fist fight. Jackson said he would fight in the manner of gentlemen. According to Overton,[42] Robards refused the invitation to a duel with a torrent of abuse, though a Donelson family tradition mentions an informal exchange of "harmless shots."[43]

Jackson left the house but not the neighborhood, transferring his belongings to the blockhouse of Casper Mansker, the hospitable pioneer who had once sheltered the entire Donelson clan. Rachel and her husband composed their difficulties and the latter part of May or sometime in June when business called Robards to Kentucky, the two parted affectionately. Jackson was then on his way to Natchez—that is, if he went at all. During the journey to Kentucky Robards astonished a traveling companion, who had witnessed the farewell to his wife, with an "ill-natured" remark that "he would be damned if ever he would be seen on the Cumberland again." "I observed," said Robards's companion, "that the friends of Mrs. Robards . . . perhaps would not consent for her to go back to Kentucky to live. He said he did not care what they liked."[44]

Rachel did go back, but only to quarrel immediately and irretrievably, and to flee. "Rachel Robards," recites the record of the Court of Quarter Sessions, Harrodsburgh, Mercer County, Kentucky, commenting on that flight, "Rachel Robards did, on the — [sic] day of July, 1790, elope from her husband, said Lewis . . . with another man."[45] The man was Andrew Jackson.

CHAPTER V

TIDINGS FROM HARRODSBURGH

I

MATTERS had not eventuated precisely as Brigadier-General Daniel Smith foretold to Estéban Miró. Mero District and the old State of Franklin petitioned for a separation successfully enough, but meantime North Carolina had ratified the Constitution and rejoined the United States. Consequently the trans-mountain region was not let loose to cast its favor where it listed, but, under the long name of Territory of the United States of America South of the River Ohio, became a subsidiary of the new Federal Government into which George Washington was infusing a likely amount of back-bone.

Thus without soliciting their approval, the United States draped the mantle of its citizenship about the surprised residents of the Cumberland. Yet the Spanish intrigue declined to die. "We cannot but wish for a more interesting connection," James Robertson assured Estéban Miró. "The United States afford us no protection."[1] And more remarkable is the number of Don Estéban's correspondents who were able to recommend themselves to General Washington for posts of preferment in the new territory. William Blount was appointed governor and Daniel Smith secretary. Robertson took Smith's baton as military commander of Mero, and John Sevier, who had miraculously restored himself to power and favor, was made brigadier-general of the Eastern or Washington District. Dr. James White represented the territory in Congress.

Having taken the oath of allegiance to the United States on December 15, 1790,[2] Andrew Jackson was retained "during good behaviour" as public prosecutor of Mero under the title of attorney-general.[3] His behavior was very good. "The thanks of this Court are tendered to Andrew Jackson, Esq., for his efficient conduct," was the entry spread upon the minutes in Sumner County after the prosecutor had preserved the dignity of the bench in a rough and tumble fight.[4]

Indians continued to suggest the blessings of a Spanish alliance. "They killed Alexander Neely at the fort where Anthony Bledsoe had lived; also a young woman of the name of Morris. They killed at Mayfield's Station John Glen who had married the widow Mayfield, and three persons at Brown's Station a few miles from Nashville. They wounded John McRory, and caught and scalped three of Everett's children and killed John Everett."[5] A man did not go for a bucket of water without his gun, and tobacco was hoed under guard within sight of Nashville's court-house on the bluff. When the wild blackberries were ripe, young blades had two good reasons for accompanying the girls on their errands.

2

Jackson's foray into Kentucky had delivered Rachel to the home of her sister Jane, wife of Colonel Robert Hays, one of the substantial citizens of the valley.[6] In this "elopement," to use the dark title it was presently to wear before a jury, Jackson appears to have acted simply as an agent of the Donelson family in the rescue of an unhappy daughter of their house from an intolerable domestic entanglement. Once before the jealous nature of Robards had made it necessary for the family to bring her away. It seems that this time Rachel's brothers consented to let one so eminently qualified by temperament as Jackson go in their stead. Events proved this to be a tragic blunder, but the harsh interpretation eventually put upon it seems an afterthought on the part of Captain Robards, or his legal adviser, United States Senator John Brown, of Kentucky. Otherwise how could he have followed his wife back to the Cumberland as he did in July or early August, 1790, to make a final plea for reconciliation? Had

Robards believed then, as he later claimed,[7] that the journey with Jackson was evidence of moral delinquency, he would not have done this.

However useful Robards's punctual reappearance may be now as evidence of his wife's innocence of wrong-doing, at the time it presented a problem. Rachel was definitely finished with her husband. But Robards stayed on, continuing his persuasions. One day he accompanied a berry-picking expedition, and something he said about Andrew Jackson flew to the ears of the prosecutor.

Jackson told Robards that if he should associate his name with Mrs. Robards's again he would cut off the Captain's ears and was "tempted to do it anyhow." To put temptation out of Mr. Jackson's way, Robards procured a peace-warrant, which a constable served. Constable, a guard, the prisoner, Robards and a file of the curious started for a magistrate's. Turning to one of the guard, Jackson asked for his hunting knife which was handed over after the prisoner had whispered that on his honor he would harm no one. Unsheathing the blade Jackson ran his thumb along its edge and directed his most penetrating stare upon Captain Robards. Jackson partizans claimed that Robards fled, and, no complainant appearing, the magistrate dismissed the charge.[8] Less friendly testimony avers that Magistrate Robert Weakley placed Jackson under bond to observe the peace toward Robards who had stood his ground.[9]

He could not have stood it long, however, for shortly he was in Kentucky again, threatening to swoop upon the Cumberland and carry off his wife by force.[10] The Donelson women were "much distressed," Mr. Overton says, and Rachel prepared for flight. A small party of traders under the elderly John Stark, an American-born Spanish subject, were fitting out for Natchez. Rachel asked them to take her away.

The trading route to Natchez was by way of the Cumberland, Ohio and Mississippi—two thousand wilderness miles dark with sagas of Indian ambuscade. One returned overland by the Chickasaw Road, later called the Natchez Trace, which for twenty years sustained the reputation of the most evil thoroughfare in the West. Though an old friend of the family, Colonel Stark shrank from the responsibility of adding a woman to his company. He mentioned his fears to Overton and then to Jackson who paced the compound at Mansker's Station with "symptoms of more than usual concern."[11] But there was no dissuading Rachel. Her determination was formed. From the deck of the *Adventure,* she had heard Indian arrows sing and seen the glint of scalping knives. She did not fear them now.

The visible signs of Jackson's anxiety increased until Overton asked him what was the matter. It was Rachel, Andrew replied, with bitter self-reproach for "having innocently and unintentionally been the cause of . . . [her] loss of peace and happiness."[12]

The peace and happiness of Mrs. Robards meant much to Andrew now, for he loved her.

Stark renewed his "urgent entreaties" that Jackson join the expedition, and, after more torments of indecision, he committed his law business to Overton and departed with the flotilla "in the winter or spring"[13] of 1791.

3

It was a flight from nothing, for the mercurial Robards had altered his course of action. Instead of dashing upon Nashville with intentions of carrying Rachel away, he closeted himself with John Jouitt, his brother-in-law. Jack Jouitt, to whom Virginia had presented a ceremonial sword for his part in the Revolution, was one of the most popular members of the Legislature. He was familiar with the estrangement over Peyton Short and believed Lewis had acted too hastily in that instance, but now he consented to sponsor Robards's petition to the General Assembly at Richmond for a divorce.

In those days divorces were usually granted by legislative act, but the committee of the Assembly to which Robards's petition was referred rejected it, and reported a bill which merely gave the husband the right to go to court with evidence in support of his allegations. This bill was passed on December 20, 1790, twelve days before Kentucky ceased to be a part of Virginia.[14]

"An Act concerning the Marriage of Lewis Roberts;

" . . . It shall and may be lawful for Lewis Roberts to sue out of . . . the Supreme Court of the District of Kentucky, a writ against Rachel Roberts, which . . . shall be published for eight weeks successively, in the *Kentuckey Gazette;* whereupon the plaintiff may file his declaration . . . and the defendant may appear and plead. . . .

"A jury shall be summoned . . . to inquire into the allegations contained in the declaration; . . . and if the jury . . . shall find in substance that the defendant hath deserted the plaintiff, and that she hath lived in adultery with another man since such desertion . . . THEREUPON the marriage between the said Lewis Roberts and Rachel shall be totally dissolved."[15]

Had Lewis Robards been an illiterate backwoodsman it would be easy to believe that he might have misinterpreted this rather unusual procedure of the Assembly, and honestly assumed that the enabling act constituted a divorce. But under the circumstances it is impossible to explain his behavior on grounds of ignorance.

Robards made no move to take his case into court, but countenanced the false report that he had obtained a divorce through the customary legislative channels. He wrote in a friendly vein to Rachel's brother-in-law, Robert Hays: "I shall depend on you and Mr Overton That theire is no advantage taken of me in My absence at Cumberland. You will plase Right by first Opportunity if the Estate is divided as I may no how to get my [due? Manuscript illegible]."[16] I can discover no reason why Robards should have anticipated a partition of his Cumberland holdings except as a consequence of a supposed divorce. This letter apparently reached Nashville not long after the departure of Jackson and Rachel for Natchez. Its tone discloses an absence of hostility toward Jackson's most intimate friends that is difficult to understand except under the assumption that, as far as Robards was concerned, bygones were bygones and Rachel had been given her freedom[17] without scandal.

Three months later, however. the scandalous nature of the Robards allegations were known to the Donelsons. Their anger flamed, and on the heels of this Andrew Jackson returned to report Rachel safely installed with the family of Abner Green, twenty-three miles from Natchez. Jackson's "first impulse was to pursue Robards and at the pistol's point make him retract."[18] That he failed to do so is not the most easily comprehended fact of his impulsive life. Instead, he besought Mrs. Donelson for "permission to offer his hand and heart to her daughter." "Mr. Jackson," said the good lady, "would you sacrifice your life to save my poor child's good name?" "Ten thousand lives, madam, if I had them."[19] And under the spur of this spirited pledge, Andrew was off again over the Chickasaw Road's perilous three hundred miles to Natchez.

Rachel had endeared herself to the rich Abner Greens who lived in a mansion that had once been the country seat of Don Manuel Gayoso de Lemos, the Spanish commandant of Natchez. Her old vivacity had begun to return and she was in demand as a guest at the homes of neighboring planters to whose prosperity, incidentally, Andrew Jackson had contributed by the introduction of slaves and Yankee goods through his trading post on Bayou Pierre.

When Andrew broke the news of the divorce the life seemed to go out of her. "I expected him to kill me but this is worse."[20] But the enveloping tenderness of Andrew's wooing soothed the bruised spirit of Rachel and her sharp anguish passed.

4

A few miles from the shaded Gayoso mansion stood stately brick Springfield where Thomas Marston Green, junior, lived. In August of 1791, Rachel Donelson Robards and Andrew Jackson exchanged the wedding vows in its tall parlor. Each was twenty-four years old. The tradition in the Green family is that Thomas Marston Green, senior, in his capacity of magistrate, performed the ceremony.[21] Mary Donelson Wilcox said that it was performed by a Catholic clergyman.[22]

In any event the couple retired to Jackson's establishment at Bayou Pierre, where a log house in a clearing on the bluff looked down on the incredible Mississippi and a summer sea of tree-tops rolling toward the horizon from the low western shore. The rhythm of the river imparted a pulse to the palpable stillness. At night a trailing image of the moon swam by in the water. Rachel's cares swam with it, and the life she had left seemed as remote as a half-forgotten, evil dream. The newlyweds entertained; and a garrulous and gay old bachelor named George Cockran wrote his hostess a flowery thank-you. "I cannot lose the remembrance of the agreeable hours . . . at Bayou Pierre."[23] Nor could Rachel—ever.

5

"Amid the joyous congratulations of her relatives and a large circle of mutual friends,"[24] Jackson brought his bride to the Cumberland in October of 1791. There were great doings. Robert Hays, "Lord Chief Joker and General Humbugger of North America West of the Appalachian Mountain," convoked his hilarious "court." A certificate of appointment as "High Marshall," countersigned by "Andrew Jackson, Attorney General," was issued to Samuel Donelson,[25] putting the three brothers-in-law in close control of this unique society whose secrets were available only to rousing good fellows of approved social standing.

The wild lands Jackson owned in the West were unsuited to home-making for the bride whom he meant to give the best the Cumberland afforded. So he bought out John Donelson,[26] whose Poplar Grove plantation filled Jones's Bend,[27] a hairpin curve formed by the sea-green, inviting Cumberland which moved so leisurely as to suggest the wish to prolong a pleasant journey. The house—its site still marked by "Jackson's Well"—stood about the center of the hairpin on land too level to reveal the river, though one could follow its course by the half-circle of haze-clad hills along the yonder bank.

Yet the honeymoon had ended too soon for Rachel. The demands of romance had kept her husband rather long from his official duties and growing private practise. A surge of activity caught up the solicitor. At the four terms of court at Nashville in 1793, Jackson appeared in two hundred and six of the four hundred and thirty-five litigations of record.[28] In 1795, he completed his twenty-second trip between Nashville and Jonesborough[29] over the Cumberland Road, a distance of four thousand, four hundred miles, representing seven hundred and fifty hours in the saddle.

An urge to riches and social rank seemed to impel this activity. Jackson was little attracted to the type of renown diffused by political office, an attitude not greatly modified during the years to come. He took pride, however, in his election as a trustee of Davidson Academy. Possibly this was because of his own irregular schooling, though more probably because it associated him with Reverend Thomas B. Craighead, master of the little school and a brother of his mother's friend in the Waxhaws. Nor did the quest for wealth obscure a flair for the profession of arms. Mr. Jackson became judge advocate of the county militia, accepting a draft on the public revenues for "Two young Likely second Rate Cows and calves . . . for Services performed,"[30] but, contrary to frontier precedent, declining casual use of the title of captain to which this distinction gave him a technical right.

In larger matters the attorney-generalship suited Mr. Jackson well. It was independent of the whim of an electorate. It brought one into contact with land and Indian problems, which meant association with a class of pioneers who were shedding coonskin caps and hunting shirts for broadcloth. Among this category of frontiersmen—the owners of slaves, the breeders of horses, the holders of local offices and titles—Andrew Jackson was born and had spent his life. This aristocracy of the border might pass supercilious remarks on the Tidewater gentility, but, nevertheless, imitated it in all that environment would allow.

Jackson had only a rough idea of how much land he owned or laid claim to. Much of it he had never seen,[31] but he knew that some day the ceaseless tide of settlers would make it valuable. Then Andrew Jackson could build himself a house with a race-path and a cockpit, such as he remembered on Charleston Neck, and follow the life of a gentleman. The waiting wife at Poplar Grove, desiring only her husband's companionship, prayed that the time might not be long.

Before that should come to pass much remained to be decided. Ultimately would the Cumberland be governed from New Orleans or from Philadelphia? What of security from the Indians? The United States had sent an emissary to the Cherokees— Colonel John McKee, a Virginian, who had spent an attractive youth among the Indians and possessed their confidence. Governor Blount believed McKee the man to persuade the Indians to peace. Mr. Jackson differed. "John McKee Dear Sir: . . . The late proclaimed peace . . . [has been] attended with . . . Depredations and Murders . . . not Less than Twelve Men killed and wounded in this District. Why do we now attempt to hold [another] Treaty with them. have they attended to the Last Treaty. I answer in the Negative then why do we attempt to Treat [again]. . . . With the highest Exteem ANDREW JACKSON."[32]

The sentiments of Colonel McKee are not available, but, if they represented the truth of the situation, Jackson may not have thought them worth preserving. Whites and not Indians had first broken the treaty of 1791, to which Jackson alluded, and several earlier treaties as well. Until 1785 not only every white settler south of the Cumberland but the town of Nashville occupied land in violation of treaty stipulations. This was in accord with the usual white procedure of making a treaty guaranteeing the Indians certain territory, breaking it and writing a new treaty to legalize the violation.

The Cherokees were perhaps the most intelligent of North American Indians, and had a feeling of nationality that was very old. They were British allies during the Revolution. We made a separate peace with them in 1785, recognizing their sovereign character and fixing the limits of their "Nation," where Cherokee law was to be supreme. Settlers punctually overran this boundary. The Cherokees first protested and then used violence as the treaty gave them a right to do. Spanish diplomacy made profitable use of the situation. President Washington was so incensed at the disregard of Western land speculators for the pledged word of the United States that he threatened to send the Regular Army to uphold the rights of the Indians. To avert this the treaty of 1791 was negotiated. Through it the Cherokee chiefs yielded more territory.[33] Land-hungry whites violated this treaty on the day it was signed, and indignant Mr. Jackson, if not then, was shortly afterward a participant in the violation.

The whites paid for this behavior. With Spanish ball and powder the Cherokees carried war into the settlements. They cut off Poplar Grove from Nashville and attacked Robert Hays's blockhouse, killing two of its defenders.[34] But the heaviest blows fell later when Knoxville, the territorial capital, was threatened. Jackson was in the neighborhood at the time. On August 29, 1793, he and Lieutenant Telford attempted a reconnaissance from Henry's Station. Hearing a fusillade in the direction of the fort they retreated only to fall into an ambush. "The Lieutenant was taken and . . . put to death. . . . Mr. Jackson made his escape" and alarmed "the whole frontier."[35]

John Sevier mobilized his militia brigade, and, after waiting in vain for Federal authorization made a dashing invasion of the Cherokee Nation. The fighting power of the Cherokees never recovered from this campaign, which also closed the military career of Nolichucky Jack—thirty-five battles, thirty-three victories.

6

In December of 1793, Sevier's success had made it possible to relax vigilance at home. Andrew Jackson and John Overton journeyed on law business to Jonesborough, where Overton said he accidentally encountered a transcript of certain proceedings before the Court of Quarter Sessions at Harrodsburgh, Kentucky, during the autumn term just closed:

"On the 27th day of September, 1793, this day came the plain tiff by his attorney, and thereupon came also a jury . . . who being

duly sworn well and truly to inquire into the allegation in the
plaintiff's declaration . . . do say, that the defendant, Rachel
Robards, hath deserted the plaintiff, Lewis Robards, and hath,
and doth, still live in adultery with another man. It is therefore
considered by the court that the marriage betwen the plaintiff
and the defendant be dissolved."[36]

This was overwhelming news. It revealed the false character
of the report of a divorce by the Legislature which sent Andrew
Jackson impulsively posting to Natchez in 1791. Robards had
waited two years before exercising his right to sue under the
enabling act.

The tidings from Harrodsburgh stunned Andrew Jackson.
When Overton suggested the "propriety" of a second marriage
ceremony Jackson refused to consider it. Before God, he declared, and in "the understanding of every person in the country,"
Rachel had become his wife at Natchez. "Nor was it without
difficulty," observed the tactful Overton, "that he could be induced to believe otherwise."[37]

7

Such is the story John Overton gave the public in 1827[38]
when Andrew Jackson's marriage became an issue in his second
contest for the presidency. Its peculiarities are inescapable. One
is asked to believe that on the return from escorting Rachel to
Natchez in 1791, Jackson, a lawyer, accepted without professional
inquiry the report that Robards had obtained a divorce from the
Virginia Assembly, and swept Rachel into an irregular marriage.
Then one is asked to believe that a man with as many gossiping
rivals as Jackson, lived on the Cumberland for two years undisturbed by the slightest suspicion of the illegality of that union,
when a simple inquiry at Richmond should have disclosed that no
divorce had been granted.

But one must believe these things for they are true. Not even
Jackson's political enemies of 1827, always merciless with the

truth and often reckless of it, claimed anything else. Evidence of the general belief on the Cumberland that a divorce was granted in 1791 is ample.[39] Evidence to the contrary is absent.

Mr. Overton has emphasized the statement that the discovery of the true state of affairs came as a surprise. In this he is corroborated by eighteen other prominent residents of the Cumberland who in 1827 united in the declaration that "neither Mrs. Jackson or Gen. Jackson ... [had] any knowledge of" the "judicial proceeding" of 1793 until it was over.[40]

This is quite possible, but in view of the court records, it is unfortunate that none of the nineteen deponents give any evidence to support their assertion.

The discovery was in December. Yet in the April preceding, Robards, through his attorney, Senator Brown, had publicly instituted his suit with a plea that the marriage be dissolved "according to an act of the Assembly ... made and provided," on the ground that "said Rachel ... did ... on the—[sic] day of July ... 1790, elope from her husband."[41] This was spread upon the records of the court and there is nothing to indicate that these records were not at all times available to public inspection.

Postponement of the case from the April to the September term of court gave more time for the news of Robards's action to circulate. On August sixth Thomas Allen, Clerk of the Court, directed the Sheriff to "summon Hugh McGary and John Cowan to appear ... at the Court House on the third day of September court next ... the truth to say in behalf of Lewis Robards in a certain matter of controversy ... between said Lewis, plaintiff, and Rachel Robards, defendant."[42] Of these witnesses John Cowan bore a name very respectable in that part of Kentucky and Hugh McGary, a frontier soldier and Indian fighter, was famous. Incidentally, he was a brother of Martin McGary, the Waxhaw Tory slayer who married Jackson's cousin.

But in one very important respect Robards, or his attorney, had not complied with the terms of the enabling act, which provided that notice of his intention to go into court should be published "for eight weeks consecutively in the *Kentuckey Gazette*." This newspaper was widely read on the Cumberland and a notice therein could not have escaped Jackson, preoccupied as Cumberland settlers were at the time with Indian raids. No publication, however, was made. This omission, which the writer finds difficult to dismiss as an oversight, lends some color to the theory that Robards sought to obtain the divorce clandestinely, avoiding a contest of his allegations.

When the case was called in September, McGary swore to a story that persuaded a jury of the truth of Robards's charge. In 1827 Jackson's defenders asserted that McGary, then dead, "must have" perjured himself. It was said that the first time he saw Jackson and Rachel together was during their return from Natchez after the marriage in 1791, Jackson and McGary quarreling over measures against a meditated Indian attack.[43] Hugh McGary was said to have taken his revenge on the witness stand. This may be true, though the act is not in character with the known annals of his conspicuous life.

8

"Know all men by these presents that we, Andrew Jackson, Robert Hays and John Overton, of the County Davidson and Territory of the United States of America South of the River Ohio, are held and firmly bound ... in the sum of one thousand pounds to be paid ... if there shall ... hereafter appear any lawful cause why Andrew Jackson and Rachel Donelson, alias Rachel Roberts should not be joined together in holy matrimony."[44]

This was the usual marriage bond and was dated January 7, 1794. On January seventeenth a license was issued and the ceremony probably performed on the same day.[45]

Thus ends the charted record, but not the human record of this romance.

The subtle attrition of an inner disquietude that began to wear upon the buoyancy of Rachel stamps the wounding character of the second ceremony. The exactions of the statute had been satisfied to the humiliating letter. Nor was Rachel joined to a mate who looked alone to such conventional forms to defend his wife's good name. Andrew Jackson's pistols were in order, and for thirty-three years they kept slanderers at bay. But a defense may be so energetic as to recoil upon the mind of the defended.

9

A military foray from Nashville in defiance of Federal author. ity completed the subjugation of the Cherokees and opened the way to riches for Andrew Jackson. The volume of new settlers doubled and trebled. It would be only a question of time until the vast and vacant lands the solicitor had acquired for ten cents an acre in services would be worth five dollars. In March, 1795, he started for Philadelphia to sell at once some thirty thousand acres on his own account, fifty thousand acres held jointly with John Overton and eighteen thousand acres on commission for Joel Rice.

John Overton sent a "Memorandum" in the wake of his part-ner. "Be canded and unreserved with the purchasers . . . and particularly inform them that" the fifty thousand acres "are situate without the [boundaries of land open to white settlement as fixed by the] Treaty of Holston"—the Cherokee treaty of 1791. In other words this land belonged to the Indians and no white man legally owned or could convey a foot of it. "If you purchase Negroes yourself in any of the northern States, be careful . . . to subject yourself to the penal Laws," added Mr. Overton, but be-fore posting the letter he crossed out the "canded and unreserved" paragraph substituting a marginal note: "This . . . to your discretion. Perhaps it would be best to raise . . . few difficul-ties."[46]

The trip to Philadelphia was Mr. Jackson's first visit to a center of culture since his descent upon Charleston with his grand-father's inheritance. He found it much less enjoyable. Jackson was an abrupt trader, used to naming his price which the other side could take or leave. This worked well enough in the West where Mr. Jackson was under no compulsion and could abide his time for bargains. Not so in Philadelphia where time was an ally of the prospective purchaser. Twenty-two days of chaffering, bickering and delays, with Jackson's temper getting shorter all the time—twenty-two days of "difficulties such as I never experienced before ... the Dam'st situation ever man was in,"[47] and the bargains were struck. David Allison, a merchant and speculator with apparently unbounded credit, bought twenty-eight thousand eight hundred and ten acres of Jackson and Overton for ten thousand dollars.[48] Payment was by a series of notes, maturing at intervals over a period of about four years.

Of the seller's candor concerning the title to the Indians' acres nothing appears, but Andrew Jackson's meanest enemy never questioned his personal honesty. Anticipating the acquisition of treaty-protected hunting-grounds was a regular part of business foresight on a frontier.

There was now a multitude of things to do and little time for them. Jackson meant to establish a trading post on the Cumberland. He bought five thousand dollars' worth of goods from Meeker, Cochran & Company, giving some of Allison's notes in payment. Allison suggested that the firm of John B. Evans & Company was also worthy of patronage—a natural sentiment, Mr. Allison being a secret partner in the concern. He walked into the store with Jackson and told Mr. Evans to let his friend "have goods to any amount." Jackson's bill came to one thousand four hundred and sixty-six dollars and sixty-six cents for which he tendered a note of Allison's. "Mr. Evans ... requested me to put my name on the back of it. I did so, but ... did not conceive I stood security for the payment of the note."[49] A rather odd conception, but Jackson was in a great haste, with the formidable shipping details still to arrange: wagons to Pittsburgh at eight dollars a hundredweight; there a boat to be bought and manned for Kentucky; thence by wagon to Nashville, bringing the total outlay for transportation to six hundred and sixty-four dollars and eighty-six cents cash.[50]

Far behind his schedule the harassed man of business reached

Knoxville in June, picked up twenty-five hundred dollars on a
quick local transaction and, "fatigued even almost to death,"
pushed on toward Poplar Grove without a day's delay.[51]

10

Politics bubbled merrily in the Territory South of the River
Ohio.[52] Mr. Jackson did not call himself a politician, but, as
a traveler with latest tidings from the nation's capital, he suggested the impeachment of George Washington, "for the Daring
infringements on our Constitutional rights"[53] by the use of his
influence to obtain ratification of John Jay's treaty which acknowledged England's right to search our ships at sea. The President
deemed the treaty preferable to war. Young Mr. Jackson would
have fought.

The Territorial Legislature ordered a census, and, if the returns should show sixty thousand inhabitants, directed the Governor to call a constitutional convention to prepare the way for
admission to the Union as a state. That was how the resolution
read, but it attracted some of its support on the supposition that
the convention might be a means of devising a separation from
the Union. Owing to the extraordinary competence of the enumerators, the census showed seventy thousand inhabitants. The
convention was ordered, and, Jackson being elected a delegate
from Davidson County, accepted the honor at some inconvenience to himself.

During the recent ascendency of his prospects, Mr. Jackson
had undertaken an expansion of his domestic arrangements. A
finer plantation called Hunter's Hill was purchased and work
begun on a new residence which tradition described as a large
one of cut lumber, a specification of magnificence. An estate
manager was engaged. "The Barer Mr. David lile is the man
I . . . send you for an Overseer. . . . Put your Negroes Under
him . . . and keep Out of the field yourself. . . . My Comp.ᵊ to
Mʳˢ Jackson. MARK MITCHELL."[5t]

This stride toward life in the Tidewater manner was imperiled by news from Philadelphia which virtually disorganized Jackson's affairs. Allison had defaulted his obligations, and the firms of Meeker and of Evans warned Jackson to prepare to cover the Allison notes with cash—not land, salt, cow-bells or other circulating media of the frontier. The one bright spot was the mercantile establishment Jackson had opened with the Meeker-Evans goods. Possibly its profits would retire the notes.

Under these circumstances, in January of 1796, the constitutional convention met at Knoxville and appropriated two dollars and a half to cover the chairman's dais with oil-cloth. Although Delegate Jackson seldom addressed this dignitary, he was one of the silent forces of the convention. He is said to have proposed the new state's name, Tennessee.[55] The proletarian aspect of the constitution alarmed eastern Federalists. Any man could vote upon six months' residence in a county, a freeholder upon one day's residence; the owner of two hundred acres was eligible to the Legislature, of five hundred acres to the governorship. Nor was this all. Tennessee declared free navigation of the Mississippi to be "one of the inherent rights of . . . this state." This the United States had specifically denied, but Tennessee said she would come into the Union on her own terms or secede. On February seventh the convention adjourned, giving the Federal Government forty-nine days in which to make up its mind.

Without awaiting the pleasure of Congress, Tennessee organized an administration under John Sevier who had graced the chief magistracy of one outlawed state. Former Governor Blount (pronounced Blunt) and William Cocke went to Philadelphia as senators, but found no red morocco chairs at their disposal. The forty-ninth day had come and gone, but Federalist members blocked the recognition of Tennessee. Washington had declined a third term, and Federalists anticipated trouble enough for Candidate Adams without raising up another state sure to vote for Jefferson and perhaps for Burr. On June first they gave in. The old Spanish threat had served its last end.

II

The first of the Allison notes was due and the store's profits could not pay it. Jackson acted resolutely. He traded the store to Elijah Robertson for thirty-three thousand acres of land and sold the land for twenty-five cents an acre to James Stuart, of Knoxville, taking in part payment a draft for four thousand five hundred and thirty-nine dollars and ninety-four cents on Senator Blount in Philadelphia who was indebted to Stuart.

Jackson had championed the Union in Tennessee, though his own county, angered by the lofty attitude of the Federalists, voted five to one against joining.[56] But now that she had joined, Tennessee was entitled to one member in the House of Representatives. Andrew Jackson was elected without opposition. With the Blount draft in his pocket he set out for Philadelphia in November of 1796.

It was a sad leave-taking for Rachel. Since the day she had said her wedding vows a second time some deep interior instinct told this woman that her hope of peace on earth lay in obscurity. Married to an ordinary man this boon would have been hers as a matter of course. But Rachel was married to Andrew Jackson. She shuddered as the world of affairs, the hostile world that had inflicted a terrible brand upon her, reached out to claim her husband.

Rachel Jackson's long flight from fame and the scrutiny that falls on the famous had begun.

CHAPTER VI

Robes of Justice

I

On December 5, 1796, Representative Jackson presented his credentials to the Speaker. Two days before a Philadelphia tailor had delivered a "black coat & breeches." Yet the pleasing impression left with Miss Nancy Jarret, of Salisbury, North Carolina, on the occasion of an earlier investiture, was not duplicated in the reflections of fastidious Albert Gallatin who looked on from his seat in the House Chamber. "Tall, lanky uncouth-looking personage . . . queue down his back tied with an eel-skin; . . . dress singular, . . . manners those of a rough backwoodsman."[1]

The backwoodsman himself seems to have carried away no memory of the occasion, however, for once in the seclusion of his lodgings his thoughts were all of Hunter's Hill. A hurried note went to Robert Hays. "I beg you to amuse Mrs Jackson. let her not fret. I am disturbed in mind about her."[2]

On December eighth Mr. Gallatin may have felt the deportment and attire of the gentleman from Tennessee in still greater contrast with their surroundings, for enough red leather chairs had been moved into the paneled hall of the House to accommodate a joint sitting with the Senate. A shining coach drawn by four cream-colored horses halted in Chestnut Street. General Washington made a stately entrance, his tall military form richly clad in black, a symbol of decorum and dignity. A deep rich voice pronounced his farewell to Congress in a lofty and, in its concluding lines, a moving address.

Three days later members of the House found on their desks a draft of the customary reply to the President's speech, prepared by a committee. Not all of the committee were Federalists, but the impending withdrawal of General Washington to private life inspired a tribute to his public services and a rather decorative expression of good wishes "for the decline of your days." The perfunctory motion for its adoption by unanimous consent failed, and for two days the reply was pulled apart line by line, and put together again with the scrupulous substitution of tweedle-de-dum for tweedle-de-dee.

To these important labors the lawgiver from Tennessee contributed nothing, but he wrote Robert Hays somewhat gleefully of the "Considerable degree of warmth" that marked the debate. The President's supporters, he added, "wish to Cultivate a close friendship with Britain at the Expense of a war with the French Republick. . . . The British are daily Capturing our vessels [and] impressing our seamen . . . but from the presidents speech it would seem that . . . all the Depredations on our commerce was done by the French. . . . Attend . . . my Dear little Rachael and sooth her in my absence. If she should want for anything [get] it for her."[3]

In silence Mr. Jackson heard a handful of unterrified patriots explain that Washington's reputation was overrated, that his tours of the country resembled "royal progresses" and hence were unrepublican. Indeed a corrupting consequence of this practise might have been cited in connection with the President's southern journey. He was entertained by Major Robert Crawford, where that sincere republican soldier had outdone himself in imitation of regal splendor, and the guest's touch had made a bed historic.

When a vote could be delayed no longer, a North Carolina statesman demanded a roll-call that posterity might know where the people's legates stood in this crisis. The journal of the House betrays that sixty-seven stood for the felicitous response, twelve opposed. Andrew Jackson was one of the twelve.

2

The points that had most impressed Mr. Jackson in the criticism of General Washington's statesmanship concerned our Indian policy, the Jay treaty and the responsibility that a governing régime always bears for hard times. Two months after Jackson reached Philadelphia, the Bank of England suspended specie payments, the signal for a world-wide depression which in the United States already was severe.

Though a rich man, Senator Blount had been caught by the stringency and was unable to honor the draft which Jackson presented. Allison did not have a ready dollar. Jackson's situation was critical. To cover his endorsements then due, he had to discount Blount's paper for what he could get. Into the chasm went the price of his store—thirty-three thousand acres of land which twenty years later were worth two hundred thousand dollars.

In the domain of public finance Mr. Jackson was more successful. A member of John Sevier's unauthorized Cherokee campaign of 1793 had asked Congress for compensation for his military services. The plea was rejected with sharp comment on the nature of the expedition by the Secretary of War. Jackson blandly introduced a resolution to reimburse Tennessee for the expenses of the entire expedition, which he supported with a crisp speech. "That war was urged. . . . The knife and the tomahawk were held over the heads of women and children. . . . It was time to make resistance. Some of the assertions of the Secretary of War are not founded in fact."

Administration parliamentarians moved to refer the subject to the Committee on Claims. "I own," countered Jackson, "that I am not very well acquainted with the rules of the House, but . . . [why] this very circuitous mode of doing business?"[4] Nevertheless, the resolution was shunted aside. On the next day Jackson revived it. His concise language held the attention of the House. James Madison came to the unknown Representative's support. The question was referred to a special committee, "Mr. A. Jackson chairman," and the treasury of Tennessee enriched by twenty-two thousand eight hundred and sixteen dollars.

The Member from Tennessee did not address the House again. For one thing he hardly had time to do so. "I am the only representative from the State. Consequently all the business of the State in the house of representatives devolves on me. . . . [I serve] on all [standing] Committees, . . . and also on Many select ones."[5]

He was disappointed when a count of the electoral ballots for a successor to General Washington revealed the triumph of Adams over Jefferson by seventy-one to sixty-eight. But Jackson was able to obtain from the incoming administration the promise of a United States marshalship for his brother-in-law Robert Hays. "Take care of my little rachael until I return," he charged the prospective marshal.[6]

Representative Jackson also voted for a proposal to build three naval frigates; against the purchase of peace by paying tribute to Algiers; against an appropriation of fourteen thousand dollars to buy furniture for the presidential residence in the new capital on the Potomac—and, on the expiration of his term, March 3, 1797, quit Philadelphia distinguished, except in the eyes of his constituents, for little more than his eel-skin.

3

Knoxville gave its Representative a rousing reception, extravagant with predictions. Not a little dismayed, perhaps, that one can not eat his cake and have it too, Mr. Jackson shook himself free of back-slapping admirers and mounted to his tavern chamber.

"My Dearest Heart

        "With what pleasing hopes I view the future when I shall be restored to your arms there to spend My days . . . with you the Dear Companion of my life, never to be separated from you again. . . . I mean to retire from . . . publick life. . . .

"I have this moment finished My business here . . . and tho it is now half after ten o'clock, would not think of going to bed without writing you. May it give you pleasure to Receive it. May it add to your Contentment until I return. May you be

blessed with health. May the Goddess of Slumber every evening
light on your eyebrows ... and conduct you through ... pleasant
dreams. Could I only know you ... enjoyed Peace of Mind,
it would relieve my anxious breast and shorten the way ...
until ... I am restored to your sweet embrace which is the
Nightly prayer of your affectionate husband."[7]

Declining to seek reelection, Jackson permitted the office to
go to William Charles Cole Claiborne, a peripatetic politician
late of Richmond, New York and Philadelphia, and in May of
1797 sequestered himself at Hunter's Hill.

Alas for Rachel, her period of happiness was brief. In July
Tennessee welcomed another returning hero: Jackson's friend
and political mentor, William Blount whose claim to the laurel
rested upon the fact that the Senate had expelled him for "a high
misdemeanor." The West ever had been engagingly indifferent
as to whether it achieved control of the Mississippi through
Spain's friendship or her enmity—which, however, did not de-
ceive Señor Miró. With the expanding prestige of the Federal
Government, one heard less talk of a Spanish alliance and more
of a Spanish war. Mr. Blount favored an economical war by
inciting the Creek and Cherokee Indians to join the British in
the conquest of West Florida, which the Senate felt to be an in-
eligible occupation for one of its members.

But Tennessee approved. It elected Mr. Blount to the State
Senate before he got home, whereupon an intricate situation over
the succession at Philadelphia enticed the Cincinnatus of Hunter's
Hill into the party councils. Jackson owed much to Blount's
influence and could not desert his patron in an hour of adversity.
After a feverish period of hesitation, the vow of political celibacy
was suspended and Rachel's husband, at thirty, accepted the
senatorial toga that had been so modishly worn by William
Blount.

Responsibilities were confronted punctually. The year before
Jackson had been a candidate for major general of militia. After
causing his defeat on the ground of inexperience, Governor Se-

vier had made an allusion to the ambitions of the aspirant which
Jackson considered incompatible with the dignity of a United
States Senator. Judge John McNairy also was concerned in the
affair. Jackson addressed to these gentlemen notes containing
the formal inquiries preliminary to a dueling summons. The
scene dissolved, however, upon the receipt of dignified but pal-
liative replies satisfying alike the demands of etiquette and of
honor.[8]

The Senator-Elect departed for Philadelphia. "Try to amuse
Mrs. Jackson," he wrote en route to Robert Hays. "I left her
Bathed in Tears . . . [which] indeed Sir has given me more pain
than any event in my life."[9]

4

Mr. Jackson made his appearance before the Upper House in
"florintine Breeches" and a black coat with a velvet collar, fresh
from the bench of his Philadelphia tailor. He attended a large
and brilliant dinner given by Senator Aaron Burr and remarked
on the excellence of the wines. They formed a fragrant memory
to be recalled on convivial occasions for many years.

A bag of trifles—a Cherokee boundary, job-seekers letters—
filled his routine, but his real interest, like that of the country,
lay across the ocean. Newspapers remained the favorite literature of the late public reader of the Waxhaws. He devoured the
foreign dispatches, sending long digests of them to Tennessee.
"France is now turning her force toward Great Britain. . . .
Should Bonaparte make a landing on the English shore, tyranny
will be humbled, a throne crushed, and a republic spring from the
wreck."[10] This soldier was the Senator's hero. A fortnight
later the news of his conduct was not so reassuring, however.
Jackson feared he might make peace with England. "Should that
Happen, Perhaps France may give america a sweap of her tail."[11]

And if France did not, the chances were that England would.
It seemed inevitable that we should be drawn into this war. But
the thing was to get on the proper side. The Federalists leaned

toward England, a name which to Andrew Jackson delineated the livid face of a dragoon lieutenant with upraised sword. The Tennessee Senator favored the French, but was obliged to confess privately that on the whole their leaders were a tricky lot.

The session dragged. David Allison went to jail for debt and more of his notes for which Jackson was liable fell due. In April of 1798 the Senator obtained a leave of absence to grapple with his personal affairs. Their aspect was so forbidding that he returned home and resigned his seat, but this proved no obstacle to the conclusion of an item of unfinished senatorial business. Although Jackson was actually the successor of Blount, and the representative of his views in the Senate, technically Joseph Anderson had been elected in Blount's place, whereas Jackson, on the same day, had taken the seat vacated rather unwillingly by William Cocke. This had led to some free expressions of opinion by Cocke. To clean the slate Jackson invited his predecessor to a duel, but Cocke wavered and friends smoothed things over.[12]

With equal resolution Jackson tackled his problem of finances. The ledger at Hunter's Hill showed a profit. Very well, increase it. Mr. Jackson verified the report that this new "cotton engine," or "gin" as the negroes called it, did the work of forty hands. He bought one. Whisky was almost the same as cash. A "distilery" was added to the plantation equipment, and its product sold at the new mercantile establishment Jackson had opened on his farm in partnership with Thomas Watson.

In six months the ex-Senator had his head above water, but little more, when he accepted an appointment to the bench of the Superior Court, often called Supreme Court because, when sitting together, its justices comprised the highest tribunal in the state.

5

"New Port, Tennessee, March 22nd 1803

"My Love: . . . Colo Christmas . . . has promised to . . . deliver some garden seeds and this letter. . . .

"On the 15th instant in Jonesborough Mr. Rawlings stable burnt down. . . . With the utmost exertion I saved my horse . . . having nothing on but a shirt . . . I wish my cotton planted between the 15th and 25th of April. I hope the apple trees . . . re-received [no] injury from the frost. . . .

"May health and happiness surround you is the sincere wish of your affectionate Husband."[13]

Mr. Justice Jackson had become a personage, his counsel sought, his favor courted. Four years on the bench saw him the most popular servant of the law that Tennessee ever has had, and perhaps the most useful. Certainly no one did more to inculcate a sentiment of respect for courts which in a border society often matures slowly. The tribunals of Judge Jackson were a synthesis of the man who presided: swift, untechnical, fiercely impartial, fiercely jealous of prerogatives and good name. "Judge Jackson, Dear Sir: The little illnature which you observ'd on yesterday evening in my language I am sorry to bring to recollection . . . and wish . . . in oblivion . . . yr Hmble Servt. GEORGE M. DEAD-ERICK."[14] "A report has been in circulation that I . . . [did] utter and speak the following words (to wit) [']As honest a man as Andrew Jackson was called he had stolen his Bull['] If I did speak the above words they were groundless and unfounded. . . . MICHEL GLEAVE."[15]

But this did not surround Rachel with happiness. She had been married eleven years, and life was still a lonely improvisation, first with Andrew absent in the quest of money, now the quest of power—which an unshakable intuition warned Rachel must some day recoil against her.

Yet how happy they could be together. The fine house at Hunter's Hill stood high, commanding a view of the beautiful river where Jackson had his store, his private landing and a ferry. Sometimes when Mr. Jackson—never "Judge" to Rachel—came home, the old-time Cumberland clan would be on hand to receive him—Rachel's innumerable connections, with their shoals of children; Overtons, Robertsons, Manskers and miscellaneous belles and beaux of Rachel's girlhood. Old friends were the best friends: a cask of whisky, a dozen pot-pies, the nimblest fiddler in Davidson County, and a rollicking dance tune such as used to make the rafters of John Donelson's blockhouse ring. The years fell away, cares fell away and Rachel was herself again.

Judge Jackson had as good a time as any. He retained his liking for companionship, a glass around, a song and a story. But the gayest night has its end, and Rachel's busy husband might ride away at dawn without touching a pillow. He would return with his friends from the encircling world of affairs. They were studiously attentive to Judge Jackson's lady and one has no reason to suspect them of hypocrisy, though Rachel made her morbid reservations. Andrew fought this shyness. He strove to draw her into the enlarging sphere of his interests. After supper she must join the gentlemen over their brandy by the fire. Jackson would fill a fresh clay pipe and light it for her with a coal, the same as when they were alone. Only for Rachel it was not the same.

As this sensitiveness grew she sought the solace of religion. No road was too bad or weather too inhospitable to keep Rachel Jackson from a household visited by sickness or death. She loaned tools and gave advice to new settlers. She was the idol of the slave quarters and the mainstay of Lile, the manager at Hunter's Hill. But her particular fondness was for children of whom there were usually from one to half a dozen about the house. She borrowed them from the overworked wives of neighbors and new settlers. The swarming progeny of her brothers and sisters came in relays to stay with their aunt who was, in fact, "Aunt Rachel" to every youngster of the countryside.

Jackson too was a favorite of the children, indulging their wants and sharing their pastimes. He was tumbling on the floor with one of the Donelson offspring when Aunt Rachel burst into tears.

"Oh, husband! How I wish we had a child!"

Andrew took her in his arms.

"Darling, God knows what to give, what to withhold."[16]

6

It was a modest account that Rachel received from her husband of the Jonesborough fire, wherein Judge Jackson had subdued a midnight panic and saved the town. His principal assistant was Russell Bean, who had rushed into the burning barn, "tore doors from their hinges to release the horses, scaled the roofs of houses, spread wet blankets and," in the estimation of one witness, "did more than any two men except Judge Jackson."[17] The fact that this hero was a jail-breaker and fugitive from justice[18] imparted a certain savor to his conduct.

Russell Bean was also a veteran of King's Mountain, and the first entirely white child born in the territory that was to become Tennessee. This, however, did not satisfy his mind as to the accuracy of Pliny's contention that babies may appear in this world from no other cause than the fertilizing effect of moonbeams. Indeed, Mr. Bean's estrangement from the law had followed his clipping the ears of an unsponsored infant born to Mrs. Bean. When the fire was out he declined to submit to arrest, and, armed to the teeth, undertook to interview his wife's seducer.

On the following morning Bean stood off a posse of ten men and Judge Jackson directed the sheriff to summon as many men as necessary and bring Bean in. The sheriff was obliged to report failure. He had found that his quarry enjoyed a certain sympathy from a public that saw the law in arms against a poor leather-shirt, while a merchant had as yet escaped any serious consequences of his amours. Jackson read the sheriff a stinging lecture and court adjourned for dinner. With two associate justices Jackson was on his way to the hotel when the irritated sheriff, taking his instructions literally, summoned the three of them to help take Bean. Two of the judges put themselves on their dignity. Jackson asked for firearms. Advancing with a leveled pistol, he invited Bean to surrender or be shot down. Bean surrendered.[19]

The rise of Judge Jackson had not been achieved without the mastery of obstacles. Tennessee was predominately Republican,

but the ascendant party lay in separate camps—the old Blount
group in which Jackson became more and more conspicuous,
the other ruled lock and stock by John Sevier. To the Jackson wing belonged most of the land barons and men of wealth,
while Nolichucky Jack, whose State of Franklin had cost him a
fortune, backed the third estate and made the clearings ring with
his criticism of the "nabobs." That was how the dice fell. Actually
Sevier was of genteel Huguenot lineage and patrician bearing,
tempered by the easy social intercourse of the frontier on which he
had spent his life. When he went to Philadelphia he wore a
powdered wig, which was something Andrew Jackson would
not do. Beneath the noisy democracy of Franklin, Sevier and
other wealthy men had scrupulously perpetuated their shadily
acquired land titles.

The difficulty between these men was that, temperamentally,
they were too much alike. Where either sat was the head of the
table.

Their gallery was enlarging. Without counting emigrants at
more than one turn of the road, census enumerators in 1800 were
able to discover one hundred and five thousand inhabitants of
Tennessee. Where Prosecutor Jackson had picked his way over
the fallen timbers of an Indian trace, Judge Jackson traversed a
"road" rutted by the broad tires of Conestoga wagons. Lines
were run. The click-clock of axes beat a ceaseless rhythm of
destruction and growth. Sawpits rasped; a new tavern rose at
the fork of the road: a new county, a new court-house, a new
court. The stimulation of these acts of creation made bodies
strong and minds buoyant. To those who fight for it daily, life
has a flavor the protected never know. Frontiersmen acquired an
unhesitant faith in themselves and their new country, and in dealing with the impediments to their progress, a convenient disregard
for the conventions.

The first settlers had come out largely on their own, in flight
from the transitory disappointments of the Revolution. Nowadays
settlers started in much as their predecessors—sheltered by a
wagon camp until the cabin was raised, eating corn-meal and

game until a crop was made. But most of them no longer took
their land first-hand from the state. They took from the big land
companies who acquired it by the hundred-thousand-acre swoop.
They were somewhat under the ægis of those monopolies, which
distributed literature fluently descriptive of the Western paradise,
offered counsel on emigrant outfits, owned stores that sold them,
sometimes roughed out roads and furnished guards for trains.
The companies were deeply and often corruptly concerned with
politics. By this nearly invisible system seaboard capital had its
hands on the entrails of Western development, and, with all its
evils, made that development more rapid, and possibly more
secure than, hit or miss, it might have been.

Andrew Jackson was on the side of the capitalists. His first
case in Nashville in 1788 had landed him as champion of the
creditors against the debtors. Jackson desired wealth. It seems to
me that this impulse led him into public life—via the constitutional
convention and Congress. But his record is clean. Barring a little
finesse in Indian matters, which was customary, no hint of irregularity renders the dim beginnings of his career of a color with
those of a few of our other Western immortals. On the bench
Jackson was rectitude embodied. His law library was presentable,[20] and his acquaintance with it ample for the time and place.
No written decision by him is known, that practise being inaugu-
rated by Jackson's successor, John Overton. But tradition preserves
the essence of his frequent charge to juries. "Do what is *right* between these parties. That is what the law always *means*."

The frontier was hailed at the time, and has been generally regarded, as a spontaneous democracy. This quality was apparent.
Less easily perceived was the cloaked influence of the land companies, peopling their fiefs with settlers, and silently imparting to
the loquacious and active pattern of Western expansion the faint
impress of a modified feudalism. When Jackson went on the
bench he abandoned his law practise, largely concerned with landowners' interests, for a salary of eight hundred dollars a year.
The legal safeguarding that his own extensive private holdings
required was entrusted to hired lawyers. But Jackson's habits of

thought—or, rather, impulse—had been formed. He belonged
with those who wore the beaver hats. Nolichucky Jack had made
a virtue of necessity by espousing the cause of those who skinned
the beavers.

7

The rift and threatened duel between these natural antagonists
in 1797 had their origin in the fact that on his way to Philadelphia
as a Member of Congress the autumn before Jackson had picked up
a piece of information involving the validity of certain large-
scale land deals in East Tennessee. As the transactions had taken
place before the separation of the over-mountain region from the
mother state, Jackson relayed what he had heard to Governor
Ashe, of North Carolina. Ashe called upon Sevier for the records.
The Tennessee Governor failed to comply but agents of Ashe obtained the papers anyhow. Whereupon Sevier, Senator Blount
and others met at Blount's house in Knoxville and formed a plan
for retrieving the documents, and if this could not be done, to burn
the building in which they were. Neither of these earnest designs succeeded, however. The land papers were carried over the
mountains to North Carolina, and then Sevier began to perceive
in Andrew Jackson a man of unsound political ideals.

In North Carolina an investigating committee quietly pursued
its study of the land papers. Stockley Donelson was found to be
involved, but when Jackson heard that his participation in the
scandal was small beside that of John Sevier he probably sensed
a deeper satisfaction of virtue rewarded. In March of 1798, when
Jackson was on his way home to resign from the Senate, the committee made its report to Governor Ashe. The Napoleonic magnitude of the attempted theft lifted it from the category of sordid
or common crimes. By forged warrants and other means Nolichucky Jack and other gentlemen of eminent good name had
labored to possess themselves of something like one-fifth of the
area of Tennessee. Ashe called upon Sevier for the extradition
of some of the guilty, which was refused. The sensational report
of the investigators was then filed away without publication and

an inexplicable hush fell over the whole affair before the public understood what had happened.²¹

Sevier kept his hold on the governorship for three consecutive terms, the limit permitted by the Constitution. In 1801 Jackson's friend, Archibald Roane, succeeded him, after which, in 1802, the Judge won another victory over his rival. The field officers of the militia were to elect a major general. Jackson and Sevier received seventeen votes each. Roane broke the tie in favor of Jackson, depriving Sevier, thirty years a soldier, of the military rank on which he had set his heart.

The new General forebore the martial airs. He preferred the title of Judge and used it except at musters of the militia. This was a prudent thing to do. General Jackson might have the rank, but the military reputation was Nolichucky Jack's.

As Governor Roane neared the end of his term, the conservatives laid careful plans for his reelection. This was crass effrontery in the eyes of John Sevier who regarded Mr. Roane's incumbency as a courtesy interregnum dictated by the letter, though not the spirit, of the Constitution. The old leader meant to have back his throne and began to stump the state with telling effect.

In this critical situation Jackson decided that the only way his man could win would be to unmask Sevier's connection with the land fraud. It was done in an article contributed by Jackson to the Knoxville *Gazette*.²² Remarkable gifts of imagination had inspired this imperial attempt at swindling. The same gifts saved John Sevier from the effects of Jackson's disclosure. The history of Tennessee was still the biography of Nolichucky Jack, who had mastered every crisis in its annals and his. He mastered this one. Evading, denying, confusing, he stormed the settlements as the persecuted friend of the poor. Jackson had made Sevier's guilt plain to any thinking person, overlooking only the fact that in the glamourous presence of Nolichucky Jack people did not think. Beating Roane easily, the old warrior resumed office in triumph, his legendary fame glowing with new luster from its brush with the "aristocrats." He pardoned the oppressed leather-shirt, Russell Bean, and, shortly thereafter, Judge Jackson arrived in Knoxville.

On Saturday, October 1, 1803, he adjourned court after hearing two prosy debt suits. There were other exits from the court-house, but Jackson chose a door that framed the gesticulating form of John Sevier on the steps haranguing a crowd which included most of the members of the Legislature. The Governor spoke of his services to the state, for emphasis shaking, in its scabbard, the old cavalry sabre he always wore. The presence of the Justice was acknowledged with an allusion which moved Jackson to in-terpolate that he himself had performed public services which, he believed, had not met with the disapproval of his fellow citizens.

"Services?" thundered Sevier before Jackson could get in a word about the land scandal. "I know of no great service you have rendered the country except taking a trip to Natchez with an-other man's wife!"

An unearthly light invaded the blue eyes of Andrew Jackson. The crowd stood as if transfixed. Sevier drew his sword.

"Great God!" cried Jackson. "Do you mention *her* sacred name?" Clubbing his walking stick, he lunged at John Sevier.[23]

8

The crowd surged forward. Pistols were drawn, shots fired and a bystander grazed by a ball before Jackson and Sevier, sur-rounded by partizans, were borne away in opposite directions.

Captain Andrew White carried Jackson's challenge to the Executive Residence. When no reply had been received on Mon-day morning, Jackson sent White to jog the Governor's memory. Not until he had called several times did he receive Sevier's answer. The Governor would be "pleased" to meet Judge Jackson, but the interview could not take place in Tennessee, which had adopted the conventional statute against dueling.[24]

Jackson replied instantly, charging Sevier with "subterfuge," and offering to fight in Georgia, Virginia, North Carolina, or on Indian territory "if it will obviate your squeamish fears. . . . You must meet me tween this and four o'clock this afternoon . . . **or** I will publish you as a coward."[25] Sevier crisply replied that the seconds could proceed with their duties relating to "time and place of rendezvous."[26] Yet he did not suit action to word, and restrained his second, young Captain Sparks. To others the Governor protested that his age, his proven courage, and the poverty which an untoward issue of events would visit upon his family should exempt him from Jackson's demands.

All very true, but not the Code. It was easy to read the discomfiture of Captain Sparks. But forces were at work. Jackson was encircled by a pressure for peace. He was importuned on the ground of respect for his judicial robes—a high consideration, but Rachel's honor was higher. He would resign from the bench, he said, but Sevier must fight, or stand publicly proclaimed a coward. Jackson wrote the proclamation, but friends persuaded him to delay giving it to the *Gazette*.

Two days passed. No word from Sevier whose friends pleaded absorption in state business. But Jackson's stock was rising. Thirty-three prominent citizens of Knoxville signed a petition asking him not to desert the bench "at this momentous crisis." Two days later a similar petition[27] attracted forty-three signers, including some old supporters of Sevier. Captain Sparks forsook the Governor's cause and left town.

Jackson did not desert the bench. On October fifth he presided at the trial of Stephen Duncan, whom a jury found not guilty of murder. On October sixth he presided at the trial of Joseph Duncan who was found "guilty of feloniously slaying . . . Joseph Remenhill." On October seventh John Stuart was acquitted of "house stealing." On October eighth a jury found John Childress guilty of murder.[28]

October ninth was Sunday again, and at the Sign of the Indian King Tavern Jackson found leisure to write Sevier what he said would be his last communication.

"In the publick streets of Knoxville you appeared to pant for combat. You ransacked the vocabulary of vulgarity. . . . You . . .

took the sacred name of a lady in your polluted lips, and dared me publickly to challenge. . . . I have spoken for a place in the paper for the following advertisement:

" 'To all who shall see these presents Greetings.

" 'Know ye that I Andrew Jackson, do pronounce, publish, and declare to the world, that his excellency John Sevier . . . is a base coward and poltroon. He will basely insult, but has not the courage to repair. ANDREW JACKSON.'

"You may prevent the insertion of the above by meeting me in two hours after the receipt of this."[29]

No answer came in two hours. On the following morning Judge Jackson sentenced Joseph Duncan and John Childress to be hanged,[30] and returned to the Sign of the Indian King where a saucy but unsatisfactory note from Sevier was delivered by the Secretary of State.[31] Jackson improved the rough draft of his proclamation and gave it to the *Gazette,* wherein it appeared on the following day at the customary rates for advertising. Knoxville was in a ferment. With one companion, Dr. Thomas J. Van Dyke of the Regular Army garrison at Kingston, Jackson set out for the Cherokee boundary at Southwest Point, in the belief that the ultimate insult of "publishing" would compel Sevier to follow.

For five days they encamped at the Point and had started to leave when Sevier appeared with several armed men. Andrew Greer rode ahead and addressed Jackson who suddenly left off speaking and drew a pistol, dismounted and drew a second pistol. Turning, Greer perceived Sevier "off his horse with his pistols in his hands advancing" on Jackson. Twenty steps apart they halted and began to abuse each other, "the Governor damn[ing] him to fire away." After a little of this both put away their arms. There were more words and Jackson rushed at Sevier saying he was going to cane him. Sevier drew his sword, "which frightened his horse and he ran away with the Governor's Pistols." Jackson drew a pistol and "the Governor went behind a tree and damned Jackson, did he want to fire on a naked man?" George Washington Sevier, the

Governor's seventeen-year-old son, drew on Jackson and Doctor Van Dyke drew on Washington.[32]

Members of the Sevier party dashed up making amicable signs. They got the three men to put away their guns and suggested that the Governor relinquish the field, which he did, swearing at Jackson and receiving the Judge's comments in return as long as either could hear.

At Kingston an alert sentry shouted, "Turn out the guard, Governor of the State!" A sixteen-gun salute in his Excellency's honor[33] restored the poise of Nolichucky Jack.

CHAPTER VII

"Truxton" against "Ploughboy"

I

Andrew Jackson voted for Thomas Jefferson in 1796 and again in 1800 when, by a narrow squeak, some good came of it. Aaron Burr was the Republican vice-presidential nominee although, as the Constitution then read, only a tacit understanding distinguished candidates for president from those for vice-president. As Colonel Burr received the same number of votes in the Electoral College as Mr. Jefferson, the choice passed to the House of Representatives before whom Burr permitted himself to stand for the presidency, and thirty-six ballots were required to dismiss his ambition. Thus the new Administration took charge, embarrassed by a coolness between the two most exalted officers of the land. This failed, however, to retard the spirited fructification of republican principles in an order forbidding army officers to wear their hair in queues—a notable badge of reaction—and in the Louisiana Purchase. These topics Judge Jackson bracketed in a single communication to his President.

"Sir, ... The golden moment ... when all the Western Hemisphere rejoices at the Joyfull news of the cession of Louisiana, ... we hope will not be ... [marred] by the scene of an aged and meritorious officer ... before a court martial for the disobedience of an order to deprive him of the gift of nature ... worn by him both for ornament and convenience."[1] Colonel Thomas Butler had distinguished himself in the Revolution. President Washington sent him to Tennessee to expel settlers from Indian lands. The courtesy and courage with which the old soldier discharged his unpopular duty won the friendship of Jackson, opposed as he was to Federal collaboration in Indian matters. "Sir the removal of such an officer for . . . his well known attachment to his locks, . . . gray in the service of his country, opens a door for the greatest tyranny."

The morale of the Army seemed important to Jackson, for the joyful news about Louisiana might entail a fight. Spain saw through the trick of Bonaparte, who had acquired the American colony only to derange a broad scheme of Spanish policy by selling out to the United States while the Spanish flag yet flew over New Orleans. Estéban Miró's successor made gestures that looked like resistance. Andrew Jackson made a gesture. Without instructions from the War Department and without cutting his hair, on the day he wrote the President concerning Colonel Butler, Jackson directed his militia "to be in order at a moment's warning to march."[2]

Spanish officialdom drew in its horns, however, and Brigadier-General James Wilkinson, author of the charges against Butler, floated down the river with a parcel of Regulars. Before a circle of unenthusiastic Creoles he unfurled the Stars and Stripes in front of the Cabildo at New Orleans.

2

A governor of the new acquisition was to be appointed and Jackson desired the post. It was important. A vast domain must be brought under our administration and a keen lookout kept for war with Spain.

Americanization of the illimitable Valley and its port of New Orleans, so profoundly altered the economic destinies of a continent that men stood breathless before the prospect. In a convulsion of speculation no scheme seemed too chimerical, no project too disproportionate to existing resources of capital to be undertaken with an enthusiasm that for the moment swept all before it. Jackson plunged in, dispatching John Coffee to offer twenty-five thousand dollars for certain salt springs "in the Illinoi" and to go as high as thirty-five thousand to get them. This came at a moment when

Jackson was so strapped that to pay three hundred and seventy-five dollars "freitage" on five tons of iron he had bought in East Tennessee he pledged his salary certificates. At Hunter's Hill John Hutchings was loading fifty-six thousand and seventy-nine pounds of cotton and a consignment of skins for New Orleans which Jackson confessed must be sold "at any market [price] . . . to save ourselves." Yet plans were for continued expansion, Jackson himself departing for Philadelphia to spend twelve thousand dollars for merchandise. He was concerned only over the thousand or fifteen hundred dollars ready money he must raise to bring it home.[3]

But the important thing he expected to bring home was the governorship of Louisiana which would end all his pecuniary difficulties. Jackson laid his route therefore by way of the new seat of government on the Potomac.

Mr. Jefferson had received Andrew Jackson's name, very respectably endorsed, but kept his counsel. Hopeful news intercepted the traveler, howevei, and he wrote Rachel to try to be cheerful until "I . . . return to your arms, dispel those clouds that hover around you and retire to some peaceful grove [in Louisiana] to spend your days in domestic quiet."[4]

In Washington Judge Jackson put up at Conrad's boarding house, the most presentable of six or seven inns at the foot of a grassy hill, wormed by paths leading to the unfinished Capitol. A miry road surmounting a gentler rise of ground a mile away revealed the Executive Mansion which Congressman Andrew Jackson had sought to deprive of fourteen thousand dollars' worth of furniture—a blank-looking edifice with pink plastered walls, striped in front by square white pillars hugging the wall in half relief. The pink house wore an air of abandonment and, indeed, had been forsaken in favor of the President's own thirty-one-room Monticello in which the architect had foreseen almost every human need except the cost of maintenance.

Judge Jackson did not go to Monticello. "A call under present existing circumstances might be construed as the act of a court· eor . . . cringing for office."[5] So the candidate posted to Phila-

delphia on a sick horse to dicker for queensware and calico, an occupation not made more congenial by receipt of intelligence that
the governorship had gone to the peripatetic William Charles
Cole Claiborne, who already had deserted Tennessee for the
fresher field of Natchez. Yet the least intimation of resentment
was precluded under the code by which Andrew Jackson lived and
died, for Claiborne was his friend. After an extravagant purchase
of parlor chairs "and a settee" for his wife, the empty-handed
office-seeker started home to recast his plans.

3

The new furniture never saw the inside of the handsome house
at Hunter's Hill. Swathed in "blanketts" it arrived with the rest
of Jackson's goods in two keel boats at Johnson's landing, Nashville, in the middle of July, 1804. Jackson was already on the
ground and the expense of transportation, one thousand six hundred and sixty-eight dollars and five cents, including twenty gallons
of whisky to sustain a crew of fourteen on the sixteen-day pull
from the mouth of the Cumberland,[6] had taken his last penny.
Hutchings crowned this with a report of the utter failure of his
crucial New Orleans expedition to realize the profits needed.

Jackson's fortunes were on the brink. He resigned from the
bench[7] on which he had served for six years, relinquishing the
office which, of all he ever held, afforded the greatest measure of
satisfaction, excepting only his military career. He sold the apple
of his eye, Hunter's Hill. "I [have] turned myself out of house
and home . . . purely to meet my engagements."[8]

From Johnson's landing a brown road slanted up the rock-
faced bluff, past a warehouse and a disused fort at the river's edge.
A rabble of cabins escorted this path until it assumed the dignity
of Market Street, accommodating ten buildings without crowding,
five to a side and no two occupying the same level. Four were
two stories high, seven were frame and two brick. De Mon-
breun's tap-room was stone, and its proprietor a son of the voy-
ageur from Quebec who was the first white man to dwell

permanently on the site of Nashville. Wooden awnings converted the fronts into shady lounging places. Horses switched flies and stamped dust at the hitching rails.

Market Street terminated in a square occupied by a stone court-house, jail, whipping-post and stocks, and a shed where farmers sold their wares from wagons. A few primitive cedars intercepted the sun and the stumps of others were handy to sit on. Facing the square stood Talbot's and Winn's taverns and Parker's new and splendid Nashville Inn at which Jackson usually stayed when in town. Next to the Inn was a cockpit where Jackson would forget his troubles for an hour. He owned a bird named Bernadotte. "Twenty dollars on my Bernadotte! Who'll take me up?"[9]

John Coffee, who luckily had not purchased the salt springs, took charge of the keel boats, and discharging some cargo that Jackson had carried as a favor to Nashville friends, pushed up the looping Cumberland to Hunter's Hill. If the boats were unloaded there, it was only to pack again and abandon the place,[10] already sold, in favor of a six-hundred-and-forty-acre tract, called the Hermitage, two miles nearer Nashville by road, but fifteen miles nearer by the river. This fertile rolling property Jackson had acquired at the height of his land-hunger days in 1795. Adjoining were six hundred and forty acres where Lewis Robards had tried to make a home in Tennessee for Rachel Donelson. In 1796 Jackson had added this to the Hermitage estate, but in his present extremity had been obliged to lump it with Hunter's Hill in the painful sale to Edward Ward.

A thousand young peach and apple trees gave a pleasing aspect to the Hermitage land, but Rachel's Philadelphia settee and her harpsichord from Hunter's Hill had hard work to give the block-house that became their new abode a look of residential formality. This did not disturb a frontier woman whose gayest memories recalled many blockhouses not unlike this—one great room downstairs, puncheon floor, hewn joists overhead, blackened by the smoke of the fireplace that would devour a cord of wood on a wintry day, two rooms above and detached kitchen. Twenty-five feet away and connected by a passage Jackson built another log house for guests. The "manse" at Hunter's Hill had harbored years of loneliness, and Rachel left it not unhappier for a change of fortunes that promised to keep her husband at her side.

4

Thomas Watson had been supplanted as Jackson's mercantile partner by young John Hutchings, whose principal qualification appears to have been that he was one of Rachel's nephews. The firm reopened at Clover Bottom where the Lebanon Road crossed Stone's River, three miles from the Hermitage and eight miles from Nashville. Branch stores were retained at Lebanon and Gallatin. Broadcloth, costing five dollars a yard in Philadelphia, brought fifteen in Tennessee. Rifles, skillets, grindstones, salt, coffee, calico and allspice went in trade for cotton, tobacco, pork, pelts and negroes that Jackson & Hutchings expected to turn into cash in New Orleans. "Sales are dull, small quantities of Cotton planted . . . [but] our A. Jackson . . . [having] made sale of his possessions . . . we flatter our selves [we] will be able to meet all our debts next spring."[11]

They might have done so had the senior partner been content to concentrate his talents upon the conduct of the store. The spring of 1805, however, found our A. Jackson caught up in another train of projects. An intoxicating incense of speculation perfumed the air. From the Upper Louisiana wilderness came a rumpled sheet with four scrawled lines that must have cost its author as much labor as a day in his pits.

"Ste Genevieve 28th Feby 1805
"Sir I have discovered a Lead mine on
    White river
                    "Wᴹ Hickman"[12]

But Jackson's new adventure lay nearer the home and as it concerned horses, nearer the heart. William Preston Anderson and his brother Patton[13] had begun the construction of a race course on the beautiful oval meadow a few hundred yards from Jackson & Hutchings's establishment—the land upon which Rachel Jackson's father had encamped his large family at the conconclusion of the voyage in the *Adventure*. Apparently the Andersons got beyond their depth for Jackson and Hutchings took over a two-thirds interest in the race course and, as was Jackson's way, enlarged the undertaking. A small army of workmen fell to building a tavern, booths for hucksters and a keelboat yard.

Thus old debts were unpaid, fresh obligations contracted. Nor was the dull state of sales all that Andrew Jackson found wrong with the cotton trade, on which he placed his principal anticipations for recruited fortunes. The cotton trade was becoming an intricate operation with the planter at one end and the manufacturer in England, or New England, at the other. Between them cropped a facile corps of factors, agents, jobbers, bankers, insurers and shippers, speaking a strange tongue in the performance of mysterious services by which the isolated planter saw his anticipated profits quartered and halved. The run of planters, encompassed by the system, submitted.

But not Jackson, "a cool shrewd man of business . . . rarely wrong; but whether wrong or right hard to be shaken." And harder still to be imposed upon. "He knew his mind. . . . 'I will take or give so much; if you will trade, say.' . . . A man . . . utterly honest, *naturally* honest; would beggar himself to pay a debt and did so."[14]

And just as ardently would he resent a charge he felt unjust. "I am truly sorry," wrote Planter Jackson, "that any of our cotton has taken its direction to Liverpool. . . . The expense will destroy the profits."[15] This transaction had been made at New Orleans by John Hutchings who had a knack for doing things almost right. The general agents for Jackson & Hutchings were Boggs, Davidson & Company, widely known cotton brokers of Philadelphia who, like most eastern firms, maintained a junior partner at New Orleans. After further inquiry Jackson accused this partner, N. Davidson, of hoodwinking Hutchings into the English shipment of one hundred bales. One hundred and thirty-three bales, however, had gone "in the brigg Maria" to Philadelphia, as Jackson desired. But the invoice showing their disposition upon arrival reached Clover Bottom two bales short and further diminished by deductions for insurance, interest and commissions which Jackson thought excessive.[16] Mr. Davidson sought to lay the blame on Hutchings. Jackson gave him a short answer: "You are regardless of truth . . . and . . . *we shall meet.*"[17]

<h2 style="text-align:center">5</h2>

On the west bank of the Hudson an acquaintance of Andrew Jackson had already "met" his man. Indicted for murder, he hid on an island off the Georgia coast to while away the warm days composing whimsical letters to his daughter and revolving audacious courses in his mind. Congress convening in December of 1804, Aaron Burr came out of concealment and with flawless composure resumed his functions as Vice-President of the United States. The Senate never had a better moderator, and at this session the trial of Supreme Court Justice Chase made the post one of conspicuous responsibility. It would have taken an unreasonable enemy to complain of Burr's conduct of this trial, marked, as a spectator said, by the impartiality of an angel and the rigor of a devil.

As March fourth, ending his term of office, approached, the Vice-President took leave of the Senate with words so dignified and, for one of his position, so moving that hearers, not the partizans of Aaron Burr, shed tears. Writing playfully to Theodosia of the legal proceedings that imperiled his safety, he vanished to reappear on the safe ground of the West.

This seemed normal. It would be nearly correct to say that Eastern disapproval constituted an endorsement in Western eyes. Burr's duel with General Hamilton had, if anything, enhanced a reputation already high in the West for the part he had played as a Senator in obtaining the admission to the Union of Tennessee. Moreover, the West prided itself as a land of regeneration for victims of inhospitable fortune.

Aaron Burr chose to exploit these facilities as no man had attempted before. Previous to leaving Washington he had surveyed the field: vast Louisiana, annexed at the displeasure of England, Spain and most of its inhabitants; Kentucky and Tennessee, lately involved in an intrigue of secession. In Washington he had whispered to the British and Spanish ministers a scheme for separating the Mississippi Valley from the Union, had spoken with a visiting junta of angry Creoles and with Brigadier-General James Wilkinson who had raised the Stars and Stripes at New Orleans. To each he had unfolded an enterprise different in detail.

Cincinnati and Louisville acclaimed the traveler. At Frankfort he was the guest of United States Senator Brown. He saw many of the leading Kentuckians, and particularly those concerned with the old Spanish plot. For public purposes Colonel Burr's mission was to recruit colonists for a Ouichata River tract in Louisiana, which all but the very naïve took as a subterfuge for a military invasion of Texas, a stroke entirely compatible with the conscience of the West. In private audiences there was a story for the palate of every hearer: England was supporting him or not; war with Spain inevitable or impossible, as the needs of the instant might require. He would seize Mobile or all West Florida, Texas or all Mexico—anything to be agreeable, or to win promises of men and of money. The certain intent of a scheme so elastic has not been ascertained to date, but the conquest of Mexico with the possible adhesion of the lower Mississippi Valley to form an empire over which Aaron I should preside with Princess Theodosia, is a vision contrived, perhaps only half seriously, for a dazzled coterie of his intimates.

After the brilliant sojourn in Kentucky, Burr could think of but one more preliminary before dropping down the river to sow his seeds in the fertile soil of Louisiana. He made a side trip to Nashville, principally to renew a half-forgotten senatorial acquaintance with Andrew Jackson.

6

Their meeting arranged itself. On May 29, 1805, all the Cumberland turned out to greet the distinguished caller. Mr. Jackson rode to town early, proposed a ringing toast at a public dinner, and carried off the honored visitor to the Hermitage. Until he heard the name in Frankfort, Andrew Jackson probably had not crossed Aaron Burr's mind in all of seven years, but the perfect houseguest was not the one to permit a hint of that. He was glad he had come. His Kentucky friends had not mistaken the latent strength of this rangy, restless Tennessean.

On the other hand Andrew Jackson remembered Aaron Burr very well: his championship of the cause of Tennessee in the tense controversy over admission to the Union, his dextrous leadership of the Republican bloc in the Senate. And perhaps as distinctly as anything else the frontiersman remembered the brilliant dinner of 1797 in Philadelphia, for he had not ceased to speak of it when the subject of table wines came under review. Jackson did his honest best to reciprocate this hospitality. The result deserves mention for Aaron Burr, as competent as any American of his generation to pass on such matters, was captivated.

"I could stay a month with pleasure,"[18] he privately assured his daughter.

Five days were enough. Jackson was his—on the basis of a highly correct colonization proposal to cloak a spring at Texas when (the now "inevitable") war with Spain should become an actuality.[19] As a Westerner with some practical knowledge of land settlement and military expeditions, Jackson did not think everything would go off as simply as Burr had outlined,[20] but the end was so laudable that he could not withhold his patronage. The most promising thing was Burr's assurance of the secret complicity of Henry Dearborn, the Secretary of War.[21]

In New Orleans the late Vice-President spoke French with the natives, charmed every one, and, upon his departure, the Ursuline sisters prayed for him. It was no longer necessary to seek out men

or to initiate proposals. Men sought him. In August he was again
on the Cumberland. "For a week I have been lounging at the
house of General Jackson, once a lawyer, after a judge, now a
planter; a man of intelligence, and one of those prompt, frank,
ardent souls whom I love to meet. The General has no children,
but two lovable nieces [of Rachel] made a visit of some days,
greatly to my amusement. If I had time I would describe these
girls, for they deserve it."[22] Showered with attentions the con-
spirator slipped eastward. Diplomatic and financial aid from
abroad was his next requirement; and the facile Colonel was
prepared, in a pinch, to reshape his program to accommodate
Spain should England fail him. In the West, however, the stage
had been set, with Andrew Jackson impulsively in the train of
Aaron Burr's dark attractive star.

7

The duties of hospitality had distracted General Jackson from
his always-heavy correspondence. Edward Ward, one thousand
four hundred and fifty-one dollars and eighty and a half cents
behind schedule with his payments for Hunter's Hill, sought to
discharge a part of the arrears with negroes. "Had negroes been
offered," Jackson wrote as soon as his guest had gone, "before Mr.
Hutchings descended the river with negroes for sale they would
have been recd." But cash had been promised, and now Jackson
must have it. "As to your offer of giving property at valua-
tion . . . if my creditors would receive their debts thus I would
meet every demand in four hours." Jackson repeated that his
"sacrifice . . . of house and home" had been to pay his debts.
"Creditors are growing clamorous and I must have money."[23]
Jackson did not exaggerate. "as a Considerable time has
Elapsed Sence we have had the pleasure to hear from you & your
acc^t. still unsettled . . . Sorry we are to say you have betrayed that
Confidence we had placed in you."[24] That from one Philadelphia
wholesaler. This from another: "we certainly have expected and
ought, according to promise to have our money . . . and we

cannot help thinking from the Character and knowledge we have of General Jackson but what ... [it] must have been sent. If not, we must beg ... "²⁵

8

Moreover there had been other disappointments, equally annoy-ing. In the spring races of 1805 over the Hartsville course, Lazarus Cotton's gelding Greyhound had beaten Jackson's Indian Queen in three heats. This was more than a blow to the flat purse of Jackson. It was a blow to his pride. The meeting had been a thoroughgoing triumph for Greyhound. He had won every race he entered, including one with Truxton, a Virginia horse of splendid repute. The victory had stripped Truxton's owner, Major John Verell, clean and his last asset, this big bay race horse, was about to be seized for debt.

Jackson yearned to avenge his own reverse. He had seen Trux-ton run. He sized up the stallion which stood fifteen hands and three inches high, was beautifully formed and had white hind feet. He searched his pedigree: got by imported Diomed out of Nancy Coleman, in the stable of Thomas Goode, Chesterfield County, Virginia. He believed Truxton had lost to Greyhound because of ill-condition. Hard up as he was, Jackson made Verell an offer of fifteen hundred dollars for Truxton on these terms: Jackson to assume Verell's debts to the extent of eleven hundred and seventy dollars and give three geldings worth three hundred and thirty dollars, with a bonus of two other geldings should Truxton "win a purse in the fall ensuing."²⁶

By this proposal Andrew Jackson staked much on his knowledge of horse-flesh, for he was near, if not within, jail bounds for debt. But as far back as he could remember, he had been accustomed to trust his knowledge of horses and only once—when he had taken his grandfather's legacy to the New Market track in Charleston—had it seriously failed him.

So he bought Truxton and matched him immediately for a re-turn race with Greyhound at Hartsville for a side bet of five thou-sand dollars. How Andrew Jackson raised five thousand dollars at this critical juncture is a point the present reviewer is unable to clarify. But he raised it and with Verell undertook to put Truxton in shape for the race. Jackson's training methods were severe. He worked a horse to the limit of endurance, but somehow implanted in him a will to win, a circumstance which, as much as anything, epitomizes the character and elucidates the singular attainments of Andrew Jackson.

The race was the last event of an already memorable season and all Middle Tennessee was there. Greyhound went to the post the favorite on the strength of his previous victory and the talk that Jackson had worn out Truxton in training.

Betting had been heavy. "Hundreds of horses," wrote Congressman Balie Peyton who had the story from Jackson himself, and "numerous 640 acre tracts were staked."[27]   Jackson accepted fifteen hundred dollars of additional wagers in "wearing apparel." His friend Patton Anderson, "after betting all his money and the horse he rode," put up fifteen horses belonging to others, "many of them having ladies saddles on their backs." "Now, I would not have done that," said Jackson,[28] making a fine distinction on the side of abstract morality. It is likely that the horses of Mrs. Jackson and her favorite niece, Rachel Hays, were among the fifteen. These ladies were ardent patrons of the turf, and once rode home from Clover Bottom without their gloves.

But everything turned out all right this time. Truxton won and Anderson treated "to a whole barrel of cider and a basket full of ginger cakes."[29]

This victory did more than ease the finances and replenish the wardrobe of Andrew Jackson. It established him in the first file of Western turfmen, a position he held for more than twenty years, and which, if Andrew Jackson had achieved no other claims to recognition, would have perpetuated his name in the fragrant memorabilia of stud-book, race path and paddock.

After beating Greyhound, Jackson immediately bought him and added him to his stable at Clover Bottom. Captain Joseph Erwin, of Nashville, offered to run his Tanner at Clover Bottom's fall meeting in 1805 against all comers for five thousand dollars

Jackson accepted and trained sixteen horses, Truxton and Grey-hound among them. On the day of the race Greyhound was led out on the track. He won in three heats.[30]

Since his defeat of Greyhound the stud fees of Truxton had been an appreciable source of revenue to General Jackson, thus cutting the income Captain Erwin derived from his famous stallion Ploughboy. After the defeat of Tanner Erwin desired more than ever to reestablish the reputation of Ploughboy, and matched him against Truxton for the best two of three two-mile heats, two thousand dollars side, eight hundred forfeit. Four persons were interested in the stake on Truxton's side—Jackson, Verell, William Preston Anderson and Captain Samuel Pryor, who was to train Truxton. On Ploughboy's side were Erwin and his son-in-law, Charles Dickinson. Before the day of the race, Ploughboy having gone lame, Erwin withdrew him and paid the forfeit.

9

Captain Patton Anderson of Bachelor Hall was as free with the reputations of his adversaries as with the horses of his friends. Shortly after the payment of the forfeit, he entertained a gathering at Bell Brothers' store in Nashville with an unpleasant story to the effect that Erwin and Dickinson had attempted to discharge their obligation with notes, not due or payable, as had been agreed. When Dickinson heard of this he asked youthful Thomas Swann, who had been present, to repeat what Anderson had said. The notice delighted Mr. Swann. It was a feather in the hat of a cub lawyer, newly come from the College of William and Mary with a lofty Tidewater attitude toward the backwoods, to be drawn into a gentlemen's controversy involving such personages as Charles Dickinson and Andrew Jackson.

As every one knew, relations between these two were strained already. Dickinson was twenty-seven years old, a man of fashion and success. John Marshall had been his preceptor in the law. At Nashville his polished manners had won many friends, but lately there had been a rift when, in convivial company, Mr. Dickinson made an allusion to Rachel Donelson's matrimonial history. Confronted by Jackson he had apologized, saying that he was drunk when he spoke. But Jackson soon heard of a repetition of the offense and begged Captain Erwin, an old acquaintance, to restrain his daughter's husband "in time." "I wish no quarrel with him," said Jackson, adding that Dickinson was being *"used* by my enemies,"[31] the Sevierites. The stimulus to talk afforded by the Sevier affray had shown Jackson that public quarrels were not the best means of casting a blanket of oblivion over the chapter in his marital relations that he wished forgotten.

In this situation Thomas Swann, whose law practise was not a burden, rode to Clover Bottom. A Saturday crowd was loafing, and probably drinking, about the fire at the store. Patton Anderson started to repeat his story of the forfeiture when Jackson interrupted to say that it was incorrect. The General then gave an account of what had happened which differed little from Anderson's, except by the absence of an imputation of trickery. Jackson said Erwin first had proffered eight hundred dollars in notes not due. Jackson protested that he must have at least half in matured notes, as Verell and Pryor needed money for their share. Dickinson then offered notes of this character for four hundred dollars, and Jackson accepted Erwin's notes for the balance[32]—all being easy to understand in a region where banks were unknown, currency scarce and notes of hand a common media in "cash" transactions of more than a few dollars. Jackson's recital was a mild rebuke to Anderson whose brother, Preston, had been present at the payment. Nevertheless, Swann shouldered into the conversation, and ran to Dickinson with an exasperating version of it. When Dickinson applied for an explanation, Jackson told him that some one had been retailing "a damned lye."

This brought from Swann a letter which usage marked as a curtain-raiser for a challenge. Jackson's reply began firmly but moderately, as a man of experience addressing a youthful stranger, to the effect that offense had been taken where none was intended, and that Swann was being used as a catspaw. Then came the thunderclap. *"The base poltroon and cowardly talebearer will always act* in the background. you can apply the latter to Mr. Dickinson. . . . I write it for his eye."[33]

Two missives reached Clover Bottom in answer. The first, from Dickinson, called Jackson an equivocator and a coward and dared him to challenge. Learning that before dispatching these provocative lines Mr. Dickinson had boarded a boat for New Orleans, Jackson did not reply. The second note was from young Swann. "Think not I am to be intimidated by your threats. No power terrestrial shall prevent the settled purpose of my soul. . . . My friend the bearer of this is authorized to make complete arrangements in the field of honor."[34]

Jackson sent word that he would not fight Swann, but would come to town and cane him for his impudence, which he did, though the devastating effect desired was modified when the General's spur caught against a chair and tripped him backward almost into the fireplace of Winn's Tavern.[35]

Jackson and his friends hoped that this might end matters, but they were disappointed. Nathaniel A. McNairy, a younger brother of Judge McNairy, immediately presented himself in Swann's interest, demanding "satisfaction" for the caning. Jackson declined. "He would not degrade himself" by accepting a challenge from one "he knew not as a gentleman." But he offered alternatives. He would repair to "any sequestered grove" and shoot it out with Swann, with the understanding that the affair should not be known as a gentleman's duel; or he would meet McNairy in a duel. McNairy repelled these proposals in a scene that furnished slender guarantees of future peace.[36] Moreover, the word had reached Nashville that on his way south Dickinson was entertaining himself with pistol practise.

The most even-tempered and least selfish of Andrew Jackson's lifelong friends was John Coffee, a big awkward man, careless of dress, slow of speech, but kindly, tactful and wise. Coffee had witnessed the assault on Swann. He had heard the conversation with McNairy and the tidings of Dickinson's target exercises. Before the eventful day was over he, John Verell and Jackson sat down together. Coffee produced a paper. "Genera! Jackson and Major John Verrell covenant with each other, that the first of them that is known to drink ardent spirits . . . is to pay the other a full and compleat suit of clothes . . . this 24th day of January, 1806."[37] It was a bargain. Coffee folded the paper and put it in his wallet.

10

Thomas Swann transferred the controversy to the columns of the *Impartial Review and Cumberland Repository,* Nashville's only newspaper, taking nearly a column to vindicate his position. General Jackson replied with two columns (the editor was one of Rachel's innumerable relatives), paying his respects to McNairy as a meddler and to Swann as "the puppet and lying valet for a worthless, drunken, blackguard scoundrel, . . . Charles Dickinson."[38] Young McNairy published a lively retort, involving John Coffee who challenged. At the meeting McNairy unintentionally fired before the word, wounding Coffee in the thigh. In reparation he offered to lay down his pistol and give his adversary an extra shot.

Clearly Jackson was reserving himself for the return of Mr. Dickinson, a circumstance which moved venerable General James Robertson, Nashville's founder, to take pen in trembling hand and write a long and painful letter. He begged Jackson not to fight. "Your courage . . . & reputation" did not require that mode of vindication. The old gentleman had the delicacy not to mention Rachel, but any issue of events, he argued, would militate against Jackson. Should he lose, "your Country besides . . . your Famnley" would suffer. Should he win it would be a Pyrrhic triumph. Jackson was besought to reflect on the gravity of taking "the life of your Fellow Mortal. might this not make you miserable so long as you lived, instant Colo Burr. I suppose if dueling Could be Jestifiable it must have bin in his case and it is beleaved he has not had ease in mind since the fatal hour. .. Once for all let me tell you . . . avoid . . . a duel."[39]

But events were in the full cry, each day adding to the public excitement. The match between Truxton and Ploughboy was rearranged, with feeling between the backers of the rival stallions more tense than ever. "Gentlemen ... would do well," counseled the *Impartial Review,* "not to put their mares to horses until after the race, as at that time will be seen ... whether or not *Ploughboy* merits the attention of sportsmen and gentlemen breeders." On the day[40] Coffee met McNairy the *Review* was able to announce the particulars of the event following:

"On Thursday the 3d of April next will be run the greatest and most interesting race ever run in the Western country between *Gen. Jackson's* horse

TRUXTON

6 years old carrying 124 pounds and *Capt. Joseph Erwin's* horse

PLOUGHBOY

8 years old carrying 130 lbs. ... For the sum of 3,000 dollars."

On the great day all roads led to Clover Bottom where Jackson surveyed "the largest concourse of people I ever saw assembled, unless in an army."

Had they come to witness his triumph or his humiliation? About Truxton's stall a knot of excited men talked and gestured. In the midst of them stood Jackson, his long face very grave. Two days before, in the course of his rigorous training, Truxton had "got a serious hurt to his thigh, which occasioned it to swell verry much."[41] No amount of liniments or rubbing or stable lore had been able to reduce the swelling. Clearly the big stallion was not himself and the positive Anderson, horse-wise Verell, conservative Coffee and Trainer Sam Pryor, in fact all of Jackson's friends, recommended that he pay the forfeit and postpone the race. Jackson went over his horse again, minutely—spoke to him, stroked his nose. When Andrew Jackson spoke to a horse he looked in its eyes, as he looked at men. No, gentlemen, he said, Truxton would run.

The Erwin stable was jubilant. Major William Terrell Lewis rushed out to offer any amount on Ploughboy. Two thousand dollars were covered. Truxton's supporters were slow to wager.

They had come on the field ready to back their choice with everything they had. One pen was filled with horses, brought for
the purpose, another with negroes, chuckling and nudging one
another in expansive enjoyment of their association with an important event; but the injured thigh chilled the ardor of Truxton
partizans. Ultimately they risked ten thousand dollars, a large
sum, but Jackson said it would have been twice as much had his
horse been in condition.

The contenders were led out under a lowering sky. The heats
were to be two miles. "All things prepared, the horses started ...
Truxton under every disadvantage." But he slipped into the
lead, held it, increased it, and passed the finish line going away.

The victory had been dearly bought. The bay horse limped
on his injured hind leg. A front leg had gone lame. Upon one
of his good legs "the plate had sprung and lay across the foot."
It did not seem that he could last another heat.

A hard-beating rain came as the horses returned to the post.
The drum tapped. Through the April downpour the crowd saw
the long bony body of the bay glide ahead of Ploughboy with
effortless ease. The Erwin phalanx was speechless. Truxton ran
away from their horse, winning "without whip or spur [by] sixty
yards ... in 3 m. 59 seconds. by two watches, by another 3 m 59
1-2, by Blufords pendulum 4 m. 1 second, by one other in 3 m.
57 seconds."[42]

The sublimity of this triumph sent the spirit soaring above the
dusty vexations of the trading house with its cloud of duns.
Something of the inextinguishable will he had imparted to
Truxton Andrew Jackson dreamed now of imparting to armies.

II

What more likely moment for a skilful letter from Aaron
Burr?

"You have doubtless before this time been convinced that we
are to have no war"—with Spain, upon which all of Burr's plans,
as Jackson understood them, depended. "The object of the ad-

ministration appears to be to treat for the purchase of the Floridas . . . This . . . is a secret to those only who are best entitled to know it—our citizens."

Yet a timid administration which shrank from an easy war of conquest was backing into a dangerous war of defense. "Notwithstanding the pacific temper of our government there is a great reason to expect hostility, arising out of the expedition under General Miranda." This flaming South American patriot had equipped ships at New York for a descent upon Venezuela. "And it would not surprise me if . . . Paris and Madrid" should retaliate by seizing "our vessels in the ports of these kingdoms" and moving against New Orleans.

Any military force to meet this invasion should "come from your side of the mountains. . . . I am glad to learn that you had your division reviewed; but you ought" to do more. "Your country is full of fine materials for an army, and I have often said a brigade could be raised in West Tennessee that would drive double their number of Frenchmen off the earth. I take the liberty of recommending to you to make out a list of officers from colonel down to ensign for one or two regiments, and with whom you would trust your life and your honor. If you will transmit to me that list, I will"—easily now, Colonel Burr—"I will, in case troops should be called for, recommend it to the Secretary of War."[43]

Burr got his list.

12

At New Orleans John Hutchings awaited a barge flotilla laden with cotton, barrel staves and negroes, upon which the year's profits depended. Jackson penned him a great account of the horse race, receiving in return a story of the barges' delay and a falling market. But New Orleans knew of Truxton's victory! "I am truly sorry that mr. Dickerson . . . left here before this pleasing nues reached me, so I might have had the pleasur of seeing . . . [his] aggoney."[44]

On May twentieth Mr. Dickinson was in Nashville. On the

twenty-first he handed a "card" to Editor Eastin of the *Review,* whose next number was due to appear on May twenty-fourth. On the twenty-second General Thomas Overton, a militia brigadier and a brother of Jackson's intimate, John Overton, took the word to Clover Bottom. Jackson bade him read the article and bring back the gist of it.

Overton returned, his face flushed with excitement. "It's a piece that can't be passed over. General, you must challenge."[45]

Jackson rode to the newspaper office and read the piece himself. Though rather long and wordy, the last paragraph came to the point. The "Major General . . . of the Mero district . . . [is] a worthless scoundrel, a poltroon and a coward." After which the writer airily announced his departure "the first of next week for Maryland."[46]

On the day before publication Overton carried Jackson's challenge to Dickinson, whose response is a model of its kind.

"May 23d, 1806

"Gen Andrew Jackson,

"Sir, Your note of this morning is received, and your request shall be granted. My friend who hands you this will make the necessary arrangements. I am etc.

"CHARLES DICKINSON."[47]

CHAPTER VIII

A Long Spoon

I

On Thursday, May 29, 1806, Andrew Jackson rose at five o'clock, and after breakfast told Rachel that he would be gone for a couple of days and meanwhile he might have some trouble with Mr. Dickinson. Rachel probably knew what the trouble would be and she did not ask. Rachel had had her private channels of information concerning the Sevier affray. At six-thirty Jackson joined Overton at Nashville. Overton had the pistols. With three others they departed for the Kentucky line.[1]

Mr. Dickinson and eight companions were already on the road. "Good-by, darling," he told his young wife. "I shall be sure to be at home to-morrow evening." This confidence was not altogether assumed. He was a snap shot. At the word of command and firing apparently without aim, he could put four balls in a mark twenty-four feet away, each ball touching another. The persistent tradition on the countryside, that to worry Jackson he left several such examples of his marksmanship along the road, is unconfirmed by any member of the Dickinson or Jackson parties. But the story that he had offered on the streets of Nashville to wager he would kill Jackson at the first fire was vouchsafed by John Overton, the brother of Jackson's second, a few days after the duel.

Jackson said he was glad that "the other side" had started so early. It was a guarantee against further delay. Jackson had chafed over the seven days that had elapsed since the acceptance of the challenge. At their first interview, Overton and Dr. Hanson Catlett, Mr. Dickinson's second, had agreed that the meeting should be on Friday, May thirtieth, near Harrison's Mills on Red River just beyond the Kentucky boundary. Jackson protested at once. He did not wish to ride forty miles to preserve the fiction of a delicate regard for Tennessee's unenforceable statute against dueling. He did not wish to wait a week for something that could be done in a few hours. Dickinson's excuse was that he desired to borrow a pair of pistols. Overton offered the choice of Jackson's pistols, pledging Jackson to the use of the other. These were the weapons that had been employed by Coffee and McNairy.

As they rode Jackson talked a great deal, scrupulously avoiding the subject that burdened every mind. Really, however, there was nothing more to be profitably said on that head. General Overton was a Revolutionary soldier of long acquaintance with the Code. With his principal he had canvassed every possible aspect of the issue forthcoming. "Distance . . . twenty-four feet; the parties to stand facing each other, with their pistols down perpendicularly. When they are READY, the single word FIRE! to be given; at which they are to fire as soon as they please. Should either fire before the word is given we [the seconds] pledge ourselves to shoot him down instantly." Jackson was neither a quick shot, nor an especially good one for the western country. He had decided not to compete with Dickinson for the first fire. He expected to be hit, perhaps badly. But he counted on the resources of his will to sustain him until he could aim deliberately and shoot to kill, if it were the last act of his life.

On the first leg of the ride they traversed the old Kentucky Road, the route by which, fifteen years before, Andrew Jackson had carried Rachel Robards from her husband's home, the present journey being a part of the long sequel to the other. Jackson rambled on in a shrill voice. Thomas Jefferson was "the best Republican in theory and the worst in practice" he had ever seen. And he lacked courage. How long were we to support the affronts of England—impressment of seamen, cuffing about of our ocean commerce? Perhaps as long as Mr. Jefferson stayed

in office. Well, that would be two years, and certainly his successor should be a stouter man. "We must fight England again.
In the last war I was not old enough to be any account." He
prayed that the next might come "before I get too old to fight."

General Overton asked how old Jackson reckoned he would
have to be for that. In England's case about a hundred, Jackson
said.

He spoke of Burr. A year ago, this day, Jackson had borne
him from the banquet in Nashville to the Hermitage. He recalled their first meeting in 1797 when both were in Congress
Jackson also met General Hamilton that winter. "Personally
no gentleman could help liking Hamilton. But his political
views were all English." At heart a monarchist. "Why, did he
not urge Washington to take a crown!"

Burr also had his failings. He had made a mistake, observed
Jackson with admirable detachment, a political mistake, when he
fought Hamilton. And about his Western projects the General
was none too sanguine. Burr relied overmuch on what others
told him. Besides, there was Jefferson to be reckoned with.
"Burr is as far from a fool as I ever saw, and yet he is as easily
fooled as any man I ever knew."

The day was warm, and a little after ten o'clock the party
stopped for refreshment. Jackson took a mint julep, ate lightly
and rested until mid-afternoon. The party reached Miller's
Tavern in Kentucky about eight o'clock. After a supper of fried
chicken, waffles, sweet potatoes and coffee, Jackson repaired to
the porch to chat with the inn's company. No one guessed his
errand. At ten o'clock he knocked the ashes from his pipe and
went to bed. Asleep in ten minutes, he had to be roused at five
in the morning.

2

The parties met on the bank of the Red River at a break in a
poplar woods. Doctor Catlett won the toss for choice of position,
but as the sun had not come through the trees this signified nothing. The giving of the word fell to Overton. Jackson's pistols

were to be used after all, Dickinson taking his pick. The nine-inch barrels were charged with ounce balls of seventy caliber. The ground was paced off, the principals took their places. Jackson wore a dark-blue frock coat and trousers of the same material; Mr. Dickinson a shorter coat of blue, and gray trousers.

"Gentlemen, are you ready?" called General Overton.

"Ready," said Dickinson quickly.

"Yes, sir," said Jackson.

"*Fere!*" cried Overton in the Old-Country accent.

Dickinson fired almost instantly. A fleck of dust rose from Jackson's coat and his left hand clutched his chest. For an instant he thought himself dying, but, fighting for self-command, slowly he raised his pistol.

Dickinson recoiled a step horror-stricken. "My God! Have I missed him?"

Overton presented his pistol. "Back to the mark, sir!"

Dickinson folded his arms. Jackson's spare form straightened. He aimed. There was a hollow "clock" as the hammer stopped at half-cock. He drew it back, sighted again and fired. Dickinson swayed to the ground.

As they reached the horses Overton noticed that his friend's left boot was filled with blood. "Oh, I believe that he pinked me," said Jackson quickly, "but I don't want those people to know," indicating the group that bent over Dickinson. Jackson's surgeon found that Dickinson's aim had been perfectly true, but he had judged the position of Jackson's heart by the set of his coat, and Jackson wore his coats loosely on account of the excessive slenderness of his figure. "But I should have hit him," he exclaimed, "if he had shot me through the brain."

With a furrow through his bowels Charles Dickinson tossed in agony until evening when friends eased him with a story that Jackson had a bullet in his breast and was dying. At ten o'clock he asked who had put out the light.

Rachel heard the news and fell on her knees weeping. "Oh, God have pity on the poor wife"—Mrs. Dickinson was with child—"pity on the babe in her womb."

3

Andrew Jackson had kept his friend, George W. Campbell, in Congress, but he could make little headway against Sevier, fortified in the governorship and licking his lips in anticipation of the fight for a fifth term against an opposition whose leader had too many irons in the fire. In the national theater Jackson's criticism of the foreign policy of the Administration had been similarly barren of result, though its tone was that of the growing voice of the West. An imperious championship of Colonel Butler, of uncut hair, had been without avail. Mr. Jefferson countenancing a court martial which disclosed a diffidence toward authority extending, alas, further than a mellow attachment to his queue. Now, despite personal misgivings, Jackson espoused the cause of Aaron Burr whose cloudy moves fell more and more under the critical scrutiny of the Government.

Nor did the smoke that curled from the poplar clearing minister to the renown of the militia general. The dead man's friends were numerous and respectable. Some also were friends of Jackson whose obdurate pride disguised the serious nature of his wound. "Oh, he pinked me," was the frivolous concession that left a public, devoured by curiosity, to turn elsewhere for details, and to hear them from Dickinson partizans: Jackson, trivially wounded, taking "illiberal and unjust advantage" of a defenseless man.[2] Jackson misled his closest friend in Tennessee, John Overton, as to the extent of his injury,[3] and neither by word nor sign did he imply that he had killed Charles Dickinson from any motive more presentable before morality than a race-track row.

The funeral had been largely attended. All the Sevierites were there. A mass meeting followed at which a petition, bearing seventy-two names, was presented to the *Impartial Review* asking the editor to dress his paper in mourning "as a tribute of respect for the memory, and regret for the untimely death of Mr. Charles Dickinson." It was proposed, however, to publish the names of only five or six signers as representative of a much

larger number. At this Jackson bestirred himself. From his bed
he wrote Eastin that a publication "so novel" should be accompanied by the names of all its sponsors, "that the public might
judge whether the true motive of the signers were a tribute of
respect to the deceased or something else." When the editor sent
word that identities would be disclosed, the Sevierites took cover,
and twenty-six names were withdrawn. But forty-six signers
stood their ground, including such old supporters of Jackson as
Alexander Craighead and Dr. Felix Robertson, a son of Nashville's founder.[4]

Summer dragged on. The barge flotilla en route to New Orleans was scattered by a storm, only four out of seven boats reaching a bad market. Jackson's wound healed slowly, with
Dickinson's bullet too close to the heart to be removed. September brought cooler weather and signs of activity. "Col. Burr
is with me; he arrived last night. . . . Say to Gen. O[verton], that I
shall expect to see him here tomorrow with you. . . . Say to Gen.
Robertson . . . I know . . . he will be happy in joining in any
thing that will show a mark of respect to this worthy visitant."[5]

The mark of respect took the form of a reception at Talbot's
Hotel at which Jackson introduced Burr to the company. They
entered arm in arm, the host an inch over six feet tall, his guest
about four inches over five. Ladies exclaimed at the courtly appearance their General made in the uniform he wore more often
now, an appearance nothing over-shadowed by propinquity to
one of the most engaging gentlemen of his day. That night Jackson indited a memorandum to his militia officers of so unconfi-
dential a nature that a copy was sent to the *Review*. Spanish
troops were "encamped within the limits of our government . . .
within the Territory of New Orleans!!! . . . They [have] imprisoned . . . five of the good citizens of the United States" and
"cut down and carried off" an American flag. Tennesseans must
hold themselves "in complete order and at a moment's warning
ready to march."

The General was grateful to his guest for the startling information from which this dispatch was derived. But the elasticity of

Burr's narratives, and the persistence of unpleasant rumors, left some of Jackson's friends frankly confused. After the worthy visitant had passed on up to Kentucky doubts began to plague shrewd old General Robertson. "He dined with me and I was several times in his company. He told me he expected to make settlements . . . on the western waters. I endeavored to find out how the Executive of our government was held with, but he was so guarded, I gained little satisfaction."[6]

<h2 style="text-align:center">4</h2>

On the score of reticence Colonel Burr had little choice. In justice to himself he hardly could divulge the entire failure of the winter's effort to obtain money, that the Executive was highly suspicious, and that, in fact, he had determined upon a hazardous throw with the help of only one confidential ally of importance. But this confederate was Brigadier-General James Wilkinson whom Burr apparently considered sufficiently deft at intrigue to insure success. Like Burr, James Wilkinson had been a colonel in the Continental line. As a trader in Kentucky after the war, he became the heart and center of the old Spanish cabal, and finally a secret agent of the Spanish crown in receipt of a salary. This machination faded and Wilkinson joined another Kentucky secession flurry in 1796. When the United States acquired Louisiana, he was back in the Army under the personal ægis of Jefferson. Through everything he had maintained his good standing with Spain and his name on its pension roll as spy No. 13.

From Kentucky Burr sent Jackson thirty-five hundred dollars with a commission to build and provision five river boats. The work was begun at Clover Bottom by John Coffee, and Patton Anderson recruited a military company for the expedition.

In the midst of this clattering activity a young man of pleasing address turned from the Lebanon Road into the level lane that led to the Hermitage. His name was "Capt Fort" and he came to Jackson "an entire stranger . . . introduced to me by letter."[7] The Captain professed "to be on his way from N. York to

join . . . Burr."[8] He spent the night at the Hermitage and a
part of the following day, speaking freely and a trifle importantly,
of the Burr project, which at length he "incautiously" characterized
as a scheme "to divide the union."[9]

If the young man's object had been to impress his host, he
succeeded. "I sternly asked how they would effect it. He replied
by seizing New Orleans and the bank, shutting the port, conquer-
ing Mexico, and uniting the western part of the union to the
conquered country." "With Warmth" Jackson demanded how
this was to be done. "He replied by the aid of Federal troops, and
the Genl at their head."

The General was Wilkinson, of whom Andrew Jackson was
prepared to believe anything evil—Wilkinson the nemesis of
Colonel Thomas Butler, who had privately attributed his troubles
to a knowledge of the Spanish connections of his superior.

"I asked him if he had this from the Genl. He said he had not,
I asked him if Col. Burr was in the scheme and he answered that
he did not know . . . that he was, that he hardly knew Col.
Burr. . . . I asked . . . from whence he got his information [and]
he said from Col. Swartwout in New York."[10]

Jackson knew Samuel Swartwout, of New York, to be one of
Burr's lieutenants. He knew Wilkinson to be concerned with
Burr's plans, though not how deeply. Fort saw that he had said
too much. With the boring blue gaze of Jackson upon him he
hedged, "attempted to take [me in] to explain &., &."[11] Too late.
"It rushed into my mind like lightning" that the treasonable
project broached by Captain Fort and the project in which Andrew Jackson was leagued with Burr were the same.[12] Like
lightning Jackson's quill flew at such a rate that one sheet would
be finished before the ink on its predecessor was dry. "In strong
tones" Burr was told that until "my suspicions . . . were cleared
from my mind no further intimacy was to exist between us."[13]

To Daniel Smith, Jackson's successor in the United States
Senate, went a long letter. "Whilst . . . not in the possession of

Testimony that would authorize names to be used ... I have no doubt but there is a plan on foot ... in concert with Spain to seize Neworleans, and Louisiana, and attempt to divide the union. . . . permit me to bring to your view how it might be" done. "A difference exists between our government and Spain, their minister at open war with our executive. A designing man forms an intrigue with him to regain the purchased territory. This designing man intrigues with the general of our army. . . . The Spanish forces under pretext of defending their frontier marches a formidable force within two hundred miles of New Orleans. Your Governor of New orleans organizes the militia ... but your general orders him home at the verry moment he is advancing to ... the Sabine." At the same time "a descent is made from the ohio and uper Louisiana on New Orleans . . . [where] two-thirds of its inhabitants [are] into the plan. The Town falls an easy pray. . . . The conquerors ... shut the Port ... and hold out to all the western world to join and have . . . profitable commerce." By stopping the mails the conspirators keep Washington in ignorance until the game was in their hands. 'I hope I may be mistaken but I as much believe that such a plan is in operation as I believe there is a god. . . . You may say to the president ... that the[y] have no time to lose ... to watch over their general, ... and give orders for the defense of Neworleans."[14]

To Jefferson himself Jackson tendered the services of his command "in the event of ... aggression ... FROM ANY QUAR-TER."[15]

He did not wait for the President's warning to reach New Orleans, but wrote Governor Claiborne direct. "I fear Treachery has become the order of the day. Put your Town in a state of defence. . . . Keep a watchful eye on our Genl., and beware of an attack ... from Spain. . . ." Jackson then subtly recognized Governor Claiborne as a confederate in the "innocent" Burr plot to subjugate Mexico. "I love my country and government. I hate Dons. I would delight to see Mexico reduced, but I will die in the last Ditch before I would . . . see the Union disunited. . . . Your sincere friend ANDREW JACKSON."[16]

5

On November 3, 1806, the day that Jackson received the order to build flatboats, United States District Attorney Joseph Hamilton Daviess petitioned the Federal Court at Frankfort, Kentucky, to arrest Aaron Burr for treason. On the bench was Harry Innes, associate of Wilkinson in the early Spanish plot and himself formerly, if not then, a pensioner of Spain. He denied the motion but granted a request to summon the grand jury to consider evidence against Burr. On Andrew Jackson's day of feverish letter-writing, November twelfth, the little court-room at Frankfort was thronged, the town agog to hear the presentation. Burr appeared with his attorney, young Henry Clay, also the legal representative in Kentucky of Jackson's trading house.

To the astonishment of every one Mr. Daviess asked the dismissal of the jury. His chief witness, he said, had fled to Indiana. Adjournment amid laughter for Daviess, cheers for Aaron Burr.

Accompanying news of this proceeding Andrew Jackson received a letter from Burr containing "the most sacred pledges that he" entertained no "views inimical to the united States."[17] Jackson was puzzled—and Thomas Jefferson no less so. For months the President had had reports of Burr's designs, but little as was the love he bore Aaron Burr, Jefferson was not a hasty man and his apprehensions, like Jackson's, were devoid of anything one could put a finger on.

James Wilkinson now overcame the deficiency. For some time this soldier had been confronted by the necessity of deciding whom he could most profitably betray—the United States, Spain, or Aaron Burr. On the eighth day of October, 1807, at Natchitoches, Louisiana, he received from the hands of Samuel Swartwout a message from Burr which he spent the night decoding. On the following morning he decided to betray Burr, but twelve days elapsed before he dispatched the cunning letter to Jefferson doing so, and another to Mexico City demanding one hundred and ten thousand dollars for the service. On November twenty-

sixth the President proclaimed the existence of a military conspiracy by "sundry persons . . . against the dominion of Spain."
"Faithful citizens" were warned to shun it, authorities to seize
boats and apprehend the unnamed guilty. With this communication on its way Joseph Hamilton Daviess, nephew of John Marshall, made his third appeal for Burr's arrest. Again witnesses
failed him; Burr walked from the court-room to a ball in his honor.

A fortnight later, however, confusion struck the Burr camps
on the Ohio. Responsive to the President's proclamation the
Governor of Ohio seized Burr's boats at Marietta. Adherents
dived into their holes, except thirty men under romantic Harman
Blennerhasset who fled down the river. Riding ahead of this
disastrous news Burr reached Nashville on December seventeenth.
The *Impartial Review* chronicled his appearance in two short
sentences.[18] General Jackson was absent when he presented himself at the Hermitage. Rachel received him coolly and did not
ask him to stay. He put up at the Clover Bottom tavern where
Jackson paid a stiff call, taking John Coffee as a witness.

"After much vehement denial Burr [assured] Jackson *upon
his honor* that his object . . . [had] the approbation of our govt
& . . . pulled from his pocket a blank commission signed by Mr.
Jefferson saying, 'Gentlemen, I suppose this will satisfy you.' "[19]

Jackson's suspicions were quelled to the extent that he released
two boats (all Burr desired), and permitted seventeen-year-old
Stockley Hays, Rachel's nephew, bound for school at New Orleans, to go on one of them. Patton Anderson's military company remained at home, however, and the Hays boy carried
confidential letters to Governor Claiborne.[20]

6

Burr and boats departed at dawn on December twenty-second.
They had gone too far to be overtaken when Jefferson's proclamation came, and Andrew Jackson learned[21] that it takes a long

poon to sup with the devil. "Last night at the hour of nine," chronicled the *Impartial Review* on January third, "commenced the burning of the Effigy of Col. Aaron Burr." There had been a similar cremation three days before. In threshing exhortations from the foot of the pyre, Thomas Swann and Charles Dickinson's father-in-law joined the names of Jackson and the fugitive. The town boiled with excitement and citizens lately flattered to be seen in Burr's company were loudest in their deprecation of his infamy.

The panic was not confined to Nashville. At Pittsburgh Captain Read reported to the War Department that an army from Tennessee with Jackson at its head was on the march to join Aaron Burr. The responsible Richmond *Enquirer* was "happy to hear that General Wilkinson had been tampered with unsuccessfully," but unhappy that it could not say the same "of a militia general in Tennessee."

While frightened friends and exultant foes proclaimed their loyalty about a fire in the court-house square, the Hermitage presented a scene of torrential activity as Jackson moved to confront the crisis believed to imperil the Union. At eleven o'clock on New Year's night he had received a communication—"I cannot call it an order"—from the Secretary of War: "a milk and water thing . . . the merest old-woman letter you ever saw."[22]
Jackson's characterizations were appropriate.

"War Department Dec 19, 1806

"General Jackson,
"Sir:
" . . . It appears that you have some reason for suspecting that some unlawful enterprise is in contemplation on the western waters. There can be no doubt, but that many persons are engaged in some such enterprise; and before this reaches you, it is not improbable, that a general movement will have commenced.—
"It is presumed that the Proclamation of the President . . . will have produced every exertion . . . and . . . that you will have been among the most jealous opposers of any such unlawful expedition, as appears to be initiated, by a set of disappointed,

unprincipled, ambitious or misguided individuals, and that you will continue to make every exertion in your power, as a General of the Militia, to counteract and render abhortive, any such expedition. . . . About Pittsburgh it is industriously reported among the adventurers, that they are to be joined, at the mouth of the Cumberland, by two Regiments under the Command of General Jackson—such a story might afford you an opportunity of giving an effectual check to the enterprise if not too late I am etc.

"HENRY DEARBORN"[23]

Contrast this nebulous, hinting thing, from the Government's responsible minister of defense, written in the light of information from a hundred quarters, with the decisive expressions of his frontier servant after one conversation with Captain Fort. The more Jackson conned it, the angrier he became. Did Dearborn really wish Burr molested?

The Secretary's letter was acknowledged: "The first duty of a soldier is to attend to the safety . . . of his country. The next is to attend to his own feelings when they have been . . . wantonly assailed."[24]

Assuming that Dearborn did wish Burr taken, Jackson put two brigades under arms. Volunteer companies were called for. Jack Morrell was dispatched with word to Captain Bissell, commanding the Regular Army post at Fort Massac on the Ohio, to intercept armed boats and to call on Jackson for reenforcements if necessary. The flames died in the court-house square, and men began to understand that a better way to prove their fealty was to put themselves at the disposal of Jackson. Old General Robertson gave this an aspect of completeness by ceremoniously tendering the service of the "Corps of Invincibles," Revolutionary veterans.

7

Major General Jackson's rôle as protector of the Republic might have electrified the country, as it did the Cumberland, had the Union been in danger. It soon fell out, however, that the military aspect of Burr's "expedition" had been comically exaggerated. Jack Morrell returned with a tart reply from Captain Bissell. The peace of the United States had not been jeopardized within his jurisdiction. Colonel Burr had passed down the river with ten unarmed boats manned by six men each. The Captain had no orders to detain him and implied that he required no instruction in his duties from a militiaman. So Burr floated down the Mississippi in ignorance of furore behind him, or the trap in front where Wilkinson was slapping dupes in jail and thunderously laying waste to the aspirations of his fellow-conspirator "Wilkinson is entirely devoted to us," wrote the Spanish Minister. "The President confides in his fidelity"—Senator Smith to General Jackson.

When his eyes at length were opened Burr deserted his boats and slipped into the wilderness.

"Burr and his expedition . . . [are] a thread bare topic," wrote a resident of the Cumberland. "The Volunteers pretty well tucked out waiting for nothing."[25] With the imagined peril of the nation out of the way, General Jackson could undertake a soldier's "next" duty. He believed Dearborn as deeply involved with Burr as himself, though wanting courage to acknowledge it—a suspicion from which time has not absolved the Secretary. Sending his army home, the Cumberland commander immersed himself in the toils of composition. Ordinarily Jackson wrote rapidly, just as he spoke. He wrote rapidly now, but nothing seemed to suit. He struck out and recast. This was unusual, for Jackson was a man who knew his own mind at all times and had the habit of expressing himself clearly in the first words that came to him. But this time he was dissatisfied and, taking a fresh sheet of paper, began anew. "Henry Dearborn, Sir. . . . Colo. B. received at my house all that hospitality that a banished patriot . . . was entitled to. . . . But sir when proof shews him to be a treator I would cut his throat with as much pleasure as I would cut yours on equal testimony."[26]

Still dissatisfied Jackson wrote a third draft, which he sent. Though slightly less quotable than the foregoing. it nevertheless holds its own place among communications from a subordinate to a Secretary of War.

"You stand convicted of the most notorious and criminal acts of dishonor, dishonesty, want of candour and justice. . . . You say Sir that it is industriously reported amongst adventurers that they are to be joined at the mouth of cumberland by two regiments under the command of Gnl Jackson. Such a *Story* might afford him an opportunity of giving an effectual check to the enterprise, if not too late. After I have given the most deliber[ate] consideration to your expressions, . . . I cannot draw from them any other conclusion but this: that you believed me concerned in the conspiracy [and] that I was a fit subject to act the traitor of traitors, as others have done, and that the . . . Secretary of war . . . [could] buy me up without honour."

The "others" Jackson identified as "yr. much loved Genl. Wilkinson" and the Secretary himself. "Was anything in . . . [the order of December nineteenth] that would have authorized . . . [Burr's] arrest? . . . There was not. . . . What . . . the Secretary at war . . . has done is unworthy of . . . a . . . man of honor. I care not where, when, or how he shall . . . [undertake to resent this language]. I am equally regardless of . . . [his] defense before the world. I know it cannot be . . . either tenable or true."[27]

Secretary Dearborn offered no defense. He made no move to resent his correspondent's language. The communication was passed over with the complete dignity of silence and Henry Dearborn said nothing more of Andrew Jackson's relations with Aaron Burr.

Jackson also labored manfully to expose James Wilkinson, but vital evidence remained elusive. Deserted by every one, Burr was taken in disguise, a few miles from the frontier of Spanish Florida, and safety. The ardor with which the Administration continued to repel the least whisper against Wilkinson, clinched Jackson's conviction that "Jamy" could hardly be the only official tarred with Burr's brush.

8

Behind the desk of the Speaker, in the graceful hall of the House of Delegates at Richmond, sat a tallish man in his fifties— jet-black hair, jet-black eyes, and the demeanor and homely dignity of a shrewd country lawyer. If his quick glance strayed to the windows it may have been to recall how as a young member of the Virginia Assembly he had pitched horseshoes on the State-House green. Before Chief Justice John Marshall bowed the accused, Aaron Burr, perfection in dress and composure. He had been escorted from a comfortable apartment in the penitentiary by a guard of honor of two hundred gentlemen. Behind him was the eminent counsel of the United States and for the accused; behind them a press of forms and faces, of powdered wigs and ruffled shirts, diffusing an odor of snuff and Madeira. Minds went back to the celebrated trial two years before when Aaron Burr sat in the seat of judgment and a Justice of the Supreme Court in that of the judged.

"May it please the Court," began Colonel Burr, very pale. He said the law for the formation of the grand jury had been evaded, William Branch Giles and Wilson Carey Nicholas being on the panel in violation of the rules of procedure. Giles was a United States senator, Nicholas a former senator, both allies of Thomas Jefferson and enemies of Aaron Burr.

John Marshall ruled for the accused, and the stillness deepened. The grand jury was formed with the lank Murat of the House of Representatives, John Randolph, as foreman—Thomas Jefferson's relative, but not his protégé. District Attorney Hay moved for an adjournment. His key witness had not appeared. On the next day he made the same request for the same reason, and on another day repeated it. The missing witness was Brigadier-General James Wilkinson, by whose testimony the prosecution promised to establish the treason of Aaron Burr. The defense sensationally demanded a subpoena duces tecum directing the appearance of the President of the United States. For four days

Marshall listened to argument, and issued the subpœna which Jefferson refused to obey. Still no Wilkinson. Public opinion began to incline toward the prisoner at the bar.

The trend was not hindered by the attitude of another witness under subpœna of the prosecution. Andrew Jackson had responded promptly and had been told to wait. In high company and low, on the thronged sidewalk of Brick Row, in smoke-fogged Eagle Tavern and the jostling crowd that trampled the State-House green, he denounced James Wilkinson; and as delay succeeded delay, asked if Thomas Jefferson held himself above the law.

After twenty days Wilkinson obeyed the summons. People lined the streets to scan the stout form in full panoply of rank, the strong face, big, brandy nose and steady eyes. They saw young Samuel Swartwout, whom Wilkinson had jailed in the South and stolen his watch, shoulder him from a walk. They heard Andrew Jackson call him "a double traitor" and "pity the sword that dangles from his felon's belt, for it is doubtless of honest steel!"[28]

The waiting witness wrote William Preston Anderson. "Tell ... Mrs. Jackson ... not to be uneasy. ... I am more convinced than ever that treason never was intended by Burr; but if ever it was, you know my wishes—that he may be hung."[29]

It required a loud explosion to penetrate the preoccupation at Richmond, but this was provided by the broadside guns of the English warship *Leopard* when they raked our unready *Chesapeake,* killing or wounding twenty-one men to get four presumed British deserters. A savage cry rang through the West. "On my Conscience and Faith and Honour," wrote one friend of Andrew Jackson, "I hope that war will take place."[30] So hoped Tennessee's Major General, and when Mr. Jefferson turned to diplomacy he announced that he "would address the people from the steps of the State-House after the adjournment of court." He spoke for an hour. "Mr. Jefferson has plenty of courage to seize peaceable Americans ... and persecute them for political purposes. But he is too cowardly to resent foreign outrage on the Republic. An English man-of-war fires on an American ship ... so near his Capital that he can almost hear the guns, and what does he do? ... A year or more ago I gave at a dinner to Aaron Burr the toast—'Millions for defence; not a cent for tribute.' They change that tune on this side of the mountains. ... 'Millions to persecute an American; not a cent to resist England!' "[31]

The prosecutor released General Jackson from his subpœna.

9

In January of 1810 Rachel stepped from her carriage at the Hermitage with a bundle in her plump arms. It was a baby, and the baby was hers—to have for ever, and not for a week or a season, to grow fond of and to lose as she had lost so many others. In 1804 Edward Butler died, making Jackson guardian of his children, Anthony Wayne Butler, Edward George Washington Butler and two girls whose names—did he resist Betsy Ross and Molly Pitcher?—are unknown to your chronicler.[32] In 1805 Edward Butler's brother, Colonel Thomas Butler, his locks still unshorn, had failed to survive his court martial. One of his last letters begged Jackson to extend a father's guidance to his boys. And when Samuel Donelson died, Jackson carried his two sons, John and Andrew Jackson, to the Hermitage, to raise and to school them as his own. Jackson felt a peculiar solicitude for these bright children. He had held the grapevine ladder by which their mother had taken silent leave of her obdurate parents for a midnight wedding.[33] The Donelson boys were at the Hermitage now with little William Smith, a pathetic child, born to a neighboring couple after the normal expectancy of such an event had passed, and grown sons and daughters were disputing over the prospective division of the estate.[34]

The new baby made four. On the third night before Christmas, the wife of Severn Donelson, had borne twins. The mother, barely surviving, could not suckle two infants. Her sister-in-law had carried one away, which Rachel and Andrew legally adopted and christened Andrew Jackson, junior. The mistress of twenty slaves submerged herself in the service of her new love. He grew strong and brightened the hearthside of the blockhouse with a promise of cheerfulness and tranquillity.

This promise was needed. As he had abandoned the law in which he prospered and public life in which he had won a name, General Jackson now relinquished trade in which he had failed. The house of Jackson & Hutchings had never rightly caught the tide that carried many to fortune with the annexation of Louisiana. As that tide ebbed, the firm struck the shoals of slack times and closed its doors. The last statement of its condition showed liabilities of twenty-one thousand four hundred and thirty-six dollars and sixty-one cents against twenty-five thousand, two hundred and eighty-three dollars and fifty-two cents in assets, mostly customers' bills, probably half of which were never collected.[35] John Coffee, a silent partner, gave Jackson notes for his share of the debts, and returned to surveying. When his friend drew upon the inexhaustible supply of Rachel's nieces for a wife, Jackson opened his iron strong-box and presented the notes to the bride.

Store debts were gradually depleted by earnings of the Hermitage plantation and racing stable. For five years General Jackson had not lost an important race without being able to compensate immediately with a victory. Truxton had won more than twenty thousand dollars in prizes and his progeny was becoming famous. During the general simplification of his affairs Jackson had sold his Clover Bottom track to the Nashville Jockey Club. In 1811 he entered Decatur, a Truxton colt, in the fall meeting. Jackson had ambitions for Decatur and was chagrined to see him beaten by three-year-old chestnut mare Maria, owned by Jesse Haynie of Sumner County. In fact, Maria lowered the Jackson colors all along the line, winning six races and losing none.

The turfman's leisure hours were spent in the company of a translation of the French army regulations, and in applying its precepts to his militia division. Again and again this division reached for its arms as the commander could not conceive of an Administration longer enduring the arrogance of England. "My only pride is [that] ... my soldiers has confidence in me, and on the event of war I will lead them to victory. Should we be blest with peace I will resign my military office and spend my days in the sweet calm of rural retirement."[36]

But Jackson foresaw only war or a perpetuation of the dishonor which he had come to regard as synonymous with the régime of Thomas Jefferson. In 1808 this had led him to support James Monroe for the presidency, perhaps on the theory that any one Jefferson opposed would be preferable to the Administration's altar boy, Madison. Actually, however, in 1808 and for a long time after, Colonel Monroe was more friendly to England than was either Madison or Jefferson. Nevertheless, the election of Madison continued a policy of non-resistance and things drifted along much as before. Each fresh climax that made drums to beat along the Cumberland splintered in futility. Acquitted of treason but reindicted for high misdemeanor, Burr had fled the country. An effort to deprive Wilkinson of his rank failed with Madison's approval. "On the eve of war and a Treator at the head of the army!"[37]

Such were the occupations of Andrew Jackson when in 1811 George Washington Campbell rode to the Hermitage to see his friend alone. Mr. Campbell had resigned from Congress for a place on the State Supreme Court of Errors and Appeals, in conse quence of which he had privately discovered an error.

The financial troubles entrammeling Jackson date from David Allison's failure at Philadelphia in 1796. Allison died in a debtors' prison after making a futile effort to free himself by mortgaging to Norton Prior eighty-five thousand acres of land on Duck River in Tennessee. Prior had asked Jackson to join him in a foreclosure against Allison's heirs, but Jackson being on the bench referred the matter to John Overton who successfully prosecuted the action in a Federal Court. In the liquidation Jackson obtained thousand acres which he sold in parcels to settlers, giving them warranted titles, binding himself, should the titles prove unsound, to buy back the land, not for what he sold it, but for what it should be worth when the titular defect appeared. The wilderness Jackson sold had become orderly fields of grain and bobbing cotton worth a fortune. Judge Campbell said that Jackson was liable for all this. His titles were not good. The Federal Court had been without jurisdiction in the foreclosure suit.

"I became alarmed and . . . went to Mr J Whitesides." United States Senator Whiteside was the most celebrated lawyer in Tennessee. He told Jackson not to worry. What the Allison heirs did not know would never help them, and in any event they were without funds to redeem the mortgage. "I told Mr. Whitesides that I had never sold any land but what I thought the title was good" and that he would perfect his titles for the protection of "those honest men" on Duck River.[38]

Andrew Jackson had been rather showy, the Administration thought, in his proffers of life and fortune to protect the nation's honor. With no show he rejected the advice of a crafty lawyer, and imperiled his fortune beyond hope of extrication to protect his personal honor. That is one aspect of the case as General Jackson's admirers in later years were pleased to point out. Another aspect of it establishes that under the proper sponsorship honesty may be not only the best policy, but the best paying one. Jackson rode to Georgia where the Allison heirs lived in poverty and told them everything. "I have a claim," he said in effect, "against the estate of David Allison for twenty thousand dollars. I will surrender that claim in exchange for your release upon these eighty-five thousand acres." Had the Allisons refused the cat would have been out of the bag and Jackson face to face with ruin. To satisfy his moral compunctions Jackson took that chance. But the heirs did not refuse, and the sagacious bargainer returned to Tennessee armed with legal instruments enabling him to convey proper titles to the purchasers of his own five thousand acres and to demand his own price for the same service to those who had sold the other eighty thousand acres.[39]

Jackson had saved himself by an act that can hardly be stripped of its attributes of courage and of honest impulse, but other acts, equally courageous, equally honest in Jackson's view, did not frame him in so fair a light: a brawl at Clover Bottom wherein Jackson covered the starting post with his pistols to prevent a race he believed had been fixed;[40] a war over the slave trade against Silas Dinsmore, government agent of the Choctaws, which constituted a rather presumptuous disregard of the authority of the

United States.[41] Then David Magness concluded a long and hitherto indecisive feud with Patton Anderson by killing him, and Jackson vowed that the slayer of his friend should hang.

The village of Franklin became a smaller Richmond, Jenkin Whiteside, John Haywood, Felix Grundy and other immortals of the border bar contending in the cause célèbre. Jackson roared upon the scene and, none too steady on his feet, delivered a tap-room harangue which a stranger would have found impossible to associate with the man who once had sustained with a pistol the prerogatives of courts in Tennessee. Jackson took the stand as a character witness for Anderson. On cross-examination alert Felix Grundy, one time to be Attorney-General of the United States, pecked away at the General's portrait of the peace-loving nature of the deceased. Had not Major Anderson frequently been in "difficulties"? Had he not made numerous enemies?

"Sir," quoth Andrew Jackson, "my friend was the NATURAL ENEMY OF SCOUNDRELS!"[42]

Magness received a light sentence for manslaughter and Jackson shook his fist under the nose of one of the jurors.

10

In a blustery February twilight the truculent Major General gazed into his great fireplace, brooding. Between his knees nestled Andrew, junior, and a lamb the master of the Hermitage flocks had carried out of the storm.[43] "From my persuits for several years past, from many unpleasant occurences . . . during that time . . . my mind . . . [has taken] a turn of thought that I have laboured to get clear of."[44]

Not money worries this time. The old embarrassments were nearly sponged out,[45] but Jackson had proof that solvency is no guarantee of felicity. George M. Deaderick was rich—president of the Nashville Bank, the only bank in Tennessee, and symbol of the retreat of the frontier. Careful as he was of fresh investments, General Jackson had taken fifty shares in it.[46] Yet Mr. Deaderick was unhappy, his wife's "use of her eyes" bringing reproaches that had caused an estrangement. "By the expressions of the eye as much levity & Viciousness can be expressed as by the tongue,"[47] the harassed husband assured Jackson, asking him to try to patch up matters. A desperate letter from Deaderick indicates the measure of the General's success. "I do solemnly declare to you that I never have conveyed an Idea to Mrs Deaderick or to any other individual that I . . . suspected you had any carnal knowledge of her." This pretty story was the work of a lady who wished to annoy her husband. "You will not I know," pleaded the banker, "Abandon a . . . friend."[48]

And other thorns sprang from seeds that should have borne only flowers of contentment. Generously had Jackson fulfilled the dying request of old Colonel Thomas Butler and become, in truth, as a father to his sons. He had seen the oldest boy Robert grow to be a fine man more than six feet tall, and an embodiment of the virtues that warmed the heart of Andrew Jackson.

Of all her nieces Rachel's favorite was Rachel Hays, a lively laughing girl in whom the older woman could see the reflection of herself in the zestful blockhouse days. When Robert and Rachel began to keep company no one looked on with more approving eyes than the couple at the Hermitage. Naturally, it was too much to expect that Robert's suit for a belle such as Rachel Hays should be undisputed. Half a dozen other blades danced attendance on her, and in this connection a foul tale reached her uncle's ears. Jackson ran it down and stood over George Blakemore who with quill and ink acknowledged himself a liar.[49]

So Rachel and Robert were married and nothing seemed wanting to insure their happiness. Robert owned lands and negroes and was looked upon as one of the coming young men of the Valley. Alack, they quarreled, and over the most sordid of matters: money. Robert wished to save, Rachel to spend. "Our friend R.B.," a cousin of the bride wrote to General Jackson, "[is] doom'd to . . . the melancholy effects of imprudence in a wife. Good God! . . . What a reward for Aunt J[ackson]."[50]

But the deepest cuts came from the slinking whispers that touched the "sacred name."

Rachel Jackson was forty-three. Her short figure had grown rather stout, but her movements were quick and agile, her olive countenance unlined, and the round black eyes young and fine. She owned a carriage but preferred the saddle. She wore good clothes, but neglected the styles. Nashville was no longer frontier, but Rachel remained a frontier woman, clinging to the fragile images of a bygone day that had witnessed her last touch with happiness—a day when something less superficial than silks constituted the resources of charm in a Cumberland belle. With these resources Rachel may have been endowed too well. In any event twenty years of piety shining in every act of her life, of boundless generosity, charity and kindness, of ministrations to the troubled, the sick and the orphaned had not erased a record at Harrodsburgh, or stilled tongues wagged by consciences enjoying an ease Rachel could not attain.

At this late time it seemed the work of her own sex. The retribution of Charles Dickinson had established that Jackson could deal with men. But women were another case as, after Mrs. Deaderick, the General had reason to suspect. He sent Lem Hutchings to Sumner County to conduct "a strict inquiry." The mission was a failure. "I cannot learn that Betsy has said anything injurious of Mrs. Jackson."[51] Jackson himself wrote to solicit the help of the wife of a neighbor. She replied in confusion. "I pledge you that Mrs Bell did not either directly or indirectly say anything tending to injure the reputation of Mrs. Jackson."[52]

A man pursuing a shadow.

II

"Unpleasant occurrences" in sooth, and, one suspects, the hidden source of much of the rancor and rashness that has left its impress on painful episodes: Dickinson, Burr, Silas Dinsmore, Patton Anderson.

The pass to which such episodes had brought the man who at twenty-one was Attorney-General, at thirty-one United States Senator and Superior Judge, all with eyes could see. Jackson saw this much and more. He saw the pass to which the pursuit of fame had brought his domestic happiness. He strove to blot out the unpleasant image "to divest myself of those habits of . . . gloomy reflections. . . . I find it impossible."[53] The poisoned arrows had struck home.

The man of action behaved with resolution. A confidential letter went to a confidential friend. "In order to try the experiment how new scenes might relieve me from this unpleasant tone of thought," Andrew Jackson was prepared to relinquish the gains of a lifetime in Tennessee and exchange the equivocal coin of public reputation for the tranquil obscurity of another frontier[54] by which he hoped to restore his peace of mind and that of the woman he loved.

One of the Donelson nephews was dispatched on a tour of inspection of Mississippi. A young Army officer at Natchitoches reported on the soil, climate and crops of Louisiana, adding, for completeness, a paragraph about the people. "The creole women . . . surpass the world at intrigue, . . . & I can only admire their taste in Generally preferring an american."[55]

The choice fell on Washington County, Mississippi. The landscape was reminiscent of Bayou Pierre where the unforgettable honeymoon had been spent and the rolling current of the great brown river washing the base of the bluff recalled the felicity of the past. The Hermitage was offered for sale to a horse-trading acquaintance, the splendid Wade Hampton of Charleston.[56] United States Senator Whiteside was petitioned for an insignificant judgeship in Mississippi Territory. "If the salary . . . is $1000 I will accept."[57]

BOOK THREE

THE SWORD

"What, retrograde under these circumstances? I will perish first!"
GENERAL JACKSON to Governor Blount of Tennessee

CHAPTER IX

Old Hickory

I

"I fear you cannot read this scroll," Jackson closed a long and depressing business letter. "I write it in the night and with the Rheumatick in my right rist so that I can scarcely wield the pen."[1]

But in seven days he had recovered the use of his writing hand.

"Hermitage, March 7 1812
"VOLUNTEERS TO ARMS!

"*Citizens!* Your government has yielded to the impulse of the nation.... War is on the point of breaking out between the United States and . . . great Britain! and the martial hosts . . . are summoned to the Tented Fields! . . .

"A simple invitation is given . . . [for] 50,000 volunteers. . . . Shall we, who have clamoured for war, now skulk into a corner? . . . Are we the titled Slaves of George the third? the military conscripts of Napolon? or the frozen peasants of the Rusian Czar? No— we are the free born sons of . . . the only republick now existing in the world. . . .

"Are we going to fight to satisfy the revenge or ambition of a corrupt ministry? to place another diadem on the head of an apostate republican general? . . . No . . . we are going to fight for the reestablishment of our national charactor, . . . for the protection of our maratime citizens, . . . to vindicate our right to free trade. . . .

"The period of youth is the season for martial exploits; and . . . how pleasing the prospect . . . to . . . *promenade* into a distant country . . . and [witness] the grand evolutions of an army of fifty

thousand men. To view the stupenduous works of nature, . . .
Niagra, . . . Montmorenci, . . . carrying the republican standard to
the heights of abraham. . . .

"ANDREW JACKSON
"Major General"[2]

2

Perhaps from a feeling of delicacy for Tennessee's pride in its
military prowess, the General omitted to mention that the "invitation" to whip England had been extended to the other states
as well.

Yet Andrew Jackson was under no apprehension as to the popularity in the East of the inevitable conflict. The fact that the
East opposed war was virtually reason enough to insure its acceptance in the West, and, regardless of glib economic theories or
ponderous ones, this spite-fence of antagonism more than anything
else produced the division of sentiment which was to embarrass
our military effort from the first. The Embargo, the Non-
Intercourse Acts, the Orders, Decrees, and the rest bore about
as heavily on the shipping and commercial interests of New
England as on the agricultural West. The personality of Napoleon
Bonaparte had more to do with it than these things. Jackson's
predilection for him, and his persevering inclination to see good
in his acts despite the allusion in the call to arms, was but a reflection of Western opinion. The Corsican was an architect of
new frontiers, let the chips fall where they may, and so were our
pioneers. He cared little for precedent. Nor did they. He was a
careerist. So were they. He created a feeling of nationalism that
Frenchmen had not known before. Our borderers did the same in
America. All this turned frontiersmen against England whom the
conservative East supported as a protagonist of the existing order
against the destructive occupations of a marauding opportunist.

The choice cost the East the leadership in affairs it had exercised
since the nation's beginning. The swift overthrow came spec-
tacularly with the organization of the Twelfth Congress in De-

cember, 1811. From the young West had swarmed young men, schooled in resentment for the humiliation that had degraded us as a neutral in the cross-fires of England's death grapple with the Emperor. The East tried to sneer at the "War Hawks," but soon discovered its inability to match for eloquence, enthusiasm and force such men as Henry Clay and Richard M. Johnson of Kentucky, Felix Grundy of Tennessee, John C. Calhoun and Langdon Cheves of South Carolina. With a scattering of Eastern allies as young as themselves, they captured Congress and swept Clay—"Harry of the West"—into the speakership of the House, an office soon to become almost second in public esteem to the presidency.

Like a bracing breeze from the mountains their ardor aroused a lethargic nation. It aroused the Administration where the War Hawks were able, by degrees, to make an ally of erstwhile pro-English James Monroe, who had become Secretary of State. In Tennessee old John Sevier once more had served the constitutional limit of three consecutive terms to be succeeded by Jackson's friend Willie Blount.[3] A change of air altogether.

The rush of these events had obliterated the plan to leave Tennessee, which one of Rachel's nephews living in Natchez had opposed from the start. "You have been able to read the Characters of men. In their actions; here another Volume will be presented to our view in which human baseness will take up a considerable part. . . . Were I in your situation [I] would not move."[4] For Rachel's sake, one hopes that he was right.

June 18, 1812, the House balloted on the war resolution. Tennessee, Kentucky, Ohio, Georgia and South Carolina did not cast a vote against it. Connecticut, Rhode Island and Delaware did not cast one for it. New York voted two for war, eleven for peace; Massachusetts eight to six for peace. But the resolution prevailed seventy-nine to forty-nine.

Anticipating the result a courier was already in the saddle. Lexington, North Carolina, saw him "tear through" without stopping, "his horse's tail and his own long hair streaming in the wind. . . . 'Here's the Stuff! WAR WITH ENGLAND!! WAR!!'" Billy Phillips had learned horsemanship under the

eyes of Andrew Jackson. He had ridden Truxton. At seven in
the evening of June twenty-first, he clattered into the dusty Square
at Nashville, having covered eight hundred and sixty miles over
primitive roads and three mountain ranges in nine days to the
hour.[5] Spreading like quicksilver, the news evoked "a unanimous
huzau. . . . Had any other sentiment been Express[d]. . . . [the
author] would have been Tarred & Feathered."[6]

General Jackson offered the President his militia division of
twenty-five hundred trained men for instantaneous service and
promised to have them before Quebec in ninety days.   "He can
most certainly do so," exclaimed Blount in an endorsement calculated to melt the antipathy of the Administration toward the
Tennessee Commander. "At the present crisis he feels a holy
zeal for the welfare of the United States, and"—in case the War
Department had not forgotten Aaron Burr—"at no period in his
life has been known to feel otherwise. . . . He delights in peace;
but . . . has a peculiar pleasure in treating his enemies as such."[7]
General Jackson's attitude toward his enemies was a matter the
present Secretary of War could establish by reference to the correspondence of his predecessor, Henry Dearborn.

Jackson's proffer was perfunctorily accepted but no orders
came to take the field. As for Quebec, the Department had other
plans. General Henry Dearborn was told off to lead the dash
against the city on the rock, and nine months after receiving his
orders took up the line of march. Meantime Hull surrendered
Detroit without a shot; Wilkinson assumed command at New
Orleans; two of Jackson's regiments and Brigadier-General James
Winchester were called to assist Harrison in the North, but there
was no call for the Commander.

Aaron Burr landed penniless in New York after four years of
wandering in Europe. Martin Van Buren who, as a law student
and a rather too carefully dressed young man, had enjoyed the
patronage of Burr, was brave enough to perform some courtesies.
"I'll tell you why they don't employ Jackson," Burr told him
"It's because he is a friend of mine."[8]

3

The Major General saw his dream of paralyzing Canada by a lightning stroke against trivial opposition—and it was trivial—come to naught. He saw an alternative plan for a descent upon the Floridas come to naught. He saw the Northwest lost and our soil invaded. "The news . . . almost killed me." His offer to march "any minute" with a thousand mounted men and retake Detroit was not accorded the civility of an acknowledgment. He saw the Indians, quick to sense the direction of the wind, swell the ranks of the enemy. As idle weeks became idle months, he beheld a decline of the esprit which for eleven years he had labored to implant in his division.

As a recreation for his mind, General Jackson interested himself in the autumn meeting of the Nashville Jockey Club.[9] Hoping for marching orders he had neglected his horses. The presence of Jesse Haynie's little chestnut mare Maria, however, recalled too vividly the humiliation of the year before. Ed Bradley's Dungannon was to race Maria and Bradley was confident of victory. To share in the triumph Jackson bought an interest in Dungannon. But Maria beat him more easily than she had beaten Jackson's Decatur in 1811.

In the same month, October of 1812, the War Department requested of Governor Blount—not General Jackson—fifteen hundred men to reenforce James Wilkinson at New Orleans. The plain implication of the Department's request was that Jackson's services were not desired.[10] And the galling part was that the troops were to be used in the occupation of West Florida, an enterprise which Jackson had originally outlined to the Department and offered to undertake alone. Dearborn for Quebec, Wilkinson for Florida: Jackson might suggest campaigns, but their execution was entrusted to the Administration's favorites.

Willie Blount turned to his friend. Would Jackson accept a subordinate command under Wilkinson?

The man who already had asked for service on every front and

advanced money from his own pocket for the purchase of rifles
until promissory notes bearing the autograph of Andrew Jackson
were currency in Tennessee, replied: "I cannot disguise my feelings. had the Secretary of War directed you to call me . . . into the
field . . . [with the] compensation of sergeant I should have been
content, but he has not even daigned to name me," or his treas-
ured division. "But . . . should your Excellency believe that my
personal service can promote" the country's welfare, "all I ask
is" a chance to fight.[11]

Blount was in a quandary. A difference of opinion had arisen
between him and the Major General over the mode of selecting
field officers for the militia. Blount favored the old and popular
method of election by the men. Jackson insisted that they should
be appointed by the Commander. "We want Men Capable of
Command—who will fight and reduce their soldiers to strict obedience."[12] This was an advanced position for a militia general in
1812. The Governor's hands fluttered over the seventy blank
commissions the War Department had sent already signed in order
to get the Tennessee force in the field without delay. He consulted lawyers, and, after agonies of indecision, took up one of the
papers and filled in the name of Andrew Jackson, who thus became a Major General of United States volunteers, in the war at
last by a small side door.

4

The sea-green Cumberland freezes at Nashville four or five
times in a century. It froze from bank to bank on December 10,
1812, the day set for the rendezvous of the fifteen hundred volunteers. Twenty-five hundred responded. From every quarter of
Middle Tennessee they came, by companies, by platoons, by ones
and twos, ahorse and afoot, in dark-blue and nut-brown homespun
and in buckskin hunting shirts. A few of the officers sported white
pantaloons and waistcoats. These men had been reared with arms
in their hands and they came with rifles. "Smooth-bore muskets,"
General Jackson had advised, "do not carry straight. They may

be good enough for Regular Soldiers, but not the Citizen Volun·
teers of Tennessee."

Against the zero cold they were not so well armed, however.
Jackson's neighbor and the army quartermaster, Major William
B. Lewis, had assembled a thousand cords of wood, expected to
last the life of the encampment. It was burned that night as
Jackson himself made the rounds to keep sleeping men from
freezing. At six o'clock he stamped the snow from his boots in
front of a tavern fire. A well-known citizen who had spent the
night in bed deprecated the lack of preparation for the troops.
"You damned, infernal scoundrel," blazed the Major General.
"More of that talk and I'll ram that hot andiron down your
throat."[13]

The War Department accepted two thousand and seventy men.
Jackson borrowed sixteen hundred and fifty dollars[14] to cover his
extraordinary personal expenses, and on January seventh Colonel
John Coffee's regiment of cavalry filed down the Natchez Trace
while the General and two infantry regiments boarded flatboats.
With "Four beautifull stand of Colours" waving and minute guns
firing, cables were slipped and the great scows glided from the view
of an huzzahing populace. "It is a bitter pill to have to serve
with ... Wilkinson ... but I go in the true spirit of a soldier."[15]
Taking his dueling pistols, however.

The Ohio was a grinding field of ice. General Jackson went
ashore to reconnoiter and to write a letter.

"My Love:
"I have this evening received your affectionate letter ... [and]
your miniature. I shall wear it near my bosom; but this was use·
less for my recollection never fails me of your likeness.

"The sensibility of our beloved son has charmed me. . . . He
will take care of both of us in our declining years. . . . Kiss him
for his papa and give him nuts and ginger cake [I send].

"I thank you for your prayers. I thank you for your determined
resolution to bear our separation with fortitude. We part but
for . . . a few fleeting weeks when the protecting hand of
Providence . . . will restore us to each others arms. . . .

"It is now 1 o'clock in the morning—the candle nearly out. . . . May the angelic hosts that reward and protect virtue and innocence and preserve the good be with you until I return, is the sincere supplication of your affectionate husband."[16]

Despite ice, an earthquake that had terrorized inhabitants and changed the currents of the Mississippi, and the loss of three men and one boat, the Commander's sleepless energy brought the flotilla off Natchez, distant two thousand miles by the route it had come, in thirty-nine days. On shore in the dark Major Carroll gave him a packet of mail.

"Your letter . . . was everything to me. . . . Where'er I go, where'er I turn, my thoughts, my fears, my doubts distress me. Then a little hope revives again and that keeps me alive. . . . Do not my beloved husband let love of country, fame and honor, make you forget [me]. . . . You will say this is not the language of a patriot, but it is the language of a faithful wife. . . .

"Our little Andrew often does he ask me in bed not to cry, papa will come again and I feel my cheeks to know if I am shedding tears. . . .

"Your dearest friend on earth
"RACHEL JACKSON"[17]

Another communication was from "Head Quarters, New Orleans."

"Sir, I have received from his Excellency Governor Blount . . . [information that] you were about to move from Nashville with one thousand four hundred infantry and Riflemen, and six hundred and seventy dragoons, destined to this city. . . .

"I beg leave to refer you to my letter of the 22nd. Inst., and must repeat my desire that you should halt in the vicinity of Natchez. . . .

"With consideration and respect,
"I have the honor to be Your Obedt Servant
"JAMES WILKINSON"[18]

The letter of January twenty-second was couched in terms that exceeded the bounds of ordinary military courtesy. "Several reasons prevent my calling you lower down the river. . . . Vizt. the impracticability of providing for your horses, . . . the health of the troops; . . . the policy of holding your corps on the alert" within equal striking distance of Pensacola, Mobile and New Orleans—wherever needed. General Wilkinson had ordered provisions to Natchez. General Jackson would find Brigade Inspector Hughes on the ground to muster the troops into Federal service, and Paymaster Knight to pay them. "Those officers [will] give every aid and facility . . . and if it is in my power to add to the comfort of the band of patriots under your orders, it is only necessary to point out the mode to me."[19]

5

Jackson perceived the military logic of Wilkinson's polite "requests" and encamped his troops. A week, a fortnight passed—and no orders. At New Orleans the subtle commandant was pondering the next phase of his problem of keeping Jackson at a distance, when news came of Winchester's disastrous defeat in Canada. Jackson asked the War Department to send him to the northern front.[20] Rachel learned of it, though not from her husband. "Oh how hard . . . Love of Country the thirst for Honour . . . is your [ruling] motive."[21]

Fifteen more days of fretful waiting for Jackson and a short letter came from John Armstrong, the Secretary of War:

"The causes for embodying . . . the Corps under your command having ceased to exist, you will on receit of this consider it dismissed from public service and . . . deliver over to Major General Wilkinson all articles of public property. . . . Accept for yourself and the Corps the thanks of the President of the United States. I have the honor to be. . . ."[22]

By countermanding the Florida venture the government had enabled the War Office to rescue General Wilkinson from his quandary as to what to do with Jackson.

Instead of recognizing the celerity with which the Tennessean had thrown an army into Natchez as the most creditable military accomplishment of the war to date, the Government had dismissed that army from service eight hundred miles from home, without pay or rations, without transportation or medicine for the sick. Nor was the blow softened by the sugary observations of Wilkinson, regretting that although "the policy of the Government" prevented "the maturation of our association in arms . . . you still have it in your power to render a most acceptable service to our Government by encouraging" his abandoned troops to enlist in the Regular Army. After which the lucky schemer wished his brother officer "pleasant weather" on his journey home.[23]

Should Jackson disband his army, he saw Wilkinson getting the bulk of Tennessee's fine soldiers without their commander by a mere promise of something to eat. Passing the word to drum from camp the first Regular recruiting officer to approach his men, Jackson posted a fiery proclamation vowing to march the Tennesseans home intact "on my own means and responsibility"[24]—at best an inglorious finale to the grand adventure his ringing words had promised the youth of Tennessee.

In strong but respectful terms he notified Secretary Armstrong and Wilkinson of his refusal to obey that part of the order calling for demobilization on the spot. His command was mostly boys. He had brought them from home, and would take them back at his own expense if they had to eat their horses on the way. Then he wrote his wife. "Kiss my little Andrew for me and tell him his papa is coming home."[25]

Though seething at "the wicked machinations of Armstrong and W—n,"[26] he repressed his feelings out of hope for service in Canada. Firmness obtained twenty days' rations from Wilkinson's quartermaster. Eleven wagons for the desperately ill were hired by the Commander, who altogether laid out more than a thousand dollars for the sick. The other ailing rode horses, three of them Jackson's own, while the General marched on foot. Such things could not be without effect on soldiers whose feeling toward their commander had hitherto been one of respect rather than affection, for Jackson was not the hail-fellow type of militia officer. The column moved at the pace of veterans—in a wilderness where streams had to be bridged and the road hacked through swamps. Jackson was everywhere—up and down the toiling line, with the sick, where the rations were distributed—and always on foot, until the men began to offer their horses.

"He's tough," an admiring voice observed in the ranks after the General had passed by. "Tough as hickory," said another naming the toughest thing he knew. The word somehow seemed to suit the tall, striding man in a mussed uniform and muddy boots. "Hickory" he became to that company. The sobriquet took, and before the first settlements were reached was the property of the army with the affectionate prefix "Old" for completeness.[27] In fine array General Jackson led his command into Tennessee to be showered with honors, but none so great or lasting as the name that had sprung from the hearts of his soldiers.

6

While on vacation from his classes at the College of William and Mary, Thomas Hart Benton had once seen Judge Jackson on the bench. The memory of it was never forgotten by this youth with the form of an athlete and a flare for Roman oratory. As a young lawyer in Franklin, Tennessee, Benton joined the local militia company of General Jackson's division and became its captain. He assisted in the prosecution of Patton Anderson's slayer and began to visit at the Hermitage. He had started on the Natchez expedition as one of the General's aides-de-camp and was not afraid to voice opinions differing from those of his chief. He returned the colonel of a regiment aglow with a desire for a military career.

Jackson gave him letters of introduction to take to Washington in furtherance of this ambition as well as Jackson's never-ceasing effort to get into the field. Moreover he was charged with straightening out the General's property accounts held up by the auditors in consequence of disregarding the order to disband at

Natchez. Henry Dearborn's tardy invasion of Canada had been defeated and driven out. Another commander for the St. Lawrence was inevitable. The War Department was raising several new regiments of Regulars. Jackson's friends in Washington were quietly working to have two of them recruited from Tennessee with their man in command.

Benton was energetic and effective. Jackson's accounts were passed. While there is little doubt of the President's desire to get along without the services of Andrew Jackson, his unjust treatment at Natchez had been due to the normal bungling of the War Office rather than collusion with Wilkinson to humiliate intentionally. Benton obtained a lieutenant-colonelcy in the Regular establishment. That was the end of success. Tennessee got only one Regular regiment—to be raised in the eastern part of the state outside of Jackson's military jurisdiction. To Major General James Wilkinson, attended by every favor and facility the War Department could confer, went the honor calculated to crown our eagles with victory on the St. Lawrence.

Another young man who returned from Natchez with the esteem of Old Hickory was William Carroll,[28] the brigade inspector. Billy Carroll had come from Pittsburgh a few years back to open a hardware store which had been very successful. He was one of the best-dressed sparks in Nashville. An inspector's rôle is not a sure passport to popularity, and a selfish streak in Carroll made his advancement more than ordinarily grating. As soon as the brigade was mustered out in May, Lieutenant Littleton Johnston challenged him. Carroll declined on the ground that Johnston was not a gentleman. The bearer of Johnston's message, Jesse Benton, a brother of General Jackson's envoy, then challenged.

Carroll asked Jackson to be his second. Jackson said he was too old for such a thing, and moreover that the quarrel should be adjusted amicably. As a matter of fact Jackson was guarding his behavior, still hoping for a crumb of favor from Washington. He rode to Nashville to act as peacemaker. He talked with Benton and everything seemed settled until others put in their oars, among them Joseph Erwin and Thomas Swann.

Jackson was indignant at the way his friend had been crowded, and above all at the rattling of Charles Dickinson's bones. "May the angelic hosts protect virtue and innocence," he had written to Rachel, and stood ever ready to extend to those hosts any mundane aid in the discharge of their duties that circumstances might seem to him to require. However faint the allusion or tenuous the trace to touch the Sacred Name, Andrew Jackson never let it pass.

To maintain his standing Carroll was obliged to accept Benton's challenge. Jackson accompanied him to the field. The affair that followed provided Tennessee with a standing jest for many years. Benton fired, and, in a fit of panic, doubled up at the waist so that the most conspicuous part of his person exposed was that covered by the seat of his trousers. Into this target Lieutenant-Colonel Carroll plumped a bullet which did far more injury to the spirit than to the flesh.[29]

7

Lieutenant-Colonel Benton heard of the duel while on his way from Washington. In Nashville he took his stand by his brother and avoided the Hermitage. Gossips made the most of this and Jackson heard that Benton had threatened to challenge him. In a fatherly letter he asked if this were true. Benton replied straightforwardly that it was not, but added that he thought it "very poor business of a man of your age and standing to be conducting a duel about nothing between young men who had no harm against each other." And there were other observations showing that Benton chose to believe the accounts circulated by Jackson's enemies. This brought a stern reply. The Bentons went home to Franklin, but busybodies kept at Jackson until he exclaimed that he would horsewhip Tom Benton the next time he saw him.

Six weeks passed. On the morning of September 4, 1813, the Benton brothers arrived in Nashville and took their saddle-bags to the City Hotel, to avoid, Colonel Benton said, a possibility of unpleasantness, as Jackson and his friends were accustomed to make their headquarters at the Nashville Inn, diagonally across the Court-House Square. Each of the Bentons wore two pistols. At about the same time Jackson, Coffee and Stockley Hays arrived at the Inn, all armed and Jackson carrying a riding whip. The news was over town in a moment. Jackson and Coffee went to the post-office, a few doors beyond the City Hotel. They went the short way, crossing the Square and passing some distance in front of the other tavern where the Bentons were standing on the walk.

Returning, Jackson and Coffee followed the walk. As they reached the hotel Jesse Benton stepped into the barroom. Thomas Benton was standing in the doorway of the hall that led to the rear porch overlooking the river. Jackson started toward him brandishing his whip. "Now, defend yourself you damned rascal!" Benton reached for a pistol but before he could draw Jackson's gun was at his breast. He backed slowly through the corridor, Jackson following, step for step. They had reached the porch, when, glancing beyond the muzzle of Jackson's pistol, Benton saw his brother slip through a doorway behind Jackson, raise his pistol and shoot. Jackson pitched forward, firing. His powder burned a sleeve of Tom Benton's coat. Thomas Benton fired twice at the falling form of Jackson and Jesse lunged forward to shoot again, but James Sitler, a bystander, shielded the prostrate man whose left side was gushing blood.

The gigantic form of John Coffee strode through the smoke, firing over the heads of Sitler and Jackson at Thomas Benton. He missed but came on with clubbed pistol. Benton's guns were empty. He fell backward down a flight of stairs. Young Stockley Hays, of Burr expedition memory, sprang at Jesse Benton with a sword cane and would have run him through had the blade not broken on a button. Jesse had a loaded pistol left. As Hays closed in with a dirk knife, Benton thrust the muzzle against his body, but the charge failed to explode.

General Jackson's wounds soaked two mattresses with blood at the Nashville Inn. He was nearly dead—his left shoulder shattered by a slug, and a ball embedded against the upper bone of that arm, both from Jesse Benton's pistol. While every physician in Nashville tried to stanch the flow of blood, Colonel Benton and his partizans gathered before the Inn shouting defiance. Benton broke a small-sword of Jackson's that he had found at the scene of conflict. All the doctors save one declared for the amputation of the arm. Jackson barely understood. "I'll keep my arm," he said.

Friends vowed to even the score. "I'm literally in hell here," Tom Benton wrote and left town.[30]

The feud was blotted out by news of a Creek uprising and the massacre of two hundred and fifty persons at Fort Mims in Mississippi Territory (now Alabama). The horrors of Indian warfare, which Tennesseans knew so well, were at their doors. A committee on public safety hastened to the Hermitage. Jackson was too weak to leave his bed but he was strong enough to make war.

"By the eternal these peple must be saved."[31]

Before the state authorities could act to save them and before the Federal Government knew what had happened, Coffee's cavalry was forming up. "The health of your general is restored," Jackson wrote, propped against a pillow. "He will command in person."[32] The Governor authorized an expedition of twenty-five hundred men and Jackson promised to march with it in nine days.

CHAPTER X

RED EAGLE

I

THE destroyer of Fort Mims was William Weatherford, a personage of unusual family history. His great grandfather, Captain Marchand, had carried the fleur-de-lis from New Orleans to the upper waters of the Alabama, thereby establishing a minute claim to immortality, which was acknowledged by a dot on a map swept by lace cuffs at Versailles where a circle of scented little men fumbled with the iron Frontenac's dream of New France. The Captain found his post of command a lonely one, but this was mitigated in 1722 when a girl of the godlike Creek Clan of the Wind consented to share his exile behind the sodded ramparts of Fort Toulouse on the River Coosa. The wilderness representative of the arms of France was less fortunate, however, in his relations with his soldiers, who mutinied and slew him, by that means removing a father's protecting hand from a small demi-French daughter named Sehoy. But the gods intervened in favor of their own. Sehoy's good looks proved to be protection enough.

A minor chief married her first. Then Fort Toulouse changed hands and Sehoy Marchand changed husbands, returning to her birthplace as consort of the English Captain Tait. The new Commander welcomed to his solitary post Lachlan McGillivray, a presentable young Scottish tourist of wealthy family. The visitor paid his host the compliment of departing with Sehoy. He built her a house on the Coosa, surrounded her with servants and accumulated a fortune in the Indian trade. Sehoy bore him a family, which one day Trader McGillivray forsook to spend life's afternoon beneath the wet clouds of Scotland, telling, one imagines, some wonderful stories.

By this time Alexander McGillivray, the trader's son, was old enough to make a man's decisions concerning life. Of commanding bearing and polished address, this youth showed little trace of his quartering of Indian blood. Lachlan had seen to his education at Charleston and desired him to be a white man. Alexander tried the life of his parent's preference, but, on the whole, it bored him so that he fell back upon the culture of the wigwam and a career in which French urbanity, Spanish deceit, Scotch thrift and Creek savagery saw him far—his boast being that no Yankee blood polluted his veins.

In the American Revolution McGillivray was a British colonel. During a subsequent recrudescence of French influence, one of his sisters became the mistress of General Leclerc Milfort. Under Miró he was a Spanish civil servant, usefully involved in the Cumberland intrigue, and so first came within the sphere of Andrew Jackson. But whatever his relation to the uncertain white counter-theme of Indian affairs, Alexander McGillivray retained the principal chieftainship of the Creeks, controlled the Seminoles, and was faithless to the interest of neither. In 1793 he died, a brigadier-general in the United States Army, worth one hundred thousand dollars, and was buried with Masonic honors in a Spanish gentleman's garden at Pensacola.

For twenty years men and nations had learned that success on the southern borderland required the good-will of McGillivray. Charles Weatherford, another Scotch trader, achieved this boon by marrying a half-sister, née Tait. Mr. Weatherford's comfortable house, his blooded horses and his hospitality were known to every traveler of distinction who fared that way. His children also were border-line cases to whom was presented a choice of races. John Weatherford chose the Caucasian and has not been heard of since. William chose the Creek.

As Red Eagle this nephew of the fantastic McGillivray won his place at the council fires, but events were several years in shaping a field suitable to the scope of his talents. In 1810 one of the remarkable personalities of American history, Tecumseh, visited the Creeks to exploit his dream of a Lakes-to-Gulf confederacy to smother the white infiltration. Red Eagle was stirred, but the glow died. There were other tribes with more cause for complaint than the Creeks. Under McGillivray the Creeks had held their own. After him Benjamin Hawkins came as agent for the United States Government—an anomaly among such officials, being both honest and able. His defense of treaty rights won him a much higher regard among Creeks than among whites.

In October of 1811 Tecumseh returned. Land-seekers had been aggressive and the red genius made the most of it. His magnetism and matchless eloquence swept away most of the young Creeks. Red Eagle, thirty-one years old, emerged from a state of moody contemplation. Then came war with England. Medicine-men said the Great Spirit had contrived this opportunity. Hawkins, the Creek's true friend, pleaded dramatically but in vain. With the crimson war-club, or red stick, dangling in the squares of their encampments, the braves rose under William Weatherford. Settlers fled to stockades. Weatherford moved against the largest of these, the fortified residence of Samuel Mims, a well-to-do Creek half-breed who had cast his lot with the whites. Seventy Louisiana militia under Major Daniel Beasley, a half-breed, guarded the fort. On August 30, 1813, the seven-eighths white leader of the Creeks surprised his half-white adversary. When the butchery was over, Red Eagle shamed his army, but before the world accepted its conduct—a duty inseparable from leadership.

2

On October seventh, Old Hickory took command of his infantry at Fayetteville. Coffee's cavalry was in Red Eagle's country. Jackson broke camp on the eleventh, and, hearing that Coffee was in danger, marched thirty-two miles in nine hours before learning that the rumor was false.[1] The next day he joined the cavalry at Ditto's Landing on the Tennessee River below the outpost settlement of Huntsville (now Alabama).

The haggard man with an arm in a sling had done more than make a new record for the movement of infantry. He had taken the first step in a bold winter campaign, all clear to his rapid mind. The second step was to move twenty-four miles along the Tennessee to its southernmost dip where part of his army began to throw up defenses called Fort Deposit, which was to be the main base of supplies. The rest of the army plunged into the wilderness with axes to hew a road across the Raccoon Mountains to the Ten Islands of the Coosa River fifty miles away where the advance supply base was to be. There Jackson planned to begin fighting.

From his bed at the Hermitage he had spread spies among the enemy. They were white men and mixed-breeds whose homes were the woods. He had sent emissaries to those Creeks who remained friendly; also to the Cherokees and to the Choctaws. In this way enough was learned of Weatherford's numbers and dispositions[2] to form the plan for an offensive, ranging southwestward from the Ten Islands, in which Red Stick towns would be destroyed and armed bands exterminated in battle. This done, Jackson would push on to Mobile, opening from Tennessee to the Gulf a highway of much importance to the United States. Then, although nothing in his orders contemplated it, the crowning stroke: invasion of Florida, seizure of Pensacola,[3] and elimination of the insidious influence of Spain, silent ally of Britain and open supporter of the Creeks.

The project of the impetuous Tennessean was complete in itself, and much more comprehensive than the suppression of an Indian insurrection. Jackson prepared to accomplish it alone. He did not ignore the fact that he was subordinate to old Major General Pinckney of the Regular Army, commanding the Department of the South; or that Georgia, Louisiana and Mississippi Territory also were dispatching militia columns against the Creeks, and that a Regular regiment at Mobile was supposed to cooperate. Neither did he rely on help from those quarters, a wise resolution as matters fell out. He did, however, count on a junction with twenty-five hundred East Tennessee troops under John Cocke.

And first of all he counted on supplies. Fort Deposit was

completed, but there was little to put into it. The civilian contractor system, in vogue in our armies, was a weak reed under
favorable circumstances. In the wild country where troops
moved with the celerity of Jackson's, it failed from the first. In
six days the road to the Coosa was cut "over mountains more
tremendous than the Alps," as a participant vowed with perfect
sincerity. Jackson stormed at the delinquent contractors, discharged one set and engaged another. Coffee was sent to forage
Indian corn. An appeal was dispatched to the inhabitants of
Mississippi: "There is an enemy I dread much more than I do the
hostile Creek, . . . that meagre-monster 'Famine.'"[4] On the next
day Jackson wrote privately, "I am determined to push forward if
I have to live upon acorns,"[5] and, publishing battle instructions,—
"the charge with the bayonet will be the signal of victory. Your
general has pledged his reputation upon it"[6]—began to march
with less than two days' rations.[7]

Red Stick scouts slipped through the trees beside the toiling
column. Chief Pathkiller of the Cherokees sent word of
Weatherford's threat to Indians who failed to espouse his cause.
"Brother," wrote Jackson, "the Hostile Creeks will not attack you
until they have had a brush with me; & that I think will put
them out of the notion."[8] To his aide, John Reid, he said he
would die rather than retreat.[9] Arriving on the Coosa in three
days, the army began to cut trees for the stockade of the advance
base which was named Fort Strother. Here General Jackson
renewed for sixty days, and sent back to Tennessee, a personal
note for one thousand dollars which he had owed for nearly a
year.[10]

Thirteen miles away two hundred Red Sticks were at the village of Tallushatchee. Coffee was sent with one thousand troops
to destroy them. The first battle of the campaign was fought the
following morning, November 3, 1813. "We shot them like
dogs," said Davy Crockett, present and shooting.[11] No warrior
escaped and eighty-four women and children captives were taken.
Coffee lost five killed, forty-one wounded. "We have retaliated
for Fort Mims," Jackson reported in literal truth.[12] Among the

prisoners a handsome child attracted the notice of the Commanding Officer. He was three, the age of another boy much in the
thoughts of the turbulent General. The Creek women would
not take care of him. His parents were dead, they said. "Kill
him, too." With his one good hand, Jackson dissolved some
brown sugar in water and coaxed the child to drink. Then he
sent him to Huntsville to be looked after at his personal expense.[13]

3

Weatherford had his hands full. Jackson's whirlwind invasion
had won Indian allies and kept others on the fence. To put his
own house in order, the red leader turned from his white adversary to the Creek town of Talladega which had declared for Jackson. On November seventh Jackson was dictating an order to
Brigadier-General James White, commanding the advance of
Cocke's East Tennessee division, to hasten to Fort Strother when
news of Talladega came from an Indian wearing a deer tail in
his hair, the sign of friendship prescribed by Jackson. Talladega
was in imminent danger, the Indian said, being surrounded by
a thousand of Weatherford's braves. The informant himself had
crept through the hostile lines in a hog's hide. Jackson added a
postscript for White to march with all speed as he was leaving his
sick and wounded in camp insufficiently protected. He told the
Indian to creep back and tell his friends that help was coming.
Talladega was across the Coosa and thirty miles to the southward. There was no road. At one o'clock in the morning, Jackson began to move his army over the river. The following sunset
the men dropped in their tracks, six miles from the beleaguered
town. Jackson was ill of dysentery. While the army slumbered
he sat against a tree in agony, questioning scouts who had been
sent to ascertain the topography of Talladega, the disposition of
the enemy and of the force he was to relieve. At midnight came
an express from White saying that "a positive order" from Cocke
would prevent his protecting the fort. This left two hundred
sick, all the stores of the army and its line of communication at

the mercy of an enemy whose intelligence service was nearly perfect, and who could outmarch even Jackson. Yet to retreat without giving battle would be a blow to white prestige that would send every doubting Indian in the region to Weatherford's standard.

Not having slept, Jackson, at four in the morning, gave word to arouse the army. As soon as light began to show through the treetops, the columns were in motion.

The sun was an hour high when they deployed for battle on November 9, 1813. The men were hungry. Half a mile away, they could see friendly Indians gesticulating from their ramparts, but no foe was visible. Jackson ordered a crescent-shaped formation, with the points toward the town, and sent three mounted companies to raise the enemy and court an attack. The men making the half-moon saw them ride warily through the brush and dead autumn grass, saw the exchange of signs with the Indians in the fort, saw two Indians rush from the fort, seize the bridle of Captain Russell's horse and point earnestly to a tree-lined creek.

The warning was not a moment too soon. A volley roared from the creek bank, and the hostiles burst from their cover "like a cloud of Egyptian locusts, and screaming like devils."[14] With the painted warriors in pursuit, the cavalrymen galloped back toward the main body. When the heedless Indians had been drawn within range, their quarry wheeled from the line of fire.

A volley from Jackson's curving battle line staggered the charge, but did not stop it. Weatherford's naked men met the whites with guns and arrows and tomahawks. The tips of Jackson's crescent pressed forward and joined. The encircled Creeks were falling in heaps before the superior arms of their adversaries when a detachment of volunteers gave way. Seven hundred Red Sticks poured through in flight.

Cavalry closed the gap and the battle went on until inside the ring of Jackson's line lay three hundred dead Indians, fifteen dead whites.[15]

4

Two stinging defeats within six days were bad for Weatherford, and although entirely without rations, Jackson wished to
plunge ahead and take advantage of his victories. Cocke's order,
which left Fort Strother defenseless, alone prevented Old Hickory
from going on to what might have been a speedy conclusion of
the war.

With eighty-seven wounded and nothing to eat, Jackson returned to the fort the second day after the battle, hoping to find
supplies and to resume operations. Not a pound of rations had
reached the stockade. Before leaving for Talladega, Jackson had
directed the surgeons to draw upon his private stores should
others not arrive. These had all been consumed except a few
pounds of biscuit. Jackson immediately ordered them distributed
among the wounded, though no one in camp had greater need
than the commanding officer for a special diet. So wracked by
dysentery that he could hardly stand, Jackson confronted his
trials with a fortitude from which his stomach never recovered.
During a paroxysm he would half-suspend himself by dangling
his arms over a horizontal sapling pole, and in this position sometimes remain for hours. The only succor of two thousand men
was a few cattle. Jackson ordered them butchered, taking for himself and staff only the offal, on which he lived without bread or salt
while moving heaven and earth to rouse the ration contractors.

Petitions came from the different commands, urging a return
to civilization to replenish stores. The troops were respectful.
No thought of abandoning the war was expressed. By one expedient and another Jackson put them off. To remove the
wounded, he said, would cause the death of many. The story
was told of a soldier who asked the General for something to
eat. "I will divide with you what I have," Jackson replied, drawing from his pocket a handful of acorns.[16]

Complaints soon grew bitter. Jackson's force was composed
of two brigades of United States volunteers, Natchez expedition

"veterans," and one brigade of militia. The militia was the first to try to take matters into their own hands and start home. Jackson threw some volunteers across their path and they returned to quarters. When the volunteers tried to leave, the militia stopped them.[17] Summoning the brigade commanders, Jackson renewed his promise of supplies, and, after a ringing appeal, asked them to ascertain if their commands would stand by the wounded and by the campaign. Coffee's volunteer cavalry voted to stick. Robert's militia would stay for three or four days. Despite all their brigadier could do, Hall's volunteers voted to go. This cut deeply. Hall's brigade was a part of the old division that had sworn to follow Jackson to Quebec. The Commander published an order. "If supplies do not arrive in two days we march back together."[18]

Two days and no supplies. Four days. With men and mounts starving, Jackson yielded on November seventeenth. Twelve miles from the fort they met one hundred and fifty beeves and nine wagons of flour. When they had eaten their fill, Jackson ordered the army to return to Fort Strother, excepting Coffee who was to take his command in search of forage for the horses. The infantry ranks formed, grumbling. At the command to march a single company moved out—toward Tennessee. Others prepared to follow. Officers were powerless.

Jackson put spurs to his horse. A detour brought him in front of the mutineers where Coffee happened to be with a handful of his cavalry. Forming them across the road, Jackson threatened the deserters with a volley unless they faced about. He did not speak twice.

Rejoining the main body Jackson rode among the men. Finding Hall's entire brigade on the point of desertion, he seized a musket and backed his horse into their path. Jackson's left arm was in a sling. Resting the barrel of the musket on his horse's neck, he swore to shoot the first man to move a step in the wrong direction. John Coffee walked to one side of his General. Major John Reid, the handsomest man in the army, took the other side. A loyal company deployed in their rear. For some grim minutes the army stood thus; then the discontented brigade trudged sullenly toward Fort Strother and Jackson returned the musket, which was found to be too badly out of order to fire.[19]

On November twenty-seventh a note for seven hundred and fifty-four dollars fell due. The General was obliged to renew.[20]

5

On December second he rejoined his troops at Fort Strother with extensive plans to move against Weatherford on December tenth.[21] He discovered, however, that Hall's brigade, comprising the bulk of his force, had made other arrangements for that date. A volunteer's term of service was one year. The brigade had been sworn in on December 10, 1812, for the Natchez expedition, after which they had been released until the recall in September. At the instigation of certain officers, a majority of the men contended that time spent at home counted toward their year of service, which would expire on the day the General had set for a resumption of operations.

Nor was this Jackson's only concern. Impossible instructions came from Major General Pinckney, viewing the situation from his headquarters at Charleston, South Carolina. The Louisiana and Mississippi expedition had accomplished little. After a brush with the Red Sticks Georgia's expedition was in retreat. A strong Creek faction which had sued for peace after Talladega was again on the war-path, and Weatherford had doubled the army opposing his vexed adversary at Fort Strother. The moral value of the two victories had been lost.

Jackson's patience, never abundant, was exhausted. Irritable and ill, he used language that failed to promote an understanding with the volunteers. Without yielding an inch, he prepared, however, to replace them, and dispatched appeals to Tennessee for reenforcements. Should the volunteers leave before new troops arrived Jackson and his one brigade of steadfast militia would be exposed to annihilation.

On December sixth a note for one thousand dollars was payable.

Jackson had renewed it the day he left Nashville. He was obliged to renew again, but omitted to do so until the eighth, a species of delay of which he was not often guilty. Sunday, December ninth, was a day of tension. A backwoods chaplain delivered a sermon which a supporter of Jackson was moved to answer in a speech that did not please the volunteers who had announced their departure from camp on Monday. Among the loyal was a nephew of Nolichucky Jack who asked a small favor. "If you can Spare as much Whiskey as will wearm a half Douzen of Good Heerited fellows you will Oblige Your friend & Hum^b, Svt CHARLES SEVIER."[22] The General himself wrote to John Coffee whose cavalry was still absent refreshing the horses: "What may be attempted tomorrow I cannot tell," but should the volunteers succeed in quitting the fort Coffee was to intercept them. Should they resist arrest "you will immediately open fire."[23]

Jackson did not have to wait until the morrow to learn the determination of the men. At eight that evening, he was informed the brigade planned to slip away during the night. With the loyal militia under arms near by, he paraded the volunteers outside the walls where the astonished brigade found their line covered by the two little brass cannon that comprised the post's artillery. Jackson addressed them. He was tired of argument, he said, and "done with entreaty." If they meant to desert, let them try it now. If they meant to be soldiers, they should return to quarters.[24] The ranks stood motionless.

With "feelings better to be Judged than expressed," Old Hickory gazed at the wayward soldiers "I once loved as a father loves his children."[25] Ordering the gunners to light their matches, he rode within the field of fire. "I demand an explicit answer." The lines stirred. Several officers hastened forward. They promised that the brigade should remain until relieved by reenforcements.

Three days later Cocke from East Tennessee marched in "with 1450 of as fine looking Troops as you ever saw," as Jackson wrote Coffee directing him to rejoin the main body ready for

battle.[26]   Hall's brigade was read from camp and they were
scarcely out of sight when Jackson was informed that the time of
most of Cocke's fine-looking troops would expire in ten days,
when they, too, expected to go home.   Old Hickory declined to
waste rations or breath on such men and wounded their pride by
packing them off in twenty-fours hours.   Everything now depended on the cavalry, ordered to come on by forced marches.
Alas for the stout Coffee, who had yet to fail Andrew Jackson as a
soldier or as a friend.   His men also were volunteers.   Meeting
Hall's brigade streaming northward, they broke camp while their
commander lay ill and joined the deserters.   "Can it be true
what I hear!" exclaimed Jackson.[27]

Then came the blow that seemed to foretell the end of Andrew
Jackson's military career.   Governor Blount threw up the sponge,
advising the evacuation of Fort Strother and a retreat to Tennessee.   It was a literal summons to join the dismal file of funking
military chieftains whose crowded march into the limbo had
distinguished our management of this war.   One ill-calculated
step and Andrew Jackson should bear company with the dim
shapes of Hull, Dearborn, Hampton, Izard, Chandler, Winder—
the list could be lengthened.

When General Jackson received Blount's letter, he had slept
only two hours in two nights, for the five hundred effective men
remaining of his deciduous military organization had begun to
falter.   Word of the Governor's loss of heart, coming in response
to Jackson's burning petition for conscription in order to maintain an army in the field, would have reduced them to panic.   At
twelve-thirty o'clock in the morning on December 29, 1813,
Jackson began his long reply by observing, in a general way, that
Mr. Blount had merely "recommended" a withdrawal.   "Still,
if you had ordered me peremptorily to retrograde with my
troops," Old Hickory declared that he would have refused to
obey.   With his back to the wall, Jackson cast everything his
passionate being possessed into the scale to restore the ebbing
courage of the Executive.

The Governor was reminded that he had "bawled aloud for

permission to exterminate the Creeks." He was reminded that
the Legislature of Tennessee had pledged the Federal Government to keep thirty-five hundred men in the field until this
was done. "And are you my Dear friend sitting with yr. arms
folded, . . . recommending me to retrograde to please the whims
of the populace. . . . Let me tell you it imperiously lies upon both
you and me to do our duty regardless of consequences or the
opinion these fireside patriots, those fawning sycophants or cowardly poltroons who after their boasted ardor would . . . let thousands fall victims to my retrograde."

To "see how you and myself would appear in the painting,"
Jackson sketched the desperate consequences of a retreat that
would add five thousand wavering Choctaws, Cherokees and
hitherto friendly Creeks to Weatherford's cause.

"Arouse from yr. lethargy—despise fawning smiles or snarling
frowns—with energy exercise yr. functions—the campaign must
rapidly progress or . . . yr. country ruined. Call out the full
quota—execute the orders of the Secy of War, arrest the officer
who omits his duty, . . . and let popularity perish for the present. . . . Save Mobile—save the Territory—save yr. frontier from
becoming drenched in blood. . . . What retrograde under these
circumstances? I will perish first."[28]

6

These lines and a supporting thrust from an unexpected quarter—the War Department—made a changed man of Governor
Blount. But before new troops could reach the Coosa, Robert's
militia, so long faithful, went home; their three months' term
was up. Jackson had declared that if two men stayed by him
he would hold Fort Strother. For a few hours he held it with
one hundred and thirty,[29] including a cavalry company under
John Coffee, composed of ex-officers who had refused to join the
men in desertion.

As the last of the militia walked off eight hundred recruits
arrived from Tennessee. Already they were beginning to sense

the irksome side of military life. Jackson gave them no time for reflection, but at once marched southward where the Red Sticks were gathering. On the night of January 18, 1814, the expedition encamped on the site of the Battle of Talladega. The men were undisciplined, the officers not much better. With such material Jackson knew he must fight now or never. He pressed toward Weatherford's stronghold at Tohopeka, or the Horseshoe Bend of the Tallapoosa River. On the night of January twenty-first he bivouacked at Emuckfaw Creek, seventy miles from Fort Strother and three from Tohopeka. Before dawn the Creeks attacked.

They hoped to take the whites by surprise, but Jackson's green men had been ready all night. By firing at the flashes of the Indians' guns, they held off the enemy until it was light enough to see. Then Jackson threw in his reserve of one company and charged. The enemy gave way and Coffee went forward with half of the command to reconnoiter the Creek position at Tohopeka. He found it too strong to attack and hastened back, fearing Jackson might be cut off. Coffee's men had scarcely thrown themselves down to rest when a clatter of musketry came from the pickets on the left of the line. Coffee called for two hundred men to flank the assailants, but only fifty-four, including the ex-officers' company, followed him.

Alarm guns sounded on the right and pickets ran in firing. This was the main attack. Jackson led the reserve, one company, into action, riding up and down the firing line. Gliding from tree to tree, the Red Sticks came on behind a stiff barrage of musketry and arrows. They prepared to charge, but Jackson charged first. The Creek line faded into the woods. Two hundred Indian allies who had joined Jackson on the march had done well in the battle. They closed the events of the day by relieving Coffee's outnumbered band which, with its leader wounded, was hotly pressed.[30]

The indecisive fight was susceptible of some military and enormous popular advantages. A diversion had been created for General Floyd's column. The report of a glorious victory for the new troops would stimulate recruiting in Tennessee. On the other hand Jackson was in a ticklish situation. Seventy miles from an unprotected base he was surrounded by an enemy in superior force. An attack on Weatherford's position at Horseshoe Bend being out of the question, he could only withdraw.

The night after the battle his men slept on their arms. Having buried the dead, who included Major Alexander Donelson, and made litters for the wounded of the skins of dead horses, their cautious retirement began. The country was wild and roadless. Weatherford's men—noiseless, invisible, a part of the leafless landscape of winter—crept alongside the nervous column. That evening Jackson reached Enotachopco Creek. The Red Sticks hovered near and the whites bivouacked in expectation of an attack. None came and on the morning of January twenty-fourth they began to cross the creek.

Enotachopco Creek was broad and cold, its banks steep and sparsely wooded. Jackson had distributed detailed orders in case of an attack on front, flanks or rear. The advance-guard, the wounded and part of the flank columns were on the other side, the artillery company with one brass cannon was in the creek, and the center column was preparing to follow when alarm guns banged in the rear. Jackson heard them "with pleasure." He had laid a trap for an attack from behind. The rear of the three columns were to hold the Red Sticks while the front of the flank columns, recrossing the stream above and below, surrounded them—a repetition of the tactical principle of Talladega.

Jackson was on the bank of the creek. Imagine his "astonishment and mortification," when "I beheld the right and left column of the rear guard precip[i]tately give away . . . in shamefull retreat," their colonels with them.[31] As the fleeing men tumbled down the declivity, the center column also gave way, despite the efforts of its commander, William Carroll. Only this officer and twenty-five men stood between the scalping knife and the panic-stricken mass splashing in the water.

Jackson's shrill oaths clove the din. "When they heard his voice and beheld his manner," many preferred to confront the

Red Sticks instead. On the far bank John Coffee staggered from a litter and brought a company to Carroll's support. Lieutenant Armstrong fired the six-pounder using the butt of a musket as a rammer and a musket ramrod to pick the flint. "Save the cannon," he cried as he fell with a ball through his body. Ordering the retreating colonels under arrest, Jackson took hold of the embattled line. "In showers of balls he was seen performing the duties of subordinate officers," wrote one who was there, "rallying the alarmed," and "inspiriting them by his example. . . . Cowards forgot their panic, . . . and the brave would have formed round his body a rampart with their own."[32]

7

Emuckfaw and Enotachopco added to Jackson's other battles afforded news in pleasing contrast to the war's established precedent. The Administration press, famished for anything that looked like a victory, printed columns in which a wealth of patriotic ardor repaired the paucity of accurate detail without, however, exaggerating the difficulties against which the Commander on the Creek front had contended. A "blue light," or anti-war, newspaper in New England might spare only twelve lines for events so remote, but its serves-us-right attitude toward defeat was deranged by a prideful swelling of hearts among common men that here at least was one soldier, named, as it appeared, Andrew Jackson, who could win battles.

But the woman waiting at the Hermitage received the news with other emotions.

"My Dearest Life, I received your Letter by Express. . . . how did it feel. I never Can disscribe it. I Cryed aloud and praised my god For your safety. . . . how long o Lord will I remain so unhappy. no rest no Ease I cannot sleepe. all can come hom but you. . . . I hope the Campaine will soon end the troops that is now on their way will be sufficient you have done now more than aney other man ever did before you have served your County Long Enough. . . . you have been gon six monthes. . . . oh Lord

of heaven how Can I beare it. Colo Hayes waites. . . . our Dear
Little Son sayes maney things to sweet papa. **. . .** your faithfull
wife untill Death. RACHEL JACKSON."[33]

Colonel Hays brought troops. Jackson had demanded five
thousand men of Governor Blount—more than he needed and
doubtless more than he expected to get. But he got them all,
hastily raised and poorly equipped. By the time half of them had
crowded upon Fort Strother the old troubles recommenced. But
when the Thirty-Ninth United States Infantry marched in, Jackson felt himself master of any eventuality. The Regulars "will
give strength to my arm and quell mutiny."[34] "With a continu-
ation of the smiles of fortune I shall soon put an end to the Creek
war."[35] A professional view of discipline began to emphasize
the distinction between Jackson's position and the position of all
subordinates. *This* army would not slip through his fingers.
When the second senior officer, Major General John Cocke,
seemed to doubt that Jackson meant it, he was relieved of his
sword and sent home in arrest. A similar fate befell Brigadier-
General Isaac Roberts.

Old Hickory was putting the final touches to his plans to end
the Creek war when interrupted by a row outside his tent. A
seventeen-year-old boy was defying the Officer of the Day with
a rifle.

"Shoot him! Shoot him!" cried Jackson.[36]

Private Woods belonged to a company that had caused much
trouble. But Jackson did not know that Woods was a new recruit,
in service less than a month as a substitute for his conscripted
brother, and not involved in the company's previous behavior.[37]
He was convicted of mutinous conduct and sentenced to be shot,
but the camp refused to believe "that a militiaman would . . .
for any offense be put to Death."[38]

After two sleepless nights[39] the Commanding General approved the action of the court. At ten in the morning of the fourteenth of March the army formed in hollow square. In the center,
a squad of Regulars leaned on their smooth-bore muskets of

seventy caliber. At headquarters Jackson penned a dispatch. "A private (John Wood) having been sentenced to death by a court martial, that ceremony is now in the act of execution. . . . I have ordered the line of march to be taken up at 12 oclock with seven days bread rations and two of meat, . . . direct for Emuckfa."[40] Having brought up to date a statement of his private indebtedness the General was now ready for battle.[41]

8

Dawn of March 27, 1814, saw Jackson's field army of two thousand men at the Horseshoe Bend of the Tallapoosa where eight hundred warriors awaited the battle upon which they staked everything. The Horseshoe enclosed one hundred acres, furrowed with gullies and covered by small timber and brush. Across the neck of the peninsula was a log breastwork with two rows of portholes. At the point was a fleet of canoes to insure an avenue of retreat.

Jackson surrounded the Horseshoe. Coffee's scouts swam the river and carried off the canoes. A thousand men were drawn upon the land side to storm the works. "Any officer or soldier who flies before the enemy without being compelled to do so by superior force . . . shall suffer death."[42] At half past ten o'clock the six-pounders' flat echo flapped through the naked woods. Their round balls sank harmlessly in the soft pine logs and Creek sharpshooters kept the gun crews close to the ground.

Jackson delayed the infantry attack until the Creek women and children could be carried across the river to safety. This took until twelve-thirty o'clock, when the drums of the Regulars beat the long roll and the infantry charged. Major Lemuel P. Montgomery of the Thirty-Ninth Regiment was the first man on the works. He reeled back dead. Half hidden by smoke, a tall boy in Regulars' blue and brass, Ensign Sam Houston, scaled the logs, and, waving his sword, leaped down on the other side.

There was a hard fight at the rampart, but it was overrun. The Red Sticks retreated in small bands into the rugged terrain where twenty battles raged at once. "Arrows, and spears, and balls were flying," recorded Ensign Houston, "swords and tomahawks gleaming in the sun."[43] The bands fought to the last man. A power more than moral sustained their courage. The Great Spirit had promised victory. Oblivious to the conflict, the priests of their religion moved among the braves, chanting the rituals, and falling as the warriors fell. The tide would yet turn, they said. The sign would be a cloud in the heavens.

In the middle of the afternoon Jackson offered life to all who would surrender. During the lull a small cloud appeared. The Red Sticks fired upon the messenger of peace and resumed the battle with passionate fury. "The *carnage* was *dreadfull*."[44] The sign of deliverance brought only a quiet shower and the "peninsular was strewed with the slain." At dusk one band held out in a little covered fortress at the bottom of a ravine. An invitation to surrender was refused "with scorn," and a volunteer storming party of Regulars driven off. Jackson set fire to the stronghold with flaming arrows; the battle was over.

Five hundred and fifty-seven Indian dead were counted on the ground and the river held two hundred more. Jackson had lost forty-nine killed and one hundred and fifty-seven wounded. From the field the victorious Commander carried "a warrior bow and quiver . . . for my little andrew."[45]

He expressed two regrets. "Two or three women & children were killed by accident,"[46] and a mischance of events had kept Weatherford away from Horseshoe on the day of the battle. Weatherford had commanded at the massacre at Fort Mims. He had been the moving spirit of the insurrection. The whites sought his corpse as evidence of the Mosaic law fulfilled.

Jackson moved south where Weatherford was reported to be rallying a few Red Stick remnants on the Hickory Ground at the junction of the Coosa and the Tallapoosa—sacred soil which, in the Creek belief, no enemy could tread and live. But on Jackson's approach, the shaken warriors scattered. The flag was raised over the moldering walls of Fort Toulouse which was rechristened Fort Jackson. One or two of the Creek leaders fled to

Florida. Others came in and surrendered. But where was
Weatherford? The thought of his quarry safely on Spanish soil
exasperated General Jackson.

A tall, light-colored Indian presented himself at the post. His
body was bare to the waist, his buckskin breeches and moccasins
badly worn. He was unarmed and on foot.

The Commanding General was leaving his quarters.

"General Jackson?" inquired the Indian.

"Yes."

"I am Bill Weatherford."

Reputed eye-witnesses have given two versions of Jackson's
response. "I am glad to see you *Mr.* Weatherford."[47] "How dare
you show yourself at my tent after having murdered the women
and children at Fort Mims!"[48]

They went inside. The General's aide, young John Reid, was
present.

"Weatherford," he wrote in a private letter, "was the greatest
of the Barbarian world. He possessed all the manliness of sentiment—all the heroism of soul, all the comprehension of intellect
calculated to make an able commander. . . . You have seen his
speech to Genl Jackson, . . . but you could not see his looks &
gestures—the modesty & yet the firmness that were in them.

" 'I am come,' he said, 'to give myself up. I can oppose you no
longer. I have done you much injury. I should have done you
more . . . [but] my warriors are killed. . . . I am in your power.
Dispose of me as you please.'

" 'You are not,' said the general, 'in my power. . . . I had ordered
you . . . brought to me in chains. . . . But you have come of your
own accord. . . . You see my camp—you see my army—you know
my object. . . . I would gladly save you & your nation, but you
do not even ask to be saved. If you think you can contend
against me in battle go & head your warriors.'

" 'Ah,' said Weatherford, 'well may such language be addressed
to me now.[49] . . . There was a time when I . . . could have
answered you. . . . I could animate my warriors to battle; but I can
not animate the dead. . . . General Jackson, I have nothing to

request ... [for] myself. ... But I beg you to send for the women and children of the war party, who have been driven to the woods without an ear of corn. ... They never did any harm. But kill me, if the white people want it done.' "

Jackson poured his guest a cup of brandy. He promised to help the women and children. Weatherford promised to try to persuade the remaining braves to peace. General Jackson extended his hand. Red Eagle took it, and strode from the ruined fort in which his mother had been born—vanishing from the view of the astonished soldiery, and from history, a not entirely graceless figure.

CHAPTER XI

STORM CLOUDS

I

RACHEL and Andrew, junior, joined the victor at Huntsville and the return became a triumphal progress. "I can but imperfectly communicate to you the feeling of the people. Your standing . . . is as high as any man in America," John Overton wrote and he added a "hint." "There are mean people whose greatest gratification is to irritate you, and thus lessen your fame if they can." Judge Overton hoped that his old friend would watch his temper.[1]

A large part of the population of the Cumberland lined the road entering Nashville to receive the first home-coming soldier-hero of the war. On the court-house steps Representative Felix Grundy did the honors, Jackson responding without vanity, in boast, or in mock modesty. A state banquet was followed by the presentation of the first of an eventual arsenal of ceremonial swords. General Jackson then treated the community to an example of what any soldier who had done his duty might expect of his old commanding officer:

"I have the pleasure to inform you that Captain Armstrong and his lady is now with me, . . . united in the holy bonds of matrimony." General Jackson addressed the bride's father, Josiah Nichols, whose brick mansion still looks upon the Lebanon Road a few miles from the Hermitage. The bridegroom was the plucky artillery lieutenant at Enotachopco. "I hear with regreat that this union did not meet with approbation. I have been acquainted with Captain Armstrong since his childhood. so have you! Is there a blemish in his charector? . . . he is honest, he is brave, he is enterprising, . . . and without a cent of property he is worthy of any lady, of any family, of any fortune. . . . Be good enough to present my respects and that of Mrs. Jackson to Mrs. Nichol, and assure her untill her daughter meets with a full forgiveness from her, she will find in Mrs. Jackson the tender care of a mother, and both will find in me the care of a father. on friday . . . I am to have my friends with me to partake of a dinner, will you and your lady do Mrs. Jackson and myself the pleasure of dinning with us."[2]

2

Speaking of Tennessee, Judge Overton was correct. Enemies had been crushed by the irrefutable logic of victory. The powerful clique of ex-officers of the autumn army that had deserted and all but succeeded in persuading Blount to call the General home, dared not make a sound. Old Sevierites said Jackson should be the next governor.[3] And the man they honored had changed. From the nadir of a tap-room shooting scrape, he had gone forth to return master of himself as well as of the Red Sticks, the sure and resolute Jackson of Mero District days.

Throughout the country Administration newspapers printed long accounts of the Horseshoe, and the opposition found itself unable to duplicate the succinct journalism that had distinguished its earlier references to the campaign. Several Administration personages would have preferred to see editorial encomiums bestowed elsewhere, but the conduct of the favorite generals had rendered this difficult. The only other military commander eligible to felicitation was William Henry Harrison, a non-favorite, who, seeing much of his good work in Canada undone by the ineptitude of James Wilkinson, resigned from the Army in disgust. After some prodding the major-generalcy in the Regular establishment thus vacated was tendered on May 28, 1814, to Andrew Jackson[4] with the command of the Seventh Military District, embracing Tennessee, Louisiana and Mississippi Territory. The War Department did not expect, however, that this should afford General Jackson further opportunities for distinction. The fighting was over on the southern front, Secretary

Armstrong said. Rumors of Spanish efforts to stir the Indians to
fresh hostility were incredible, and "the report of a B. naval force
on our Southern coast . . . of nearly the same character." Jackson
was instructed to dismiss all troops, except a thousand men, and
rest from his exertions.[5]

The new Commandant had other plans. When he left his bed
to lead the expedition against Weatherford, Andrew Jackson's
true goal had been Pensacola. It was Pensacola now. But another matter came first. The War Department had announced that
General Pinckney, Jackson's nominal superior during the Creek
campaign, and Benjamin Hawkins, the veteran United States
agent of the Creeks, would make the treaty of peace with the defeated Red Sticks. The choice was not popular in the West.
Pinckney was a decent old Charlestonian whose martial force had
been usefully spent in the Revolution. Hawkins was an appointee
of George Washington and embodied the Father's views of Indian
affairs. By a series of blunt moves, Jackson supplanted these
gentlemen as peacemaker and the frontier was assured of a representation of its own ideas.

On the day that a tailor in Murfreesborough measured the General for "one suit of full dress uniform, . . . [with] Gold Epaulettes, . . . all of the best quality," an express arrived with Florida
news through Jackson's own channels: British marines arming
and inciting Indians to a renewal of hostilities. "We ought to be
prepared for the worst," Jackson warned the Secretary of War.
"*Query*. . . . Will the government say to me, . . . 'proceed to ——
[*sic*] and reduce it. If so I promise the war in the south has a
speedy termination and the British influence forever cut off from
the Indians in that quarter."[6]

3

Twelve days later he was at Fort Jackson, inviting the chiefs
to council. "Destruction will attend a failure to comply."[7]

They came, chieftains and sub-chieftains of the war-party who
had surrendered at discretion, and expected a stern peace; leaders

of the Creeks who had sided with Jackson, anticipating reward for their loyalty—all attended by the retinues that their rank required. The retinues of the Red Sticks were pitiful. "Could you only see the misery and the wretchedness of those creatures," Jackson wrote to Rachel, "perishing from want of food and Picking up the grains of corn scattered from the mouths of horses."[8] Yet to complain would have been beneath the dignity of an occasion when one must assume a brave appearance at any inconvenience. Their lean faces masks of oriental reserve, they gathered their robes of ceremony over empty stomachs and confronted the man with whom they must barter for their fate.

The mind of the Indian was a deep mind, perhaps at its best in a council of this kind. He reasoned subtly and rather well, clothing his thoughts in language which for beauty and color is surpassed by that of no race on earth. He would contend cunningly for an advantage, but an agreement was quite as likely to be respected by him as by the frontiersmen through whom his ideas of civilization were formed. In the present instance the negotiators knew the man with whom they dealt. The Indian name for Jackson was Sharp Knife.[9] He was hard, but, having given his word, he kept it.

The Creeks reposed their hopes in ceremonious delay, a strategy already begun with Pinckney and Hawkins. They had no opportunity to continue it with Jackson who called the delegations before him and addressed them briefly, speaking first to the loyal Creeks. "Friends and brothers, you have fought with the Armies of the United States, many of you ... by my side." Then to the Red Sticks: "Friends and Brothers, you have followed the counsel of bad men." The war, he said, had been expensive. To pay for it and to avert the possibility of future war the United States must indemnify itself with land from the whole Creek people. "Brothers, the terms of peace I hold in my hand. . . . [They] will be read to you."[10]

The translators performed their task. An Indian was schooled from childhood to control the lines of his face against a betrayal of surprise or dismay, and so without comment, when the reading ended, the Creeks withdrew to their foodless camps. They were thunderstruck. In all the checkered narrative of our dealings with the Indian people, General Jackson's terms are unequaled for exorbitance. They cast a long shadow, giving the authority of distinguished approval to a precedent that was to accomplish the ultimate ruin of the red race more quickly than otherwise might have been. Since the result was inevitable, perhaps it was better thus. The Indian was of flint; one could only break him for he would not bend. But one issue was possible in his struggle against the Caucasian who always has conquered. Because of its directness and swiftness, the method of Andrew Jackson was probably the more humane in the long run. At least, he did not clothe it in the diaphanous disguise of nice excuses.

Jackson demanded the surrender of twenty-three million acres, or half of the ancient Creek domain. This territory now comprises one-fifth of the state of Georgia and three-fifths of Alabama. There was slight distinction between the lands of friend and foe. Nearly half of the territory demanded belonged to tribes whose braves had fought throughout the war under the banners of the whites. To the government Jackson perfunctorily explained his terms on grounds of policy. The frontiers of Georgia and Tennessee were removed from hostile threat. The remaining Creek lands were separated from the deleterious influence of Florida. The coveted highway from the Cumberland to Mobile was assured. To the West explanations were superfluous. The frontier gazed with hungry eyes upon a land speculator's New Jerusalem.

In private council the hearts of the Creeks sank. An attempt to ameliorate the brutal terms was delegated to two chiefs who had fought with Jackson in the late campaign. On the following day the General and his suite received them. The eloquence of Big Warrior and of Shelokta touched every white man who heard it. Jackson answered them at considerable length. The interest of his country, he said, would permit no amendment to his demands. Through the territory the Creeks must relinquish "leads the path that Tecumseh trod. That path must be stopped. Until this is done your nation cannot expect happiness, mine security."

Those who signed the treaty would be received as friends, those who refused, as enemies. They must decide that night, but whoever declined to sign would be given safe-conduct to Pensacola.[11]

"Face" was important to an Indian. The negotiators could not return to their people without a concession, however trivial. Of the land they were asked to surrender, they proposed that three square miles be given to General Jackson "as a token of gratitude." Similar gifts were suggested for Benjamin Hawkins and two others. Jackson replied in a friendly speech. With the consent of the President of the United States, he would accept the gift and "appropriate its value to aid in clothing their naked women and children." The chieftains replied that "they did not give to General Jackson land to give back to them in clothing; they want him to live on it, and when he is gone his family may have it; and it may always be known what the nation gave it to him for."[12] There is subtlety in the last words.

On August 9, 1814, thirty-five friendly chiefs and one who had been hostile signed the extraordinary treaty.[13] A "disagreeable business" was done, the General wrote Rachel, and "I know your humanity would feel for them."[14]

4

Not for an instant had Jackson taken his eyes from Florida. His first act on arriving in the Creek country was to dispatch observant and reliable John Gordon, a man of the woods and captain of a scout company, to Pensacola. He bore a letter to the Commandant demanding the surrender of two fugitive chiefs and an explanation of the British proceedings on Spanish soil. "Disagreeable consequences" were intimated in event of an unfavorable answer.[15] Gordon's interview with the Spanish officer was brief. Don Matteo González Manrique observed that Jackson's communication was "Impertinent" and that the hospitality of Spain would not be withdrawn from the chiefs. On his return, Gordon further reported that the British were establishing a military base at the mouth of the Apalachicola, and that a

Spanish fleet was expected to join the British men-of-war off the coast.[16]

From other sources the observations of Captain Gordon were confirmed. British marines had landed and a captain of their number was drilling the Indians while regiments of black troops were being mobilized at Jamaica. "I calculate on some warm work with them and the Indians in the course of the fall season,"[17] Jackson informed John Coffee. To Secretary of War Armstrong he wrote: "You will pardon me for suggesting that the months of September and October are those in which we may anticipate a blow."[18]

Jackson had received no reply to his "*Query*" for tacit consent to strike at the root of the trouble in Florida and this puzzled him. The Secretary was equally puzzled. He had written a sleek letter, explicit enough to send the Commander of the Seventh District into Florida, but vague enough to support a disavowal should this become diplomatically desirable. But when General Jackson received this communication the war was over. The delay has the color of intrigue, though in later years Armstrong declared it was Madison who held up the letter.[19] Jackson was left, therefore, to act on his own responsibility, which is probably what he would have done in any case.

The day after the Indian treaty was signed he had made up his mind to act.

"My love

"This is the last letter you will receive from this point . . . as tomorrow at 12 I embark for Mobile." But the separation was nearly at an end. From Mobile Colonel Robert Butler, Rachel Hays's husband and the General's ward, would return to Tennessee "for the purpose of bringing you to me." "I have wrote John Hutchings to have you a good pair of horses procured, and I wish your carrige repaired or exchanged for a new one—you had better vissit Nashville and make this arrangement with the carriage maker yourself— you must recollect that you are now a Major Generals lady in the service of the U. S. and as such you must appear elegant and plain, not extravagant, but in such state as

Strangers expect to see you— a good Supply of Eatable such as our
country yields will add verry much to our comfort. . . . Let a
house be built for your Sister Cafferry." She was Mary, the oldest
of the Donelson sisters, who with her young husband had journeyed from Virginia to Louisiana by the rivers in 1780, reared a
family and in her widowhood come to Tennessee to enjoy the protection that Jackson extended to so many of the numerous
company of his wife's relations. "Say to Genl Overton he knows
I would write if I had time. May heaven protect you is the prayer
of your affectionate Husband."[20]

General Jackson was aware that he invited his wife to a theater
of lively scenes. He had asked Blount to summon troops. "Dark
and heavy clouds hang over us."[21]

5

The storm those clouds foretold had already broken, though
it was a month before Jackson began to receive the news.

"Wellington's army to America! . . . Bonaparte dethroned.
Peace in Europe; English coming to swallow U. S."[22] So recorded
a diarist of Dedham, Massachusetts, who refused to speak to his
brother, the distinguished Fisher Ames, because of his opposition
to the war.

Ten thousand Peninsular veterans disembarked at Quebec to
invade the East, while Sir Alexander Cochrane's fleet was to divert
attention along the Atlantic littoral. As a finishing blow the most
formidable military and naval expedition the New World had seen
moved toward its secret rendezvous at Jamaica to subjugate the
South. A fringe of this stupendous effort was what Andrew
Jackson had detected in Florida.

Cochrane struck first. He seized and annexed most of Maine.
He burned Eastport, captured Nantucket, sacked or laid under
tribute the Cape Cod towns and made a foray into Long Island
Sound. New England shuddered. Banks buried their specie and
people fled. A good many Blue-lights renounced their British
sympathies and the scurrying of militia companies contributed to

the confusion. Other reformed lukewarms, groping for a scheme of resistance, began to prepare the way for the Hartford Convention. A few border-line traitors among them, supported by a wide-spread sentiment in New England, were to give this assembly the hard name of a secession conspiracy. Believing the worst Andrew Jackson declared that had he been in the East, he would "have hung every man of them."[23] Later he graciously modified this opinion, saying he would have hanged only "the three principal leaders."[24]

But with Andrew Jackson on the Alabama and an English fleet off Boston harbor, sufficient of the anti-war party in high places stood its ground to present a bewildering spectacle—Paul Revere's copper-clad dome atop the State-House illuminated in honor of the Allies' victory over Napoleon!

The Quebec army marched and Cochrane entered the Chesapeake for an experimental thrust toward Washington, defended by a force of militia thrice the size of the invaders. The government disappeared by as many exits as the city afforded. The militia proved almost as nimble. A band of Navy seamen sold their lives dearly but Washington was leisurely occupied and the Capitol and President's House burned. Alexandria was plundered, Baltimore shelled and the middle seaboard clutched by panic. Philadelphia frantically fortified, New York fortified. Then came tidings of an American defeat at Plattsburgh by the expedition from Quebec.

It was false. By an astonishing victory on Lake Champlain, Commodore John McDonough had broken up the invasion, and sent ten thousand Wellington veterans limping back to Canada. One could count on the Navy! Bonfires flared and flags flew in great celebrations, as if such din could substitute for self-respect or repair the naked objects of degradation that scarred our coast from Penobscot to Potomac. The menace from Quebec was removed and Cochrane stood to sea—for Jamaica and New Orleans, it transpired. At the time it was enough to know that he had gone. New England dismissed her homeguards, dug up her money and resumed a sophisticated stare upon allusion to what a crude man like Andrew Jackson styled "our nation's Honour."

6

With the Third United States Infantry, five hundred and thirty-one strong, General Jackson reached Mobile on August 22, 1814, two days before the fall of Washington. He sent a runner to over-take Butler, en route to fetch Rachel from Tennessee.

"His B. M. ships Hermes, Carron and Sophy has arrived at Pensacola ... and taken possession. The Orpheus is expected in a few days with 14 sail of the line and many transports with 10,000 Troops. It is further added that 14 sail of the line and Transports has arrived at Barmuda, with 25,000 of Lord Wellingtons army &c. &c., before one month the British and Spanish forces expect to be in Possession of Mobile and all the surrounding country.

"The[re] will be bloody noses before this happens. I have ordered the different Indian agents to enroll every warrior that will take the field. I have called on all the militia I am authorized under orders of the Government. ... See Captain Deaderick and Captain Parish and say I expect them in the field with . . . a Betalion and the favorite six pounder. . . . I want about 1000 horse with Genl Goffee." A page of this, calling up men. "Cause the Contractors to . . . [forward] 6 months rations for three thousand men. . . . Say to Mrs. Jackson I have not time to write. . . . Before this reaches you we may have a brush."25

Next day he found time to write Rachel. She must defer her visit. "I pray you be calm and Trust to that superintending being who has protected me in the midst of so many dangers and kiss little Andrew for me affectionately adieu."26 With a British fleet at hand the Commandant of Pensacola sent Jackson an insolent reply to the message delivered by John Gordon. Jackson's re-joinder contained a sentence that captivated his imperiled little army: "An Eye for an Eye, Tooth for Tooth and Scalp for Scalp."27 But before the Old Testament could be employed as a guide for the regulation of affairs at Pensacola, Jackson surmised he would meet the British at Mobile. Major Lawrence was sent with one hundred and sixty men to repair abandoned Fort Bowyer on the spit commanding the pass that connected Mobile Bay and the Gulf. To hold the pass was Mobile's only chance of safety.

Lawrence strove day and night at the fort. In the drowsy little waterside town, Jackson's cyclonic energy confirmed the easy-going French-Spanish inhabitants' worst opinions of "Americans." They chattered knowingly in groups and helped when they were paid for it. Soon it became impossible to pay them. "I have not a dollar," Jackson informed the Government, "to purchase an Express horse, nor can the Quarter Master procure one on credit, and the Mail arrives here only once a month."[28]

7

Intelligence of the enemy, however, arrived daily. Spain had shed the pretense of neutrality. At Pensacola, a few hours' sail from Fort Bowyer, an English fleet rode at anchor and in the casemates of Fort Barrancas lounged English marines. Captain George Woodbine distributed scarlet jackets and sought to instruct his astonished Indian allies in the manual of arms! The Cross of St. George was unfurled beside His Catholic Majesty's standard over the residence of Don Matteo Manrique. The Commandant's guest was Lieutenant-Colonel Edward Nicholls, an Irishman whom Wellington thought well of. The Colonel had not been long on the scene when he penned—and composition seems to have presented few difficulties to this soldier—an order of the day:

"You are called upon, . . . to perform long marches through wildernesses, swamps and water-courses; your enemy, . . . inured to the climate, will have great advantages. . . . But remember the . . . glory of your country."[29]

This was followed by a proclamation:

"Natives of Louisiana; on you the first call is made to Assist in Liberating . . . Your paternal soil. . . . American Usurpation . . . must be Abolished. . . . I am at the head of a large body of Indians, well armed, disciplined and commanded by British officers—

good train of artillery, seconded by . . . a numerous British and Spanish squadron. . . . Be not alarmed at our approach. . . . A flag over any door, whether Spanish, French or British, will be certain Protection."[30]

With these engaging documents there came to Jackson's hands the letter of a resident of Pensacola intended for a business friend in Mobile. "Great events are in embrio. . . . I tremble for what you already have at stake in case of resistance. . . . All the Mobile will fall an easy prey and before one month it will be your inevitable fate again to change masters."[31]

The American Commander had been following the moves of Colonel Nicholls since he had appeared in Havana a month before. Fortunately for Jackson, the Colonel loved the sound of his own voice. In Cuba he had talked too much for a military man, and his words had found their way to the alert Commander at Mobile. According to Nicholls the British would occupy Pensacola as a base, then seize the mouth of the Mississippi and Mobile, and, marching on Baton Rouge, cut off New Orleans from above and below. Slaves were counted on to join the black regiments of Jamaica and help was expected from the Louisiana Creoles.[32] With the landing at Pensacola the first step in this broad program had been taken.

Fortunately also this opportune disclosure of British intentions was no surprise to Jackson, who, putting himself in the enemy's shoes, had come to virtually the same conclusion as to the most practicable way to move on New Orleans. During the Indian conference Jackson had warned Claiborne to prepare for an attack. But the Governor was not impressed. As a courtesy to a friend, he ordered his militia to be "ready," but nullified the force of his act with an opinion that the idea of an invasion was too "chimerical" for serious attention. By now he had changed his mind, however. While Nicholls was addressing the Louisianians, Claiborne addressed Jackson. "I have a difficult people to manage, . . . Native Americans, Native Louisianians, Frenchmen, Spaniards (with some English). . . . *That ardent Zeal* which the Crisis de-

mands" was lacking. Unless "Louisiana [militia] is supported by
a Respectable Body of Regular Troops . . . I fear . . . we shall be
enabled to make *but a feeble Resistance*."[33]

<h2 style="text-align:center">8</h2>

Serious as Jackson knew his situation to be it was not possible
to follow every tentacle of the vast British effort that was encom-
passing him. On the second day after Colonel Nicholls had signed
his proclamation, His Majesty's brig *Sophie* sailed under the guns
of Barrancas and stood to sea. On September 3, 1814, she approached with care a narrow strait between two low green islands
of the Louisiana coast.

A small brick fort materialized against the foliage. It flew no
flag. The *Sophie* fired a signal gun and a boat containing four
men at the oars and a fifth in the bow left the beach. It was
met by a gig carrying two English officers. One of them requested
"Monsieur Laffite." He was told, in French, that Laffite might be
seen on shore.

On the yellow beach a motley press of barefooted seamen
crowded to the water's edge. The King's servants did not like their
looks and were glad when a glance from their guide dissolved this
gallery. On a breeze-swept porch overlooking Barataria Bay, the
guide turned to his visitors.

"Messieurs, I myself am Laffite."

Captain Lockyer of the brig *Sophie* and Captain McWilliams
of the Royal Colonial Marines introduced themselves. Perhaps they
appraised rather closely the man of whom they had heard so much.
He was thirty-four years old, tall and sunburned. His countenance
was pleasant, his address polite, and he had a peculiar habit of
closing one mild brown eye when he spoke. He wore a green
shirt, open at the throat. His wavy brown hair was tossed by the
wind.

The time of the Englishmen's visit had been happily chosen,
said Jean Laffite. It was the hour of dinner.[34]

9

Possibly Governor Claiborne might have sensed more quickly the peril of a British invasion had it not been for the dust of his lesser war against Jean Laffite. "Emboldened by the impunity of past trespasses," the Barataria pirates "no longer conseal themselves ... but setting the Government at defiance in broad daylight carry on their infamous traffic."[35] Mr. Claiborne offered five hundred dollars for the capture of Laffite.

Ten years among them had failed to acquaint William Charles Cole Claiborne with his Latin constituents. Five hundred dollars! Monsieur Laffite redeemed the dignity of the scene by offering thirty thousand dollars for the apprehension of Mr. Claiborne, and the Hôtel du Trémoulet chuckled over its coffee and cordials. Laffite's sail continued to comb the Gulf for Spanish ships, his only quarry, and to bring them into Barataria. The cargoes were offered for sale to New Orleans merchants, who sometimes were apprized of their arrival by advertisements in the *Louisiana Gazette,* inviting an inspection of goods before buying. While Jackson, with a weather eye on the Gulf, wrote his Creek treaty, Mr. Claiborne labored with a handpicked Grand Jury. This body terminated its toils with a broad deprecation of piracy and an expression of regret that convictions should be "difficult . . . even where the strongest presumptions of guilt are offered."[36]

From his comfortable quarters at Barataria, Captain Laffite noticed the activities of the Grand Jury in a letter to the *Gazette,* adding: "Please to inform the public that several prizes have latterly been brought to Barataria. . . . Notes of any of the Banks of New Orleans will be received for goods sold."[37] Whereupon Pierre Laffite was arrested. The Laffites' lawyer, Edward Livingston, sought his release on bail. It was refused. This depressed Jean, who was fond of his brother. He himself had spent four years in a Spanish prison, and to his misfortune attributed his present attitude toward society.

Jean Laffite was a native of Bordeaux, the second of five brothers.

After short terms in the British and the French navies and in Napoleon's artillery, he turned his hand to piracy in the Caribbean where an English house-cleaning had brought the profession to low estate. Laffite restored it to a plane not enjoyed since the royal patronage of Elizabeth. He had a warehouse in Royal Street, New Orleans, and a blacksmith shop in St. Philip Street, where skilled slaves fashioned grills for French and Spanish houses. Jean was little at sea, the maritime branch of the business being in the charge of Pierre Laffite and Dominique You, a dandified little fellow with a hot temper. For the touch it afforded with gentility, Jean instructed the youth of first families in the use of the sword. He brought his younger brothers from France, intending that their acquaintance with the polished world should penetrate beyond the fencing ground. Marc Laffite promised to fulfill these expectations. He studied law and was elected a local magistrate.

But all the quiet influence, by no means small, that Jean could bring to bear failed to open prison doors for Pierre Laffite. Claiborne was elated. His "difficult" population might not support him against England. Against Laffite he did not require their support. In New Orleans were a handful of Regulars and a few small gunboats. Governor Claiborne conferred with Master Commandant Patterson of the Navy and with Colonel Ross, Forty-Fourth Infantry. An expedition to destroy the fort at Barataria was arranged.

Jean knew of this plan almost as quickly as it was made, but he lay in his hammock on the cool porch and lifted not a hand to forestall it. His first desire was the release of his brother. Unusual means would be necessary, but there were ways by which such means might be applied. He was turning over expedients in his mind when the *Sophie's* signal gun boomed off Grand Terre.

The English officers long remembered the delicacy of the food and wines and the splendor of the plate that graced the table of Jean Laffite. Over fragrant cigars Captain Lockyer unfolded his papers.

The first was the proclamation of Colonel Nicholls.

The second was a letter to "Monsieur Lafite or the Commandant of Barataria:" "I Call upon you, with your brave followers, to enter into the Service of Great Britain, in which you shall have the rank of Captain.... I hope to cut out other work for the americans than oppressing the inhabitants of Louisiana. Your property shall be guaranteed to you, and your persons respected. ... Be expeditious in your resolves, and rely on the verity of your humble servant, EDWARD NICHOLLS."[38]

Another letter was from Sir William H. Percy, commanding the squadron at Pensacola. Sir William addressed Laffite in a different tone. He must be England's ally or her enemy. "Monsieur Le Feete . . . I hold out [to you] a War instantly destructive ... but trust that the inhabitants of Barrataria, consulting their own interest, will not make necessary . . . such extremities . . . [but will] assist Great Britain in her just and unprovoked war against the United States." In this event "the security of their property [and] the blessings of the British Constitution" would be their reward. "Given under my hand on Board H. M. Ship Hermes."[39]

So the rumored descent upon New Orleans was to be a fact. Moreover, the British offer seemed a solution to all the difficulties that beset Jean Laffite. He would be protected against the meditated attack by Patterson and Ross. Pierre would be free.

Jean told Captain Lockyer he would reply to his proposals in writing. The officers returned to their ship and a letter followed them.

"If you could grant me fifteen days . . . to put my affairs in order . . . I will be entirely at your disposal."[40]

10

The *Sophie* departed from Barataria on September fourth. With the *Hermes, Carron* and *Childers,* she stood off Mobile Point on September twelfth. Colonel Nicholls landed marines, Indians and a howitzer in the rear of Fort Bowyer. On the thirteenth he exchanged shots with the fort at long range. The men of war moved into the pass and began to make soundings. Sir William H. Percy had hoped for Jean Laffite as an ally in the attack impending.[41] His small vessels would be in no danger of grounding. But the British Commander was confident, nevertheless. His guns outnumbered those of the fort seventy-eight to twenty.

Major Lawrence watched these preparations through a glass and when darkness fell dispatched Lieutenant Roy in a small sailing vessel for reenforcements. Mobile was thirty miles away and against the high wind Roy had a difficult passage before him.

But it was a good night to journey in the other direction. Jackson was still at Mobile. Knowing nothing of the presence of the British at the Point, he decided to slip over and inspect Lawrence's preparations for defense. At ten o'clock boarding a schooner with a small guard, he headed for the pass.[42]

CHAPTER XII

"PUSH ON THE TROOPS"

I

AFTER ten thousand miles on the curling currents of Western rivers, this was Andrew Jackson's introduction to salt water. The wind stiffened, and at one o'clock in the morning the schooner hailed the vessel of Lawrence's messenger beating up the bay. From Lieutenant Roy, Jackson learned that Fort Bowyer was besieged by superior forces on land and on water. Timely news! Sixty minutes more and the wind might have carried into the pass a prize of more consequence to Sir William Henry Percy than Lawrence's awkward little fort on the sand spit.

Jackson's schooner put about for Mobile to hasten reenforcements to Lawrence. For fourteen hours the small vessel tacked against the storm, making land at two in the afternoon, September 14, 1814, at the mouth of Dog River. Jackson leaped into a pirogue and ordered a course to Mobile. A pirogue on a river is one thing, on Mobile Bay in dirty weather another, but Jackson reached the town by nightfall. He called Captain Laval's company to arms. There was not a sea-going craft in the port. Jackson embarked them on a boat he had used to descend the Alabama, with instructions to transfer to the schooner should they meet it, but at all hazards to reach Fort Bowyer.[1]

The next day was one of anxious waiting. If the fort fell Jackson meant to resist at Mobile. "Lose no time," he ordered the Governor of Mississippi, "in facilitating the arrival of five hundred infantry and the *four troops of Cavalry*."[2] The sixteenth dawned without news, and Jackson sent confidential officers by land and by water for intelligence from the front.

A few hours later Captain Laval and his company returned by schooner. Their story threw garrison and town into a state of excitement. On the afternoon of the fifteenth they had run up within four miles of the fort, but were unable to land because the battle was on, the four British vessels letting loose their broadsides against the walls, while the force of marines and Indians waited on the land side to attack when ships' bombardment had done its work. "Great was the exertions & valiantly the action fought."[3] Laval's men cheered when they saw the British flag-ship disabled and abandoned. Then the flag on the fort went down. Had Lawrence struck? The marines and Indians advanced. The flag reappeared on a makeshift staff, the enemy's land forces retired, and the battle was resumed with new fury. Toward midnight the firing slackened, both fleet and fort seeming to have spent themselves. A glowing light revealed the angular contours of the works, followed by a vivid flash and a roar. Something had blown up. Laval declared the magazine of the fort had gone and started for Mobile. But some of the sailors on the schooner thought the explosion was on board the disabled British ship.[4]

The night brought no more explicit news, and General Jackson learned to appreciate something of the trials of Claiborne with his "difficult population to manage." Spies in regular correspon- dence with the enemy reported Jackson's every move.[5] A visiting merchant from New Orleans, suspected of complicity in this business, was lodged in the guardhouse. The belief that the fort had fallen was received with undisguised satisfaction, and Lieu- tenant Guillemard, of the Spanish Army, who had brought Man- rique's latest to Jackson, became an object of friendly attention.[6] Jackson's answer to this was: "Push on the troops from Ten- nessee."[7]

A few hours later saw Lieutenant Guillemard at Jackson's head- quarters in a nervous sweat for his passport. The word had come, proving Laval mistaken and the sailors right. The British them- selves had blown up the *Hermes* to avert its capture. Lawrence's victory was complete,[8] and Jackson was jubilant. "Sir Wm. has lost his ship, and the Col [Nicholls] an eye . . . and have retired to Pensacola to rest.... We will be better prepared to receive them on the next visit."⁹

2

Having put the British off for two weeks, Jean Laffite wrote a lengthy letter to Jean Blanque at New Orleans. "I make you the repository of a secret on which perhaps depends the tranquility of our country." Monsieur Blanque was a member of the Legislature and one of the political powers in Louisiana. Laffite enclosed the documents of Captain Lockyer. "Our enemies exerted on my integrity a motive which few men would have resisted. They have represented to me a brother in irons, a brother who is to me very dear! of whom I can become the deliverer! ... From your enlightenment will you aid me in a circumstance so grave."¹⁰

With this was also enclosed the following communication for Blanque to deliver:

"A Son Excellence Monsieur
"Wᵐ C, C, Clayborne, Gouverneur
"del' Etat de la Louisiane:

"MonSieur
"In the firm persuasion that the choice which was made of you for ... Office of first Magistrate ... has been by the Esteem & accorded by Merit, I address Myself to you with confidence for an object on which can depend the Safety of the State. I offer to Return to this State many Citizens Who perhaps have lost to your eyes that sacred title. I offer ... Their Efforts for the Defense of the country.

"This point of Louisiana that I occupy is of Great Importance in the present situation. I offer myself to defend it.... I am The Lost Sheep who desires to return to the flock ... for you to see through my faults such as they are. . . .

"In case, Monsieur Le Gouverneur, that your Reply should Not be favorable to my ardent wishes I declare to you that I leave immediately so Not to be held to have Co-operated with an in-

vasion. . . . This can not Fail to take place, and puts me entirely
at the judgement of my conscience.

"I have the Honor to be, Monsieur Le gouverneur,

"LAFFITE"[11]

The outlaw had the quality of loyalty to friends and most of
his friends in New Orleans, notably his legal adviser, Edward Livingston, were supporters of the United States. Moreover, alliance
with the British would involve peace with his implacable enemy
Spain.

Claiborne was deeply impressed by Laffite's correspondence,
which contained the clearest disclosure of British intentions yet
known in America. Hard as it was on his pride, the Governor
agreed that this put a new face on the pirate's affairs. "There
is in this city a much *greater Spirit of Disaffection* than I had
anticipated, and among the faithfull Louisianians There is a *De-
spondency* which palsies all my preparations. . . . Laffite and his
associates might probably be made useful to us."[12] The sailing
of the Patterson-Ross expedition to destroy Barataria was therefore delayed and the commanders summoned to a council at the
Executive Residence. These officers denounced Laffite's papers as
forgeries and a design to outwit justice. They dominated a stormy
conference. Claiborne yielded and the expedition sailed. But
that very night Pierre Laffite mysteriously escaped from jail, and
the impertinent *Gazette* twitted the authorities.

Pierre joined Jean at Barataria with word of the impending
attack. Jean made no move to resist, though a British fleet was
within call. Pierre was free and the promise implied was kept.
With a few personal followers the Laffites slipped away to the
Côte Allemand, a stretch of river above New Orleans, to await
events. On September sixteenth, the day after Lawrence's victory
at Fort Bowyer, Barataria was rifled and burned. Goods worth
half a million dollars were carried to New Orleans, the spoil of
a bloodless raid, a circumstance which detracted but little, however, from the stirring prose of Colonel Ross's official report to
General Jackson.[18]

Though Mr. Claiborne permitted the raid on the assumption that the Laffite papers had been forged, he sent copies of them to Jackson on the assumption that they were genuine and contained military intelligence of first importance. General Jackson was not a man readily to see himself in error and this drew him also into an equivocal position. Jackson had denounced Laffite and seconded the plan for the destructon of Barataria. Now he used the pirate's information and enjoyed a gift of claret from his confiscated cellar[14]—with no thanks to Laffite for either. He roundly rebuked Claiborne because "those wretches, the refugees from Barataria ... should find an asylum in your city. ... Cause them to be arrested."[15]   And if this were not enough the Laffites were noticed in a proclamation Jackson sent to New Orleans in answer to Colonel Nicholls's literary composition. "Can Louisianians, can Frenchmen, can Americans ever stop to be Slaves or allies of Britain ... [or] place any confidence in the honor of Men who have courted an alliance with ... the Pirates of Barrataria? ... Have they not insulted you by calling on you to associate ... with ... this hellish Banditti?"[16]

Governor Claiborne reported the address "well received," despite comment of the *Gazette,* a journal never unfriendly to the interests of Laffite.[17]   Claiborne may have been so deficiently informed as to believe what he said, though the fact is General Jackson's allusion to the Baratarians was a blunder.[18]   That the consequences were not disagreeable is due to the good management of Edward Livingston. A curious odor of ships attends this distinguished family, Edward's brother having financed Robert Fulton and his grandfather Captain William Kidd. Edward himself had served with Andrew Jackson in the House of Representatives, being one of the twelve immortals to vote, with Jackson, against a congenial reply to Washington's address of farewell. In 1804 a scandal in municipal politics and the ruin of his private finances had driven Mr. Livingston from the mayoralty of New York City to seek a restoration of his fortunes in Louisiana, and to find it in a law practise which, among other things, imparted respectability to the calling of Laffite.

Louisianians who might not listen to Claiborne would listen to Livingston. Elected chairman of a committee of defense created with Gallic éclat in the coffee room of the Hôtel du Trémoulet as a result of Laffite's disclosures, he became Jackson's most effective champion at New Orleans. The committee did little except to vote a sword to Lawrence, but Livingston did much. While Claiborne congratulated himself on the "victory" over Laffite and bombarded Jackson with alarms over the undefended state of the city, the questionable loyalty of its cosmopolitan population, and rumors of a slave insurrection,[19] Livingston strove to repair these conditions. He sent Jackson a useful description of the six water approaches to the town with suggestions for the defense of each, requiring four thousand men. He asked Jackson to pay the city a visit—"Tho' short it would have an happy effect"[20]—solicited a place on the General's staff for himself and sent a bottle of Laffite's claret, without, however, calling the "hellish banditti" by that name.

In Congress the relations of Jackson and Livingston had been close. In 1804 Jackson felt that if he himself could not get the governorship of Louisiana, Livingston should have it.[21] The formal though polite tone of the letters now passing between them gave no indication of their earlier intimacy. Jackson studied the water approaches, but it was to Claiborne he applied for additional enlightenment.[22] He drank the claret as honest booty, but declined Mr. Livingston's proffer of official services[23] and turned to other things.

3

General Jackson did not think the British would use a water route to New Orleans, but would advance on the city by way of Mobile. "A real military man, with full knowledge of the geography of . . . this country, would first possess himself of that point, draw to his standard the Indians, and march direct to the walnut Hills [site of the present city of Vicksburg] . . . and being able to forrage on the country, support himself, cut off all supplies from above and make this country an easy conquest."[24]

The activity at Pensacola, the attack on Fort Bowyer, everything the British had done, and all that Jackson or any one[25] had learned of their intentions could be construed as supporting this view. A glance at the broad instructions to the army and naval commanders at Negril Bay, in Jamaica, where the great expedition was taking form, would have left one little wiser. To enable the English Government "to exact its cession as a price of peace," orders were to occupy Louisiana by advancing directly upon New Orleans or through Mobile, at discretion. Nicholls's free talk in Havana had indicated an attempted advance through Mobile.

Jackson moved, therefore, to meet the enemy in that quarter, and moved alone, because for a month during and after the occupation of Washington, he was, in effect, without a Government to report to. On his own responsibility Jackson demanded troops from Mississippi, Tennessee and Kentucky, though Kentucky was outside his military jurisdiction, using all his passionate art to stir in Western hearts the will to battle. Stricken with fever and unable to sign his name,[26] he dictated one of these letters. The response was rather encouraging, except in the matter of arms and supplies. A "patriotic" letter from Rachel was worth a new regiment. "The burning [of] the capitol," her husband replied, "may be a disgrace, . . . but it will give impulse and energy to our cause, the change too, in Secretaries of war will add much. . . . Say to my son . . . he must never cry. . . and learn to be a soldier. I wish the horses kept in good order and my coalts well fed."[27]

Salutary, indeed, had been the change in the War Department. The first officers of the Administration upon the scene of desolation after the retreat of the British from Washington were Madison and Monroe. The President was on the verge of nervous prostration and Monroe took charge. Expelling Armstrong from the Cabinet, he assumed the duties of the War Office without relinquishing those of Secretary of State and planned to wage the war as it had not been waged before. The Treasury was empty, recruiting for the Regular establishment discontinued for want of funds, and the cry of disunion raised in New England.[28] In the blackest hour since Valley Forge, James Monroe pinned his hope for deliverance on emergency measures for raising money, federal conscription for raising men—and on Andrew Jackson. He found one hundred thousand dollars to place at the Southern Commander's disposal and his validated levies for troops, adding Kentucky and Georgia to the territory from which he could draw.[29] "A war of seven years," an attaché of the War Office informed Jackson, "may be expected."[30]

Simultaneously Jackson found time to outline to a friend in Congress his own idea of the government's duty. "The whole force Britain can bring into the field we are now contending against [and] it is daily increasing." To meet this there must be "unanimity of feeling . . . and . . . action in the deliberative councils of the nation." Men must be provided without "calculating the expense." "The spirit of mutiny and desertion that pervade our militia" must be removed, and "their term of service [extended] to one or two years," making them, for all practical purposes, Regular troops.[31] Had the two men conferred, General Jackson's recommendations could not have been more agreeable to the energetic Secretary of War.

Meantime peace negotiations had been opened at Ghent where the British Commissioners displayed an attitude somewhat similar to that of Andrew Jackson toward the Creeks. And despite all that Madison and Monroe could do to pump new life into the war, New England was for ending it on any terms. But the West chose to keep up the fight. Brigades, regiments and isolated companies began to people the wilderness above Mobile—their frontier dress and weapons forming a picture in acute contrast to the British Regulars on board the transports en route to the rendezvous at Jamaica. Jackson's illness passed almost as quickly as it had come upon him.[32] He began to station the gathering units strategically, and to reiterate the old plea for supplies. From a Tennessee regiment came the monotonous militia story of insubordination and mutiny. Jackson ordered two hundred men in arrest and convoked a court martial to sift for the guilty. But on the whole the news was good. "Coffee's near approach gives . . . confidence to me."[33] Coffee led eighteen hundred men, each riding his own horse and carrying his own rifle. "Every one of my boys wants to get within fair buckrange of a red coat!"[34]

On October twenty-fifth the General quit Mobile for Pierce's Stockade on the Alabama, where a large force of the new troops was concentrated. A frontier dream of twenty years was in the execution: Jackson meant to strike at Pensacola. "As I act without the orders of the government, I deem it important to state to you my reasons. . . . The safety of this section of the union depends upon it . . . [and] Pensacola [has] assume[d] the character of British Territory. . . . I feel a confidence that I shall stand Justified to my government. . . . Should I not . . . the consolation of having done the only thing in my own opinion which could give security to the country . . . will be an ample reward for the loss of my commission."[35] This letter to Mr. Monroe had several possible uses. In case of diplomatic consequences it would give an innocent appearance to the record. In any case it would be an excellent nerve tonic for Mr. Madison, and for Monroe too, if he should heed it, though in reality Jackson had private assurances that the Secretary personally would approve of the expedition.[36]

On November second Jackson marched with three thousand men, seven hundred of them Regulars. On the sixth he was before Pensacola. Major Peire of the Forty-Fourth Infantry accompanied a flag of truce "to require that the different forts, Barrancas, St. Rose, and St. Michael, should be immediately surrendered, to be garrisoned . . . by the United States, until Spain . . . could preserve unimpaired her neutral character."[37] The flag was fired upon—by the English, it later came out—and Major Peire retired without delivering his message.

4

Jackson stormed the town in the morning. The principal defenses of Pensacola were constructed to meet an attack from the west along the white beach, the beach on the east side being narrow and difficult of access. Jackson was encamped on the main road entering the town from the west, just out of range of the guns of

St. Michael and seven British men-of-war in the bay. An hour before dawn he led the bulk of his army out quietly and began to circle the town, while five hundred of Coffee's men started a noisy demonstration on the west.

When sunrise disclosed the maneuver the dispositions for as-sault on the east had been made. There was no time for the fleet to change its position, but a battery was posted at the head of a street and garden walls looking eastward were manned by in-fantry. The Americans advanced in three columns, one on the beach and two above it. Captain Laval of the Third Infantry captured the battery after its third fire. The assailants swarmed up the streets, clearing garden walls and roofs as they went. The General was standing over Captain Laval, who had been seriously wounded, when he was told that Commandant Manrique, old, infirm and trembling, was stumping about with a white flag in distracted quest of Jackson. The two met at the Government House where the surrender of the forts was arranged while a Brit-ish sally in small boats was beaten back. The Spanish killed time and displayed such bad faith in the surrender of Fort St. Michael that Jackson was obliged to defer until the following morning a projected attack on Barrancas, fourteen miles away and garrisoned by the British. At three A. M. Jackson was ready to march when an explosion rocked the earth beneath his feet. The British had blown up Barrancas. Whereupon they fled to their shipping which put to sea.

The bird Jackson had hoped to bag had flown, and, fearing it was headed for Mobile, he dropped his useless prizes and in three and one-half days was on the Tensas ready to support Fort Bow-yer.[38]

The dash upon Pensacola was a daredevil thing, and the Gen-eral's personal historians have confessed disappointment "in the object he had principally in view."[39] Washington was shocked, not so much over a violation of the nominal neutrality of Spain, as over Jackson's absence from the vital points of Mobile and New Orleans, not even Monroe reckoning upon the celerity with which this man could move an army. But the immediate and local results were wholesome. The expedition exalted Coffee's men, who failed not to note how punctiliously the Red Coats had kept out of "buck range," leaving the honor of defense to the Spaniards. It ruined British prestige among die-hard Creeks and Seminoles. Deserted by allies who had promised so much, they fled destitute into the Florida wilderness. It disgusted Manrique with the same allies and mightily altered the tone of his communications. "Exmo Señor D^n. Andres Jackson. . . . Permit me . . . to sign myself, with additional consideration and respect, your most faithful and grateful servant, who kisses your hands."[40] It thrilled the West, the only part of the country properly supporting the war. It enhanced Jackson's confidence in his troops and theirs in him.[41]

5

New Orleans continued to call. "I renew the entreaty," wrote Livingston, "that you will pay us a visit . . . and overawe disaffection."[42] Claiborne was little more cheerful. "The Legislature has not as yet done anything to damp the public. . . . But I fear, I much fear, they will."[43] These fears wearied Jackson, who adhered to the belief that the enemy would move on the city through Mobile.[44] "The Citizens of New Orleans have addressed me," he informed Monroe. "My whole force would not satisfy the demands they make."[45]

Jackson had not neglected New Orleans. He had requested Claiborne to embody the militia, and the War Department to send arms by way of the Mississippi. He had directed Lieutenant-Colonel McRae of the Regular Army to take command of the city and put the forts in condition for resistance. He had sent his inspector-general, Colonel Arthur P. Hayne, to report on this work. But despite all this Livingston's plea that the situation required the dominating presence of the Commander himself was not without basis.

Returning to Mobile from the Pensacola excursion, Jackson decided to go, though not until he had placed Mobile and surrounding country in a bristling state of defense. Militia and friendly Indians ranged westward to keep hostile Seminoles and Creeks at bay.[46]   Fort Bowyer was strengthened "until I feel a conviction . . . that ten thousand troops cannot take it."[47]   Other Regulars and militia were stationed at Mobile and posts to the northward from whence they could be thrown where needed in event of attack.   Command of the whole was given to Brigadier-General James Winchester, trained in Jackson's Cumberland militia division before the war.   "Fort Bowyer . . . [is] the Key of communication between . . . [Mobile] and New Orleans," Jackson instructed him. . . . "[It] must be maintained."[48]

To cover New Orleans proper Jackson sent Coffee toward Baton Rouge to await reenforcement by Carroll's newly mustered militia from Tennessee and Thomas's from Kentucky.   With these dispositions in the making, General Jackson glanced at the politico-military situation as a whole.   With specie payments suspended by nearly all banks west of the Hudson, with New England Federalists crying for peace at any price, and the Governor of Massachusetts upbraiding the American commissioners at Ghent for rejecting the British demand for the cession of the Northwest, Andrew Jackson felt sufficiently unterrified to forward to Monroe a suggestion for the reduction of Canada.   "I leave for N. Orleans on the 22d [of November, 1814], and if my health permits, will reach there in 12 days."   The leisurely pace was to afford "a view of the points at which the enemy might effect a landing."[49]

General Jackson was five days on his way when the British armada—ten thousand seamen, fifteen hundred marines, nine thousand six hundred troops—sailed from Negril Bay.   The presence of officers' wives gave decks a holiday air.   They brought their prettiest frocks, these ladies, prepared for a lengthy sojourn in New Orleans concerning the social tone of which they had made diligent inquiry.   The attitude of Major General Keane reflected this expression of confidence.   Counting on another Bladensburg victory, he had decided to forego the tactically superior route through Mobile and to embarrass Jackson's calculations by disembarking directly on the Louisiana coast.

This posture of affairs was certain to bring disappointment to some one. For the altered blockhouse at the Hermitage was also astir with preparations of departure. Confident that Mobile would be the scene of the fighting, General Jackson had written his wife to descend the river to New Orleans. In the thirteen months past they had been together fewer than thirty days. Mrs. Jackson asked her vivacious niece Rachel Hays Butler to accompany her, and none could say that Aunt Rachel had not taken to heart her husband's suggestions as to the style of travel suiting "a Major Generals lady in the service of the U. S." She had a thirty-ton keel boat fitted out at an expense of four hundred and fifty dollars.[50]

CHAPTER XIII

THE ESCAPE OF GABRIEL VILLERÉ

I

A CREOLE[1] lady of New Orleans, whose identity seems lost to history, surveyed the dining-room of J. Kilty Smith with an eye of serene approval. Formal silver and Sèvres patterned the white damask. The kitchen steamed with a "rich and savory" breakfast, "prepared in that style of cookery for which the Creoles are renowned."[2] Madame had fulfilled her duties in distinguished style. Monsieur Smith could be proud of the hospitality he was about to tender le grand Général Jackson.

The host was one of the first "American" merchants to come to New Orleans and one of the most successful. His home, a few miles north of the city near the junction of the Carondelet Canal with the Bayou St. Jean, had been the country seat of an affluent Spaniard of an older day. But as a bachelor who surmised that his preparations for welcoming Andrew Jackson to the gates of New Orleans might profit by a feminine touch, Mr. Smith had solicited the collaboration of the wife of a wealthy neighbor.

It was the morning of December 1, 1814.[3] The chill night mist breathed up by the swamps reluctantly dissolved beneath a sullen sky, revealing the old road past the Smith place following the Bayou St. Jean into New Orleans. This stream twisted through the swamp like a dark green serpent and the road was muddy and broken. But General Jackson had traversed worse thoroughfares on his journey from Mobile. He had come slowly, integrating the troublesome topography with the map that Claiborne had sent him. His observations had confirmed him in the opinion that it would be the part of wisdom for the British to attempt their invasion through Mobile, or at nearest make a landing at the mouth of the Pascagoula,[4] thirty miles west thereof, and attack New Orleans from above. At Fort St. Jean on Lake Pontchartrain, a few miles from the Smith place, Major Hughes of the Seventh Infantry and Major Chotard of the Louisiana militia had joined the party. There were not more than three or four others, including Jackson's adjutant-general, Robert Butler, and his military secretary, handsome John Reid.

At Mr. Smith's reins were thrown to stable-boys and the party welcomed on the merchant's spacious gallery. The young officers chatted gaily, but the appearance and demeanor of the Commanding General was a shock to Mr. Smith and the temporary mistress of the manse who observed him narrowly: "A tall, gaunt man, very erect, . . . with a countenance furrowed by care and anxiety. His dress was simple and nearly threadbare. A small leather cap protected his head, and a short blue Spanish cloak his body, whilst his . . . high dragoon boots [were] long innocent of polish or blacking. . . . His complexion was sallow and unhealthy; his hair iron grey, and his body thin and emaciated like that of one who had just recovered from a lingering sickness. . . . But . . . [a] fierce glare . . . [lighted] his bright and hawk-like eye."[5]

The elaborate breakfast was wasted on the guest of honor whose querulous digestion permitted him to eat only a few spoonfuls of boiled hominy. Moreover, he was eager to be at his work of the day. Glancing at his watch, he "reminded his companions of the necessity of their early entrance into the city."[6]

Mr. Smith's neighbor was piqued, but the General received no hint of it in the smooth alloy of her drawing-room manner. Madame was not sure whether she had been the victim of a jest or her friend the victim of a hoax. She who had seen officers of Napoleon knew a "grand général" by the outward signs—"plumes, epaulettes, long sword and moustache." "Ah! Mr. Smith . . . you asked me to . . . receive a great Général. I make your house comme il faut, and prepare a splendid déjeuner, . . . all for . . . an ugly old Kaintuck flat-boatman."[7]

When a Louisiana lady said Kaintuck flatboatman there was little one could add to the degree of disparagement.

2

At the last moment carriages appeared to convey the shabby General and his staff to the city. He had initiated his own arrangements for quarters in New Orleans, however, a circumstance that had come about in a curious way. The dismay of the Spanish over the nimble retreat of the British from Pensacola had been genuine. During his short stay in that city, Jackson was entertained by the elegant Don Juan Ventura Morales who had been Spanish Intendant at New Orleans before the transfer of Louisiana to the United States, and later was expelled by Claiborne for plotting against the American régime. Surely Jackson knew Don Juan's history. Yet he believed his protestations of friendship which indeed may have been sincere in that Don Juan was prepared to accept the Americans temporarily as the lesser of a choice of evils. Jackson left Pensacola carrying a letter of introduction to Don Juan's son-in-law, Bernard de Marigny de Mandeville, of New Orleans. From Fort St. Jean Jackson had sent this letter into the city, with an intimation that he would appreciate the use of Marigny's residence as his personal headquarters.[8]

But the carriages had not been sent out by Marigny and they did not convey the General to the Marigny house. They conveyed him to the residence of the lately deceased Daniel Clark, an Irish adventurer picturesquely involved in Louisiana politics since the Miró conspiracy. On the gallery of this large house, Jackson was formally received in the presence of a crowd that filled the street despite the unheralded nature of his arrival, the early hour, and the threatening sky. Governor Claiborne was there, tall, immaculate and truly happy to shed his responsibility for the safety of the city. Commandant Patterson was there, "a compact, gallant-bearing man, in the neat undress naval uniform, his manner slightly marked by hauteur,"[9] and none too popular as the "conqueror" of Laffite. Rotund, affable little Mayor Girod bowed and bobbed about. But the personage of the occasion was tall, high-shouldered, ungraceful Edward Livingston. The welcoming committee was of his choosing. Bernard Marigny, the only person in New Orleans whose hospitality Jackson had solicited, was not invited to the gallery, and dark reflections filled his active Latin mind as he hung on the fringe of the crowd.

Claiborne addressed his fellow-citizens with "fluent elocution." Girod addressed them with fluent elocution plus gestures. The rain began to fall and soon "all present," as Monsieur Marigny recorded, "were wet, muddy and uncomfortable; but the Mayor (given to singing madrigals to persons in power) assured the General that 'The sun is never shining more brilliantly than when you are among us!' "[10] The General responded briefly. Edward Livingston advanced to render his remarks into French. When this man spoke one forgot his unprepossessing exterior. His manner was assured, his voice rich, his diction flawless. General Jackson, he translated, pledged himself "to protect the city, . . . drive their enemies into the sea, or perish in the effort."[11]

The effect was "electric. . . . Countenances cleared up. Bright and hopeful were the words and looks of all who . . . caught the heroic glance of the hawk-eyed General."[12]

The hawk-eyed General mounted his horse, and, with Livingston at his side, rode to the Place d'Armes where four gorgeously uniformed companies of New Orleans militia waited in the downpour. The élite of the town comprised this battalion—sons of planters, merchants, bankers—with a sprinkling of soldiers of fortune and refugees from Santo Domingo (now called Haiti), where the slave uprising under L'Ouverture had uprooted French dominion. Jackson passed down the line: the Carabiniers d'Orléans of Captain Plauché; the Dragons à Pied of Captain St. Gême, a salty little French rooster whose five feet of stature was exalted by a twelve-inch plume in his cap; the Francs of Captain Hudry; the Chasseurs of Captain Guibert; the Louisiana Blues of Captain Maunsel White, an Irishman. Seasoned soldiers in the ranks, and there were men who had followed Napoleon, felt a wordless unity with the one that had come to lead them.

At the three-story building at Number 106 Royal Street set aside for his headquarters, Jackson made Livingston an aide-de-camp with the rank of colonel, and began to consider the situation.

The total of arms in the city did not exceed twenty-five hundred muskets and seventy-five hundred pistols, the latter captured from the Baratarians.[13]   No government rifles had arrived, but a shipment of molasses had come overland from Boston in the same barrels in which it had left New Orleans two years before.[14] This much the War Department had contributed toward the defense of the city whose warehouses bulged with cotton, sugar, and sirup, accumulated in consequence of the British blockade. The Commander also began to sense the quicksand of jealousies and doubtful loyalty that had mired Claiborne.

He was to dine with Colonel Livingston whose wife, a Santo Dominican of exotic beauty, had repelled the idea of bringing "that wild Indian-fighter" in contact with polished society. "He will capture *you* at first sight," said her husband dryly.

Madame Livingston could have spared herself the worry that her dinner would be anything but a success. Andrew Jackson's first appearance in New Orleans society was a triumph which was to repeat itself many times. Colonel Livingston discovered the secret of the General's easy victory at his wife's dinner.

"I ushered General Jackson into the drawing-room . . . in the full-dress uniform of his rank, . . . a blue frock-coat with buff facings, white waistcoat and close fitting breeches. . . .

" 'Madame and Mesdemoiselles, I have the honor to present Major-General Jackson of the United States Army.'

"I had to confess to myself that the new . . . uniform made another man of him. He had two sets of manners: One for headquarters . . . the other for the drawing-room. . . .

"Of the twelve or more young ladies present . . . not more than three could speak English. . . . However, . . . we placed the General between Madame Livingston and Mlle. Eliza Chotard, an excellent English scholar. . . . Of our wines he seemed to fancy most a fine old Madeira and remarked that he had not tasted anything like it since Burr's dinner at Philadelphia in 1797. . . ."[15]

But despite the success of General Jackson with Madame Livingston's guests, a tactical error had been committed at the dinner, from the effects of which the General was to suffer in‑ numerable embarrassments. Bernard Marigny had not been in‑ vited.

Colonel Livingston was the acknowledged leader of the "Ameri‑ can" element, but his influence with the Creoles, though consider‑ able, has been exaggerated. Under his chaperonage Jackson could not hope to complete the conquest of "society" in New Orleans, a not unimportant adjunct to the coordination of all preparations for the defense of the city. True, Madame Livingston was French and therefore could be a great aid, but—and what a difference this made in a social hierarchy almost as rigid as the courts of the Louis—she was a Santo Dominican.

There was no prouder name in Louisiana than de Marigny de Mandeville, about which the lambent traditions of Creole aristoc‑ racy cluster in their finest flower. Bernard was twenty-nine, unassailably rich, and a leader of the faction in the State Legisla‑ ture that had effectively checked attempts at a rampant Ameri‑ canization of Louisiana. He accepted the snub and abided his time. In the morning, as he understood, General Jackson and staff were to take up their residence in the Marigny town-house by the river—which should alter very materially the sudden as‑ cendency of the parvenu Colonel. Monsieur Marigny, who knew the salons of Paris and of London, would show General Jackson what correct entertainment was, and would acquaint him with the real rulers of Louisiana. For Marigny was impressed with Jackson and wished him well—under the proper auspices, naturally.

On the morning of December second Bernard Marigny paced his spacious drawing-room. The apartments set aside for the General and his official family were in order. Breakfast had been prepared. When Jackson had not arrived at noontime Marigny went abroad for news. "M. Pelletier Delahoussaye . . . told me that the General had changed his mind and would remain at Dr. Kerr's on Esplanade Street. I was astonished."[16] A call at the Kerr residence verified this intelligence. Firm in the clutches of the "Americans," General Jackson was poring over a map. The hospitality of a Marigny had been rejected. Incredible happenings are a part of war.

3

General Jackson was also astonished, but for a different reason: "the total ignorance I have found among all descriptions of persons of . . . [the] topography" of the country[17] surrounding New Orleans. This topography is unique, and knowledge of its peculiar intricacies indispensable to any plan for the defense of the city. Jackson clung to the belief that if New Orleans were attacked it would be from above, a contingency that could arise only after Winchester's defeat at Mobile, which the Commander regarded as improbable. But now that he was on the ground his duty was to fend against the other alternative, a direct assault on the city from the Louisiana coast.

New Orleans lies about one hundred and five miles from the mouths of the Mississippi. For the most part the country intervening is neither land nor water, but a geological laboratory where land is being made. If one would behold the completed product, however, he must wait for another fifty thousand years. At the present moment, the more finished parts of this leisurely labor of Nature comprise dank cypress swamps peopled by alligators and muskrats and lugubrious pelicans. In the less finished parts where the forming soil is too unstable for trees, marsh reeds rear their bright green blades six feet high, tough as hemp and sharp as knives. The whole is schemelessly patterned and webbed by streams and sloughs and lakes, which in 1814 afforded no less than six definable approaches to the environs of the city. This much Jackson had known from his study of an imperfect map and from information supplied by Livingston before his departure from Mobile.

The map I have provided to assist the reader's understanding of these six routes is, I hope, much clearer than the one General Jackson was obliged to use. Glancing from west to east one first encounters the Bayou La Fourche. This narrow deep stream is in reality a mouth of the Mississippi. It breaks away from the parent river about midway between New Orleans and Baton Rouge, entering the Gulf eighty miles west of the delta.

Next is Barataria Bay which lies seventy miles west of the mouths of the Mississippi, and by a series of water courses affords communication with the Mississippi at a point opposite New Orleans. This was the route Laffite used to bring his booty to the city.

Then comes the Mississippi River which was the usual mode of approach.

East of the Mississippi are River aux Chênes and Bayou Terre aux Bœufs. These sluggish streams, navigable to small boats, almost touch the Mississippi in the vicinity of English Turn, a bend in the river fourteen miles below the city.

The next approach is Lake Borgne. This arm of the Gulf scallops the east side of the delta, reaching within six miles of the Mississippi just above English Turn. Its possession would afford an enemy two possible routes to the city: first, by ascending Bayou Chef Menteur to the Plain of Gentilly, a treeless belt of dry land about a mile wide, and second, by crossing the six miles from the lake shore to the Mississippi. Approximately five miles of this was swamp, passable only by a series of finger-like bayous concerning which Jackson could get little precise information. But having passed this swamp an enemy would find himself on a strip of firm ground bordering the river, the seat of some of the richest cane plantations in Louisiana, with a road along the levee leading directly into the town.

The last route General Jackson had to consider is through Lake Pontchartrain, which is reached from Lake Borgne by the narrow strait of the Rigolets. Mastery of the lake would admit an enemy to the city by way of Bayou St. Jean and the road leading along its bank which Jackson had recently traversed. The bayou itself was navigable for vessels of a hundred tons to a point within two miles of the city. The route of the lakes and the Bayou St. Jean ranked next to the Mississippi River as an artery of the city's water-borne commerce.

Not until his arrival in New Orleans did Jackson comprehend the difficulty of defending these six routes. He had spent his life among a frontier race whose security depended upon unsleeping vigilance. At fourteen he had been sufficiently familiar with

Waxhaw trails to serve William Richardson Davie as a courier. But this was not the state of affairs in New Orleans, "an opulent and commercial town," as Jackson said, made soft by "the habits...of wealth."[18] "The numerous bayous & canals"—the only roads through the swamps—"appear almost as little understood by the inhabitants as by the Citizens of Tennessee. True every man will give you an exact description of the whole & every man will give you an erroneous one."[19] Such is the General's own statement of the case, which is not, however, to be taken altogether literally. Perhaps only by contrast to backwoodsmen could citizens of New Orleans be called ignorant of the unique geography of their country; and in any event, despite the handicaps, within twenty-four hours after his arrival Jackson had gathered a vast fund of reasonably accurate topographical information.

The next move was to send detachments armed with axes to fell trees and obstruct the smaller streams—Bayou La Fourche, the waterways from Barataria Bay, Bayou Terre aux Bœufs, Bayou Chef Menteur, and the innumerable creeks—called coulées—which, like so many treacherous fingers, stretch from Lakes Pontchartrain and Borgne toward the Mississippi.[20]

There remained the lakes themselves and the Mississippi River, through which progress of an enemy could not be hampered by such elementary means. Five small gunboats cruised Lake Borgne under command of Lieutenant Thomas Ap. Catesby Jones of the Regular Navy. This force was too slender for fighting. Its duty, therefore, was one of reconnaissance—to watch for a sight of British sail at the mouth of the lake, and, should enemy vessels enter the lake, to stand back out of range and keep New Orleans informed of the movements of the invader. It was calculated that the shallow waters of Borgne, necessitating the transfer of a landing force from sea-going transports to vessels of light draft, would afford time for the gunboats to perform their mission. The route of the lakes long had given the military authorities of Louisiana the greatest concern, but Jackson felt that his precautions in this direction were sufficient for the time being at least. Indeed, with the means at his disposal, there was nothing more that the Commander could have done.

This sweeping activity, the spreading of men from Bayou La Fourche on the west to the mouth of Lake Borgne on the east, was the work of forty-eight hours after leaving the breakfast table of J. Kilty Smith. But the task was only fairly begun. Jackson now turned his personal attention to the Mississippi, which he descended on December 3, 1814, the day following the chilly call of Bernard Marigny.

Wisely he determined to attempt no defense of the river below Fort St. Philip, fifty miles from the mouths. There he ordered two auxiliary batteries erected. At English Turn, fourteen miles below the city, he designated additional batteries, which planters turned out their negroes to erect. On his return to New Orleans, after an absence of six days, there was no indication of the designs of the enemy. The General was able to assure Secretary Monroe that the military situation was in hand. The works projected would render the Mississippi impassable for hostile troops. "The Gun Boats on the Lakes will prevent the British from approaching in that quarter.... Fort Bowyer will be their point of attack."[21] So confident was Jackson of this that he hoped for word that Rachel had begun her journey.

But on the next day there was news of the enemy to engage his attention. Lieutenant Jones reported their vessels arriving off Cat and Ship Islands, near the mouth of Lake Borgne. The news threw New Orleans into a state of alarm, though Jackson was not surprised or disturbed. "I expect this is a faint," he informed Coffee near Baton Rouge, "to draw my attention to that point when they mean to strike at another—however I will look for them there and provide for their reception else where."

And while waiting to see which way the cat should jump, here was a morsel for General Coffee to chew on. "I see in the Nashville Gazette that *'Packolett has beat the noted horse Doublehead with great Ease.'*"

True, this was not the best turf news that Old Hickory, who owned Pacolet, could have wished, but it took some of the sting from the triumph of Jesse Haynie's little chestnut mare Maria which continued to beat every horse that Andrew Jackson or any one else sent against her.

"I have only to add," concluded General Jackson, "that you will hold your Brigade in compleat readiness to march. . . . We may, or may not have a fandango with Lord Hill in the christmas holidays."[22]   Originally the British ministry had intended that Lord Hill should command the expedition against Louisiana.

4

Next morning Jackson departed for the reedy shores of the lakes, Chef Menteur and the Plain of Gentilly, where old fortifications were strengthened, new ones begun and lines of resistance projected. This required four days. Jackson's accomplishments, in the face of his illness from dysentery, had amazed the people and drawn the majority of them to him. "General Jackson, his presence revived spirits . . . and rescusitated Clabo [Claiborne] the very day he entered the town," Pierre Favrot wrote to his wife. Like most Creoles Monsieur Favrot had slight use for the Governor. "He is good for nothing, . . . a third rate lawyer."[23]

Yet the benefits of Jackson's labors were not conceded on all hands. There still remained the wounded sensibilities of Bernard Marigny who was a power in the Legislature and this body adopted a critical attitude toward the measures of the Commanding General. Water-front lodging houses abounded with sailors, but Commandant Patterson was unable to recruit crews for the naval schooner *Carolina* and the ship *Louisiana* that lay in the river. It was subtly intimated, no doubt by Livingston, that a word from General Jackson would repair this difficulty. Jackson had steadfastly declined to receive the services of the Laffites or their followers, though some of the latter who were out of jail slipped past complaisant mustering officers. It was argued that infantry might be improvised, but artillerymen and sailors were another matter. Jackson needed both, and the Baratarians were skilled cannoneers and intrepid seamen. The General insisted, however, that he would get along without the "hellish

banditti," and asked the Legislature to permit him to impress
seamen. The Assembly airily replied by asking Jackson to procure an amnesty for the Baratarians.[24]

Evidences of defection, if not treason, were visible in the city.
Consternation followed the circulation of a story that the object
of the British expedition was to return Louisiana to Spain, a
suggestion not displeasing to a good many Creoles. Jackson
thought the situation grave enough to warrant a blunt warning.
"Believe not such incredible tales—your government is at peace
with Spain—it is the . . . common enemy of mankind . . . that . . .
has sent his hirelings among you with this false report. . . . The
rules of war annex the punishment of death to any person holding
secret correspondence with the enemy."[25]

This was published on the morning of December 15, 1814,
after which Jackson repaired to the Plain of Gentilly to resume
his survey of the terrain. Should a battle be fought near New
Orleans he believed that this would be the place.

A hard-riding courier found him there. The news was bad
and wholly unexpected. A swarm of British vessels had overwhelmed Jones's five gunboats. Lake Borgne was in the hands of
the enemy.

5

Panic threatened New Orleans.[26]   "The enemy was on our
coast with a presumed force of between nine and ten thousand
men; whilst all the forces we had yet to oppose him amounted to
no more than one thousand regulars and from four to five thousand militia."[27]   Two thousand militia would be about accurate.[28]
Jackson galloped to his headquarters in Royal Street, and for
thirty-six hours the place shook with his tumultuous energy. Too
ill to stand he lay on a sofa, and, whipping up his strength by force
of will and an occasional sip of brandy, exhausted a corps of
robust aides with the dictation of orders, the enlistment, concen-
tration and dispatch of troops, and the multitudinous details
which before another sun had set were to transform frightened
New Orleans into an armed camp.

A battalion of free Santo Dominican negroes who had stood with the whites against the legions of L'Ouverture, marched to reenforce the defenses of Chef Menteur. Captain Newman of the Regulars, guarding the pass to Lake Pontchartrain, was ordered "to defend his post to the last extremity."[29] Fort St. Philip was told to resist "while a man remained alive to point a gun."[30]

To Coffee near Baton Rouge: "You must not sleep until you reach me."[31] To Billy Carroll who had left Tennessee by water two months before with a division of raw levies and had not been heard from since: Hasten! "Our lakes are open to ... the enemy, and I am prepared to ... die in the last ditch before he shall reach the city."[32] Similar orders to Hinds's Mississippi Dragoons and Thomas's Kentucky militia. Yet the man of action remained a calculating strategist, viewing the campaign as a whole, which, were the British to exercise the same degree of caution, must be a long one. Provisions for six months were ordered. To Winchester at Mobile: "Fort Bowyer ... must be ... defended at every hazard. The enemy has given us a large coast to guard; but I trust ... to ... defeat him at every point."[33] To the Secretary of War went a reassuring account of the posture of affairs concluding: "We have no arms here. Will the Government order a supply?"[34]

Crowning these labors of a night and a day, Jackson proclaimed martial law and a levée en masse.

"No persons will be permitted to leave the city.... No vessels, boats or other craft will be permitted to leave.... Street lamps shall be extinguished at the hour of nine at night, after which time persons of every description found in the streets, or not in their respective homes ... shall be apprehended as spies."[35]

The panic subsided. "General Jackson had electrified all hearts," one witness recorded. "New Orleans presented a very affecting picture ... [of] citizens ... preparing for battle, ... each in his vernacular tongue singing songs of victory. The streets resounded with *Yankee Doodle, the Marseillese Hymn, the Chant du Depart,* ... while ... at the windows and balconies ... beauty applauded valour."[36]   The Ursuline sisters said special prayers.[37] Editor and staff of the newspaper *Friend of the Laws* repaired to camp, informing subscribers that they could be "more usefully ... employed in defending the country than satisfying the public appetite for news."[38]

6

Yet one class of recruits, equally eager, Jackson stubbornly declined to accept—the Baratarians.

Livingston exercised his persuasive wiles in vain, although the story was about that Dominique You, the most celebrated of Laffite's sea captains, had offered the solicitor fifteen thousand Spanish dollars to procure his release from jail.[39]   Major General Jacques Phillippe de Villeré of the Louisiana militia had no better luck than Livingston.[40]   Jackson thought well of the courteous old Creole, however, and well of the soldierly qualities of many of his command, notably cocky little St. Gême, with the foot-high plume in his cap.   General Villeré refrained from mentioning that in his non-military character Captain St. Gême was a partner of the proscribed Laffites.   A committee of the Legislature, Messieurs Marigny, Rafignac and Louaillier, visited the headquarters in Royal Street.   They were accompanied by Auguste Davézac, a brother of the beautiful Madame Livingston. These gentlemen enlarged on the patriotic services already rendered by Captain Laffite, and the unsurpassed qualifications of his followers as swamp guides and artillerymen.   To no purpose.   "The General was inexorable," reported Marigny.   "The committee retired, saddened by ... his decision."[41]

But the committee did not despair.   It sought Judge Dominick Hall of the United States District Court, a magistrate who would have been at home on a Tennessee bench when Andrew Jackson rode the circuit.   The offenses of the Baratarians, being in contravention to Federal laws, came within the purview of Judge Hall.   "I am general under these circumstances," said Hall

He advised his callers to obtain from the Legislature a resolution suspending proceedings against the buccaneers.[42]   This done, the Judge released Dominique You and the others from jail—at a possible saving to Captain You of fifteen thousand Spanish dollars.

Thus Jean Laffite, who had made a pretense at hiding, was provided with a safe conduct to walk the thoroughfares of New Orleans in security until nine o'clock at night.   He walked to 106 Royal Street and requested an audience with General Jackson. After all others had failed, the mild-mannered pirate had resolved to state his own case.

It was an audacious resolution, but audacity was a feature of the trade of Jean Laffite.

No narrative of the interview appears outside the pages of fiction, a circumstance for which history is the poorer.   Major A. Lacarrière Latour, Jackson's chief of engineers, knew Laffite well and immediately after the campaign collected his military correspondence.   The brief and bald sentences of Major Latour tell all that we shall probably ever know of the singular meeting of these singular men.   "Mr. Laffite solicited for himself and for all Baratarians, the honour of serving under our banners, that they might have an opportunity of proving that if they had infringed the revenue laws, yet none were more ready than they to defend the country. . . . Persuaded that the assistance of these men could not fail of being very useful, the general accepted their efforts."[43]

Artillery detachments were formed under Dominique You and Captain Belluché.   The defenses of the route from Barataria Bay to the city of New Orleans were strengthened.   "Fortify yourself at the . . . Temple," Jackson commanded Major Reynolds.   The Temple was an Indian mound made by oyster shells.   "M^r. Jean Lafite has offered his services to go down and give you every information. . . . Dismiss him as soon as possible as I shall want him here."[44]

The chief of the hellish banditti was succeeding with his new associate in arms.   This was a habit of his.

7

A soft breeze stirred the fronds of the palm-trees, a warm sun brightened the gray towers of St. Louis Cathedral, and the time-stained walls of the solid Cabildo. The streets enclosing the Place d'Armes were thronged with people. It was Sunday, December 18, 1814, and they had been called from their beds, not alone by the Cathedral bells' unfailing invitation to mass. Since dawn the town had echoed the roll of drums, the music of bugles and the tramp of marching men, as General Jackson prepared to review his troops. All routes led to the revered Place which had witnessed the formal authentication of much of the volatile history of Louisiana. Here, fourteen years before, James Wilkinson had raised the Stars and Stripes before an audience that smiled when the halyards fouled and the flag stuck half-way up the staff. But now the flag flew high, and the ring of people parted as the "Battalion of Uniformed Companies"—Major Plauché, Captains St. Gême, Guibert, White, Roche—swung into the Square. They cheered again, though with less abandon, for the "Battalion of Free Men of Color," Santo Dominican negroes under white officers. Their mobilization had been Jackson's own idea, carried out in the face of a considerable body of local opinion as to the propriety of placing arms in the hands of former slaves.

The General appeared, splendidly mounted.

"Vive Jackson!"

His "eye brightened, the careworn expression of his face cleared up"[45] at the enthusiasm of the populace. Colonel Edward Livingston read the General's address. The rhetoric probably was Livingston's but the spirit was Jackson's and both exactly what the people wanted.

Two mornings later, on December twentieth, John Coffee halted his advance-guard of eight hundred men on the Avart plantation four miles above the city. He had marched one hundred and thirty-five miles in three days.

Louisianans had heard much about Coffee. They beheld "a

man of noble aspect, tall and herculean in frame, yet not destitute of a certain natural dignity. . . . His appearance . . . on a fine Tennessee thorough-bred was striking." Equally striking to the city-folk who flocked to see them pitch camp was the aspect of Coffee's weary men "in their . . . dingy . . . woollen hunting-shirts, copperas-dyed pantaloons, . . . hats . . . of the skins of raccoons and foxes, . . . belts . . . in which were stuck hunting-knives and tomahawks, . . . [and] unkempt hair and unshorn faces."[46] These veterans had traveled light, carrying "nothing but their pieces, cartouch-boxes and powder-horns—their bullets were usually in their pantaloons pockets. . . . They had no idea of military" drill, but spectators found comfort in the tale that these soldiers were concerned only with "the more important part of their calling which . . . was quietly to pick out their man . . . and 'bring him down.' "[47]

Nor was this all the good news. A few hours behind Coffee, Carroll's long-unreported flotilla, bearing the new Tennessee division three thousand strong, hove in sight.[48] Until thirty hours before, Jackson had been without word of Carroll beyond the bare fact that he had left Nashville on the seventeenth day of November. Carroll had made the trip by water in violation of orders from both Jackson and Governor Blount, "but neither when I arrived or at any subsequent period has the General mentioned the subject to me."[49]

There were reasons. Carroll had embarked with raw recruits. He arrived with fairly disciplined men. While half of a company plied the oars, the other half drilled on the boat decks. Starting virtually unarmed, they had overtaken and brought along a shipment of eleven hundred muskets that a War Department contractor had sent by slow freight to minimize the carrying charges. On a boat fitted with forges, Tennessee blacksmiths had put all guns in order and fabricated "fifty thousand cartridges in the best manner, each containing a musket ball and three buck shot."[50] Jackson's failure to receive word of his subordinate's progress was due to no fault of the latter. Carroll had sent messengers overland, but, on account of storms and high water, had beaten all except the fleetest of them to New Orleans.

The same causes delayed the Eastern mails. Jackson had heard nothing from Washington for sixty days. Perhaps this was just as well. Any news from that distracted quarter would have been dismal news. The efforts of Madison to rally the country continued to meet opposition at every step, the call for the Hartford Convention crowning all. Congress refused to create a national army and refused the means to pay what troops we had. The Conscription Bill which Jackson had urged so vigorously was on the road to defeat. The Treasury was bare. James Monroe rode from bank to bank in Washington soliciting loans in the banks' own depreciated currency, adding his personal credit to the guaranty of the United States. New England Federalists called for peace at any price. They would accept the humiliating terms by which the British demanded a third of Maine and a large slice of the Northwest. They stormed against the American commissioners at Ghent for rejecting them. By the Eternal! Had Old Hickory heard of that!

Cheered by the presence of Coffee and Carroll, he returned to Royal Street, easier in mind than he had been since the loss of the gunboats. His military position was correct. With every approach to the city, as he imagined, either blocked or guarded, he had only to await an alarm that would betray the direction of the enemy's contemplated advance. Although he believed the British would attempt the route of the Plain of Gentilly, Jackson was not committed to that line of defense. He was committed to nothing except to attack the British when and where they should show themselves. His best troops—those of Coffee, of Carroll, the Regulars, Hinds's Mississippi Dragoons and Plauché's Uniformed Companies—he kept under his hand at New Orleans ready to throw in any direction.

Early on the morning of Friday, December twenty-third, the waiting General wrote Robert Hays a family letter, tranquil in the belief that "since . . . the capture of our gun boats . . . the British had made no movement of importance. . . . *All well.*"[51]

But all was far from well, as by mid-forenoon Jackson received an inkling from Colonel Pierre Denis de La Ronde,[52] in com-

mand of militia pickets assigned to watching all possible routes
through the swamp from Lake Borgne to the Mississippi. The
Colonel's courier reported "several sail of vessels" in a position
that suggested the possibility of a landing that would threaten
the vital point of English Turn. Forthwith Jackson dispatched
his chief of engineers, Latour, to reconnoiter.[53]

Latour left at eleven. He had been gone about an hour and a
half when Augustin Rousseau flung himself from a lathered horse
in front of 106 Royal Street and dashed inside with the most overwhelming news of the campaign. He told Jackson the British
were eight miles from town. They had captured Villeré's plantation, five miles above English Turn. Rousseau himself had witnessed the surprise of an American picket belonging to the regiment of Colonel de La Ronde.[54]

The story was incredible. Every approach in that region Jackson had ordered blocked and had received reports that his directions had been executed. Yet Rousseau had the air of a man
telling the truth. The General retired to his sofa to turn the
matter over in his mind. A sentry rapped at the door and announced "three gentlemen . . . having important intelligence."

Colonel de La Ronde, Major Gabriel Villeré and Dussau de la
Croix, a friend of Edward Livingston, rushed into the room.
The clothing of the officers was stained with mud and they were
nearly breathless. Their appearance prepared Jackson for the
worst.

"What news do you bring, gentlemen?" he asked.

"Important! Highly important!" cried de la Croix. "The British have arrived at Villeré's plantation! . . . Major Villeré was captured by them and has escaped!"

Young Villeré was a son of the ranking officer of the Louisiana
militia and the son-in-law of Colonel de La Ronde. A cataract
of French tumbled from his lips, de la Croix translating. The
English had accomplished what Jackson had labored day and
night to avert. Unseen they had landed on the shore of Lake
Borgne. Undiscovered they had penetrated the five miles of
swamp which Jackson believed his vigilance had transformed into

an impassable barrier between the lake and the sugar planta
tions along the Mississippi.

Whose blunder or treachery, or what military skill or luck or
magic had got them there was more than the agitated militiamen could explain. Nor was this a moment to probe for explanations. It was enough to know that the enemy stood in force on
the river, eight miles by highway from the city. Already Villeré's story had corroboration. Latour had seen the British troops
and dispatched Major Howell Tatum to headquarters with the
news.

Jackson sprang from his sofa. "With an eye of fire and an
emphatic blow upon the table," he cried:

"By the Eternal, they shall not sleep on our soil!"

This flushed mood passed with the abruptness of a summer
storm. Jackson's tone grew calm. Inviting his visitors to sip a
glass of wine with him, he called his military secretary and his
aides.

"Gentlemen, the British are below. We must fight them to-
night."[55]

It was then two in the afternoon.

CHAPTER XIV

THE MUD RAMPART OF RODRIQUEZ CANAL

I

By a bold scheme tenaciously carried through, the British had landed from Lake Borgne with a degree of secrecy that has not favored another modern military expedition.

On December 10, 1814, ten days after Jackson's arrival at New Orleans, the wooden walls of England came to anchor off the white beaches of Ship and Cat Islands at the mouth of the lake: fifty-odd sail of various rigs and sizes, from the huge *Tonnant*, Nelson's prize at Abouquir, to restless gun-brigs pitching in the swell. Ladders went over the sides, and down them streamed lines of red-tunicked men, as Keane crowded his troops on board lighter craft for the invasion of the lake. They were tried troops: four regiments of the Army of the Chesapeake which had fought at Bladensburg, burned Washington and fought again at Baltimore; a brigade of Wellington's veterans, straight from their victories over Napoleon's armies in Spain; the kilted Ninety-Third Highlanders, a "praying regiment" fetched from a detail of Empire building at the Cape of Good Hope; two West India regiments, mainly Jamaican negroes supposed to be adapted to the Louisiana climate; complete trains of artillery, a rocket brigade, sappers, engineers.

The little islands were uninhabited, but from the *Tonnant* Vice-Admiral Sir Alexander Cochrane perceived that his arrival had been observed. Just out of range, the fast gunboats of Lieutenant Thomas Ap. Catesby Jones hovered impudently about the British front, meanwhile informing Jackson of the enemy's arrival. From Maine to Maryland our shores had felt the quick and hard hand of the acrid old admiral. With the same promptitude he moved to efface the obstacles to his mastery of Lake Borgne. A fleet of gun-brigs in battle line sailed forth, making a show calculated to gladden the eye of the Admiral and correspondingly disconcert Mr. Jones with his five gunboats. But Jones was clever and he knew the lake. Dexterously he lured the fleet aground in shallow water and darted out of sight. Admiral Cochrane lost no time in taking another tack. He manned barges and cutters with volunteers under Captain Lockyer. This enterprising mariner had been duped by Jean Laffite and he had been defeated at Fort Bowyer, but now his time had come to be served by better fortune. After rowing thirty-six miles, Lockyer found Jones becalmed and unable to maneuver. With forty-five boats and twelve hundred men, he attacked the American's five boats and hundred and eighty-two men. The fighting was savage. Lockyer was wounded. Jones was wounded and every fourth man on his slippery decks went down.[1] After two hours of battle, British boarders carried the day. The last of the gunboats struck at twelve· forty o'clock, December fourteenth.

Jackson was now without "eyes" on Lake Borgne. Under the prodding of Cochrane, General Keane wasted not a moment in starting his army toward New Orleans. Pea Island in the upper reach of the lake was selected as a rendezvous. For six days and six nights the seamen of the fleet plied from ships to island and island to ships. It was a pull of thirty miles, but Cochrane was relentless, and some of the crews were at the oars four days without relief.

Their passengers had no holiday excursion. "Than this spot," wrote a subaltern, "it is scarcely possible to imagine any place more completely wretched, . . . a swamp containing a small space of firm ground at one end, and almost wholly unadorned by trees of any sort of description, . . . the interior a resort of wild ducks and . . . dormant alligators. . . . The army . . . without tents or huts, or any covering from the . . . heavy rains such as an inhabitant of England cannot dream of, and against which no cloak can furnish protection. . . . As night closed . . . severe frosts . . . [congealed] our wet clothes to our bodies." There was no fire-wood. The only ration was "salt meat and ship biscuit ... moistened by a small allowance of rum."[2] Many of the Jamaica negroes died from exposure.

"Yet, in spite of all this, . . . from general down to youngest drum-boy, a confidant expectation of success seemed to pervade all ranks." A similar expectation pervaded several citizens of Louisiana who shared with the visitors the discomforts of Pea Island. They "entertained us with accounts of the alarm experienced at New Orleans, . . . the rich booty that would reward its capture," and promises of "a speedy and bloodless conquest."[3] Veterans of the Chesapeake campaign who had seen the Americans fly before Washington could believe the bloodless part. On December twentieth, while Jackson was meeting Coffee and Carroll, General Keane managed a review of his army on the dry end of the island.

The vital question confronting the British commanders was answered. A place to land in secret had been discovered. The route of Chef Menteur and the Plain of Gentilly was too obvious and too closely watched by Jackson. Naval Captain Spencer and Army Captain Peddie had cruised the coast-line in search of a likelier spot. At first their quest was disappointing. Bayou after bayou that might have afforded a route through the swamp had been blocked with fallen trees. But at length they came upon one, the only one apparently, on the whole coast that was open— the Bayou Bienvenue.[4] This almost fatal neglect on the part of Americans remains unelucidated. The existence of Bayou Bienvenue was known to Jackson who had issued "express orders in writing" for its obstruction.[5] Another peculiarity of the case is that one of the sources of this stream was on the plantation of Major General Jacques de Villeré, commandant of the Louisiana militia, to whom the execution of Jackson's orders had been entrusted.[6] General Villeré was the father of Major Gabriel Villeré.

Near the bayou's mouth Spencer and Peddie came upon a collection of palmetto huts raised on piles above the marsh and inhabited by Spanish and Portuguese fishermen. With these fishermen the English scouts quickly reached an understanding. The fishermen made daily journeys to New Orleans with their wares, Villeré and other landowners affording them right-of-way. Disguised in blue smocks obtained from their guides, the British officers and three fishermen ascended Bayou Bienvenue on the night of December eighteenth, branched off on Bayou Mazant and emerged on Villeré's plantation. So enthusiastic was Peddie over his coup that when he took a drink from the Mississippi he pronounced the water cool and sweet. Back at Pea Island he communicated the exhilarating intelligence that New Orleans was defended by less than five thousand men. The estimate was nearly correct.

At dusk on the evening of December twenty-second, the British advance-guard of two thousand and eighty men and two guns[7] appeared in small boats off the mouth of Bayou Bienvenue. "The place ... was as wild as it is possible to imagine. Gaze where we might nothing could be seen except ... tall reeds. ... Yet it was such a spot, as above all others, that favored our operations. No eye could watch us, or report our arrival to the American General."[8] Or so the invaders imagined. They learned, however, that since the visit of Spencer and Peddie, an American picket of twelve men had been stationed a short distance up the bayou. The success of the whole British plan hinged upon the suppression of this outpost. The job was expertly done and one of the prisoners was led before Keane and Cochrane for interrogation.

His name was Joseph Rodolphe Ducros and his brief turn beneath history's proscenium had a share in important consequences. Ducros said that Jackson commanded from twelve to fifteen thousand men in New Orleans and had four thousand at English Turn. He stuck to his story, and, for that matter, probably believed it, Jackson being the last general on earth to understate his numbers. Other prisoners corroborated Ducros. Curiously enough this estimate of the American strength tallied almost exactly with the one Cochrane had received from emissaries Jackson had sent to inquire about prisoners taken in the gunboat battle.[9] The repetition of this exaggeration of Jackson's force had its effect.

Could the fishermen be mistaken? The white-haired fighter in worn sea-clothes was disturbed, something that did not happen every day.

At daybreak on the twenty-third, when, so far as Jackson knew, the British army was still aboard shipping at Cat Island, the red-coated column began to pick its way through the swamp. Engineers went ahead, clearing an excuse of a road over the narrow rim of soggy ground that hugged the bayou. At length, however, the soil grew firmer and the mud-spattered men moved more rapidly through a cypress woods, from which they emerged on to the Villeré plantation. Before them stretched a field of cane stubble. Beyond this stood the white Villeré house, its low rectangular lines half-concealed by an orange grove.

Colonel William Thornton of the Eighty-Fifth Light Infantry, one of the ablest regimental commanders in the British Army, deployed a few companies under cover of the woods. They swept forward in a semicircle to surround the house.

It was ten-thirty in the morning. Major René Philippe Gabriel de Villeré sat on his father's gallery contemplating the river through the smoke of a Spanish cigar. His brother, Célestin, was cleaning a rifle. The Major commanded the picket at the fishermen's village, and, under his father, was responsible for the security of Bayou Bienvenue. He deemed it secure enough until a file of British infantrymen, traversed his line of vision. A few moments later the crestfallen young Creole surrendered to Colonel Thornton.

This energetic officer begged Keane not to halt. They could reach New Orleans in two hours, probably before Jackson was aware of their presence on the mainland. Thornton believed the fishermen had given a correct idea of the size and scattered state of Jackson's army, with its main body four miles above the city. But Keane was afraid Ducros had told the truth. He was in the enemy's country with only two thousand men, and, moreover, a reenforcement of three thousand was due from Pea Island at midnight. So strong outguards were posted and the troops ordered to bivouac.

A clatter of musketry in the plantation yard brought the General to his feet. Gabriel Villeré had leaped a fence and escaped.

2

Andrew Jackson was not a Keane. In the face of Villeré's tremendous news, he made the most daring and most far-reaching decision of his career, when on the instant, he concluded to attack. "I will smash them, so help me God!"[10]

Couriers flew along the roads and drums beat the assembly. The hawk-eyed Commander remained tranquil. Orders were issued with "no unnecessary words, even of excitement or encouragement."[11] Preparations for the battle completed, he ate a little boiled rice, dropped on his sofa and was asleep in a moment.[12]

At four o'clock he was in the saddle beside the road that surmounted the levee near the old French barracks below the city. A thousand men under Carroll stood in the cane stubble near by. This was the reserve, in readiness to march where needed. Hinds's Mississippi dragoons had already disappeared at a gallop down the levee road to reconnoiter. In their wake had gone the Seventh Infantry with orders to engage the British should they advance, and to hold them at any cost until Jackson could get up with his main body. These troops had not as yet arrived on the field and every moment of waiting was critical. Any instant Jackson expected to hear firing on his front and he was none too sanguine as to his rear, which the enemy could fall upon by way of a branch of the Bayou Bienvenue; but Carroll was supposed to take care of trouble in that locality. Anxiously, too, Jackson gazed across the yellow river at the schooner *Carolina,* moored to the western bank. Seamen clambered among the rigging, the vessel cast off and drifted slowly down with the current in the direction of the enemy.

At five o'clock the December sun had slipped behind the treetops. With half of his main body—five hundred-odd mounted gunmen under Coffee, two six-pound field pieces under escort of a company of marines, and eighteen Choctaw warriors under half-French, half-Indian Pierre Jugeat—Jackson joined the advance-guard at the Rodriquez Canal, two miles from the British position. Hinds sent good news. The enemy was not more than two thousand strong, he said, and was preparing to camp for the night. Plauché's picturesque battalion arrived panting, having run most of the ten miles from Fort St. Jean. The Forty-Fourth Infantry, Daquin's Santo Domingo blacks and Beale's excellent New Orleans militia company made Jackson's force complete.[13] He now had on the field two thousand one hundred and sixty-seven men.

Dusk deepened, faintly outlining a misty moon. The damp air grew chill. Jackson moved forward until Versailles, the plantation château of Colonel Denis de La Ronde came into view. A double row of oaks,[14] planted in 1783 on the Colonel's twenty-first birthday, led from a private boat landing on the levee to his gate. Behind this screen Jackson arranged his army for battle.[15]

The field of cane stubble grew darker. Versailles and the slave village behind it surrendered their identity, and, lingering for a few moments as nebulous dark lumps, dipped into the uniform blackness of the night-conquered plain. Accouterments were muffled, orders passed in whispers. So silently did Jackson's men move out that the pickets of the enemy, five hundred yards away, suspected nothing. Keane's camp-fires "burning very bright," recorded Jackson, "gave a good view of his situation."[16] The guns and the marines remained on the levee. The Seventh Infantry, the battalions of Plauché and Daquin, and the Forty-Fourth Infantry formed in that order on the left, reaching as far as the gardens of Versailles. Coffee's men filed noiselessly into the black plain. Guided by Denis de La Ronde and Pierre Laffite,[17] they passed behind the château, and began a wide detour calculated to bring them in position to strike the enemy's flank and rear.

At six-thirty the shadowy bulk of the *Carolina* floated abreast Jackson's position. Livingston went aboard and gave Commandant Patterson orders to open fire on the British main position at seven-thirty. At eight Jackson would attack.[18] "The Caroline," wrote

Jackson, "passed in Silence, . . . sliding gently down the current."[19]
A cold fog, seeping in from the river swallowed her up and began
to dim the moon and the camp-fires of the unwatching enemy.
Jackson inspected the line to see that every soldier had "plenty" of
ammunition, and then returned to his post behind the guns on
the levee. Men drew their coats closer about them and strained
their eyes in the wake of the vanished *Carolina*.

At exactly thirty minutes past seven o'clock a great red patch
glowed through the fog and faded; a roar and a rolling echo: the
Carolina had opened fire.

The consternation in the British camp was apparent. Jackson
waited his full half-hour. When the British, feeling that they
had only the schooner to deal with, had concentrated most of their
forces against it, the American infantry advanced. From his
post on the levee, Jackson could see nothing more than the shapes
of the artillerymen and the rumps of their horses, but he could
hear in the dark to his left orders and oaths in French and in English. The infantry had got off badly. They stumbled into a
stake-and-rail fence and a wet ditch which the militia battalions
were slow getting over. The line opened a ragged fire and the
British outposts replied with a stiff volley. From the Seventh
Infantry came the cry that the lagging militia "are firing into us."
Yet the Regulars pressed on and the British fell back. The six-
pounders opened and a quarter of a mile ahead the *Carolina* continued her raking bombardment. Gun flashes far out on the black
plain revealed that Coffee was engaged. This much, and this much
only, could the Commanding General discern of his battle, a lieutenant's fight from the start, every platoon for itself.

Staff officers dressed the infantry line and directed the militia's
fire toward the enemy. But the British resistance stiffened. Keane
had sent up reenforcements under Thornton, and wherever that
soldier appeared an adversary had his work cut out for him. The
heaviest fusillade yet sprayed the six-pounders. Our fire slackened.
The British line moved up. Our marines gave ground. A
wounded horse reared, overturning one of the limbers. The
guns were in imminent danger.

Jackson dashed into the fight.   The air was stiff with lead.[20]
"Save the guns!"[21]

The marines rallied about their General, a company of the
Seventh Infantry rushed to the rescue and the guns were saved.[22]

"Charge! Charge! Push on the bayonet!"[23]   The Regulars
leaped forward.

"*A la bayonette!*"[24] Plauché and Daquin were in the thick of
it. On the left things were going better now.

And Jackson traced Coffee's progress, a thousand yards away,
by the twinkle of his rifles.

3

Between twelve and one o'clock Coffee was back on the levee
without his horses,[25] but with a parcel of prisoners including
Major Mitchell who had applied the torch to the Capitol at
Washington. The gunmen had ranged through the British
position, roughly describing a circle two miles in extent, and fighting wherever an enemy presented. Friend could not be distinguished from foe much beyond a saber's length. "In the whole
course of my military career I remember no scene at all re-
sembling this," a British officer related. "An American officer,
whose sword I demanded, instead of giving it up . . . made a cut
at my head."[26] Captain John Donelson, junior, substantiates the
Englishman's complaint of unprofessional conduct. "I charged
on near Lord Pakenham's quarters [meaning Keane's, in the
Villeré house], made several prisoners and killed several. . . .
The enemy having discovered my position immediately fell on
my rear . . . [shouting] that they were General Coffee's men,
having by some means learned the General's name. They advanced within about ten steps, ordered us for d—d rebels to lay
down our arms. . . . I answered them, they be d—d, and ordered
my men to open a fire."[27]

While Coffee was making his eventful tour, the battle line
on the river bank drove the enemy advance-guard behind a fence
and a ditch separating the de La Ronde and Lacoste plantations.

Colonel de La Ronde returned to enjoy the personal satisfaction of finding the enemy evicted from his property.

At nine-thirty firing had begun to diminish. At midnight the black field was still. Ominously still, suspected Jackson, who knew that Keane was being reenforced. British prisoners put his strength at six thousand. Above all, Jackson was still uncertain of the enemy's plans. Keane had surprised him on Bayou Bienvenue, and, fearing he might attempt the same feat elsewhere, Jackson declined to draw men from Chef Menteur and other posts to strengthen his present force. A determination to resume the offensive at dawn was therefore abandoned, and Jackson consulted his engineers about a protected position where he might await the enemy's pleasure.[28] At four o'clock in the morning he began to withdraw his army, and daybreak saw it behind the Rodriquez Canal with only a façade of cavalry in front to observe the movements of the British two miles away.

The Americans had lost twenty-four killed, one hundred and fifteen wounded and seventy-four prisoners. Keane's losses were forty-six killed, one hundred and sixty-seven wounded, sixty-four prisoners.[29] Jackson had displayed unusual generalship, first in his instantaneous decision to attack, turning a surprise into a counter-surprise, a phenomenon so rare that it has no name in the glossary of military terms; and second, in his present decision to take the defensive. On the morning of December twenty-fourth, Keane had four thousand seven hundred and three effectives on the field, exclusive of staff, against whom Jackson's nineteen hundred and fifty-four might have fared differently from the night before.

4

General Jackson's next move was to have "the whole city and country ransacked for intrenching tools,"[30] horses, vehicles, muskets and men. The provost guards redoubled their vigilance. Every person found abroad without a pass was ordered under arrest, this measure being enforced against the careless as well as the suspect. "Before two days," expostulated Mayor Girod, "the Guard House will be full."[31] The inexorable Jacksonian will was unleashed—an instrument by which he believed he could accomplish anything. Had Charles Dickinson shot him through the brain, Andrew Jackson counted on the power of sheer resolve to sustain him long enough to kill his adversary. This mood possessed him now. His determination was formed to fight below New Orleans; if beaten there, to fight in New Orleans; if beaten there, to fight above New Orleans—to fight until no living thing could withstand his ineradicable impulse to victory.

This was fury—but of the cool, calculating sort. "As the safety of the city," he assured Monroe, "will depend on the fate of this army, it must not be incautiously exposed."[32] Dawn of December twenty-fourth groped through a sullen fog. The conditions were ideal for a hostile attack, but none came. At four in the afternoon Hinds in command of cavalry pickets, reported the British still receiving reenforcements, but making no preparations to advance. "I expect the enemy is pretty sore to day," Jackson informed Governor Claiborne.[33] The army had found the Rodriquez Canal a dry grass-grown ditch twenty feet wide and about four feet deep. It was an abandoned mill-race running from the levee to the woods on the plantation of Augustin Macarté. Thirty yards in the rear of this ditch Jackson made his line which by nightfall on the twenty-fourth bore some resemblance to a field entrenchment stretching from the river to the woods. The work went on in the darkness, one rank sleeping on its arms while another toiled at the rampart. Jackson slept none at all. He was never off the line. He ate his rice in the saddle.

So opened Christmas Day. At a salvo of artillery in the direction of the British camp, spades were dropped and rifles caught up. A messenger from Hinds reported, however, that the red coats merely were saluting the arrival of a new commanding officer, whom rumor quickly identified as Wellington himself.

He was, in fact, the Duke's brother-in-law, Major General Sir Edward Pakenham. Born in a mansion in County Antrim, where Andrew Jackson's parents also first saw the light of day, the hero of Salamanca had justified by valor and ability the exertions that family and friends had made for his advancement. He had fought his way up from subaltern, and something of a subaltern he remained, in appearance and in the simplicity of his manner. A round boyish face belied his thirty-seven years and a mischievous glint in his blue eyes shielded the methodical brain behind them. No unpleasant story of Ned Pakenham survives, and singularly enough Andrew Jackson had heard many stories about him. Dr. Redmond Dillon Barry and Pakenham had gone to college together in Dublin, the latter to leave for fields of glory and the former for the orderly hills of Sumner County, Tennessee, to practise medicine, to race horses, and open his home to Rachel and Andrew Jackson during the meetings at the Gallatin course.[34]

The presence of the popular Commander infused spirit into the British troops whose disturbed state of mind since the night of the battle General Jackson had rightly surmised. They had landed prepared to take over the civil administration of New Orleans, with appointments from tide-waiter to collector of customs already designated. An inspection of the dispatch case of General Pakenham would have disclosed the enlarging scope of English aims. He had brought a commission as governor of Louisiana and the Regent's promise of an earldom to adorn the office.

The methodical soldier moved discreetly toward a realization of these rewards. He perceived the injudicious position of his army and the disagreeable result of its not having advanced on the twenty-third. The report was that he spoke of withdrawing and landing in another quarter, only to be crushed by the scorn of the weather-beaten veteran in a seaman's rough coat. The lower ranks of the British Army shared Admiral Cochrane's opinion of the inferior military qualities of the Americans. Their not entirely misleading name for them was Dirty Shirts, inspired by the homespun raiment of the prisoners they had taken from Coffee in the night battle. The belligerent Admiral declared that if the army shrank from the risk his sailors would carry the Dirty Shirt lines and march into the city. "The soldiers could then bring up the baggage," the old tar added.[35] But he agreed that no advance should be attempted until the *Carolina* and the *Louisiana,* which lay in the river above the British position, were removed. Guns from the fleet were sent for and Pakenham began to dig emplacements for a battery.

Along the American line of defense, Jean Laffite cast an appraising eye. The retired pirate had learned the art of entrenching from engineers of Napoleon Bonaparte. The plan of Jackson's works was the conception of Major A. Lacarrière Latour, an able man, and Captain Laffite hesitated to raise an issue of its virtues with the General. He pointed out to Livingston, therefore, that the line which ended at the cypress woods was too short. It should be carried through the woods to the impassable swamp. "Otherwise, [the enemy] might turn our left."[36] Livingston conveyed the suggestion to Jackson at once and the extension was ordered. Hinds's scouts saw the work on the British batteries and reported the enemy to be fortifying. At the same time word came that the enemy was landing troops on the Plain of Gentilly and driving the Americans before them. From the first Jackson had feared the Bayou Bienvenue demonstration might be a feint. Claiborne was in command at Gentilly. Jackson sent two hundred Tennesseans under Latour to reenforce him and spent another night without sleep and without news. "Uncle Jackson . . . looks very badly," observed Captain Donelson, "and has broken very much."[37]

On December twenty-sixth Latour returned to report that the alarm at Gentilly had been a ruse. A few sailors had landed and set fire to the grass. Jackson was now convinced that Pakenham's main attack would be against his present position. A part of Carroll's division was called up to help prolong the rampart through the woods. Other outlying posts were stripped to reenforce the river end of the battle line, and Jackson slept for the first time in three nights.

5

He slept more soundly than did a good many residents of New Orleans, four miles away, where the restrictions of martial law and the strain of suspense were beginning to tell. An underground current of criticism rasped nerves already raw. "While . . . explosions of musketry and artillery reminded them that their sons were facing war-like soldiers, . . . old inhabitants . . . lamented that the protection of the city had been confided to an utter stranger . . . who . . . had hardly ever met any but an Indian enemy."[38] And what of the march of events? Jackson had lost the gunboats. He had been surprised by the landing at Villeré's. He had promised to sweep the enemy into the lake and failed to do so. Curbstone Vaubans viewed the mud bulwark behind the Rodriquez Canal and returned to town with long faces. They spoke with some of General Jackson's young gentlemen volunteers who had flown to the front to risk life and fortune on the field of honor only to have shovels thrust in their hands, and, what is more, required to use them. The connection between military glory and blistered palms remained obscure.

Suppose the mud rampart should not hold. "Jackson . . . openly declared," said Vincent Nolte who was there, "that he would imitate the example of the Russians at Moscow, and consign the whole city to the flames" rather than see its rich stores fall to the enemy.[39] Jackson openly declared nothing of the kind, although the secret of his intentions had been rightly guessed by Mr. Nolte. A great quantity of powder was placed aboard a vessel manned and ready to stand up-stream.[40] Jackson's "conduct in this respect was considered by some as an evidence of his deeming his defeat a probable event."[41] Captain Thomas L. Butler represented the commanding officer in New Orleans, charged, among other things, with the enforcement of martial law. Thomas Butler was a nephew of the Revolutionary colonel of uncut hair, a ward of Andrew Jackson and a close-mouthed young man. Subterranean whispers continued to carry the ominous refrain of Moscow. The wealthy of New Orleans feared for their property. When Fulwar Skipwith, president of the State Senate, demanded the nature of Butler's orders in case of an evacuation of the city, the Captain declined to give them.[42]

On the evening of December twenty-seventh Colonel Declouet,

commander of a militia regiment, was in New Orleans on leave from duty. Declouet was a member of a distinguished Creole family and a former state senator. Before the street lights were extinguished, he repaired to the home of his old friend Magloire Guichard, Speaker of the Lower House of the Legislature, and heard from that gentleman's lips some remarkable observations. He understood Guichard to say that certain members of the Legislature were prepared to make terms with the British to preserve New Orleans from the fate of Moscow.[43] Among the names mentioned was that of Bernard Marigny. Declouet was frightened. He was aware of the risk any man took in questioning Andrew Jackson's authority at this desperate juncture. Moreover, the Colonel had come straight from the mud line and was loyal to his indomitable Commander.

6

This conversation took place at the close of a day when the news from Jackson's army had increased the apprehensions of New Orleans.

Early that morning of December twenty-seventh, at his headquarters in the Macarté plantation mansion, Andrew Jackson had awakened from the first repose he had enjoyed since taking the field. This galleried house and its trampled garden stood a hundred yards behind the rampart of the Rodriquez Canal. From an up-stairs window he could survey his line, and, after an old Frenchman lent him a telescope, he had a view of the British encampment. He had hardly risen on December twenty-seventh before a mighty blast of artillery brought him to his post of observations with the telescope. Pakenham's new batteries were letting go at the *Carolina*. In thirty minutes the schooner was in trouble. Her fire had ceased and the crew began piling over the sides. They departed none too soon. With an explosion that rattled windows in New Orleans and threw flaming fragments the width of the river, the *Carolina* blew up.

Then the batteries turned upon the *Louisiana*. Jackson had

anticipated this and had sent word that she must be saved at any risk. Already he could see Lieutenant Thompson frantically spreading sail. But against the current the whisper of a breeze did not serve to slacken the ship's cable. Under a rain of red-hot shot the boats were launched and manned and lines passed to them. A shell tore up the *Louisiana's* deck. Boat crews pulled at the oars. The next moment was like an hour. On the tattooed arms of these striving seamen depended, perhaps, the fate of New Orleans, for half of Jackson's remaining artillery was aboard the *Louisiana*. The American line watched breathlessly. Could the sailors do it? . . . Then, vaguely perceptible, the big ship moved. A mighty cheer from the mud line. They towed her out of danger.

The day continued one of industry for the Yankees. A twenty-four pounder and an old brass twelve-pound howitzer, slightly out of repair, were established behind the Rodriquez Canal by seamen from the late *Carolina*. Jackson began a second line of defense along the Canal Dupré, two miles in the rear of the first and only two miles from the city. This precaution provoked fresh alarms in New Orleans.

Preparations in the British camp seemed to foretell an attack in the morning. In the evening strong enemy outposts were pushed forward in an effort to insure a night of rest for the main body. Jackson upset this plan for a comfortable night, sending down small bodies of snipers to harry the English with false alarms. "Scarcely had the troops lain down," wrote a British lieutenant, "when they were aroused by a sharp firing at the outposts." Columns were formed, ready to meet an attack of the entire American army. In the stubble the snipers lay on their bellies as still as deer hunters. "But as soon as . . . [our columns] were dispersed, the same cause for alarm returned and they were again called to ranks. Thus the entire night was spent . . . [without] the main body . . . obtaining any sound or refreshing sleep, . . . than which nothing is more trying to . . . [the] spirits of an army."[44]

The eastern horizon began to glow behind the British position and the black plain to turn to purple. Jackson was at his window. Rice birds in the orange trees set up their morning chatter and a shout turned the Commander's glance to the levee. He saw a band of "red-shirted . . . desperate-looking men, all begrimed with . . . mud, hurrying . . . toward the lines."[45] Baratarians under Dominique You. They knew their business and promptly swabbed and charged a second twenty-four that had been heaved into place during the night. It was hardly day when a messenger from Hinds brought word that the British were advancing. At twenty-five minutes past eight a cloud of singing meteors rimmed arcs of fire across the sky. *Crash!* The meteors pelted about the mud rampart and the Macarté house. Their detonations shook the earth. The enemy had opened with Congreve rockets, a new and terrifying, but seldom fatal, bit of pyrotechnics on which they laid great store.

The rockets were attended by a cannonade from ten guns and this barrage was not without effect on the Americans, half of whom were in battle for the first time in their lives. On rearing horses Jackson's aides patrolled the entrenchment, warning the men to hold their fire. Jackson caught sight of the infantry of the enemy. In two compact columns it advanced, one column next the river, the other bordering the woods. Carroll and Coffee *must* be reenforced. They held the weakest part of the line against which the British right was aiming. Dropping his telescope, the Commander leaped into the saddle and dashed through the shower of rockets toward the swamp.

Abner Duncan, a prominent lawyer of New Orleans and a volunteer aide, halted him.

"I am the bearer of a message from Governor Claiborne," gasped Duncan. "The Assembly are about to give up the country to the enemy!"

"Have you a letter from the Governor?" demanded Jackson.

"No, General."

"Who gave you the intelligence?"

"Colonel Declouet."

"Where is Declouet?" screamed Jackson's high voice. To be

heard above the din the men were shouting at the top of their lungs. Soldiers began to gather around. Partly for their benefit, Jackson yelled that he did not believe the news and that Declouet should be arrested.

The Commander glanced over his breastwork. On came the British columns. The red and green and tartan of their regimentals bright against the gray cane stubble, the bayonets agleam in the morning sun presented quite the majestic spectacle that General Pakenham intended it to be. The right column next to the woods, not half a mile away now, spread forward a fan of skirmishers. Carroll's and Coffee's men lay behind that flank of line, where the mud rampart was hardly waist high and the canal a ditch that a man could leap.

"The Governor expects orders what to do!" screamed the aide.

"I don't believe the intelligence, but tell the Governor to make a strict inquiry, . . . and if they persist to blow them up!" Jackson shouted back.[46]

The colorful mass flattened with impersonal precision from column into line, the formation of assault. The sight effaced the yelling Duncan from Jackson's thoughts. He loosened his reins to gallop toward his imperiled left.

CHAPTER XV

THE SILVERY CARPET

1

FROM the deck of the *Louisiana* Master Commandant Daniel T. Patterson trained his glass on the advancing British infantry. The enemy's artillery raised yellow plumes in the water, but the square-built seaman favored them with little notice. His orders were to break up the infantry assault, and this involved a nice piece of timing. He must fire not too soon and not too late. The gunners held their matches ready. Not a fortnight ago this crew had been swept up from the streets of New Orleans—"men of all nations, English excepted"[1]—and much depended on them to-day.

The left column of infantry, nearest the river, continued to advance. It was within five hundred yards of Jackson's line. On the border of the woods, the right column was deploying to attack and Jackson, having just got rid of Duncan, was riding toward Coffee's menaced flank. Patterson's primary business was with the left column. He made a signal and a wall of flame leaped from the starboard guns of the *Louisiana*. Five puffs of smoke rose from the mud rampart behind the Rodriquez Canal: the land guns had joined in.

Pakenham's splendid left column wavered, halted. Mounted officers reassuringly scurried beside it. The column began to melt into line, presenting a less compact target. Patterson's gunners ripped that line with the accuracy of sharpshooters. It fell apart like a broken string of beads and men began to take cover wherever they could find it. The advance on the left was stopped.

But the British right did not waver. Small-arms crackled on the edge of the woods. Less exposed to our artillery, a spirited young colonel was able to lead a thrust at a detachment that Carroll had sent into the woods in front of the rampart. The Tennesseans were falling back on their entrenchments and the flank was in danger. Then, inexplicably to the Americans, the attack ceased and the British halted just out of rifle range. Orders had come from Pakenham for his right to wait until the riddled force by the river could resume its advance. To expedite this Sir Edward pushed forward two field pieces near the levee.

2

The lull at the edge of the woods gave Jackson a chance to strengthen Carroll and Coffee, and when this was done he returned to his headquarters. There he found Bernard Marigny pacing the floor.

The Senator had been waiting some little while for the General. He had arrived with a "heart enraged,"[2] but the wait during the thunder of bombardment had subdued his emotions considerably. However, he greeted Jackson with a demand for his reasons for closing the State Legislature.

Abner Duncan had been gone from the battle-field less than two hours, and, if Jackson was astonished to learn the drastic turn events had taken in New Orleans, he gave no sign. Instead, he listened to Marigny's passionate defense of the Assembly and was rather favorably impressed. This increased Senator Marigny's confidence in his powers of persuasion until presently he asked the forbidden question. What were the General's plans in case the battle should go against him? Jackson closed the interview:

"If I thought the hair on my head knew my thoughts on that subject I would cut it off and burn it. . . . Return to . . . [your] Honorable body and say to them from me, that if I was so unfortunate to be beaten from they [sic] lines . . . and compelled to retreat through Neworleans, they would have a *warm session*."[3]

Senator Marigny did as was told, apparently quite satisfied with the results of his mission. He had faced the fire of British batteries. He had faced Andrew Jackson. And he lingered on the field long enough to bring to the anxious city assurances that the enemy's attack had failed.

Not until after the battle did the Commander learn that Abner Duncan had taken large responsibilities on his shoulders, Andrew Jackson himself seldom displaying greater originality in the interpretation of the orders of a superior. What had happened was this: Early in the morning Colonel Declouet had come to the camp to apprize Jackson privately of his conversation with Magloire Guichard. Failing to find him, he imparted his story to Duncan who relayed it to Jackson as a message direct from Claiborne. Jackson's instructions to have Claiborne look into the matter had been communicated to the Governor by Duncan as an unconditional order to prevent the Legislature from sitting. Claiborne acted immediately and Marigny, confronted by the barred doors of the Assembly chambers, had posted to the battlefield.

The assurances of a victory that he carried back to New Orleans were not exaggerated. The awesome British attack never recovered from the blows of Patterson's artillery on its left, and sputtered out like a display of fireworks. When the field guns, with which Pakenham hoped to restore his fortunes, were within range, the *Louisiana* wrecked them and resumed its vicious sweep of the inactive infantry. The five land guns also combed the plain for troops crouching behind fences and the ruined buildings of Chalmette plantation. Unable to reestablish his left, Pakenham ordered it back, and the men crept to the rear as best they could. The right, however, withdrew in formation, bitter in the belief that had the command been "Forward" it could have turned Jackson's flank.

So ended, on December 28, 1814, the second battle for New Orleans. A discriminating use of the military vocabulary saved General Pakenham from a confession of defeat. He called the engagement a "reconnaissance in force." In later years a subordinate could speak with more candor. "In spite of our sanguine expectations of sleeping that night in New Orleans, evening found us occupying our negro huts at Villeré's, nor was I sorry that the shades of night concealed our mortification from the prisoners and slaves."[4]

3

Three days and three nights of dazzling activity followed the victory. Every house in New Orleans was searched for firearms and entrenching tools. But tension in the city relaxed when the Legislature was permitted to resume its sittings. Three batteries of naval guns were erected across the river. The number of guns in the mud line was increased from five to twelve, affording protection to the left which Pakenham might have turned on the twenty-eighth had he known how weak it was. The emplacement of these guns was a work of great labor and considerable ingenuity. Cotton bales were sunk into the yielding soil and wooden platforms built upon them. The cheeks of the embrasures in the rampart were faced with cotton bales plastered with mud.[5]

The soul of this preparation was Jackson. "Although . . . ready to sink under the weight of sickness [and] fatigue, . . ." wrote his chief of engineers, "his mind never lost for a moment that energy which [caused] insurmountable obstacles" to melt before him. This "energy . . . spread . . . to the whole army, . . . composed of heterogeneous elements . . . speaking different languages, and brought up in different habits. . . . There was nothing . . . it did not feel capable of doing if he ordered it to be done."[6]

By day a desultory fire from Jackson's cannon made life miserable in the British encampment. By night he kept the enemy's nerves on edge, sending down "hunting parties" to stalk sentries as a frontiersman stalked his game—the first extensive use of the raiding party, now a common feature of minor tactics. The British appeared so cowed and inactive that Jackson arranged a treat for his hard-working troops and a tonic for the citizens of New Orleans. A formal review was announced to take place behind the lines on New Year's morning.

But the British were not cowed or inactive, and they had their own plans for New Year's Day. The air of idleness that overhung their camp had masked the almost incredible toil by which Cochrane's sailors brought naval guns from the fleet seventy miles away—guns with which the short-tempered Admiral expected to silence Jackson's cannon, breach his mud wall and open the way to New Orleans. The British had not counted on a long delay at the threshold of a well-provisioned city, and their ration stores were low. The night of December thirty-first closed in foggy and pitch dark. Under a strong escort of infantry, seventeen pieces of ordnance were painfully dragged forward. Seven hundred yards from the Rodriquez Canal batteries were set up within easy range of the American front. The men worked quietly. Only the dull sound of their sledges reached Jackson's lines where, for some reason, the Dirty Shirt hunters rested from their exertions.

4

The fog's fleecy veil threatened to dim the splendors of Jackson's review. Shortly before eight o'clock the first of the visitors, several ladies among them, arrived from the city. A band was playing. The troops assigned to parade were forming up, their uniforms and accouterments scrubbed clean of the stains of the less engaging aspects of military life. Jackson had completed his morning inspection of the rampart, and, stretching himself on his couch, awaited the beginning of the review. Suddenly the room grew lighter. The fog dissolved as if touched by a hand of magic. Parade weather after all.

A thunderous clap drowned the music of the band. The Macarté house rocked amid a shivering of glass and a rain of plaster. Jackson rushed to a door. The sky was aflame with rockets. The walled-in garden was being plowed by shells. The troops assembled for the parade were dashing toward the safety of the rampart. Spectators went flying in every direction. Shouting to his aides to follow, Jackson started for the garden gate. A ball erupted a geyser of earth that almost buried Robert Butler.

At Battery Number One by the river Captain Humphrey, a veteran Regular, "dressed in his usual plain attire [and] smoking that eternal cigar [was] cooly levelling his guns." The British batteries erected during the night were guarded by low mounds of earth and hogsheads filled with sugar. They presented small targets, and it was some moments before Humphrey was satisfied with the aim of his twelve-pounders.

"Let her off," he said at length.[7]

Jackson passed on. At Battery Number Three fierce little Dominique You examined the enemy works through a glass. A cannon shot grazed his arm.

"I'll make them pay for that!" exclaimed the pirate.[8]

The picked gunners from the English fleet, veterans of Nelson and of Collingwood, were superior to the army artillerists against whom Jackson had contended on the twenty-eighth. One hundred balls struck the Macarté house. In the river a boat laden with supplies was disabled. Along the rampart cotton bales were torn apart and set on fire. The carriage of one of Dominique You's twenty-fours was broken. A thirty-two and a twelve were silenced. A rocket blew up a caisson of ammunition. At this tremendous explosion the British gunners, believing their work was done, suspended their fire. The infantry, behind them waiting to attack, sent up a cheer. It was answered by a broadside from Jackson's guns.

The pungent smoke blotted out everything. The Americans blazed into it by guess. An infantry thrust against the left of the line in the woods was warmly received by Coffee's riflemen. The chance that Pakenham had on the twenty-eighth against that flank was not to be his again. Toward noon the enemy artillery fire began to slacken. At one o'clock their guns in the center and on the right ceased to fire. At three the battery on the levee had quit and Cochrane admitted another failure.[9] The defenders had won the third battle for New Orleans.

General Jackson rummaged the ruins of the Macarté house. He had lost his overcoat,[10] and overcoats were at a premium in his army. The search was futile, and, throwing himself on his couch, Jackson asked John Reid to take an order. "The Major General Tenders to the troops he has the honor to command his

good wishes for a happy new year, and especially to those officers
& men at the pieces of Artillery. . . . Watch Word Fight on——
The Contractor will issue half a gill of whiskey round."[11]

That night, while the men drank it, the British hauled their
guns to the rear.

5

"The enemy occupy their former position," Andrew Jackson
wrote to James Monroe two days after the battle, "and are engaged in strengthening it; Our time is spent in the same employment and in exchanging long shot with them. . . . I do not
know what may be their further design—Whether to redouble
their efforts, or apply them elsewhere. . . . I am preparing for
either event."[12]

The pounded first line was repaired, the second line was
strengthened, a third line just below the city was begun. Under
the relentless pressure of this preparation, the yeasty enthusiasm
of some of the militia organizations began to droop. One battalion laid down its shovels. Jackson gave the officers of the
recreant organization a talking to that enabled them to persuade
their men of the intrinsic nobility of lowly labor in an exalted
cause.[13] Nor did he soften his words to the Secretary of War.
"The Arms I have been so long expecting have not yet Arrived,
All we hear of them is that . . . the man . . . entrusted with their
transportation has halted on the way for the purpose of private
speculations. . . . This negligence . . . [threatens] the defeat of
our armies."[14]

On January fourth the long-delayed Kentucky division under
Thomas began to arrive. Livingston reported them unarmed.

"I don't believe it," exclaimed Jackson. "I have never seen a
Kentuckian without a gun and a pack of cards and a bottle of
whisky in my life!"[15]

Nevertheless, these particular Kentuckians had only seven hundred guns to twenty-three hundred and sixty-eight men.

On the sixth Jackson learned from deserters and from the
evidence of his own telescope that the British were preparing

another attack. The arrival of a fresh brigade had put new heart into Pakenham's weary troops. Boats were being dragged from Lake Borgne to the Mississippi, which added a new element of uncertainty. Did Pakenham mean to attack on the west side of the river, where Jackson had a rude line defended by only five hundred and fifty Louisiana militia under Brigadier-General David Morgan?

On the seventh the British were detected bundling cane stalks into facines and making ladders. From this Jackson decided the real attack would be against his main line with perhaps a demonstration against Morgan. Accordingly, he reenforced this officer with five hundred Kentuckians, only one hundred and seventy of whom, however, had arms. The main body of the Kentuckians went into bivouac in the rear of Jackson's line as a reserve. Four hundred rusty Spanish *escopetas* were taken from the Veteran Guard, on police duty in New Orleans, so that every second man of the reserve possessed a fowling piece of some kind.

Toward evening Jackson received information from which he concluded that the British intended to attack before dawn. He ordered half of the force at the rampart to remain at their posts while the other half slept. The General himself turned in early. On the floor of the same room lay his aides Butler, Reid, Livingston and Davézac, with only their sword-belts unbuckled and pistols laid aside.

They had not been asleep long when a figure entered the dark hallway and spoke to the sentry at the door. Jackson was awake before the sentry could call him.

"Who's there?" he demanded.

It was a courier with a note from Commandant Patterson who reported strong enemy detachments preparing to cross the river toward Morgan's position. "I would therefore beg leave most earnestly to recommend an increase of our present force."[16]

"Tell General Morgan," Jackson replied, "that . . . the main attack will be on this side, and I have no men to spare. He must maintain his position at all hazards."[17]

The General glanced at his watch. It was after one in the

morning of January 8, 1815. "Gentlemen," he said, addressing his
aides, "we have slept enough."[18]

The group passed out into the creeping cold of the clammy
night for a last survey of the lines. Lieutenant Billy Phillips, of
Phillips's Ride remembrance, led the General's horse. On the
extreme right by the river, a bastion protruded some thirty yards
to the front, flanking the Rodriquez Canal. It had been built
three days before at the earnest suggestion of subordinates, Jackson yielding against his own judgment, as he said, "for the first
time in my life."[19] It was held by Beale's City Rifles, a crack
militia company from New Orleans, and one company of the
Seventh Infantry. Next was Battery Number One, commanded
by Captain Humphrey of the "eternal cigar," then the Seventh
Infantry, then Battery Number Two, Lieutenant Norris of the
late *Carolina.*

The men spoke in low tones and they did not speak much.
Their laughter was a little off key. The wait before a battle pro-
duces a sensation for which there is no name.

Next were Plauché's Uniformed Companies; then the Baratarians' battery where a circle of men crouched about a mound
of red embers dripping coffee in the Creole way.

"That smells like better coffee than we can get," remarked
Jackson. He turned to Dominique You. "Smuggle it?"

"Mebbe so, Général," rejoined the little captain, filling a cup
for his commander.

"I wish I had five hundred such devils in the butts," said
Jackson.[20]

Lacoste's negroes. . . . Daquin's negroes. . . . Battery Number
Four, Lieutenant Crawley of the Navy. . . . The Forty-Fourth
Infantry. . . . Battery Number Five, Colonel Perry. . . . Battery
Number Six, Lieutenant Spotts. Rank had little to do with
Jackson's selection of battery commanders. It was ability to
handle the guns.

Carroll's division was next. Old Hickory espied a grandson
of Nashville's founder. "Joe, how they using you? Wouldn't
you rather be with Aunt Lucy than with me?" Aunt Lucy was

Joe's mother "Not by a damned sight, General," retorted Private
Robertson. "Stick to 'em, Joe." He clapped the boy on the back
and passed on. It was astonishing how many of the Tennesseans
Jackson could call by name.[21]

The visit to Battery Number Seven called for a different style
of military etiquette. Its commander, General Garriques Flau-
geac, had led a division in Egypt under Napoleon. Battery Number Eight, a few yards away, was manned by Tennesseans, in
charge of a Regular Army corporal.

Here the line entered the stubby cypress woods and Coffee's
sector began. For a few yards the moss-hung trees grew from
ground fairly firm and then the swamp began. For two weeks
Coffee's men had breathed its odors of decay and, standing to
their waists in the viscous slime, had cut trees to prolong the
mud line with a breastwork of logs for a distance of six hundred
yards. In front of this rampart, trees had been removed to afford
a field of fire. Back of the rampart was a log walk for the men
to stand on. They crowded about the General, who called out
names by the sound of voices and exchanged greetings in the
intimate vernacular of the West. If Andrew Jackson had a favor
ite corps in his army it was Coffee's which had taken the most
difficult post in the battle line and borne the hardest labors with
the least complaint.

At three o'clock Jackson stopped at Battery Number Eight
to dictate an order for Brigadier-General Adair, acting in the place
of Thomas who was ill, to bring up the Kentucky reserve and dis-
tribute it in two lines at the point behind the works where the
commands of Carroll and of Coffee joined. Here, near the margin
of the woods, he believed the British would make their real attempt to break through. This gave Jackson a total of five thousand one hundred and seventy-two men on his line, or about all
he could crowd in.[22]

At six o'clock a milky light paled the little fires over which
men rubbed their hands for warmth. Noting the direction of the
wind, Major Latour said the fog would clear in an hour. Pickets
reported the enemy formed in column on the plain of Chalmette

plantation not half a mile away. Jackson sent Billy Phillips for his telescope and stood on the parapet with Carroll and Adair. From the field in front a rocket rose with a shrill sigh and burst into a bluish silver shower. It was answered by a rocket from the river bank.

"That is their signal for advance, I believe,"[23] said Andrew Jackson, whose life until now had been a preface to this moment.

6

Edward Michael Pakenham was not a man ordinarily to take counsel of his fears, which he had done when he fired that *"fatal ever fatal rocket,"* as a British officer afterward named it.

Sir Edward had been up nearly all night only to witness one miscarriage of arrangements after another. First, Colonel Thornton, commanding the forces that were to assail Morgan across the river, had got off four or five hours late and then, because of a shortage of boats, with less than half of his force of fourteen hundred men. He was to make the first attack, plow through Morgan, seize Patterson's batteries and turn them on Jackson's rear. Pakenham's advance against the mud rampart was to consist principally of two columns. Twelve hundred men under Keane would make a demonstration by the river, while twenty-one hundred under Gibbs breached the line near the margin of the woods. To occupy Coffee further a regiment of West Indian negroes was to attack through the trees. A third column of fourteen hundred under Lambert would remain in the center of the field to go where the fortunes of battle might call. It was a devastating scheme to box in Jackson's position with hostile fire. And the crux of the whole plan was that all attacks should take place in the dark. The British had had enough of Dirty Shirt marksmanship in broad daylight.

Mismanagement trod the heels of delay. At the head of the main striking force under Gibbs was placed the Forty-Fourth Regiment to carry facines for bridging the canal and ladders for scaling the rampart. The selection of this corps is unaccountable;

its lack of discipline was notorious. The column was in position, though late, and awaiting the signal to move when General Gibbs discovered that the Forty-Fourth had neither facines nor ladders. Three hundred men were sent back to get them.

With the thin January dawn breaking about him, Pakenham was almost frantic. There was no sign from across the river that Thornton had begun his attack. The chance to fall on Jackson's line in darkness was slipping away. Yet, in his exasperation, he dared not face old Cochrane with a proposal to postpone the assault.

So his signal flared. Keane answered. Of them all he alone was ready. The Forty-Fourth had not returned with the facines and ladders. For an instant, Gibbs hesitated, then sent his column forward in the blundering but brave British way. Still no sign of Thornton. Could Pakenham have but known—his Colonel was just landing on the opposite shore, having been dragged far from his objective by the unexpectedly strong river current.

A breeze broke ragged patches in the fog—one more tragedy for Pakenham, a God-send to the Americans.

General Jackson was standing on the parapet when a caprice of the wind unmasked the British advance. They were immediately in front, not more than six hundred and fifty yards away, and headed straight for the point behind which Jackson had massed his reserve. Andrew Jackson never forgot the sight that met his eyes. A heavy frost had embossed the cane stubble with silver. Across this shining carpet moved a field of red tunics latticed by white cross-belts, and a pulsing hedge of bayonets that gave an impression of infinity.

The American rifles were ineffective beyond four hundred yards. Jackson called to Carroll and Adair to pass the word for each man on the fire-step to pick out his target and "to aim above the cross plates."[24]

"The men were tense, but very cold," related one of them. "The enemy was now within five hundred yards. . . . Then— boom! went ou~ first guns, . . . the long brass 12-pounder . . .

commanded by Old General Fleaujeac. . . . Then all the guns opened. The British batteries, . . . concealed from us by the fog replied, directing their fire by the sound of our guns, . . . their flashes light[ing] up the fog . . . into all the hues of the rainbow."[25]

Cannon smoke billowed forward and "spoiled" the aim of the riflemen. This was as bad as the fog, shouted Adair. Jackson directed Batteries Seven and Eight to cease firing. When the air cleared the red line was within three hundred yards and coming at a run. Shells from the center batteries furrowed the ranks. They closed up and came on. Jackson could not suppress his admiration of the sight.[26] Carroll's and Coffee's men pressed their cheeks to their rifle stocks, each bringing his "bead" to bear above the belt-plate of a British soldier.

"Fire!"

A sheet of orange flame flared from the parapet. The rank stepped down to reload. Another took its place.

"Fire!"

The second rank gave way to the third.

"Fire!"

The solid front of the British column was now a skirmish line. But this came on. The ranks behind it thinned, like teeth snapping from a comb. But they came on. The shining field was red with British coats. Advancing ranks tripped over them, the precise lines began to buckle, to bunch, and open a premature and ragged fire. "Never before," related an English lieutenant, "had British veterans quailed. But it would be silly to deny that they did so now. . . . That leaden torrent no man on earth could face. I had seen battle-fields in Spain and in the East . . . but nowhere . . . such a scene" as this.[27]

A figure on horseback appeared in the van—Gibbs, shouting to the men to push on with the bayonet. But the foreranks had turned toward the rear, throwing the column in confusion. Two more horsemen dashed to the front—Pakenham and his aide, Captain McDougall. Sir Edward's horse went down. A ball shattered the rider's right arm. He threw himself on McDougall's black pony. But the column was in retreat.

Out of range it reformed, the men throwing off their heavy knapsacks. Keane, on the left, perceiving the plight of Gibbs, obliqued across the field with the praying Ninety-Third Highlanders. This regiment, in which every man was six feet tall, was ordered to lead the second assault. Its commander, Colonel Dale, handed his watch and a letter to a surgeon. "Give these to my wife," he said.

With swinging kilts the Scots came on across the stubble.

Blasts of grape rutted their line. They came on.

"*Fire!*" A musketry volley mowed them. Those who were left trailed arms and came on.

"*Fire! Load! Aim! Fire!*" There is British corroboration for Jackson's statement written on the field that his riflemen fired "with a briskness of which there have been but few instances, perhaps, in any country."[28]

The Scots stumbled among their dead and the dead of the first attack. Colonel Dale was dead. Pakenham and Gibbs were dying. Keane was down, with a ball through his neck. One hundred and fifty yards from the rampart the leaderless Highlanders halted and huddled together. Other corps pressing up from behind bred confusion, then panic. Officers shouted and struck men with the flats of their swords. Major Wilkinson of the Twenty-First North Britain Fusiliers ran forward. Perhaps a hundred men followed and perhaps two-thirds of these gained the Rodriquez Canal, thirty yards from the black line's smoking face.

Twenty clambered up the bank and charged the works. Wilkinson scaled the parapet and fell gasping into the arms of Major Smiley of the Kentucky militia. He lived for two hours and the Kentuckians covered him with their colors.

When Keane went to the relief of Gibbs he left the left column along the river to Rennie, the gallant young colonel who had threatened Coffee's sector on the twenty-eighth. More favored by the fog than Gibbs had been, Rennie stormed the lines almost on the heels of the American pickets. He penetrated the bastion protruding from our line and perished there.

The last order Pakenham gave before he received his third and mortal wound was for Lambert to throw in the reserve. But this officer decided the battle was beyond redemption. As best he could he withdrew the whole British army from the stricken field.

At half past eight the American infantry ceased to fire. The batteries ceased at two. The silvery carpet had changed back to gray cane stubble. "I never had," said General Jackson, "so grand and awful an idea of the resurrection as . . . [when] I saw . . . more than five hundred Britons emerging from the heaps of their dead comrades, all over the plain rising up, and . . . coming forward . . . as prisoners."[29]

Andrew Jackson was not called a religious man, but when he looked upon those British dead and heard the report that his own loss was seven killed, six wounded,[30] his heart was filled with awe and his mind with wonder. "The unerring hand of providence shielded my men."[31]

7

Yet the battle was not ended. Across the river the long-delayed Thornton was moving against Morgan's works. Jackson climbed on top of his scarred parapet and peered anxiously into the mist.

"Take off your hats and give them three cheers!" he shouted, though Morgan's men were a mile and a half away.[32]

The cheers were given too soon. Gun-flashes showed that Morgan was falling back. Jackson's enthusiasm yielded to wrath and then to alarm. In the rear of Morgan's line were Patterson's batteries, still playing across the river on the retreating British. Morgan's withdrawal turned into flight. As Thornton pressed on the batteries ceased to fire. Patterson was spiking his guns. Should Thornton find even one of them undisabled, he could rake Jackson's position from river to swamp, Pakenham's original plan.

Hinds was begging Jackson for permission to pursue and cut up the fugitive army in front of him,[33] but Jackson refused until he could see how matters should eventuate on the western bank. General Jean Humbert, a Napoleonic exile, was sent across the river with four hundred men to drive back Thornton. He returned to say that the troops objected to the leadership of a foreigner.

After his almost incomprehensible victory, the night of January eighth was one of anxiety for Jackson. Thornton still held a position of enormous tactical possibilities. But on the morning of the ninth, Jackson learned, to his relief and astonishment, that Thornton had recrossed the river and joined the main body. General Lambert had called him back, considering the army too low in morale to attempt the exploitation of its success on the western bank.

Over the showing of his own army on the western bank, Jackson was bitter. In anger he dashed off a note to Monroe that Morgan's defeat had averted "the entire destruction of the enemy's army."[34] The entire destruction of a British army had been an accomplishment for which General Jackson had lived since he was thirteen years old. Monroe was further informed that the responsibility lay squarely on "a strong detachment of the Kentucky troops . . . [which] ingloriously fled." To this conclusion Jackson clung, despite protests of Adair and others, including a court of inquiry, presided over by William Carroll, which later was to find the conduct of the Kentuckians "not reprehensible." General Morgan blamed "Major Arnaud of the second brigade of Louis[a] militia . . . [who] abandoned his post in a most shameful manner."[35] The court of inquiry also placed the blame on Major Arnaud.[36]

Nothing is easier than armchair criticism after a battle. Jackson has had enough of it to relieve the monotony of hero-worship, but the fact remains that in matters small and large his generalship was excellent and considerably superior to that of the English. As to fighting qualities there was no comparison. But the responsibility for the failure on the western bank was Jackson's.

He placed the incompetent Morgan in command there, permitted him to locate his line badly, and then refused sufficient troops to defend it.

8

With Thornton gone from the other side of the river, Jackson was ready to carry out Hinds's suggestion of the day before and complete the ruin of the British army. Livingston declared it would be a useless exposure of lives. "What do you want more? . . . The city is saved."[37] Even Coffee and Adair hesitated to "hazard an attack with raw militia on the open plain."[38]

As for the British, their only desire apparently was to quit their forlorn camp unmolested. For ten days they made elaborate preparations to protect their narrow avenue of retreat to Lake Borgne. On the night of January eighteenth, leaving fires alight, Lambert piloted his broken command over the five miles of swamp, the soldiers stumbling and struggling to extricate their feet from an entangling evergreen called Laurel of the Conqueror. At the mouth of Bayou Bienvenue shallow boats awaited them. Already on its way to the fleet was the body of "General Pakenham in a casket of rum to be taken to London. What a sight for his wife who is aboard and who had hoped to be Governess of Louisiana."[39]

The next morning when Jackson rode toward the littered encampment a British surgeon met him with a petition for considerate care of eighty badly wounded who could not be removed. They were carried to New Orleans and given the same attentions as the American sick and wounded.

A few days later Jackson received a communication from General Keane, who was with the British fleet off Cat Island, offering "any price" for the return of the sword he had lost in battle.[40] Jackson marveled at the lapse of pride that could permit a request so exceptional.[41] He sent the General his sword promptly and with it a letter, entirely correct and military, and on the whole perhaps one of the most satisfying epistles Andrew Jackson ever wrote.

"The General Commanding the American forces, having learned that Major General Kean ... has expressed a wish for ... his sword, ... feèls great satisfaction in having it ordered returned to him. .... The undersigned, feeling for the misfortunes of the brave, begs that Genl Kean will be assured of his wishes for his speedy restoration."[42]

CHAPTER XVI

"THE UNITED STATES VERSUS ANDREW JACKSON"

I

JANUARY of 1815 was one of the bleakest months it has been the lot of a President of the United States to endure. Behind the eight walls of Colonel Tayloe's Octagon House to which the British had driven him when they destroyed the Executive Mansion, James Madison shifted his anxious gaze between two remote points on the map—Hartford, Connecticut, and New Orleans. From either locality might issue news that would be the doom not only of his Administration, but of the Union.

Disaster had followed upon disaster. The war was a failure, the armies unpaid, the Treasury empty. Our coast was blockaded, business disturbed, taxes doubled. From Albany to Savannah banks had suspended specie payments. Then in December, like twin clouds obscuring the last gleam of hope, the great expedition equipped at an expense of one million pounds sterling converged upon Louisiana, and the "New England Convention" sat in the State-House at Hartford. The Administration press branded the latter as a plot to dismember the Union, an allegation the journals of New England did little to repel. "Throwing off all connection with this wasteful war," said one, "[and] making peace with our enemy ... would be ... a manly course." [1]

A dearth of news increased the tension. A discreet observer sent to Hartford by Mr. Madison might as well have remained at home for all he learned, so closely did the delegates guard their deliberations. As for Louisiana, after news of the loss of the gunboats three Southern mails in succession failed to arrive. Then a post that had left New Orleans at daylight on December twenty-

271

fourth brought the word which appeared to confirm the worst forebodings. The British had made a surprise landing "with 6,000 men;" a battle was in progress.[2] And after that silence. An army officer employed the time to demonstrate to an Administration congressman that New Orleans was indefensible.

On January fifth the Hartford Convention adjourned and published its report, which was received with mixed emotions. With old George Cabot in the chair, the Convention had been kept in leash by the moderates. The report contained ample sop for the radicals—the iniquities of the Administration set forth, the war denounced, defeat conceded—but considering the temper of New England, the body of recommendations was conservative. A strong argument in favor of union prefaced the opinion that secession should be contemplated only as "the work of peaceable times and deliberate consent." This on one hand. On the other a peremptory demand that Congress empower each state to carry on the war to suit itself, raising and directing armies independently of Federal authority.

Harrison Gray Otis and two other gentlemen departed from Boston on February third to lay the Hartford report before the general Government. They meant to take a firm tone with Mr. Madison. New England had been patient, for two and a half years remaining aloof from the major concerns of the war. No applause for Lundy's Lane, for Plattsburgh or Tohopeka. A motion for a vote of thanks to Captain Lawrence for the capture of the *Peacock* was rejected by the Massachusetts Legislature as "not becoming . . . a moral and religious people to express any approbation of military or naval exploits."

But now reserve had been discarded. New England had spoken and did not intend her breath should be wasted.

What, indeed, could little Mr. Madison do except listen and submit!

Supremely confident, Mr. Otis and his companions proceeded toward the capital. At any hour they expected to meet an express with news from the South which would finish the Administration.

Sunday Blue Laws detained the envoys for a day at New Haven.

Ice in the Hudson put them back another twenty-four hours. And still no news. Three black crows preceded their coach into Philadelphia. "These are *ill omened* birds," observed Otis, "and . . . when augury was in fashion would have been considered sad precursors of three Ambassadors."[3]

Augury, it seems, had gone out of style too soon. At Gadsby's Hotel in Baltimore the three ambassadors learned of "The *Miraculous* success of our arms at N Orleans . . . [which] will probably put the Administration on stilts, and augur no favorable issue for our mission."[4]

The gentlemen who had expected to shake Washington with their tread tiptoed through a scene of celebration, ringing with the name of Jackson. The Administration was on stilts a mile high, and Mr. Otis was thankful for the shelter of a respectable Georgetown boarding house where several other bewildered New England statesmen also waited for the fever to pass. It did not pass. On February fourteenth Otis wrote his wife. "At this moment a rumor of peace . . . throws the natives into a great bustle." Mrs. Otis was cautioned to remember, however, that Madison had been taken in by such rumors before. Still, the letter remained unsealed until post-time, in the hope of later advices.

They were not long coming. Cannon boomed, bells rang, men paraded. "Peace! Peace! Victory!" A disciplined New England conscience guided the pen of Harrison Gray Otis. "Gods holy name be praised. . . . I say again, Gods name be praised."[5]

For ten days the august embassy withstood the lampooning its ridiculous position evoked and then left town. Mr. Otis grimly resumed his seat in the Massachusetts Legislature in time to vote for a resolution giving the Lord exclusive credit for the battle of New Orleans. General Jackson was not mentioned.

2

The Almighty was already aware, however, that the General entertained similar views. Riding from the deserted British camp on the morning of January nineteenth, he dictated a note to the Abbé DuBourg, head of the Catholic clergy of Louisiana. "Revd. Sir, The signal interposition of heaven . . . requires . . . some manifestation. . . . Permit me therefore to entreat that you will cause a service of public thanksgiving to be performed in the Cathedral."[6]

Two days later Jackson returned to New Orleans and the city gave him a Latin welcome. Pierre Favrot, seated by a window overlooking the Place d'Armes, undertook to describe it to his wife. "At this moment there are more than 2500 people in the Place awaiting the arrival of the General . . . at least 1000 women, ladies & young girls." New Orleans gave itself over to fêting the heroes and Monsieur Favrot wrote no more that day. The rigors of the siege were forgotten, Jackson suspended the nine o'clock curfew and the gaiety lasted into the night. In the morning Favrot finished his letter. "8 A.M. Never my dear, have I seen such a crowd. . . . All the troops arriving to the strains of military music & of the cannons, . . . more than 12000 people of whom 8000 were armed. . . . Tomorrow they . . . will crown the General; twelve young girls will strew his path with flowers. . . . They are practicing at Mme. Floriant's."[7]

Madame Floriant fulfilled her duties with imagination. Two of the little girls took their places under a triumphal arch, one holding a wreath of laurel, one a paper inscribed with the words of a song. From the arch to the door of the gray cathedral stood two lines of children, "all dressed in white, . . . and wearing a silver star on their foreheads. Each . . . held in her right hand a flag . . . and in her left a basket . . . of flowers."[8] The sight touched the heart of the child-loving soldier. When the little girl under the arch had sung her song (to the tune of *Yankee Doodle*), General Jackson bent down and requested a copy of it, which he sent with an affectionate note to one of the Hays youngsters in Tennessee. At the door of the church he was received by the Abbé DuBourg in his robes of office and attended by a college of priests. A transcript of his remarks went to the little Hays child's father with this modest comment: "The language is good and the sentiments sublime altho' . . . as it respects myself too flattering."[9]

The choir began to chant the majestic lines of the *Te Deum*. The people in the church took up the hymn. It spread to the lips of the throng that filled the square as all New Orleans poured forth its gratitude for deliverance.

3

On the following day New Orleans awakened somewhat amazed to find itself, to all intents, once more in a state of siege. The tight restrictions of martial law were reimposed. Militia companies which had looked forward to prompt disbandment were marched into camps and set to drilling. Reserve companies not under arms before because there were no arms to give them were called out, the dilatory cargo of War Department rifles hav-ing arrived. Andrew Jackson expected his victory to have bear-ing on the tedious negotiations he assumed to be in progress at Ghent, but he took no chances.[10] He knew the tenacity of the English and their reputation for losing every battle except the last one. Moreover, boarding their boats on Lake Borgne, they had recovered sufficiently to boast a little. "We have missed the victory," a captain was heard to declare, "but we are going to get General Wellington, and . . . come back. . . . We did not count on having to do with Frenchmen. Your . . . Dirty Shirts are not much."[11]

The army in Louisiana was not alone to feel the hand of dis-cipline. When Jackson left Mobile in November, two hundred Tennessee militiamen were under arrest for mutiny. In Decem-ber they were tried. The court condemned six of the ringleaders to death and the others to penalties less severe. The papers in the case reached Jackson probably about January first. After the vic-tory of the eighth there was time to study them. On the day before he was crowned with laurel at the Cathedral, Jackson dic-tated a lengthy memorandum which shows that he had considered the findings of the court with scrupulous care. He approved the sentences.[12]

Jackson foresaw a need for discipline on the Alabama. "The last account from the enemy," he wrote, "they were steering towards Mobile," evidently in contemplation of a "stroke." But "Winchester is prepared and must defeat them. . . . If they return [here] I am ready."[13]

This state of readiness was maintained at a sacrifice of much popularity. The Lower House of the Louisiana Legislature voted Jackson a sword, but the proposal was killed in the Senate, no one working harder to that end than Bernard Marigny. A lengthy resolution of thanks, however, was adopted. It was studded with names—captains, majors, colonels, generals—the author must have written with a roster of the army before him. But in this long list of the conspicuous and the obscure nowhere appeared the name of Andrew Jackson. The Legislature had taken its revenge for December twenty-eighth.

Martial law bore cruelly upon the population. "General," the patriotic Abbé DuBourg wrote in unaccustomed English, "a Number of unfortunate half starved women of Terre Aux Bœufs fall at your feet to redemand you their husbands."[14] Civil authorities chafed to resume their functions and picked quarrels with the military. Claiborne urged the discharge of some of the militia. Jackson refused like a shot, reminding him that the enemy was only four days' sail away. The reminder had little effect. The militia began to desert, Private James Harding taking the trouble to state his reasons in writing to the Commanding General. "Dear Sir, My wife was turned into the Street by the land lord . . . and she wrote me to go home."[15] A court martial ordered him to be shot, but Jackson quietly withheld his approval of the sentence.

On February nineteenth word came that Fort Bowyer had fallen to the English, but, before Jackson could give effect to his flaming determination to recapture it, Edward Livingston returned from a mission to the British fleet with a rumor that the war was over.

New Orleans forgot Fort Bowyer as completely as if it were in China. But Jackson did not forget it. He published a proclamation warning that the report of peace might be a "stratagem" on the part of "an artful . . . enemy . . . to put you off your guard. . . . Fort Bowyer . . . must and will be speedily retaken."[16]

New Orleans declined to attach importance to Fort Bowyer. It had ears only for the news of peace. Counting houses, coffee houses, offices and shops seethed with milling throngs. Bids on cotton, bids on sugar, tobacco, pelts. Prices climbed and the truth or falsity of the rumor of peace would spell the difference between riches and ruin to some of the bidders. The wharves and warehouses of New Orleans were piled with the accumulations of two years, cut off from export by the British blockade. On confirmation of the rumor of peace the value of exportable products would jump one hundred per cent. Manchester's looms were starved for American cotton, and New England's little better off. Peace would deflate the prices of imports in the same proportion.

At Washington, at Philadelphia—almost any place one pries into this subject of the peace news, one finds that a favored few by underground means were informed in advance of officials for whom the dispatches were intended. Some such leak seems to have occurred at New Orleans. Livingston arrived on February nineteenth and publicly gave out a report based on a copy of a London newspaper that had just reached the British fleet. But he knew more. Admiral Cochrane, with whom Livingston was personally acquainted, had exhibited a Foreign Office bulletin announcing a treaty at Ghent "by [which] hostilities will cease as soon as . . . ratified by the President of the united states . . . and the Prince regent."[17] Indeed Cochrane had given Livingston a copy of this bulletin to deliver to Jackson with a hasty note of "sincere congratulations."[18] When Colonel Livingston reached New Orleans he turned his dispatch case inside out before the Commander. The note from Cochrane was not there. It did not arrive until the morning of February twenty-first, by a British launch flying a white flag. Meanwhile had Edward Livingston seen fit to tell his friends privately that the peace rumor rested on a foundation more substantial than a newspaper report, the information would have been priceless. An incident suggests that some such thing occurred.

Jackson hardly had time to acknowledge Cochrane's message when he heard boys crying handbills in the streets: "A truce-boat from Admiral Cochrane . . . has just brought to General Jackson official news of a treaty concluded at Ghent . . . and a request for a cessation of hostilities."[19]

The handbills were issued by the Louisiana *Gazette* whose editor enjoyed the confidence of Colonel Livingston. Jackson sent John Reid scurrying through crowded Royal Street with a bristling order for the *Gazette* to destroy "every copy of so *unauthorized and improper a notice*" and to publish the retraction which General Jackson had dictated.

"The only official news . . . received by no means declares that a truce is to take place until the treaty be . . . ratified. . . . The Commanding General again Calls upon his fellow Citizens and Soldiers to recollect that . . . until . . . [peace] is properly announced" there can be no "relaxation in the army under his command."[20]

These words had no effect. The tide of speculation reduced Louisiana militia commands to skeletons as brokers, planters and merchants in the ranks declined to see themselves outdone by rivals not in service. Cotton rose from six to sixteen cents. The river front whitened with sail as ships long idle were loaded and made ready for sea, but Jackson forbade them to weigh anchor, though it is probable that some of his own cotton lay on the wharves. The stronger he was opposed the more tightly he clutched the mace. Each day brought nearer the inevitable eruption that was to display the defects of the qualities that had made Andrew Jackson the savior of Louisiana.

4

On to this taut stage stepped Rachel and Andrew, junior, after "a tollerable pasage in 25 days"[21] on the refurbished Cumberland keel boat. In December their departure had been postponed by news of the British landing, but they had left the day following receipt of the tidings of the eighth of January.[22] Rachel's coming was a signal for a partial suspension of hostilities between the General and the militia and, for the moment, supplanted the treaty rumor as the pièce de resistance of drawing-room small-talk, while the Creole community prepared to entertain a lady who had been preceded by such engaging descriptions of her virtues. Rachel seemed unaware of the especial attention. Joy alone consumed her. At last, she was reunited with the husband who had been gone from her side more than seven months.

Madame Livingston took her in charge. This family had become truly devoted to Andrew Jackson who reciprocated with his confidence and his friendship. Their home was a quiet harbor where he could shed the cares of headquarters, take their little daughter Cora on his knee, and send her to bed with a story. At first Cora's mother was rather alarmed by the responsibility of rendering Aunt Rachel presentable to New Orleans society. Mrs. Jackson was forty-seven. Her short figure had grown so stout that in describing her the natives repeated an old French saying, "She shows how far the skin can be stretched."[23]

It was skin honestly tanned by the wind and sun of Tennessee, for during her husband's absence Rachel had been the active manager of Hermitage plantation. Her black hair was without a strand of gray, her large dark eyes still young, her generous lips ready for a frank warm smile, revealing teeth that would have been the pride of a duchess. But her clothes—*mon Dieu!* Mrs. Jackson's wardrobe ignored the pageant of style even as revealed to remote Nashville. With invitations to plays and dinners pouring in, not to mention the great celebration of Washington's birthday, Madame Livingston surrounded her guest with folds of goods and a corps of French needlewomen. When General Jackson lifted the censorship from the press, a caricaturist represented Aunt Rachel standing on a table while Madame Livingston tugged at the strings of a pair of stays in an effort to re-establish her waist-line.[24]

It was Mrs. Jackson's first visit to a city larger than Nashville.

"I have seen more already than in all my life past it is the finest Country for the Eye of a Strainger but a Little while he tir[e]s of the Disipation. . . . So much amusement balls Concerts Plays theatres &c &c but we Dont attend the half of them. I herd a band of musick a few Evinings since."[25]

The elegant Creole ladies smiled behind their fans, but very soon Rachel's simplicity and her unaffected kindliness won them.

Preparations for the Washington's birthday dinner and ball were bewildering. For days the upper floor of the French Exchange had been in the hands of a Committee on Arrangements whose selection resulted in the usual contest for supremacy between the French and "American" contingents of society. "to give you a disseription [of their handiwork] is beyond the power of my pen," Rachel asserted, but her fresh, frontier eyes caught details that were lost to the sophisticated. "The Splendor, the brilliant assemblage the Magnificenc of the Supper and orniments of the room with all our greate Characters in Large Letters of Gold on a Long Sheet of Glass about four Inches wide with Lamps behind that they might be read as we Sat at Supper I was placed opposit the Motto Jackson and Victory ar one on the table a most Ellegant piremid on the top was Vivi Jackson in Large Letters on the other Sid the Immortal Washington— ther was a gold ham on the table . . . to say nothing . . . [of] the orniments and S[u]pper."[26]

After the supper, to say nothing of the gold ham, had disappeared the merry company formed for dancing. The guests of honor finally consented to treat their hosts to a pas de deux as it was done in blockhouse days in the Mero District. A member of the Committee on Arrangements observed them, perhaps still a little resentful because Jackson had allowed him only the pre-peace-rumor price for his cotton used to mount guns behind the Rodriquez Canal. "To see these two figures, the general a long, haggard man, with limbs like a skeleton, and Madame le Generale, a short, fat dumpling, bobbing opposite each other . . . to the wild melody of *Possum up de Gum Tree* . . . was very remarkable."[27]

5

"I have given you," concluded Rachel, "some of the flowers now the thorns." The nights of vigilance and days of toil in the swamps were taking their toll of the unacclimated troops from Tennessee and Kentucky. Hospital tents were full. "Major Read tells me this morning nearly one thousand have died." Yet, with the Louisiana militia approaching a state of mutiny, these soldiers bore their lot without complaint. Jackson labored incessantly. "of all men in Erth he Does the most Business from Day Light to ten at night."[28]

He had much business to do. French citizens in the militia had found that they could obtain discharges by registering their nationality at the French consulate. Creoles were quick to perceive the advantages of this arrangement and the obliging consul, Louis de Tousard, began a land-office business in French citizenship papers. Jackson matched the trick by deporting the holders of such papers to Baton Rouge.[29] Tousard made a theatric protest and was deported also.

Any number of actual French subjects, having neglected to obtain certificates, remained in the city. They sympathized with their exiled compatriots. Moreover, at the first ebb of Jackson's popularity, Governor Claiborne had made himself accessible to those opposed to the measures of the Commander. Relations between the two had become strained during the campaign. *La Courrière de la Louisiane* strode boldly into the breach on March third, publishing a lengthy communication which gave a formal cast to coffee-house criticism. Did General Jackson forget that Frenchmen and men of French blood had virtually won his battles? "It is high time the laws should resume their empire; .. that citizens accused of any crime should be rendered to their natural judges; ... that having done enough for glory the moment for moderation has arrived."

This was defiance and it acted as a match to powder. Louisiana troops at Chef Menteur mutinied, and a company in the city ordered to replace them refused to march.[30]   Jackson demanded the name of the author of the *Courrière* article and was surprised to hear that it was Louis Louaillier, a member of the Legislature who had distinguished himself by his support of the war.   Louaillier was a naturalized Frenchman.   Jackson ordered his arrest and on Sunday, March fifth, a file of businesslike Regulars closed about him on the steps of the Exchange Coffee House.   The prisoner threw up his hands and shouted that he was being borne away against his will by armed men.   A Creole lawyer offered his services on the spot and sped to the residence of Federal Judge Hall with a petition for a writ of habeas corpus.   It was granted. The Major General's answer was to arrest Hall for "a[i]ding abetting and exciting mutiny within my camp," and to lock him in the Barracks with Louis Louaillier.

Rachel wrote on that day that her husband, though "busy," seemed much improved in health and spirits.

6

Morning found the town in an uproar.   A crowd filled Royal Street in front of General Jackson's headquarters.   It parted to admit the passage of a horseman, a road-stained stranger in the uniform of a Regular captain.   The rider was a courier, twenty days from Washington, with a sealed packet for General Jackson and a letter identifying him as the bearer of official news of peace. An hysterical cry went up:

"*La paix! La paix!*"

In the mind of the populace there could be no doubt of it now. Jackson ripped open the packet.   Several official papers tumbled out, but there was not a line in one of them about peace.[31]

Jackson accepted the situation as a clerk's blunder and hurried a note to General Lambert at Fort Bowyer.   "I have . . . little doubt in my mind that the treaty . . . has been ratified. . . . I pray you to receive . . . [assurance] of the satisfaction I feel in reflecting that our Correspondence begun as Commander of hostile armies should terminate as officers of nations in amity."[32]   No assurance or any word whatever, was addressed to the perplexed citizens of New Orleans until the following day when General Jackson admitted the probability of peace, and, with soldierly words of praise, released the drafted militia of Louisiana. The exiled holders of Tousard's certificates were permitted to return.

But volunteer troops were retained and Louaillier was placed on trial before a court martial on seven fearful-sounding charges, ranging from mutiny to "general misconduct." The president of the court martial was Brigadier-General Edmund P. Gaines of the Regular Army, a competent and conscientious officer. After two days of deliberation the court declared itself without jurisdiction in six of the seven charges, and on the remaining charge, that of being a spy, acquitted the prisoner.

In a black rage Jackson rejected the findings and sent Louaillier back to the Barracks. The Major General appreciated, however, the futility of trying Hall even by a court of his own choosing, and detailed a squad of soldiers to escort the Judge out of town and let him go.

Forty-eight hours later, at daybreak on March 13, 1815, New Orleans awakened to the boom of minute guns. At last General Jackson had received official notice of the ratification of peace. With the same paralyzing promptitude with which he had gathered them into his hands when the crisis came, the Commander laid aside his extraordinary powers. Martial law was revoked and military prisoners released, including Louaillier and Private James Harding. The Mississippi, Kentucky and Tennessee troops were told to make ready for home, and the remainder of the Louisiana militia was dismissed. "Farewell, fellow-soldiers. The expression of your General's thanks is feeble."[33]

The volatile city surrendered to the emotions of jubilee, an about-face in which self-congratulation assumed the sublimer form of hero-worship. Huzzahing crowds enveloped the Royal Street headquarters. Coffee houses that two days before had rumbled with denunciation rang now with toasts to Old Hickory. The Sister Superior of the Ursuline nuns who viewed the carnival from their latticed windows begged that General Jackson would visit them again. The officers of the Battalion of Uniform Companies, representing most of the distinguished Creole families, presented a glowing and significant address, which indicates the unspontaneous nature of much of the recent opposition. "Leaving to others the task of declaiming about ... *constitutional rights, we are content with having fought ... for them.*"[34]

In a carefully worded reply in which he admitted with disarming candor infringement on personal rights guaranteed by the Constitution, Andrew Jackson developed his hypothesis on the subject of authority. "The laws must sometimes be silent when necessity speaks. ... My first wish ... has been to be useful to my country."[35]

In the midst of these occupations General Jackson celebrated his forty-eighth birthday on the fifteenth of March. A few old friends came to offer their felicitations. They found the chief in a mellow mood. The years rolled back to the scenes of childhood and he spoke of his mother. "How I wish *she* could have lived to see this day." He told of her heroic resolve to nurse the prisoners of war at Charleston and repeated her farewell: make friends by being honest, keep them by being steadfast; be truthful, be sincere, be brave. ...

"Gentlemen. ... [those] words have been the law of my life."[36]

7

Dominick A. Hall did not subscribe to the imperial doctrine of authority enunciated by the Major General. Hall was born in England, but neither the United States nor the prerogatives of the bench had a stauncher defender. He had braved the frown of Jackson in preparing the way for the participations of the Baratarians in the late campaign. He had welcomed the Louaillier case as an opportunity to contest the Commander's right to supersede habeas corpus proceedings by martial law. Returning to the city during the rejoicing, he quietly resumed his seat on the bench and permitted the hero to enjoy his hour.

But on March twenty-first he issued a summons directing Andrew Jackson to show cause why he should not be held in contempt for his refusal to recognize the writ of habeas corpus in the case of Louis Louaillier. Ten days of legal fencing followed, Jackson's counsel (Edward Livingston, et al.) disputing the jurisdiction of the court over acts of their client during the period of martial law. Popular opinion was as strongly on the side of Jackson as it had been on that of Hall and Louaillier a fortnight before. Nor was Judge Hall any more terrified by threats than General Jackson had been. He ruled against Jackson on every count and directed the defendant to appear and receive the sentence of the court.

Andrew Jackson was not ignorant of the force of the theatrical values in a court-room. Faultlessly attired in civilian dress, he left his carriage and made his way on foot through the throng that packed Royal Street in front of the little red-tiled Spanish building where Judge Hall presided. The room was crowded almost to suffocation. In their red shirts and holiday sashes, the Baratarians were present in force ready for anything. The General had no more zealous partizans than these mariners, many of whom, but for Dominick Hall, would still have been in jail. Jackson reciprocated this loyalty. In his most sprightly contributions to the belles-lettres of the war, the "hellish banditti" had become "my comrades in arms," and the brothers Laffite, "those gentlemen."[37]

The General entered amid perfect decorum, but as Judge Hall emerged from his chambers a storm of jeers broke from the Baratarians. Leaping to his feet, Jackson silenced them with a gesture reminiscent of the public prosecutor of Mero District. Then he turned toward the bench and inclined his head in a slight bow.

Judge Hall lowered the dramatic tone of this spectacle by dryly directing the clerk to proceed.

"The United States versus Andrew Jackson."

The defendant arose. "When called upon to show cause why an attachment for contempt of this court ought not to run against me, I offered to do so. . . . You would not hear my defense. . . . Under these circumstances I appear . . . to receive the sentence of the court. . . . Your Honor will not misunderstand me as meaning any disrespect, . . . but as no opportunity has been furnished me to explain . . . my conduct, so it is expected that censure will form no part of that punishment which your Honor may imagine it your duty to perform."[38]

It was an astute protest, but the urbane Dominick Hall was undisturbed by this representation of a patriot entangled by a manipulation of the law's machinery. Judge Hall had the measure of his man. It was impossible to forget, he said, the important services of the defendant to the country, and for that reason imprisonment would form no part of the sentence. "The only question was whether the Law should bend to the General or the General to the Law." The defendant had declined to respond to the interrogatories of the District Attorney. This left the Court no alternative but to adjudge him in contempt. A fine of one thousand dollars and costs was imposed.[39]

Jackson walked out of the court-room the idol of the cheering crowd. They unhitched the horses and dragged his carriage to the Exchange Coffee House. The General stood on the seat of the vehicle and signed for quiet.

"I have," he said, "during the invasion exerted every one of my faculties for the defense and preservation of the constitution and the laws. . . . Considering obedience to the laws, even when we think them unjustly applied, as the first duty of a citizen, I did not hesitate to comply with the sentence you have heard, and I entreat you to remember the example."[40]

Dominick Hall not being present, the scene was wholly Jackson's.

CHAPTER XVII

A Changing World

I

With the nation as well as New Orleans at his feet the hero bore his honors becomingly. If anything, he grew a little weary of the laurel. The departure from New Orleans was taken in triumph—public farewells, private leave-takings, exchanges of costly gifts. A purse was raised to discharge the fine imposed by Dominick Hall, but Andrew Jackson waved it aside requesting that the money be distributed among the families of soldiers who had fallen in battle. Rachel, too, had her farewells to say and she addressed some lines "To the ladies of Orleans,"[1] which may have come from the pen of John Reid, though, if it were possible, one should suspect Madame de Staël.

On the evening of May 15, 1815, General Jackson, Rachel and little Andrew descended from their coach at Nashville into a changing world. The bounteous blessings of peace and prosperity lay upon a smiling land—trade reviving, crops moving, coin clinking across the counters in Market Street and the Square. From a pit of disillusionment the new order had issued with the celerity and perfection of a miracle. Peace and Victory! It mattered not that the victory was gained fifteen days after the commissioners had put their names to the articles at Ghent, and had had no bearing on the negotiations. It mattered not that the peace secured to us scarcely one specific trophy promised by the enthusiasts whose buoyant rhetoric had swept the republic into War in 1812. Enough to know that Andrew Jackson had met the British and sent them reeling. Through his agency a treaty, "honorable," yes, in that it failed of national humiliation, was touched with the wand of glory and transformed, redeeming the self-respect of a spiritually bankrupt people. Not even Rachel could resist. She dropped her "Mr. Jackson" and began to speak of "the General."

Once more she was looking forward to a quiet life with her husband at her side. This time it seemed as if she were really to have it. The General had declined to show himself about the country and retired to his log residence to resume the management of his plantation. The Army was reorganized into two divisions, Jackson retaining command of the South, where his military duties promised to be nominal since the detail work devolved upon capable Edmund P. Gaines. The Major General's pay of twenty-four hundred dollars a year, with forage and rations allowances of sixteen hundred and fifty-two dollars more, had got him out of debt for the first time since 1796.

Thus the old financial worries were gone. Truly, Rachel and her husband now had nothing to stop the flow of their lives into the normal ways of the contented countryside. They visited back and forth among the neighbors and their old friends, comfortably and without ostentation. The pride of the General's heart was Andrew, junior, now five and a half, and Jackson was pleased to observe that "he behaved like a soldier" in the face of danger. Andrew's horse had run away, but the plucky child "stuck to him for half a mile" and when thrown "never hollowed."[2] The late Samuel Donelson's two sons still lived at the Hermitage, but Junior's especial playmate was Lincoyer, the little Creek Indian boy General Jackson had found half-starved among the dead at Tallushatchee and fed with his own hands.

His indifference to applause stimulated curiosity and the victor of New Orleans remained the most talked-of man in the country, interest undiminished by the fact that the public knew, and apparently could learn, very little about the man it honored. The War Department was obliged to write for a portrait before it could proceed to design the gold medal Congress had voted.[3] A resident of Lexington, Kentucky, wagered a "Considerable" sum that he was born in Ireland,[4] whereas an Eastern newspaper de-

clared him a native of Devonshire.[5] North and South Carolina
asserted their divergent claims. As a general response to such inquiries Jackson turned John Reid loose among his papers to write
a biography, and addressed himself to preparations for the forthcoming meeting at the Nashville Jockey Club.

2

Much was at stake here. During the war Jackson had made
an effort to maintain his stable, with the immediate object of
defeating Jesse Haynie's chestnut mare Maria just as soon as he
could send the British about their business. When Maria humbled
his colors so thoroughly in 1811, the General punctually inaugu-
rated a search for a horse to beat her and with this quest the
fighting of three campaigns interfered only slightly. Pacolet had
been acquired while Jackson was with the Natchez expedition.
From that front the General wrote Colonel William R. Johnson
of Kentucky to send to the Hermitage "the best 4-mile horse in
Virginia, without regard to price."[6] Johnson had bought the
dapple-gray six-year-old Pacolet for one hundred and seventy-nine
dollars. He sold him to Jackson for three thousand. At home
in the summer of 1813, Jackson did not think he had made a bad
bargain. The grueling training began, but the Creek uprising
kept Old Hickory from the fall meeting that year. It was just
as well, for Pacolet injured an ankle and Jackson paid a forfeit
of five hundred dollars rather than risk defeat.

While facing the British at Mobile in the summer of 1814,
Jackson purchased Tam O'Shanter in South Carolina and Stump-
the-Dealer in Georgia to train with Pacolet. Meantime a Kentucky sportsman named DeWett turned up in Nashville with a
mare that observers thought should distance Maria. Jackson
ordered the Hermitage stables placed at his disposal. But to no
purpose. Stump-the-Dealer was scratched and Pacolet reserved
to race Doublehead. Maria easily won from Tam O'Shanter and
from the DeWett mare. But there was some balm in the fact that
Pacolet beat Doublehead, which news Jackson included in his

order to Coffee announcing the arrival of the British off the Louisiana coast.

The battle of January eighth out of the way, the General filled his letters home with expressions of solicitude for his horses and directions for their training. Yet, as the autumn meeting of 1815 approached, he felt that he had nothing fit to contend with Maria, and so gave his support to the DeWett mare and to Edward Ward's Western Light in whom he had a partnership interest. Maria was first matched against the DeWett entry in a half-mile dash for three side bets, five hundred dollars on the first quarter, five hundred on six hundred yards, and five hundred on the finish. She won all wagers, the last by a hundred feet. Then she beat Western Light, taking for her owner a bet of one thousand dollars.

But Jackson was not done. Himself an old rider, he believed that with the right jockey in the saddle the DeWett mare could best Maria over a two-mile course. Accordingly, he hired of Colonel Lynch in Virginia a negro rider named Dick who bore a great reputation. Unquestionably General Jackson was unaware of the secret of Dick's consistent triumphs, for Jackson's most unbending enemy never accused him of shady work on the track. A salient factor in Dick's success was his reputation among fellow jockeys as a conjurer. Most professional riders were negroes, usually slaves, drenched with the superstitions of their race. They were privileged and sometimes pampered characters. A skilful jockey, such as Lynch's Dick or Colonel George Elliott's hunchback Monkey Simon, would command on the block a price equal to that of a first-class race-horse. As in the case of Dick they were frequently hired at fancy figures for a single race or for a season.

The race in which Dick was to ride the DeWett mare attracted more attention than any turf event in Tennessee since Truxton had beaten Ploughboy. The match was for a side bet of one thousand dollars, Maria giving her opponent one hundred and twenty yards distance. Maria's trainer was Berry Williams, who had served in Jackson's Creek campaign and was destined for fifty years to be a figure on Western and Southern tracks. He instructed his rider to give Maria her head at the tap of the drum, take the lead and never relinquish it.

To Williams's amazement **Maria started leisurely, and the De-**Wett mare passed the stands at the end of the first **mile a good** hundred and twenty yards ahead. Williams yelled to his rider to give her the spur, but Maria kept on at the same speed until she struck the back stretch. Then the spectators saw a sight that taxed the credulity of their senses. The chestnut mare leaped forward like lightning. Such a burst of speed had never been seen on a Tennessee track. The hundred-and-twenty-yard lead diminished, vanished. Maria went ahead and thundered home the winner by one hundred and eighty yards. When Williams demanded an explanation, his rider declared that Dick had put a "spell" on him, saying that should he attempt to pass him before they had gone a mile and a quarter, he would lift him from the saddle by a wave of his whip.

Jessie Haynie offered to match Maria against any horse on earth, one to four mile heats, for five thousand dollars.

"Make it fifty thousand," exclaimed Jackson, "and consider me in with you. She can beat any horse in God's whole creation."[7]

Maria had licked Old Hickory, a circumstance so unusual that he could never forget the little mare. Twenty-two years later an old friend sat with Jackson at the Hermitage enumerating his triumphs, and no other American, before or since, has enjoyed so long or so stormy a reign as a popular idol. Was there anything Jackson ever had seriously undertaken and failed to accomplish? the friend inquired.

"Nothing that I can remember," he said simply, "except Haynie's Maria. I could not beat her."[8]

There was consolation in the fact that neither could any one else. The chestnut mare never lost a race, or a heat.

3

Five months of rest restored General Jackson's health. His fortunes were restored by the rise of tobacco and cotton prices and a timely assertion of his claim to the Duck River land obtained from the Allison heirs in 1811.[9] On October 2, 1815, his cash balance with the Nashville Bank was twenty-two thousand one hundred and seventeen dollars.[10] He yearned for activity, and poor Rachel could see there was no want of opportunities to satisfy this yearning. Meantime he seemed to have overcome, to an extent, his diffidence toward the plaudits of the multitude.

Officers of the New Orleans army, scattered to every quarter of the country, kept interest kindled with expanding sagas of their Commanding Officer, and boomed advance subscriptions for John Reid's book. "You are the favorite . . . in the *New England* States," wrote Arthur Hayne;[11] and there was much truth in the statement. Federalist leaders who had staked the political future of their party on an inglorious termination of the war found themselves deserted by their followers, with the national elections only a year away. Returning from a trip in October, William Carroll reported "many of the leading characters of . . . K.y OHio and Penna, . . . are solicitous that you should become a candidate for the next President. . . . I should be glad to know your views."[12]

What views General Jackson imparted are not known, but a few days later when, with his wife and son, he departed for Washington, ostensibly on military business, the pulses of Jackson men quickened. Another friendly observer reported that even General Adair, whose sensibilities had been ruffled by Jackson's reference to the behavior of the Kentucky troops on the west bank, "had little doubt with proper management . . . you might be elevated to the highest office in the American Government. . . . I have friends in Balto . . . of the same sentiments. . . .Will you be good enough to call on those gentlemen?"[13] Anthony Wayne Butler also sent a letter in the wake of his guardian. "On my way through Pennsylvania and Virginia I had numerous conversations with persons of the first consideration . . . and found a strong disposition . . . to run your Name for the Presidency. . . . I . . . [urge] you to stand a candidate."[14]

The reference to congressmen was important in view of the

approaching caucuses at which, according to custom, the members of Congress would designate the candidates of their respective parties. The dramatic termination of the war and the crowning misfortune of the Hartford Convention had so disorganized the Federalists that it seemed as if they might let the election go by default. Thus it only remained for the Republicans to agree on their man. James Monroe had emerged from the war with the highest prestige of any member of the Administration, not the least conspicuous feather in his cap being his mettlesome support of Jackson at New Orleans. In this way, he had associated himself with the great event that imparted a rosy cast to what otherwise would have been the unstimulating end of a war, about which the less said the better. This state of affairs placed Colonel Monroe in a position that no aspirant except William H. Crawford of Georgia dared to challenge. Although the abler man, Crawford's post as war-time minister to France had deprived him of opportunities for popular distinction. During the crisis Monroe had been both Secretary of State and of War, but when the rewards in the War Office had been reaped, Crawford was summoned home to take over this portfolio. He made considerable headway against the claims of Monroe, though it appears that many congressmen secretly hoped for a new man with sufficient popular appeal to the imagination of the electorate to justify the desertion of both announced candidates.

A collateral factor in the situation was the increasing distrust of the system of congressional nominations which the people, afflicted with the growing pains of democracy, felt excluded them from the councils that governed the nation.

In New York Aaron Burr, an outcast to whom personal aspirations were impossible, pondered the case with singular clarity and detachment. He had lost his talented Theodosia, whom he had loved even more than he had loved ambition. He desired an occupation for his mind and an activity to arouse his son-in-law, Governor Joseph Alston of South Carolina, from his brooding. And he had not forgotten the conduct of Andrew Jackson at Richmond. He wrote to Alston.

"A Congressional Caucus will, in the course of the ensuing month, nominate James Monroe for Pres'. . . . I have often heard your opinion of these Congressional Nominations. . . . Independently of the manner of the nomination . . . the Man himself is . . . Naturally dull & stupid, . . . indecisive, . . . hypocritical. . . . Pretends, I am told, to some knowledge of military matters, but never commanded a platoon. . . . In the revolutionary war . . . he acted a short time as aide to L^d. Stirling who was regularly drunk, . . . Monroe's whole duty being to fill his Lordship's Tankard. . . . As a lawyer Monroe . . . never . . . [tried] a cause of the Value of a hundred pounds.

"The Moment is extremely Auspicious for breaking down this degrading system. . . . If then there is a man in the U. S. of firmness and decision & having standing enough to afford even a hope of success it is Your duty to hold him up to public view—— That man is Andrew Jackson—— Nothing is wanting but a respectable Nomination . . . [prior to] the Proclamation of the . . . Caucus, and Jackson's success is inevitable. . . .

"Exhibit yourself then & emerge from this State of Nullity—— You owe it to yourself—— You owe it to me—— You owe it to your Country—— You owe it to the memory of the dead——"

Before posting this letter, Burr learned that Jackson was on the way to Washington. "If you have any confidential friend . . . [there] charge him to caution J against the perfidious Caresses with which he will be overwhelmed." Then a second postscript: "Our project is wonderfully advanced." Alston was to inform Jackson that "Communications have been had with every State to the Northward," and to solicit the "names of persons in the Western States . . . whom you may address."[15]

4

Joseph Alston replied that he was too encompassed by grief, "too entirely unconnected with the world," to interest himself in "anything." It did not matter, for, in his own way, Andrew Jackson had disposed of the cloud-castle of his aspiring friends.

On the first stages of the journey to the capital, he maintained a silence that was beginning to wear a significant aspect when Lynchburgh, Virginia, was reached. Here a prodigious reception awaited, to which Thomas Jefferson had come, a long day's ride from Charlottesville. This was an event in itself. Mr. Jefferson seldom had need to leave his curious mansion on the mountain. The world had pressed a path to the door, coaxing from his books, his violin and his memories an untidily attired old man richest in honors of living Americans, though master of Monticello only by the indulgence of creditors. Mr. Jefferson and General Jackson had not met since 1798, and, since Jackson's speech on the State-House green at Richmond, few had been willing to sponsor a reunion—a situation that very nearly had kept Andrew Jackson out of the war.

At a banquet attended by three hundred persons, the founder of the Republican Party lifted his glass.

"Honor and gratitude to those who have filled the measure of their country's honor."

General Jackson responded.

"James Monroe, late Secretary of War."[16]

The estrangement was over, and without loss of countenance by either party. Jackson had supported Monroe for president against Jefferson's candidate, Madison, in 1808. But the philosophic Jefferson possessed the seemly faculty of retaining a personal regard for some of the men from whom he differed politically. James Monroe had studied law in his office and the exigencies of politics had failed to disturb their social relations. Now Mr. Jefferson supported his old pupil's aspirations for the presidency, and was delighted to see that General Jackson did so.

A mind less embittered than Aaron Burr's might have discerned a motive beneath the shining surface of the welcome the Administration gave Andrew Jackson in the capital. Young John Reid could hardly find time for a personal letter. "To tell every thing would require a book. . . . This week . . . two *special invitations* to dinner; one . . . from *Jimmy* [Monroe] *himself*, the other . . . from Dolly and her husband." At first the traveling biographer

was more than a little apprehensive over the outcome of his sub
ject's call on the Secretary of War. There had been some talk of a
polite, though official, request for additional enlightenment on
the Hall-Louaillier business at New Orleans. Jackson ascended
the steps of the War Office *"fully prepared"* to give it. Mr. Crawford was not in the city and the acting Secretary, Mr. Dallas, received the General who launched impulsively into his exposition.
Mr. Dallas interrupted. Explanations were not in order. Anything General Jackson had done at New Orleans was quite all
right. "The President as well as the heads of departments" were
happy and satisfied. John Reid breathed easier. "I think now I
see the horizon *blue before me.*"[17]

And so thought Andrew Jackson when his sojourn in the
city was ended and his carriage jolted over the frozen January
roads toward Tennessee. So thought Rachel from whose spirit
a weight of dread had been lifted by that toast at Lynchburgh.
But her husband had plowed and sown another field.

Next to New Orleans Andrew Jackson regarded the Creek
treaty as his most enduring claim to fame. Speaking from the
conviction of experience, he had fired the mind of Monroe with a
vision of this wilderness empire transformed into homesteads, a
perpetual diadem for the crown of the new Administration. The
old frontiersman's blood raced to contemplate the sweat and
smoke and hurly-burly of it all. Through the management of
Mr. Monroe General Jackson was charged, in broad language,
with the pacification of the Southern border, where, under British
and Spanish influence and the crushing terms of the treaty, the
Indians were becoming restive again. Commissioners had been
ordered into the field to survey the conquered lands. Jackson
was delegated to protect them. And upon himself he took the
additional responsibility of seeing that their lines should embrace
the ultimate acre nominated in the bond.

Yet this could not be the end. No open-minded person could
devote an hour's consideration to the subject without appreciating
the futility of efforts for permanent peace in the South as long as
Florida remained in the hands of Spain. Mr. Jefferson had

initiated pourparlers for purchase of the province, but the matter lagged. At the head of an army on the border, Jackson might become a providential instrument for bringing these negotiations to a satisfactory conclusion; and certain it seems that he and Monroe had discussed this delicate contingency without reserve.[18]

Thus the scope of the alluring task Andrew Jackson had set to round out his public career.

5

At Nashville a letter awaited from John Coffee, the only one of the three commissioners designated to run the Creek treaty lines who was at his post. The Indians were in bad temper, and, without waiting for his colleagues, Coffee had begun work alone. Warmly complimenting his old friend, Jackson told him to proceed irrespective of the other commissioners. To the Indians he dispatched a succinct warning and himself started south to make a general reconnaissance.[19]

He rode with a heavy heart, having just received news of the death of John Reid. Jackson had grown extremely fond of this gifted young man. They had parted at Reid's home, in Virginia, where John desired to remain at the bedside of a sister hopelessly ill of consumption. The General and Rachel had slipped away leaving a note of farewell. "How can I apologise for not taking leave of your amiable mother & sisters? I have but one [excuse]. I saw their distress I was fear full (if Possible) it would heighten their sorrow—— I could not bear to take leave of the family and not bid adieu to the *amiable* the *dying Maria.*"[20] A fortnight after the burial of Maria her brother was stricken with a mysterious fever and died in twenty-four hours. Jackson resolved that the biography should be finished and the proceeds reserved for Reid's widow and little children in Tennessee. He volunteered to advance the cost of printing. Deluged with offers to complete the book, he accepted that of John Henry Eaton, a wealthy lawyer and planter of Franklin, Tennessee, with a frontier reputation for scholarship.

The tour of observation inevitably brought the General to New Orleans. At a private gathering Judge Hall offered his hand. "I received it and . . . my mind . . . tells me I have done right. . . . The hatchet is buried."[21]

Prospects for peace in other quarters, however, were not so re-assuring. British agents, operating from the safe refuge of Florida, had spread the report among the Creeks that the treaty of Ghent required the United States to restore the lands Jackson had taken from them. Another source of alarm was Negro Fort on the Apalachicola River in Florida sixty miles below the Georgia line. This stronghold had been built by the British during the war. With three thousand small arms and a thousand barrels of powder, it was now in the hands of fugitive slaves under the determined leadership of one of their number named Garçon. With the horrors of Santo Domingo fresh in Southern minds, Georgia was in a state of excitement. Jackson told Gaines to awe the Indians with a show of force and gave him permission to destroy Negro Fort "regardless of the ground it stands on."[22]

En route home he wrote his old partner in trade, John Hutchings. "A great speck'l [speculation] . . . on the allabama" seemed imminent and was more than the old fortune hunter could resist. "I have been making some conditional contracts for land on the coast, and am . . . [contemplating] the purchase of a sugar estate."[23]

The great speculations and the private plans and public policies of General Jackson were thrown into confusion by the action of Secretary of War Crawford in modifying the celebrated Creek treaty.

With the preoccupations of war past, the drum-head nature of the procedure by which Jackson had "negotiated" this instrument had gradually become apparent. To effect his ends the American peacemaker had snatched at will lands from friendly as well as hostile Creeks. This was well known. Now it transpired that in the twenty-three million ceded acres were four million belonging to neither Creek faction but to the Cherokees and Choctaws who had been Jackson's allies in the war against Weatherford. Indian boundaries were always vague, and the General had recognized a shadowy Creek claim to this territory solely that he might include it in the booty.

Crawford returned the four million acres to the Cherokees and Choctaws. The announcement was made a few days after the Congressional Caucus had given Monroe, by the surprisingly narrow margin of eleven votes, the Republican nomination that was equivalent to election. It probably afforded the Secretary additional satisfaction to endow his act of justice with the color of a rebuke to his successful rival's agent in the Southwest.

The effects of the admonishment were short-lived, however, and gained for Mr. Crawford only the unrelenting enmity of Andrew Jackson. A howl went up from the West, and Madison sent Jackson to get the land back. He succeeded, naturally, though not without having to pay the Cherokees and Choctaws one hundred and eighty thousand dollars. Jackson bargained as closely over this indemnity as if it were to come from his own pocket.[24] Meantime Gaines had blown up Negro Fort, killing two hundred and seventy of its occupants, and a measure of peace settled on the Southern border.[25]

6

But an uncertain peace in more ways than one, and President-Elect Monroe began to choose his Cabinet with care.

He declined to select as Secretary of War the man of Jackson's choice, William H. Drayton of South Carolina, turning to Henry Clay who loftily refused the place as unworthy of his attainments. Clay wished to be Secretary of State, a post also coveted by William H. Crawford, whose presidential hopes, though deferred, had not been abandoned. Mr. Monroe disappointed both of these men, however, and earmarked the Department of State for John Quincy Adams, late minister to England and member, with Mr. Clay, of the peace commission at Ghent. This son of the second President was a singular man—polished, learned and lonely—who after three decades of unselfish and distinguished devotion to the public service remained virtually without one intimate personal or political friend. Yet a youthful aloofness, deepening to austerity, masked a wistful heart and at times an almost romantic turn of mind. Adams was fifty, but years of unremitting labor and intellectual solitude had given a drawn and set cast to once-handsome features, and he looked older than he was. To see him now it seemed incredible that he should have confessed, even in the privacy of his thoughts, to a secret boyhood passion for a Parisian actress.

Mr. Monroe made a restrained gesture of tendering the War Office to Jackson, "tho' I doubted whether I ought ... to draw you from the command of the army to the South, where in case of any emergency no one could supply your place."[26] Jackson did what seems to have been expected of him and declined. "I have looked forward to that happy period when ... I would retire from public life" as soon as the frontier should be safe.[27]

The interim of superficial tranquillity continued big with change. In the East, the gilded aura of lush prosperity had begun to pale as our young factories met the strangling competition of European imports. This swelled the torrent of settlers plunging toward the Edens of the frontier—Ohio and Indiana in the North and, with the Administration's especial benediction, General Jackson's Alabama acquisitions in the South. In the face of great rivalry for this choice site, the Cypress Land Company bought at government auction an immense acreage below the Muscle Shoals of the Tennessee River toward which architects of empire had cast longing glances since the days of John Donelson, the elder. John Coffee was a leading spirit of the Cypress Land Company and Jackson owned a few shares of its stock. This concern laid out the town of Florence where speculation reached its climax, town lots selling for thirty-five hundred dollars and near-by cotton land for eighty dollars an acre. Jackson acquired a lot or two and some of the cotton land, paying for the latter two dollars an acre which was the lowest bid the government would entertain.[28] But by common understanding, when the great benefactor who had made this land available came forward with an offer, no one bid against him. John Henry Eaton and Captain John Donelson, junior, likewise expressed their confidence in the ultimate issue of events by making a heavy purchase in Florida.

Money for these ventures gushed from the strong boxes of Western banks. Tennessee's banking policy remained fairly conservative, only two institutions being chartered in addition to the now celebrated Nashville Bank in which Andrew Jackson was a small stockholder. But across the line in Kentucky were fifty-nine banks, or seventeen more than in the State of New York, all of them printing their own currency. This display of fictitious capital made credit easy. Farms uncleared were mortgaged, crops yet unsowed were pledged and the money used to enlarge the ever-expanding rainbow of speculation.

A Tidewater atmosphere began to drift with the blue mists across the Appalachians. The Cumberland Valley was frontier no longer. The début of William Carroll's steamboat, the *Andrew Jackson*, on the sea-green water was a spectacle as certain to draw an audience as the General himself. Sons were building fine houses on the sites of their fathers' cabins. Life slipped into a slower tempo, gaining in grace what it lost in robustness. One generation had tamed the land, another was being tamed by it. The Cotton Kingdom was being planted, its astonishing harvest to bring forth, to subjugate, and one day destroy an era.

Change, change. Within the same month two youthful faces vanished from the Hermitage family circle. John—"Jacky"—Donelson III died in military service on the Alabama and his brother Andrew Jackson Donelson departed for West Point. "On these children," confided General Jackson to their grandfather, old General Daniel Smith, "I had built my hopes for happiness in my declining days. . . . They . . . always appeared as my own."[29]

Jackson looked back upon his own student days at Salisbury with a degree of perspective. "I was but a raw lad then."[30] He hoped Cadet Donelson might be something better. "in your intercourse with the world . . . be courteous to all, but make confidents of few [as] a young man is too apt to form opinions on speecious shows . . and to bestow confidence . . . [unwisely].

Amonghst the virtuous females you ought to cultivate an acquaintance, and shun ... the others. ... I recommend economy ... [but] shun parsomony. ... You are authorized to draw on me for money."[31]

Mr. Monroe's difficulties in filling the War Office to his satisfaction continued, and for several months the post remained in the hands of an acting secretary, George Graham, a hold-over from the Madison régime. On the day Monroe assumed the presidency, March 4, 1817, Jackson wrote him a lengthy letter, departing from the theme of ardent congratulation only long enough to pick a bone with the War Department. Graham had ordered a major of engineers from Jackson's jurisdiction to New York without consulting the Southern Commander. To Monroe Jackson remonstrated against this irregularity. Had the President replied by return post Jackson would not have had his letter in less than forty days. He waited forty-nine days and then issued an order forbidding subordinates to obey the commands of the War Depart ment unless they should come through him.[32] This remarkable military paper made the rounds of the press, and in August the New York *Columbian* published an article characterizing it as an effort by Jackson to protect his favorites. An anonymous correspondent forwarded this to Jackson, with the salty observation that it had been written by Winfield Scott who had called the order "an act of mutiny."[33] This drew from Jackson a courteous letter to Scott expressing disbelief in the report, but asking Scott's assurance to that effect.[34]

Winfield Scott was an ambitious major general without command, and he seems to have been very badly informed as to the character of his Southern colleague. Otherwise it is difficult to believe that he would have replied in a vein so condescending and contentious. Though disclaiming authorship of the newspaper article, General Scott admitted having privately pronounced the order in question "mutinous ... and ... a reprimand of the ... President"—a sentiment he was quite at liberty to entertain, but his manner of expressing it was subtly provocative.[35] Jackson's rejoinder was a challenge to a duel in language that does not materially enhance his reputation for moderation. Disdaining the use of "tinsel rhetoric" he undertook to render his meaning clear by calling the Northern general *"a hectoring bully"* and one of an undisclosed number of *"intermeddling pimps and spies of the War Department."*[36] Scott replied that his correspondent had the better of him as a master of epithet and declined an affair of honor on religious grounds, adding that his life would be risked to a better purpose in "the next war."[37]

General Jackson enlivened this period of military inactivity with further proof that his talents for unproductive controversy amounted, at times, to genius. In Kentucky a history of the war had appeared, with some critical observations on Jackson's attitude toward the Kentucky troops on the west bank at New Orleans, which the General noticed in a letter to the *Kentucky Reporter*. "A forgery of the blackest kind," "wicked, willful and corrupt" and "Spanish dish" were some of the gems that dropped from his pen. John Adair came forward with a defense of the Kentuckians. After a spirited exchange of letters, Jackson prepared a third communication which William Carroll apparently was able to persuade his chief to withhold, on the well-reasoned assumption that "You stand on too high an emminence to gratify the Editors of the Kentucky news papers."[38]

Meanwhile another of the General's wards, Edward George Washington Butler, took his departure for West Point, and the prolific correspondent paused in the midst of the Kentucky conflict to indite a word of counsel to Andrew Jackson Donelson. "My son, I wish you ... and Edward ... to live in the harmony of brothers ... and by ... obedience to your superiors ... merit ... the Esteem ... of all."[39]

7

Over these scenes crept the shadow of Florida, rendered more portentous by the rumble of revolution that rocked Spain's fabulous empire from the Louisiana border to Tierra del Fuego. During his sojourn in Washington, General Jackson and Colonel Monroe had discussed the prospect as practical men, and allusions to the subject continued in their correspondence. Monroe referred to his subordinate's unsponsored seizure of Pensacola in 1814. "I was not very severe on you for giving the blow, nor ought I have been for a thousand considerations, which I need not mention."[40] In point of fact very little need be mentioned between these gentlemen who understood each other perfectly. Monroe expressed his pleasure at the swarming of settlers upon the Jackson treaty lands. "As soon as our population gains a decided preponderance in those regions Florida will hardly be considered by Spain as a part of her dominions."[41] Very well put, Mr. Monroe.

Mexico was in revolt, affording fresh employment in freedom's cause to a number of military characters of vague nationality who had stood behind the mud wall of Rodriquez Canal. Weary of repose and honors, Jean Laffite sailed for Galveston Bay and once more the diversion of Spanish cargoes contributed to the prosperous appearance of Royal Street. From the cluttered desk of Edward Livingston emanated proof of the impeccable legality of everything. He kept Jackson informed, and, carried away by the clarity of his demonstration of the high-minded zeal of his clients, importuned the General to go to Texas and lead them.[42]

This activity served the useful purpose of inserting one more thorn in the flesh of Spain. But with the sure instinct that so often enabled him to pick the essential thing from a jungle of miscellaneous detail, Andrew Jackson kept his eyes on Florida. There was much of interest to follow: fortifications stripped of troops to oppose dominions in revolt; Pensacola with "not enough Gunpowder to fire a salute;"[43] Spanish authority sunk to a charade of shabby grandeur.

Then as now the lazy waters of St. Mary's River formed part of the boundary between Florida and Georgia. In the Atlantic, off the mouth of this international stream within gunshot of shore, lay Amelia Island on whose sands sprawled the village of Fernandina. It was a poor and impermanent-looking place of wood and thatch and sunburnt plaster, but these appearances were deceptive. The current value of chattels stored in the flimsy shacks was something like five hundred thousand dollars. Fernandina was the

Barataria and the Galveston of the Atlantic, maintaining about the same cordial relations with merchants in Savannah, Charleston and Baltimore as did the Laffites with New Orleans. A decent regard for some of the freer traditions of smuggling enabled the Fernandians to surpass in volume the commerce of their rivals in the Gulf. Perhaps the high mark of conservatism in the profession was established when Messrs. Laffite and Livingston declined traffic in negroes, who, since the war, had become one of the most profitable items in the American import trade. The result was a scarcity of field-hands in Louisiana. Livingston purchased a plantation, and, hearing that Jackson had forty negroes for sale, he offered twenty-four thousand dollars for the lot, eight thousand down.[44]

In June of 1817, an attractive professional adventurer from South American fields named Gregor MacGregor convinced a coterie of Baltimore business men that, without injury to their interests, they could assist the sacred cause of liberty by financing the deliverance of Fernandina from the "yoke" of Spain. Accordingly, he "captured" the town, wrote some marvelous proclamations and departed in quest of reenforcements. During his absence "Commodore" Louis Aury, late client of Edward Livingston and associate of Jean Laffite, dropped in from Galveston with a stolen ship, the *Mexico Libre,* and declared Amelia Island a part of the Mexican Republic. These incidents so disturbed the settled order of smuggling along the Atlantic coast that persons of influence began to complain. Meantime our perpetual negotiations for the purchase of Florida emerged from a period of hibernation, and President Monroe saw in the Amelia Island situation a chance to apply pressure upon Spain. A naval expedition was ordered to send Aury on his way and to hold Fernandina in trust for His Catholic Majesty.

While this sturdy feat of diplomacy was being realized, Brevet Major General Gaines attacked a party of Seminoles at Fowltown just north of the Florida border. These Indians had declined to vacate lands included in the Creek cession of 1814. The Administration had expected trouble with them, and was prepared for it, entirely aware that the Seminoles, like the buccaneers of Amelia, might serve as convenient pawns in the larger gamble for Florida. The War Department ordered Gaines to continue his offensive against the Indians, pursuing them into Spanish territory if necessary, but to molest no Spanish military post without further instructions.

8

Andrew Jackson had declared he would resign from the Army, rather than withdraw his celebrated order forbidding subordinates to obey commands of the War Department unless transmitted through him. With the Florida crisis looming the President wrote a long and conciliatory letter, begging Jackson not to leave the service at such a moment, but stating frankly that he could not accept "this order [which] involves the naked principle of the power of the Executive over the ... army."[45] Jackson's friend, Congressman John Rhea, intervened in behalf of the President. Every member of the Administration, he said, including William H. Crawford, now Secretary of Treasury, wished Jackson to retain his command.[46] With the naval force against Aury on the sea, a compromise was arranged in which Monroe went as far as a President could go without abdicating his authority.[47]

In this arrangement the President was skilfully counseled by the man he had finally selected for Secretary of War—John Caldwell Calhoun—and if one may judge by the vigor with which the Secretary attacked his duties, Mr. Monroe must have been glad he had taken his time to fill this post. The new Cabinet officer was a restless man, with darting eyes, and a swift speech in which lingered a trace of something Andrew Jackson would have recognized instantly. For Calhoun was Back-Country Scotch-Irish from South Carolina, his forebears even more obscure than Jackson's. After Yale and a marriage that ended financial anxieties, he had gone to Congress in 1811 as a War Hawk. His career in the House was sufficiently distinguished to cause him, at thirty-five, to think twice before taking the War Office.

On December 26, 1817, Mr. Calhoun ordered General Jackson to

Georgia. His instructions were very broad. "Adopt the necessary measures to terminate . . . [the] conflict."[48]

While Mr. Calhoun's communication was on the way to Tennessee, General Jackson received a copy of the Gaines order which the Department had previously forwarded as a matter of information. At a glance he perceived its weakness, and, not for the first time in his life, undertook to stiffen the spine of an executive. "Suppose," he wrote Monroe, "the Indians . . . take refuge in either Pensacola or St. Augustine. . . . General Gaines . . . has to halt before the . . . [town and] communicate with his Government; in the meantime the militia grows restless, and he has to defend himself with regulars. The enemy, with the aid of Spanish friends and Woodbines British Partizens, or, if you please, with Aury's force, attacks him, what may not be the result? defeat and massacre."

General Jackson proposed a simpler plan. "The whole of East Florida [should be] seized and . . . this can be done without implicating the Government." How? "Let it be signified to me through any channel, (say Mr. J. Rhea) that the possession of the Floridas would be desirable . . . and in sixty days it will be accomplished."[49]

Five days after this letter had started north the order for Jackson to supersede Gaines reached Nashville. By the same post came a note from the President. "The mov'ment . . . against the Seminoles . . . will bring you on a theatre where you may possibly have other services to perform. . . . Great interests are at issue. . . . This is not a time for repose . . . untill our cause is carried triumphantly thro'."[50]

"Other services. . . . Great interests. . . . Our cause." Mr. Monroe seemed to be himself again.

CHAPTER XVIII

THE FLORIDA ADVENTURE

I

MR. MONROE's patriotic importunities were scarcely necessary to stir the General from his "repose." A brigade of New Orleans veterans was called to arms. The Governor of Tennessee being absent, Jackson swore them in on his personal responsibility. When funds for their equipment gave out, he advanced four thousand dollars from his private purse. Eleven days after receiving the orders from Washington he was on the road with the advance guard of two mounted companies. "My love, . . . I have left you . . . with greater regret than I have ever done. I hope that God who controls the destinies of nations . . . will permit me to return to you in a short time. . . . With my prayers for your preservation and happiness. . . . adieu."[1]

On the night of February 13, 1818, the advance-guard bivouacked on the bank of Big Creek, four miles from Hartford, Georgia. There Jackson received a packet of mail among which, as he always claimed, was a letter from Representative Rhea transmitting President Monroe's "approval" of Jackson's suggestion to effect an unofficially authorized seizure of Florida and let the diplomats sweep up the débris. In later years, when the incident became the core of a muddy controversy, Monroe denied that he had empowered Rhea to convey any such assurances. In my opinion the evidence favors Monroe's contention on this specific point. On the other hand—and this is far more important—the evidence is clear that the Administration understood General Jackson's intentions toward Florida, and, by the absence of any restraining sign or syllable, gave its consent to them. For instance, after he received word of the occupation of St. Marks, Secretary of War Calhoun wrote Governor Bibbs of Alabama: "General Jackson is vested with full power to conduct the war as he may think best."[2] Mr. Calhoun knew perfectly what Andrew Jackson thought "best" for Florida, having, indeed, read the General's unambiguous letter to Monroe, the answer to which, Jackson asserted, was received at Big Creek.

Be that as it may, during the night of March ninth, General Jackson reached Fort Scott, near the Florida border, and at dawn took formal command of eight hundred Regulars and nine hundred Georgia militia. The militia was restless and all were hungry, but Andrew Jackson was no stranger to such conditions. With one quart of corn and three rations of meat per man, the army took up the line of march for Florida at noon. Streams were bank high and the trail was a quagmire. In five days the struggling column gained the site of Negro Fort, where a boat-load of army flour ascending the Apalachicola, by permission of the Spanish authorities, provided the first square meal the troops had eaten in three weeks. The next day they were put on half rations and set to repairing the fort while the Commander took stock of his situation.

"It is reported to me that Francis and Peter McQueen," Creek leaders who had fled to Florida after their defeat in 1814, "are now exciting the Seminoles to ... acts of hostility.... With them it is stated ... [are] Woodbine, Arbuthnot and other foreigners."[3]

2

Francis, Woodbine, Arbuthnot. . . .

When General Jackson traced those names, he struck deeply into the dark pattern of Florida politics where the practised hand of England had not ceased from troubling. After the battle of New Orleans Colonel Edward Nicholls had returned to his old stamping-ground. He negotiated a military alliance with the Florida Indians—Spanish subjects and American fugitives—and sailed in triumph to London with the chief Francis. This was a bit too raw and the Foreign Office felt compelled to repudiate the treaty, but sent Francis home with marks of friendship including the scarlet regalia of a brigadier-general. Then came Captain George Woodbine, whose official connection with Whitehall was more tenuous, though when occasion required he signed himself "on His Britannic Majesty's service in the Floridas." With an eye for his own prospects as well as those of his sovereign, the Captain had acquired a grant of land which would be his to enjoy only in the event that the province remained out of American hands. The transaction brought the interests of Captain Woodbine in collision with those of General Jackson's Tennessee neighbors, Eaton and Donelson, whose Florida investments had been made with other expectations in view.

The last personage on the scene was Alexander Arbuthnot, a Scottish merchant of Nassau who appeared in the province as a trader, and, by charging the Indians honest prices and taking an interest in their welfare, established a profitable commerce. This abuse of the ethics of the Indian trade estranged other mercantile interests in Florida, notably the celebrated Scottish house of Forbes & Company, which, seeing how the wind was blowing, had begun amicable intrigues with the Americans. Arbuthnot went his way. In his seventy years he had acquired a suit of flowing white hair and a gentle though confident air with the world. He had no official connection with his government, and regarded Woodbine as a man of low principles. His only friends were Indians. "They have been ill treated by the English," he wrote in his diary, "and robbed by the Americans," but he regarded the Americans as the worse offenders and made no effort to conceal his opinion. Beside secret council fires he became immersed in Indian statecraft, and, by accepting a power of attorney from the Creek refugees, gave to his utterances a cast that brought upon his person a burden of responsibility. The wildest rumors concerning him reached the United States. The authoritative Niles's *Register* of Baltimore declared Alexander Arbuthnot to be Woodbine in disguise, and, if captured, that he should suffer the fate of "a sheep-killing dog."

Jackson received word that the Indians had demanded arms of

the Spanish commandant at St. Marks and were probably now in possession of the town. He marched at once, sending Naval Lieutenant Isaac McKeever with a few small gunboats to blockade the west coast of the peninsula and prevent escape of the fugitives by water. Without resistance, Jackson lowered the Spanish colors from the stone fort at St. Marks. But the Indians had departed and the Americans' only prisoner was an old gentleman with snowy hair, taken in the commandant's quarters while preparing for flight. Mr. Arbuthnot accepted arrest quietly, and General Jackson spared a moment to record the events of the week.

"St. marks, April 8, 1818
"My Love, on the 1st of april I . . . had a small affair with the Indians in which we lost one man killed (Tucker) and four wounded all Tennesseens. . . . Entered the Town of St. marks on yesterday. . . . Capt [Lieutenant] McKeever . . . was fortunate enough to capture on board his flotilla the noted Francis the prophet and Homollimicke [another Creek chief and leader in a recent massacre]. . . . The Capt having the British colours flying they supposed him to be part of Woodbines Fleet. . . . These were hung this morning. I found in St. marks the noted Scotch villain Arbuthnot. . . . I hold him for trial. I leave Tomorrow in hopes . . . with the smiles of heaven to put an end to the war. . . . Kiss my Two sons and accept my prayers for your health and happiness until I return yr affectionate Husband."[4]

"My two sons" were Andrew, junior, and his Creek Indian playmate, Lincoyer.

General Jackson left St. Marks on schedule. Plunging into a jungle that had changed little since De Soto's time, he hoped to surprise the Indians at the village of Chief Boleck (or Bowlegs) on the Suwanee River, one hundred and seven miles away. Two skirmishes barely interrupted the march. Boleck's place was reached in eight days. The reed huts were empty. The Chief and his people had scattered like quail into the swamps. But during the night there blundered into an American picket Lieutenant Robert C. Ambrister of the Royal Colonial Marines, and another

Englishman, Peter B. Cook, probably the two most astonished persons in Florida.

On one of their negro servants was found a letter from Arbuthnot to his son. "Tell my friend, Bowleck, that he is throwing his people away to attempt to resist such a powerful force as will be drawn on Sahwahnee."[5] Cook admitted that the letter had been read to the Indians, and General Jackson began to understand why he had advanced two hundred and thirty miles into Florida's wet wilderness without meeting the Indians in a proper battle.

3

The one hundred and seven miles from St. Marks to the Suwanee, over which no white army had passed before, had been covered in eight days. Returning, Jackson made it in five, and, on the morning of April 26, 1818, issued an order for the trial of Arbuthnot and Ambrister. The court met at noon in the stone fort. Eight of its members were officers of the Regular service, five of the militia or volunteers. The president was General Gaines who had presided over the court martial at New Orleans which disappointed the anticipations of the Commander in the trial of Louis Louaillier.

Arbuthnot was arraigned on charges of exciting the Indians to war, spying and giving aid to the enemy. Two witnesses for the prosecution were agents of Forbes & Company whose hostility to the prisoner impairs faith in their testimony. A third witness was Ambrister's companion, Peter B. Cook, who bore Arbuthnot a grudge. His story that Arbuthnot had warned Boleck of Jackson's advance was corroborated, however, by John Lewis Phoenix, master of the prisoner's schooner. Moreover the documentary evidence found aboard this vessel was clear and uncontroverted. In Arbuthnot's handwriting were appeals from Boleck and other chiefs to the British Governor at Nassau for troops, arms and ammunition with which to fight the Americans; communications in the Indians' behalf to the British Minister at Washington and to the Governor of Havana; statistics on the strength of the hostile

Indians and the munitions they needed to wage war.[6] On the twenty-seventh the case against Arbuthnot was completed and he was given until four o'clock the following afternoon to prepare his defense.

The second prisoner to face the court presented an appearance in contrast with that of the aged and anxious merchant. Robert Christy Ambrister was a well-born English adventurer who had lived by the sword in many lands and climes. Wounded on the field of Waterloo he was made a member of Napoleon's guard at St. Helena. Then, in the Orient, he had been suspended from command for a year for dueling. Coming to Nassau to pass this enforced vacation as a guest of his uncle, Governor Cameron, he fell in with George Woodbine. As a soldier Ambrister knew the gravity of his position and the weight of the evidence against him. To a charge of "assuming command of the Indians in . . . war with the United States," he pleaded "guilty, and justification."[7]

At four o'clock on April twenty-eighth Arbuthnot was called in to offer his defense. His language was dignified. He wished to avoid, he said, an appeal to sympathy, "though I am persuaded that sympathy no where more abounds than in a generous American breast." With some justice he argued against the admissibility of certain evidence. He admitted the sale of ten kegs of powder to Boleck, but contended this was no more than the Indians needed for hunting. No explanation of the damaging contents of "sundry letters purporting to be written by myself" was attempted, however, and the manifest evidence that they had been written by Arbuthnot remained unchallenged. "May it please the honorable court I close my reply . . . fully persuaded that should there be cause for censure my judges will . . . lean on the side of mercy."[8]

He was found guilty and sentenced to be hanged. Such was the retribution of "the noted Scotch villain" whose principal villainy had been to treat the Indians decently, without regard for the United States, his own country, General Jackson, or any one. Yet, taking a military view of the evidence, he was guilty as charged.

At five o'clock Ambrister faced the bar   The attractions of this prisoner's personality had won him many well-wishers among the officers of General Jackson's army. Ambrister was an excellent talker. His cell was crowded every evening. Summoned to plead for his life, he detained the court no more than sixty seconds with a word of appreciation of its courtesies and a frank petition for mercy.

The verdict of a court martial is determined by the vote of two-thirds of its members. On a poll of the court Ambrister was sentenced to be shot. After the finding had been recorded, one member asked to reconsider his vote with the result that the sentence was reduced to fifty lashes and confinement for one year.

The following morning, while the army was falling in to march, Andrew Jackson approved the sentence of Arbuthnot "and . . . the finding and first sentence . . . of Robert C. Ambrister, and disapproves the reconsideration."[9] The prisoners received the word of doom stoically. A drum beat assembly for the platoon assigned to conduct the executions.

"There," said Ambrister, "a sound I have heard in every quarter of the globe, and now for the last time."[10]

A girl in London was waiting to marry him.

4

In four days Jackson was back at Fort Gadsden, as the new post on the site of Negro Fort had been named.

On May fifth he notified Calhoun that he would invade West Florida and probably take Pensacola. On the seventh he marched. "The continued wading of water . . . first destroyed our horses, and next our shoes, the men are literanny barefoot."[11] On the twenty-fifth Pensacola was invested. On the twenty-eighth it surrendered. On the twenty-ninth, in the most sweeping exemplification of imperial powers he had exercised in Florida, Jackson seized the royal archives, appointed one of his colonels military and civil governor, and declared in force "the revenue laws of the U. States."[12]

On May thirtieth he departed for Tennessee and the frontier's acclaim of his exploits billowed across the mountains. It was the diplomats' turn now.

5

They had their work cut out. One dispatch after another, like chapters of a swashbuckling serial, apprised Washington of Andrew Jackson's career in Florida. "The storm," wrote John Quincy Adams, "is rapidly thickening."

On the night of July seventh the Secretary was routed from his bed by a message that Don Luis de Oñis, the Spanish Minister, had rushed back to the city. Members of the Administration, Mr. Adams excepted, stood a little in awe of this vigorous official whose commanding presence breathed a semblance of life into the hollow shell of Spanish power. Only a fortnight before James Monroe had begun to rest easier when the smooth assurances of his Secretary of State sent the Minister away to enjoy the cooling breezes of his summer place in Pennsylvania. He returned in the middle of the night with a surging communication on the subject of Florida. "In the name of the King, my master, I demand a prompt restitution of St. Mark's, Pensacola, Barrancas, and all other places wrested by General Jackson from the Crown of Spain. I demand . . . indemnity for all injuries and losses, and the punishment of the general."[13]

For three days the Cabinet met at noon and continued in session until five, the members dispersing exhausted by the heat of the weather and of their discussions. At the outset, as Adams recorded in his diary, "the President and all the members, . . . except myself, are of the opinion that Jackson acted not only without, but against his instructions; that he has committed war upon Spain, . . . which if not disavowed" would ruin the Administration. Calhoun and Crawford took the lead in urging the restoration of the captured forts and a flat disavowal of Jackson's acts, the Secretary of War going so far as to intimate that the General was a party to the Eaton-Donelson land gamble. Their arguments impressed the President. Jackson had not made out a case for himself, de-

clared Mr. Monroe, with an anxious allusion to what the newspapers were saying about the danger to the Administration's prestige. He referred to the Crawford organs in Virginia and Georgia
which already had set themselves to advance the political fortunes
of their man at the expense of the Florida campaign.

Against them all stood the thin-lipped, perspiring New Eng-
lander, who had spent a third of his life abroad and had not the
remotest connection with the mottled Western intrigue against
Florida from which Monroe now sought to disengage himself.
Adams contended that Jackson was guilty of "no real ... violation
of his instructions; that his proceedings were justified by ... necessity." Did the Administration, he asked, wish to deal with him
as Elizabeth had dealt with Walter Raleigh—to have the benefit
of his services, and then abandon him? Thus John Quincy Adams
championed Andrew Jackson's cause at every turn, until, at the
end of the third day, his hands trembled from fatigue so that he
was obliged to neglect his famous diary.[14]

On the fourth day, June 18, 1818, the Cabinet made its decisions.
Though his opinion had prevailed in part, Adams characterized
them as "weakness and confession of weakness." He prepared a
note to de Oñis stating that in taking the posts Jackson had acted
on his own responsibility for which, however, he could not be cen-
sured, and that the forts would be given up. Attorney-General
Wirt drafted for the press a paragraph calculated to conciliate all
shades of popular opinion. So much for the Administration's endeavor to appease Spain and the public. Another, and equally
delicate, task remained—that of appeasing Andrew Jackson. The
President took this upon himself.

6

His long letter opened with the interesting assurance that
"nothing" would be withheld. General Jackson had been called
into service, wrote Mr. Monroe, under orders previously issued to
General Gaines. These instructions sanctioned an invasion of
Spanish territory, but precluded the occupation of military posts.

"An order to attack a Spanish post would ... authorize war" which was more than a President could do. "Congress alone possesses the power." Therefore, "in transcending the limits prescribed by those orders you acted on your own responsibility."

But on this point the President sought to put his subordinate at ease. "I am aware that cases may occur when the commanding general, acting on his own responsibility, may safely pass the limit ... [of his orders] with essential advantage to his country." For instance: "The officers and troops of the neutral power forget ... their neutral character; they stimulate the enemy to make war; they furnish ... arms; ... they take an active part in their favor. ... The general ... pursues them to their post, ... attacks and carries it, and rests on those acts for his justification."

The flaw in this justification was that the General had not thought of it first. His dispatches omitted to aver that Spanish officers had incited the Seminoles to war, furnished arms or participated in the struggle. True Jackson had said something about the occupation of St. Marks and Pensacola being necessary to the pursuit of the enemy, but his words were not explicit. The President dropped the subject for a moment, however, and addressed himself to the more ticklish business of excusing the return of those posts to Spain.

"If the Executive refused to evacuate . . . [them] it is not improbable that war would immediately follow, . . . and we do not foresee that we should have a single power in Europe on our side. Why risk these consequences? . . . There is much reason to presume that this act will furnish a strong inducement to Spain to cede the territory, providing we do not wound her too deeply. . . . The manner in which we propose to act will exculpate you from censure, and promises to obtain all the advantages you contemplate."

Now back to the matter of justification. The President said it would be necessary to establish that the posts had been seized in retaliation for the misconduct of Spanish officers. "You must aid in procuring the documents necessary for this purpose. Those you sent ... do not, I am satisfied, do justice to the cause.... Your letters to the Department were written in haste, under the pressure of fatigue.... If you think it proper to authorize the secretary or myself to correct ... [certain] passages, it will be done with care."[15]

Unlike Napoleon, whom he admired for many things, the Commander of the Southern Division did not regard history as a fable agreed upon. His Florida dispatches remain in the files of the War Department as he wrote them. Nor is this the only evidence of the Jacksonian touch that illuminates the reply to James Monroe. The elaborate war scare was not mentioned. The President's concern over the Spanish officers was dismissed with scant respect, though Jackson promised to get up stronger evidence of their rascality. The body of the letter dealt with the President's disclaimer of responsibility. Accompanying the copy of the order originally issued to Gaines, which forbade the violation of Spanish forts, Calhoun had sent a letter directing Jackson to "adopt the necessary measures to terminate ... hostilities." This letter did not state that Gaines's order was to be binding on Jackson. Always a latitudinarian in such matters, the General had followed the letter and not the order. For this Old Hickory was ready to accept responsibility. "I never have shrunk from it and never will."[16]

A break with the Administration seemed to impend. Jackson wrote in confidence to a Philadelphia politician. "Being a sincere friend of Mr. Monroe ... it is not my desire to injure him unless impelled in my own defense.... Had the government held the posts until the guarantees were given stipulated in the Articles of Capitulation ... I would have been more than willing to have taken on myself all responsibilities, but when my country is deprived of all the benefits resulting from my acts I will not consent to bear ... responsibility that ought to be those of another. My situation is ... delicate. I must for the present be silent."[17]

Was Jackson holding over the head of the President the celebrated Rhea letter said to have been delivered at Big Creek? In any event Monroe was afraid of the General, and he had reason to be. What an explosion if Old Hickory should learn that during

.iose warm days in July both the President and Mr. Calhoun had
proposed to save their skins by throwing Andrew Jackson to the
wolves. The Secretary of War also was uneasy, and nimbly he
changed his course and deftly he covered his tracks. Within
sixty days after he had argued by the hour to break down Adams's
stubborn refusal to accede to a disavowal of Jackson a complete
somersault had been achieved. Meeting Captain James Gadsden
of the Regular service and one of Jackson's confidential officers
in Florida, Mr. Calhoun praised the results of the campaign and
deplored the fact that certain of his unfeeling Administration
colleagues would sacrifice "their best friend" to "screen them·
selves."[18]

Mr. Monroe's difficulties increased. A timid attempt to induce
Jackson to confess that he had "misunderstood" the Secretary's
instructions failed to budge the adamant soldier an inch.[19] On
top of this came an ultimatum from Madrid. The restoration of
the posts was not enough, exclaimed His Majesty's Minister for
Foreign Affairs. Jackson's actions must be disavowed and Jackson
himself "suitably punished" or negotiations for the purchase of
Florida were at an end.

James Monroe turned to his Secretary of State. Mr. Adams
had defended General Jackson to his fellow Cabinet officers in
July. Let him do it now.

Gladly John Quincy Adams undertook the task and composed a
withering dispatch that would fill twenty pages of this volume,
all of it excellent—and much of it true. Mr. Adams labored alone,
without the connivance of any one. No subterranean request for
doctored documents or planted evidence. The Secretary of State
interpreted documents to suit his requirements and extemporized
testimony by the power of assertion.

"The President," he said, "will neither inflict punishment nor
pass censure upon General Jackson for that conduct—the vindication of which is written in every page of the law of nations, . . .
self defense." On the contrary, "suitable punishment" of the
commandant of St. Marks and the governor of Pensacola was demanded for their "defiance and violation of the engagements of

Spain with the United States." If these officers were powerless, "the United States can as little compound with impotence as with perfidy, and Spain must immediately make her election" and properly defend Florida, "or cede to the United States a province of which she retains nothing but the nominal possession."

Jackson's occupation of the forts was contrasted with that of Nicholls in 1814, who had not only seized the defenses of Pensacola but had blown up the largest of them. "Where is his Majesty's profound indignation at that?" The subsequent history of Florida was reviewed—Woodbine, Amelia Island, Arbuthnot, Ambrister—"this narrative of dark and complicated depravity; this creeping and insidious war, this mockery of patriotism, these political philters to fugitive slaves and Indian outlaws. . . ." The paper closed with a threat. Should it become necessary again to take "forts and places in Florida," the unconditional surrender of them must not be expected.[20]

Thus a Jacksonian spirit in the Cabinet to support Jacksonian measures in the field.

7

The General prepared for a quiet winter at the Hermitage. "My eyes are weak and my hand trembles."[21] He needed recreation, and on a Sunday in October, 1818, drove to Nashville where a Methodist Conference was in session.

Peter Cartwright had rounded out twenty of the two score years as a circuit rider that made him the frontier's most celebrated priest of religion. Subtler persuasions failing, he had been known to knock a sinner down and drag him to the throne of grace. Not without misgivings, a local pastor had invited him to fill the pulpit on this Sunday morning. The announcement brought out the town. Reverend Cartwright read his text in a ringing voice.

"What shall it profit a man if he gain the whole world and lose his soul?"

He paused to let the words sink in. General Jackson entered the church and walked slowly down the aisle. Every seat being taken, he stood for a moment leaning against a pillar.

Mr. Cartwright felt a tug at the tail of his coat.

"General Jackson has come in!" the Nashville minister whispered. "General Jackson has come in!"

The whisper was audible to most of the church. Peter Cartwright's hard jaw tightened. He gave the minister a look of scorn and confronted his congregation.

"Who is General Jackson? If he don't get his soul converted, God will damn him as quick as a Guinea nigger!"

After the sermon Reverend Cartwright was advised to leave town. "General Jackson will chastise you for your insolence."

"Two can play at that game," said Cartwright, and accepted an invitation to preach at a country church near the Hermitage. Jackson invited him to dinner.[22]

Certain other critics of the General were not to get off as easily. It was too early to judge of its effect abroad, but the domestic success of Mr. Adams's Florida dispatch had been instantaneous, and of this William H. Crawford and Henry Clay took particular note. With Mr. Adams, these gentlemen aspired to the presidency in 1824. They were pained to see a rival winning so much applause. Nor did they fail to consider that General Jackson's undimmed popularity boded no good to their expectations. When Congress convened the two were soon at work. In the House a resolution was prepared disapproving the execution of Arbuthnot and Ambrister.

His renown as Andrew Jackson's biographer had helped to elevate to the United States Senate John Henry Eaton who advised the General to leave Florida matters in the hands of his friends. But Colonel Robert Butler urged his guardian to come to Washington and direct the fight for his military reputation. Representative Felix Grundy wrote in the same style. "It is natural that you (now near the close of an illustrious life) should feel sensibly for your fame—and . . . I have no doubt but yr presence would inspire many with correct sentiments."[23]

On the morning of January 23, 1819, a gaunt figure on horseback muffled in a borrowed greatcoat thumped across the Long Bridge that spanned the Potomac. At Strater's Hotel General

Jackson dismounted cold and ill, but resolved so 'defeat these hellish machinations,"[24] if it were his last accomplishment on earth.

8

Machinations they were. On January twelfth the House Committee on Military Affairs had reported against the executions of Arbuthnot and Ambrister. In a savage onslaught Thomas W. Cobb of Georgia, Crawford's spokesman in the lower chamber, broadened the issue to include disapproval of the occupation of Pensacola, and proposed bills prohibiting the execution of captives taken in an Indian war, or the invasion of foreign territory without authority, except in fresh pursuit of an enemy. Men less consumed by the fires of ambition might have awaited the tranquillization of our foreign relations before attempting the destruction of their country's greatest soldier and of any member of the Administration who should stand with him. The situation does not render more difficult of belief a rumor that came to Jackson's ears that, unwilling to wait until 1824, Crawford and Clay plotted to overthrow Monroe in 1820.[25]

The House dropped all other business. Galleries were crowded, aisles packed and cuspidors overturned. It was feared that the temporary edifice in which Congress met pending the rebuilding of the Capitol might not stand the strain. Not since the trial of Aaron Burr had the country's interest been captured by such a spectacle. Jackson's defenders were on hand and they made their points well. On the twelfth day of the debate Speaker Clay descended from his dais to crush them. The Kentuckian and General Jackson had long been casual friends, viewing Western problems through Western eyes, as during the Burr affair, which, in its most innocuous guise, contemplated a violation of Spanish sovereignty. At Ghent Mr. Clay would sit too late at cards to please John Quincy Adams, though he was invariably on hand in the morning bearing his part to get the better of the third-rate Englishmen at the other side of the table. Returning to Kentucky he was warmly received, but there was no blinking the fact that another Westerner had gained the first place in the admiration of his countrymen. This became more apparent when Mr. Monroe passed over Henry Clay in his quest of a Secretary of State.

The Speaker began by disclaiming any ill-will toward General Jackson. He was actuated, he said, by principle. His first attack was directed against the Creek treaty, which, though it had been a subject of discussion for four years, Mr. Clay read for the first time on the eve of this debate. The Creek treaty is a vulnerable document, but so superficial had been Mr. Clay's perusal that he missed or overshadowed the most assailable points by a rhetorical, and incidentally baseless, outburst that Jackson had sought to deprive these worthy barbarians of the consolations of their native religion. The Florida part of the speech showed more careful preparation, but here again the orator failed to make the most of his opportunity, except in the use of language. He closed with a murky implication which every act of Andrew Jackson's life, good or bad, refutes. "Recall to your recollections the free nations which have gone before us. Where are they now and how have they lost their liberties? If we could transport ourselves back to the ages when Greece and Rome flourished, and, . . . ask a Grecian if he did not fear some daring military chieftain, covered with glory, some Philip or Alexander, would one day overthrow his liberties? No! no! . . . [he] would exclaim, we have nothing to fear for our heroes. . . . Yet Greece had fallen, Caesar passed the Rubicon. . . ."[26]

Mr. Clay's utterance caused a sensation. Three days after its delivery, General Jackson reached Washington, and, declining public hospitalities, closeted himself with his supporters. From that moment until the end of the twenty-three days of argument, Jackson's lieutenants dominated the declamatory scene. Old Hickory sat in his hotel room, the center of an ever-increasing press of homage-bearers, guiding, inspiring, directing. Mr. Clay was answered in kind by Poindexter of Mississippi, and while the Jackson proponents did not disdain oratory they did not rely on it as the opposition did. Every truth and half-truth that could be regimented in support of their position was used and generally used well.

In granting that personal ambition played a conspicuous part in the Clay-Crawford assault on Jackson's Florida raid, it should not be assumed that, by contrast, loftier motives were the sole spur of the General's defenders. Many vehicles already were hitched to the soaring star of Old Hickory, and individual aspirations played their part in his defense. On the face of the facts it would be nearly as easy to make out a case against Jackson as for him, and the careful student of the record may well be astonished at the inherent weakness of an attack engineered by such resourceful men as Crawford and Clay. At the outset they underestimated their task, which, with Adams brazening and bluffing his way with the diplomats and Jackson himself bringing lieutenants in the House under the hypnotic sway of his will, was not one to be approached as casually as Mr. Clay, for one, approached it.

On February eighth the votes were taken.

"Resolved, That the House of Representatives . . . disapproves the execution of Alexander Arbuthnot and Robert C. Ambrister." Ayes, 54; noes, 90.

"Resolved, That the Committee on Military Affairs . . . prepare . . . a bill . . . prohibiting" the execution of captives in Indian warfare without executive authority. Ayes, 57; noes, 98.

"Resolved, That the late seizure of Pensacola was" unconstitutional. Ayes, 65; noes, 91.

"Resolved, That" a bill be prepared prohibiting the invasion of foreign soil, without authorization of Congress, except in fresh pursuit of an enemy. Ayes, 42; noes, 112.

It was the greatest triumph since New Orleans.

9

The victor left Washington with the ostensible object of visiting his godsons at West Point. Philadelphia waylaid him with an ovation, which, gathering momentum, lasted four days. The modest manners of the guest pleased every one. At a vast public dinner, speakers electrified the air with controversial allusions. Thanking his hosts briefly, General Jackson raised his glass.

"The memory of Benjamin Franklin," he said.

New York had more time to prepare. Beginning with the presentation of the freedom of the city in a gold box, its reception lasted five days. The guest was amenable, but he kept his bearings. A banquet at Tammany Hall, many of whose leading lights were active Crawford men, was thrown into confusion when General Jackson blandly offered a toast to Governor DeWitt Clinton whom he had never seen, but knew as the head of the anti-Crawford wing in New York.

At four o'clock in the morning of February twenty-seventh, residents of Baltimore were roused from their slumbers by salvos of artillery hailing the approach of the hero. Here Jackson received great news. In Europe Adams's aggressive note on Florida had carried all before it. England had dropped her protest over Arbuthnot and Ambrister. Spain had renewed the purchase parley, and on February 22, 1819, Adams and de Oñis had signed a treaty ceding Florida to the United States for five million dollars. At five o'clock on the evening of March first, Jackson took his place beside the Mayor of Baltimore at a banquet. At nine he took leave of the company and boarded a stage which entered Washington before day.

It was not the tidings of the Florida treaty, however, that called the General to the capital in such haste. Unmindful of the verdict of the House, the popular approval of the same, or, indeed, the Adams-de Oñis treaty, the United States Senate had undertaken to pass upon the propriety of General Jackson's late campaign. John Henry Eaton was a member of the committee to whom the task was delegated, but Abner Lacock, of the Crawford camp, was the chairman and ruling figure. This quiet and effective Pennsylvanian had gone about his duties, undeterred, as he later said, by a story that General Jackson meant to establish the purity of his motives in Florida by "cutting off the ears" of critical Senators.[27]

Though calm in tone, the report of the Lacock committee was

penetratingly critical of the invasion. The Administration, however, conceived the idea of forestalling action until Congress should
die on March fourth. Jackson's precipitous appearance on March
second did not promise to facilitate this velvety stratagem, especially when the rumor reached the streets that he had come to
town to cane Senator Eppes of Virginia, a member of the Lacock
committee and a nephew of Thomas Jefferson. Captain Stephen
Decatur, with whom Jackson had struck up an instantaneous
friendship, has been pictured dashing across Washington in a cab,
and intercepting the General on the steps of the Capitol, where
he was able to dissuade him from his intention.[28] In any event
no caning occurred, and, when Congress and the report faded from
the scene together, the hero graced a levee at the reconstructed
Executive Mansion gleaming with its first coat of white paint.
"The company pressed about him" until it seemed to observant
John Quincy Adams that General Jackson was giving the reception.[29] How it seemed to Mr. Monroe is something Mr
Adams did not attempt to sav.

CHAPTER XIX

General Jackson Calls on Colonel Callava

I

The silvering logs of Hermitage blockhouse had begun to confess their years. "Say to my overseer that on my return I will expect my house . . . prepaired in such a way as will prevent the nothern blast from entering."[1] But the tide and tone of the times prescribed that the family seat of the most popular man in America be something more than a shelter against the northern blast. Twenty years before, as an industrious frontier solicitor, Andrew Jackson's Hunter's Hill was the equal for elegance of any residence in the Cumberland Valley. Misfortune had brought him to the Hermitage and the threshold of oblivion, but the years of flailing struggle against debt and disappointment had bred a retrospective tenderness for its logs, and General Jackson was content to spend the remainder of his days in their friendly company. Returning from Florida enfeebled by dysentery, he reflected that these days would not be many, and that Rachel deserved a better home.

As soon as he was able to be about he showed a neighbor, William B. Lewis, the site of the new house, a stretch of pasture land almost perfectly level, a few hundred yards southwest of the blockhouse and screened by a wood from the highroad a quarter of a mile away.

Lewis suggested a more commanding situation which, indeed, had been the General's personal choice.[2]

"No, Major," he said, "Mrs. Jackson chose this spot, and she shall have her wish. I am going to build this house for *her*. I don't expect to live in it myself."[3]

Commanding situations formed a small part of Rachel's desires in this world, and the house was built in the secluded meadow—a plain rectangular structure of brick which was burned and oak timbers for the most part cut and shaped on the plantation. It faced south, with a front of about eighty-five feet, the depth being somewhat greater. From a small porch, such as were more commonly seen on New England than on Southern houses, one entered a hall which ran the length of the house. On the right and left, in front, were the parlors. Back of the parlor on the left was the dining room, back of the parlor on the right the bed chamber of General and Mrs. Jackson, a northeast room. Upstairs were five or six sleeping rooms. The General's office was a small brick building on the west side of the house; the kitchen and house-servant quarters in the rear.

On his return from the East in April, 1819, General Jackson engaged William Frost, a "regular bred english Gardner," [5] to lay out the grounds. The result was a beautiful lawn, shaded by gigantic trees, and, on the east side in view of her bedroom window, Rachel's particular sanctuary—an orderly acre of flowers, traced by curving brick-edged walks.

The guest chambers were seldom vacant and Rachel and Andrew rarely sat at their table alone. Judge John Overton—who had known Mrs. Jackson as the bride of Lewis Robards—Senator Eaton, Governor McMinn, youthful Gaston Davézac of New Orleans clicking his heels and conveying his father's respects; Edward Ward talking horses and Alabama land; a cloud of Donelson kin; Sam Houston, a tall handsome young lawyer in whom the General was beginning to take an exceptional interest; Dr. James C. Bronaugh of the Army, flint-and-trigger duelist, beau sabreur and the General's personal physician; officers reporting from distant posts; politicians, speculators, a Sunday-School picnic; the traveling curious with letters of introduction from persons who had shaken the General's hand, say, at the stage station in Perth Amboy the winter preceding; brisk young aides-de-camp on fancy horses, plying to and from Division Headquarters at

Nashville: the new Hermitage was not an idle place. And it rang with childish laughter, for Rachel and Andrew had taken another ward to raise, Andrew Jackson Hutchings, the six-year-old orphan of the junior partner of Jackson & Hutchings of Clover Bottom memory. General Jackson had kept the President waiting for an answer to a letter while he journeyed by forced rides to Alabama to comfort the last hours of his dying friend with a promise to care for his boy.[6]

There were other domestic problems. "Dear Uncle I am . . . confined in the Common Jaoll . . . for an assault on John McKinley in which I displayed the patriotism which should be engrafted in the bosom of every free born American. . . . S. D. HUTCHINGS."[7] "D^r. Uncle Herewith you will find enclosed a letter . . . on the subject of my Brother Anthony's suspension from Yale College. . . . C[AROLINE] S. BELL."[8] But the Hermitage mail pouch was not without its compensations. "I send you a Barrel of what I think good old Whiskey. . . . Respect & friendship. EDWARD WARD."[9]

Ralph E. W. Earl, an itinerant portrait painter, and member of a talented though eccentric family of artists, caught Rachel's fancy. "I can say with truth a more Correct young man I never knew."[10] Jane Caffery, a niece of Rachel, caught the fancy of the artist. He married her and prepared to settle down to confine the practise of his profession to meeting the active demand for likenesses of General Jackson. The bride died a few months after the ceremony. "My Friend," wrote Rachel, "you have not to weep as thos who have no hope. Angels wafted Her on Celestial wings to that blooming garden of roses that has no thorns."[11] Like his father before him Earle had been a wanderer from boyhood who had never known a home. Mrs. Jackson carried him off to the Hermitage where he remained for seventeen years.

In the summer of 1819, General Jackson rode to Georgia to greet another visitor. Earle went to Nashville for a few days, and a letter followed him. "Pleas to Look in the post office for Letters for me. I feel Lonely and unhappy. . . . I have lived a life of hope, I hope to Die in the Faith. . . . I would write you a long letter but perhaps not so as to be all together Exceptable Adieu Dear sur and believe Me your Sincere friend RACHEL JACKSON"[12]

But not to Mrs. Jackson alone did the persisting lamp of fame bare the imperfections inherent in the human plan. The General had gone to Georgia to welcome James Monroe to Tennessee. Two years before the President had undertaken the experiment of showing himself to the country, which no Executive since Washington had done. He had promised to visit Nashville then, but wrote Jackson that the Spanish situation would not permit. This tour was a success. The raw-boned, six-foot President was a shy man, an able lieutenant though a mediocre chieftain, whose timidity had grown with the exactions of independent leadership until one could scarcely recognize in him the draconian Secretary of War of 1814, braced by the shadow of Mr. Madison's responsibility. Applause seemed to renew his failing self-assurance, but, like most men with an interior sense of insecurity, he was jealous. In 1819 a second journey carried the Executive through the Carolinas and into Georgia where Jackson joined the entourage. Immediately the crowds were larger, the plaudits heartier, altogether a salutary thing until the presidential party made the unfortunate discovery that this was because of the presence of Andrew Jackson. Over the War Path to Knoxville, over the Cumberland Road to Nashville, the procession filed amid continuous ovation; and thence by the Kentucky Road to Lexington, where General Jackson turned back, and the homage, if less strident, was at least the President's own.

2

Having put on a brave face for Mr. Monroe (and for General Jackson), Tennessee turned again, amid a clamorous conflict of counsel and convictions, to the infinite perplexities of a life disordered.

Moving westward the creeping paralysis of hard times had reached the frontier. To put currency on a sounder footing, the government-supported Bank of the United States had opened its doors in 1817 with branches from Portsmouth to New Orleans. The Bank of the United States redeemed its paper in coin on demand, and, as fast as the currency of wildcat banks fell into its hands, they were pressed to do the same. The wildcat banks began to call loans and the financial house of cards in the West toppled. A cry of rage went up against the government bank. Tennessee excluded its branches from the state by imposing a tax of fifty thousand dollars a year, and, departing from a policy of moderation, chartered a "litter" of independent banks to accommodate the imagined financial needs of the communities. For a little while every one was flush; then came a reckoning. Throughout the West independent banks fell like nine-pins in the face of the demand that they honor their paper money. The Nashville Bank was obliged to suspend specie payments, though it managed to keep open. The government bank's demand for the redemption of the paper that flooded the West revealed conditions that would have fascinated a finance minister of Louis XVI. One bank had twenty-seven thousand dollars in specie with which to redeem three hundred and ninety-five thousand dollars in notes; another thirty-five thousand dollars to cover five hundred and thirty-four thousand dollars' worth of paper.

The collapse had come at an awkward moment for General Jackson. The new Hermitage had drained his reserve of cash. He had loaned money freely. He was deep in Alabama specula- tions on his own account and with partners, notably John Coffee and the late John Hutchings. Over the latter's interests he estab- lished a protectorate for the benefit of the Hutchings boy. On the eve of the débâcle, he had joined his old friends, John Overton and James Winchester, in the founding of Memphis, "on the American Nile," as the prospectus defined it. The promoters spent a good deal of money clearing the bluff, laying off squares and streets—one named Jackson, naturally—and building a court-house and jail. Russell Bean, hero of the Jonesborough fire, was en- gaged as marshal to keep the peace. His duties were not arduous. The queen of the American Nile attracted few investors, peace- able or otherwise, though it proved a suitably isolated asylum for

General Winchester's son when he married the quadroon mistress of Colonel Thomas Hart Benton. Before the reviving river trade established the fortunes of Memphis, Jackson had disposed of his interest.

Middle Tennessee was prostrate. Between five and six hundred suits for debt clogged the courts in Davidson County. In a single action Andrew Jackson brought the law upon one hundred and twenty-nine persons who owed him.[13] His situation was serious. He must meet obligations maturing in Alabama or sacrifice thousands of dollars he had poured into his ventures there.[14] Debtors cried out for relief from the public funds. Bills went before the Legislature to set up loan offices and to stay the collection of debts. Jackson and Edward Ward were the only men of prominence in the Cumberland Valley to oppose them, Jackson sending the Legislature a protest which it declined to receive on the ground that the language was disrespectful.[15] The bills were passed.

To this turmoiled scene came the news that America had congratulated itself too soon on the acquisition of Florida. Spain hesitated to ratify the treaty. Jackson's impulse was to rush to Washington, but he did not have the money for the journey.[16]

3

He wrote to James Monroe. "I am wearied with public life. . . . I have been accused of acts I never committed, of crimes I never thought of, and secretly . . . charged . . . in the Senate . . . of doing acts in my official capacity to promote my private interest." This was an allusion to the Eaton-Donelson land purchase in Florida, from which the Lacock committee had sought to draw false inferences. Jackson was deeply hurt. "I have laboured through life to establish an honest Charactor. . . .

"I had hoped that our affairs with Spain would have been finally settled by her ratifying the treaty, and nothing would have arisen to prevent me from" leaving the Army. "But Sir you know my services is my countries as long as" the country should need them. Yet he prayed for peace. "I have therefore to request

that you ... say to me ... at what time it will be proper ... to
tender my resignation. ... Have the goodness to present Mrs. J.
and myself to your amiable lady ... and believe me to be Yr mo.
ob. serv."[17]

The storms that beat about the haughty spirit beat more fitfully
now. The intervals of calm were longer. An old slave Peter pined
for his children and grandchildren. General Jackson located them
in East Tennessee and increased his debts eighteen hundred dollars
in order to unite the family at the Hermitage, "object, humanity."[18]
At West Point Andrew Jackson Donelson joined other cadets in a
protest against "kicks and cuffs" and the use of the ball and chain
as aids to the mastery of the military profession. This precipitated
a controversy during which young Donelson wrote home for permission to resign rather than embarrass his uncle by a scene. He
remained at the Academy, however, and eventually was graduated
second in the class of 1820.

Andrew and Rachel followed with pride the progress of this
studious, spirited youth and his letters were an event at the busy
Hermitage, General Jackson's only complaint being that they did
not come oftener. "Your aunt and myself ... [were] fearfull from
your long silence that you were sick. ... You can attend to
nothing more beneficial than writing. It ... expands the mind,
and will give you ... an easy habit of communicating your
thoughts. there is nothing so beautiful in writing as a plain easy
stile. ... Altho Mr. Jeffersons writings has met with the approbation that they merited I have always thought that the chasteness
of Mr. Madison excelled any american author I ever read." The
man preparing to withdraw from the world could judge impar-
tially, untroubled by the remembrance of how many times the
chaste style had been employed to defeat the desires of Andrew
Jackson. "It is by habit that this ease and plainness of stile which
I call elegance is to be acquired. ...

"When you know the pleasure it gives me to read your letters
why not amuse yourself by writing to me. Choose you own subject—and handle it in any way your judgt may direct. ... This will

give you confidence in yourself, which to become great you must acquire, keeping you mind allways open to reason, . . . but never yielding your opinion until the Judgt. is convinced. Independence of mind and action is the noblest attribute of man. . . . [It] gives a peaceful conscience, and when the public voice, being misled, disapproves the course, innocence smiles . . . at . . . clamour [until] time dispells the mists of error from their eyes . . . truth ultimately prevails. . . .

"If we remain at peace I wish you to study law and live with me. if we have war . . . I will have you with me, but . . . war is a great evil . . . and a curse to any nation. . . . I enclosed you in my last one hundred dollars in a bill of the Branch bank of the U States— I am anxious to know whether it reached you, there are so many roberies of the mail."[19]

Within three weeks the philosopher of the Cumberland came to the assistance of Time to dispel the mists of error from the Florida issue. The bad faith of Spain was apparent, and she had potential allies in Crawford and Clay who seemed willing to go to any lengths to feather their nests at the expense of Adams and the treaty. Adams pressed the President into a position of defiance, and Jackson received confidential instructions to prepare a military movement calculated to awe the Spanish. He replied instantly. "My health is very precarious, but . . . with the smiles of heaven I will endeavour to place once more the american Eagle upon the ramparts of the Barancas Pensacola, St. Marks and reduce Ft St augustine and then beg leave to retire if I survive."[20]

The first person awed by these sentiments was the President of the United States.

But there was no retreat. Mr. Calhoun asked for details of a program involving only Regular troops, and twenty-four hours after his dispatch had reached Nashville the answer, in Jackson's slanting scrawl, was on its way. This compact and able military document embodied a plan for war against the full power of Spain, no less, on a front from New Orleans to Charleston, complete to an "Estimate of the Teams . . . required . . . for the Field Artillery"—the rapid work of a man who knew his resources, those of the enemy, and his own mind exactly. The Commander was under no delusion that Florida would prove the easy prey that she had been in 1818. "Garrisons at Pensacola and Barrancas . . . may be estimated at 500 regulars and 300 militia. . . . St. Augustine is one of the strongest Fortress in the World with the exception of Quebeck and Gibraltar. . . . St Marks is a strong place, . . . and well defended will cost many lives to take by Storm. . . . I might be 75 days employed in the reduction of the . . . posts, . . . but with the Smiles of Heaven I hope not to be half that time." As ever with Jackson to think was to strike. Orders had gone, he said, and, by the time this communication should reach the Secretary, the troops would be in motion.[21]

Then taking a fresh sheet of paper, Old Hickory indited a private letter to the Secretary of War. Would it embarrass the government if he should seize Cuba also? Mr. Calhoun treated the request with elaborate deference to Jackson's views. He, also, favored the acquisition of Cuba, but felt "we ought at present limit our operations to Florida."[22]

Mr. Monroe had had his lesson. He halted the movement of troops against Florida, determined to consult Congress before turning Andrew Jackson loose on Spanish soil again. Secretary of Treasury Crawford declared our finances would not bear the strain of war and Congress hesitated. Jackson fumed. "Had Congress acted with the . . . feeling . . . our national charector demanded the Don long since, cap in hand, would have paid his respects to our President, with the treaty ratified."[23]

Something like this eventually happened when, in February, 1821, Francisco Dionisio Vives, the Spanish Minister, delivered the ratified treaty. Before the document was actually in his hands, Mr. Monroe offered Jackson the governorship of the new acquisition. His communication reached the Hermitage on the ninth or tenth of February with a request for a prompt answer, as the President must send his nomination to the Senate on March third. Jackson answered at once declining the office, and the letter went to Nashville to await the departure of the bi-weekly mail.

4

This letter, had he received it, would have dissipated the web of dilemma which increasing vacillation and a nervous fear of Jackson had spun about James Monroe. A President owes something to his public, and Mr. Monroe was not without a feeling that he did not appear at his best in the company of Andrew Jackson. As early as 1818, a solution was suggested that seemed to possess so much intrinsic merit that Monroe took it to his old preceptor, Thomas Jefferson. How about sending General Jackson on a mission to Russia? The patriarch threw up his hands. "Good God, he would breed you a quarrel before he had been there a month!"[24]

Jackson's repeated requests for Monroe to name the day of his retirement had been sincere. Had the compliments with which the President sugared his correspondence during the two years past been equally sincere, there would have been no problem. Congress had reduced the Army which required the demotion of one major general commanding troops. There were only two such, Jacob Brown, head of the Northern Division, and Jackson. Brown had hastened to Washington, and, with Winfield Scott and other friends of William H. Crawford, waged a campaign in his own behalf. Jackson had done nothing, but, by accident or design, the oft-stated plea for retirement dropped from his letters. Now that the skies were serene, Monroe would be more comfortable with the comparatively colorless Brown at the head of the Army, but a high regard for the amour propre of the Southern Commander caused him to hesitate. The governorship was a way out and Mr. Monroe called Senator Eaton to the White House, flattered him, and declared that Jackson could remain in the Army if he wished, but that he hoped he would undertake the more important, the much more important, work of organizing an administration in Florida.[25]

The Florida landowner was easily persuaded. Other political and military satellites of Jackson were quick to perceive the ad-

vantage during these lean times of a patron in a position to dis-
tribute public appointments. Off to the Hermitage sped a letter
from Eaton saying that Jackson's friends in Congress were determined to have him appointed whether he would accept or not,
and hinting at a "strong political reason" for the step.[26] On the
heels of this missive a delegation from Nashville hurried up the
guitar-shaped drive. Over Rachel's remonstrances,[27] Jackson consented to reverse his decision on condition that his letter of refusal
had not left the post-office. A horseman was off to Nashville like
a bullet. He brought back the letter. Jackson crumpled it and
"reluctantly" wrote another, accepting the appointment on condition "that I may resign as soon as the Government is organized."[28]
Willing hands sped this to Nashville, the delegation departed,
and the weary old soldier fell to reckoning the speed a post rider
should make to Washington over the long red road that Andrew
Jackson knew so well. At best he would not make it before March
first. A forty-eight-hour delay, then, and Mr. Monroe would name
another man. "My hopes are that the letters will not reach there
[in time]."[29]

5

But they did.

In the remarkable space of eight days, General Jackson and
Rachel arrived in New Orleans by steamboat on April 22, 1821.
On board was their carriage, newly glassed, curtained with "Broad
Lace" and upholstered in "Moroco Skins," at an expenditure of
one hundred and sixty-three dollars. A new set of harness had
cost another one hundred and sixty dollars, less an allowance
of twenty-five dollars for the old.[30]

This equipage was not out of place in New Orleans. "Great
Babylon," wrote Rachel, "is come up before me. Oh, the wicked-
ness, the idolatry of this place! unspeakable riches and splendor.
The attention and honors paid to the General far excel the recital
of my pen. They conducted him to the Grand Theatre . . .
[which] rang with loud acclamations, Vive Jackson. Songs of
praise were sung by ladies, and . . . they crowned him with . . .
laurel. The Lord has promised his humble followers a crown

that fadeth not away; the present one is already withered the leaves
falling off. . . . Oh, farewell! Pray for your sister in a heathen
land."[31]

Mrs. Jackson found their next tarrying place, Montpelier, Ala-
bama, smaller than New Orleans, but as sinful per capita. "The
Sabbath entirely neglected and profaned. The regiment [of
United States troops] . . . no better than the Spaniards. . . . The
General, I believe, wants to get home again as much as I do. . . .
[He] wishes he had taken my advice. . . . Amen. RACHEL JACK-
SON."[32]

She was right about her husband. The General had regretted
that letter of acceptance since the instant it left his hand. His impulse was to recall it "but my word is out and I must comply."[33]
For another thing, he could not disappoint the President whose
"solicitude . . . arose from feelings of friendship, and a desire to
give evidence that he fully approved my course in the Seminole
campaign, as well as believing that my name would have some
weight in establishing the Government over the Floridas."[34] A
third reason for taking the office was to help his friends. A list of
suggested appointments to subordinate posts had been forwarded
to the President. Andrew Jackson knew the advantage steady income gave a man starting out in a strange country. Under such auspices he had come to the Cumberland in 1788. But as soon as Congress could meet and extend a territorial form of government to
Florida, friends must fend for themselves. "I retire to my farm
and there spend my latter days."[35] Through the efflorescent aura
of official compliment, General Jackson had begun to discern that
it required a lenient view of the facts to construe his present mission
as a promotion in the public service. Twice he had borne the
flag into Florida under circumstances that had made the world
look on. Now he carried it as a figure in a ceremonial. A gust
of pride eddied up in a private line to Coffee. "I never can con-
descend to become a governor of a Territory after the office I have
filled."[36]

Moreover, despite all his protestations, as the day neared for
Andrew Jackson to lay aside his sword, a singular depression of

spirit weighed upon him. In nine years of active service he had
grown accustomed to command. Army life had opened natural
avenues of expression for talents always a little robust for ordinary
pursuits. He loved the camaraderie of camp and barracks and
was loath to leave it. He had formed more and closer ties of
friendship than in any other period of his life. Though American
soldiers had not known such discipline since the day of Von Steu-
ben, Jackson's men adored him.

The General found it equally hard to part from his superiors.
Mr. Adams's challenging loyalty was apparent to the world, while
the mellifluous phrases of Messrs. Monroe and Calhoun obscured
a shadowy hour when but for Adams the conquest of Florida
would have been repudiated. "I have my D'r Sir read your letter
with great pleasure, the principles you have laid down for political
guide through life will ... lead you to compleat triumph over your
enemies and your country to safety and happiness." The quick
eyes of John C. Calhoun must have glowed at these lines, for he,
too, was in the lists for the presidency. "Before this reaches you
our military relations will have ceased, but my breast will allways
cherish ... that friendly feeling ... your honourable conduct towards me ever since you have been placed in the Department of
war was well calculated to inspire. this feeling for you will never
cease during life."[37]

Andrew Jackson had hoped to enter Pensacola again as a
soldier—a soldier seated beside his wife in a carriage, it is true,
rather than riding at the head of a barefooted army—but even this
was not to be. The day designated for his retirement, June 1, 1821,
found him marooned at Montpelier where he penned a moving
order of farewell. It had not been distributed, however, when
the late Commander of the Southern Division chanced upon an
address to the troops elucidating an easy theory of discipline which
was susceptible of the interpretation that General Jackson had
been too severe on the men. Moreover this order was signed
"Jacob Brown, Commander-in-Chief, under the President, of the
Armies of the United States." This title Jackson had never
achieved. the office having lain vacant until the announcement of

Jackson's retirement, which was in reality a compliment to Jackson as Brown was his senior in the service. Although his name had passed from the Army rolls, Jackson recalled his order of farewell and added a stiff "P. S." of a hundred lines to say that, contrary to the opinion of the Commander-in-Chief, the trouble with the military establishment was that discipline was too lax.[38]

6

The vertical rain crushed down like a water-fall compressing the elastic forms of the Pride of China trees and making a pond of the Plaza. Rachel had seen rain like this every day since she had come to Pensacola. But in no time the flood would run off into the bay, or sink into the porous white sand, and the sun reveal the premeditated brilliance of the walled-in gardens. Before her gallery had ceased to drip, people were abroad and bare feet whispered on the damp sand beneath her windows like the sound of a little stream.

"Fine flowers growing spontaneously, for they have neglected their gardens expecting a change of government.... All the houses look in ruins, old as time."[39] Mrs. Jackson was somewhat mistaken as to the age of those sun-washed, shuttered houses with plastered walls of faded blue and green and yellow. Their time-stained appearance was the work not so much of years or neglect as of the extraordinary powers of tropical nature to triumph over human endeavor.

"The inhabitants all speak Spanish and French. Some speak four or five languages. Such a mixed multitude you, nor any of us, ever had an idea of. . . . Fewer white people by far than any other. . . . I am living on Main Street which . . . [gives] me an opportunity of seeing a great deal from the upper galleries." There was a great deal to engage the eye. "We have a handsome view of the bay, . . . the most beautiful water prospect I ever saw." Languorous movement, vivid colors—the sea, the foliage, the houses, the garb and the complexions of people. Seamen strolled with knives in their belts and coins burning their pockets; absurd' little Spanish soldiers; yellow women with well-turned limbs and insinuating glances; Jamaica blacks bearing prodigious burdens on their heads; a fish peddler filling the street with incomprehensible cries; a Seminole Indian with a set expression of unfriendliness; a grandee in his carriage. "And must I say the worst people here are the cast-off Americans?"[40]

"The Sabbath profanely kept; a great deal of noise and swearing in the streets; shops kept open; trade"—a broad term—"going on, I think, more than on any other day."[41] This disturbing environment so carried away Mrs. Jackson's mulatto maid Betty that Rachel was obliged to report her delinquencies. "She can behave herself," wrote General Jackson, "or Mr. Blair . . . [will] give her fifty lashes and if he does not . . . as soon as I get possession I will order a corporal to give it to her publickly."[42]

The General was not, therefore, in possession.

After five weeks of delay at Montpelier, he had sent Rachel and her household into the city alone, expecting almost every day to follow. But delay succeeded delay, and nothing takes more from the imposing character of a ceremonial than a want of punctuality. The first postponement was occasioned by the tardiness of the United States sloop of war *Hornet,* which was to bring from Havana the authorization for Don José Callava, Governor of West Florida, to make the formal transfer. Jackson was certain that the officials were purposely "amusing" our Colonel Forbes in Havana, in order to detain the *Hornet* while Florida slave smugglers and miscellaneous importers took advantage of the last benevolent days of Spanish sovereignty. "How Irksome . . . to remain here with my arms Folded not able to prevent those illegal practices."[43] Nor was the tedium relieved by the arrival of a copy of the *National Intelligencer* containing a roster of the President's appointments to subordinate situations in General Jackson's Florida government. Not a name that Jackson had suggested was on it. Not one. Jackson wrote to Doctor Bronaugh, in Pensacola, with Mrs. Jackson, and for whom he had solicited the office of Receiver of Public Money. "I am determined never to be associated with such men. . . . Say to my friend Call [another of the Jackson candidates] not to despond. . . . I am too sick to write more."[44]

Eventually the *Hornet* reached Pensacola, and, in an exchange of flowery letters, the formal negotiations with Callava began. They struck a snag promptly when Callava proposed to remove the cannon from the fortifications. Jackson said that by explicit instructions from the President the cannon must be considered a part of the fortifications, specifically ceded by Article II of the treaty. Callava replied that by explicit instructions from the King, under no circumstances could the cannon be considered as a part of the fortifications, ceded by Article II of the treaty. The difference of opinion was given time to expand by failure of the vessels, which were to carry away the Spanish garrisons, to arrive on schedule.

Never a man to pursue a long-range discussion when he could meet the other party face to face, General Jackson entered Florida without invitation, but with the Fourth Infantry, encamped fifteen miles from Pensacola and in courteous terms invited an interview with Don José. The Governor's reply breathed those exquisite compliments before which the oafish bulk of the English language retreats in confusion. Only a violent illness, threatening to extinguish life itself, deprived Señor Callava of the pleasure of visiting General Jackson's camp. "I have the honor to acquaint your Excellency, that in your quality as Commissioner, you may when it suits your pleasure, and in the manner you deem most expedient, exhibit your credentials to me."[45]

So that was it. If General Jackson wished to see Colonel Callava, he must pay the first call—not omitting to bring his credentials.

General Jackson's idea of the formalities, like his ideas concerning the cannon, differed from those of his Spanish colleague. "Etiquette due me as a stranger and to my rank" required that the first call should come from Callava.[46] For the present, however, he limited himself to a fervent prayer for the restoration of His Excellency's health and the hope of a meeting (at his camp) before long.[47] A letter to Coffee used up less ink. "I would sink the place and him with it before I would visit him."[48]

It is a pity that some one like Coffee was not there in the place of the General's young and ornamental aides-de-camp—some useful friend with the forthrightness to tell his chief that he was on the wrong side of this etiquette issue. By international usage Callava was entitled to receive the first call. On occasions, there could be no greater stickler for punctilio than General Jackson, and this was an occasion when, had he been properly enlightened, certainly no Spaniard would have surpassed him in politeness.

While Callava continued diplomatically indisposed, Jackson fell ill in reality. Doctor Bronaugh recommended his immediate removal to Pensacola. He refused to go. Rachel came out from town. Her persuasions were futile. "He said when he came in it should be under his own standard, and that would be the third time he had planted that flag on that wall."[49]

Jackson moved his camp to a mosquito-ridden flat two miles from the wall and pressed Callava for a settlement of the artillery question. After first making sure that Jackson would accept, the Governor "proposed" an elaborate "compromise" (which Jackson had already suggested), the guns remaining in our possession, Jackson giving receipt for them. Ruffled by Jackson's failure to call, the urbane Callava continued to take his revenge by those subtle tactics of postponement for which the Spanish seem to possess an especial genius. Finally he proposed to deliver the province on July seventeenth at ten in the morning. Jackson replied that unless the delivery was made at ten A. M. July fifteenth certain small money penalties would be invoked. Callava replied with an air of offended innocence. He would pay the fines, but delivery could not take place before the day and hour he had specified. "God preserve Your Excellency many Years."

"My feelings as a soldier," replied General Jackson on his last day with the mosquitoes, "correspond with yours, death before an undue condescension. . . . I will be in Pensacola early tomorrow morning to breakfast with Mrs. Jackson, whom our unfortunate misunderstanding has prevented me from visiting since she has been in Pensacola. . . . Will you . . . breakfast with . . . [us] . . . at half after Six or Seven, when I shall have the pleasure of introducing you to my Officers, who know well how to appreciate a soldiers merits." Yet, these hearty words did not go without a final and rather strained effort to bring the Spaniard to General Jackson's terms in the matter of official precedence. Would Callava visit the camp that evening? Jackson asked in a tone strangely akin to entreaty. "I am without a horse, or I should meet you and conduct you: but I send my nephew Lt. A. J. Donelson . . . to conduct vou to the Camp, where you will meet a cordial welcome, . . . but be assured that I have no wish to expose your health. . . Should we not meet . . . before 10 o'clock tomorrow, . . . I shall then take you by the hand as a soldier and a friend, and am certain that after further acquaintance we will know how to appreciate each other."[50]

7

They did not meet until ten o'clock—on July seventeenth. From her balcony Rachel saw the American and Spanish troops facing each other in front of the Government House with flag staff between them. A silent crowd lined the boundaries of the square. Respectfully, but silently, it made a lane for General Jackson and his suite which moved splendidly accoutered and mounted (the General having found a horse) to the steps of the Government House. "O how solemn was his pale countenance when he dismounted," noted Mrs. Jackson. "Recollections of perils and scenes of war . . . presented themselves to view."[51] Quite possibly, though all that the crowd could see was General Jackson in the act of calling on Colonel Callava.

In a few moments they descended the broad steps together. The sternness of the General's countenance had relaxed a little. Callava was smiling. He made a striking appearance—tall, well-formed, blond, not more than forty, and seemingly recovered from the malevolent illness which had prevented him from breakfasting with General Jackson. The dignitaries passed between the lines of troops who raised their arms to salute. The Fourth Infantry band began *The Star Spangled Banner* and the royal standard of Spain fluttered to half-staff.

The Stars and Stripes were raised to a level with it. Aboard the *Hornet* in the bay boomed the first of twenty-one guns, after which the Spanish flag came down and the American ensign went up. Florida was ours.

On the Sunday following, Colonel Callava and staff gave themselves the pleasure of dining with Governor Jackson. They were enchanting guests.

CHAPTER XX

THE BORDER CAPTAIN

I

THE President had not stinted his Governor of Florida as to the extent of his authority. He was clothed with "all the powers . . . heretofore exercised by the Governor and Captain-General and Intendant of Cuba, and by the Governors of East and West Floridas," with the exception of granting land and laying "new or additional" taxes.[1] No American civil servant, before or since, has held in his hands such regal rights. General Jackson expressed himself as satisfied.

On assuming the duties of his office, the Governor found that, despite the delays of Callava, none of the Monroe appointees to subordinate offices had arrived. General Jackson was not greatly dismayed. The town was filled with place seekers—Army officers left without employment by the reduction of the military establishment, politicians, adventurers and the various driftwood of hard-times, many of them without a dollar in their pockets. "The vessels are daily coming in loaded with people," observed Rachel.[2] Before the General's entrance into the city one poor wretch had thrown himself on Mrs. Jackson's mercy. She promised that her husband would do something for him. Jackson made him Port Warden, and the other posts of the absent appointees were promptly filled with friends.

This relief was transitory. Twenty applicants contended for every position. As the Monroe men began to arrive and appropriate the more desirable spoil, the ranks of unemployed Jackson adherents swelled and the Governor began to perceive his gleaming scepter a thing of paste and brass. The positions he could fill with any degree of permanence were few and their rewards small.

Every aspect of the Florida business was small. The white population of the territory did not greatly exceed in numbers the armies Andrew Jackson had created and commanded in the New Orleans campaign. It was segregated in communities remote from one another—the most feasible communication between Pensacola and St. Augustine being by water around the tip of the Cape—rendering the tasks of administration largely the work of local functionaries. This left little for an executive of Jackson's caliber to do, as, until Congress should meet, the Spanish machinery of government remained intact, with no extension of the United States laws except those dealing with the customs and with slave smuggling. For Jackson this was the labor of a few days, after which many an official in his situation and state of health would have given thanks for the opportunity to enjoy the sunshine, and the Gulf breezes that cooled the broad galleries of the Government House. Even Rachel, whose enthusiasm for Florida was tempered by many reservations, said their domicile was "as pleasant as any in town," and that Pensacola was the most healthful place she had ever seen.

The Governor was in no mood for relaxation, however, and before a week was out there was something in his activities that vaguely suggests the occupations of the Emperor at Elba. He undertook the duties of a town constable, demolishing gambling houses and closing the shops and bazaars on Sundays. "Fiddling and dancing not heard any more on the Lord's day," wrote Rachel in triumph. "Cursing not heard. What, what has been done in one week!"[3]

2

Other officials were more inclined to yield to the mutation of destiny and accept the restful nature of their responsibilities. Spanish residents of quality abandoned their reserve, finding some of the American Army officers and their families indeed quite presentable. One of these was Lieutenant Andrew Jackson Donelson. Another member of the Governor's household not wanting for polite attentions was Mrs. Jackson's niece and companion, Narcissa Hays. Rachel bought her a pair of silk slippers to wear to parties. Colonel Callava who remained as a Commissioner of the King proved eminently popular with the military set, whose duties were not arduous. The tedium was abated by an affair of honor between two young officers, in which Doctor Bronaugh acted in his professional capacity. He brought the news of the result to the Executive. Lieutenant Randal had shot Lieutenant Hull through the heart, Hull's pistol, of the hair-trigger type, having stopped at half-cock. "By God," exclaimed the experienced Jackson, "to think that a brave man would risk his life on a hair trigger."[4]

Under the terms of the "compromise" whereby the cannon were left on the fortifications, Jackson had given a receipt for the guns, pending their eventual disposition, and Colonel Callava was to receipt for the provisions which, under the treaty, the United States furnished the Spanish troops while en route to Cuba. When Jackson's aide called on Callava for his signature acknowledging an inventory of the rations, he was put off by a plea of a return of the Colonel's enigmatic illness. Eventually a document from Callava was delivered to the Government House, which, when translated, proved to be no receipt. Whereupon, Jackson declared his own receipt for the ordnance void, warning Callava that his duplicity "can injure no one but Your Excellency and Your Government. . . . This closes my correspondence on this subject forever."[5]

The incident had its influence on the lively pattern of social life in Pensacola, though without diminishing the popularity of the Colonel who managed to retain in his circle several officers of the Fourth Infantry as well as some of the civil appointees of Mr. Monroe, notably Judge Eligius Fromentin of the Federal District Court. To this company belonged John Innerarity, a member of the Cabildo or town council of Pensacola. For ten years this tall, Hispanicized Scot had been resident manager of Forbes & Company. Royal Governors, British soldiers, international adventurers came and departed, but since the reign of Alexander McGillivray Forbes & Company remained the actual rulers of Florida. The Scottish house had dealt with McGillivray by making him a partner.[6] It had covertly assisted Andrew Jackson in removing Alexander Arbuthnot as a troublesome commercial rival. Like a white shadow John Innerarity glided through the weaving labyrinth, never on the losing side.

3

John Quincy Adams used to tell how he dreaded the arrival of the Florida post, never knowing what strange, new problem would spring from the mail bag. When Henry M. Brackenridge, Alcalde of Pensacola, waited on the Governor on the twenty-first day of August, 1821, he brought an interesting story that was destined to sharpen the Secretary's apprehensions. Mr. Brackenridge had received a caller, he told Jackson, in the person of Mercedes Vidal, a free octoroon, the natural daughter of Nicolas Maria Vidal, a Spanish official who had died in 1806 leaving large holdings of land in Louisiana and other property in Pensacola to his half-caste children. The estate had gone into the hands of Forbes & Company for settlement. Some years passed, and, when the beige-complexioned Vidals received nothing, they applied to the courts for an accounting. A number of judicial orders were served on John Innerarity to deliver the records in the case to the courts, but the merchant complied with none of them until peremptory demand was made in 1820. Then he produced a few papers which a court auditor pronounced irregular and presumptive of fraud. Governor Callava signed a decree directing Innerarity to bring forth his accounts as executor under Vidal's will within ten days, and to deposit in the royal treasury certain sums of money within five days. He evaded this decree and presently Governor and trader were on their old terms of intimacy.

Meantime Mercedes Vidal had not been inactive. By the exercise of personal wiles, she had obtained copies of sufficient of the records to substantiate her story. The originals, she said, along with the papers bearing on other estates, had been spirited from the municipal archives, and were now at the residence of Lieutenant Domingo Sousa, a clerk of Callava, in readiness for transportation to Cuba.[7]

Jackson immediately sent Brackenridge to demand the papers of Sousa, who refused to relinquish them without an order from Callava. The Governor slept on the matter and the next morning sent Colonel Robert Butler to bring both Sousa and the papers before him. He brought Sousa, but not the papers, which the terrified Lieutenant admitted he had conveyed to the residence of Colonel Callava.

Jackson had every right to the Vidal and other estate papers. Callava had no right to them. The Governor did not hesitate. He sent Butler, Brackenridge and Doctor Bronaugh to demand the documents of the Commissioner and to say that, if the demand were refused, Sousa would be imprisoned. The four reached the Callava house at four o'clock. They were informed that the Commissioner was dining with Colonel Brooke of the Fourth Infantry. When Callava had not returned at five o'clock, the party proceeded to Colonel Brooke's a few doors away. Mr. Brackenridge entered the house.

The dinner was over. Colonel Callava, John Innerarity, Judge Fromentin and several ladies were on the gallery fronting the bay. The Alcalde stated his errand and Callava jumped up and began to declaim on the inviolability of his person as Royal Commissioner. He declared that he would neither surrender the papers nor return to his house, and Colonel Brooke announced that no civil process should be served on his premises. He followed the Alcalde to the gate complaining about the way his guests had been disturbed.[8]

Later the American emissaries found Callava at his home with John Innerarity and courteously renewed their request. An hour was consumed explaining and trying to bring the slippery Spaniard to accede. At length Callava said that his illness, which had returned coincidentally with the appearance of the Americans, had become so severe that he must refrain from further discussion

Jackson's aides were on the point of leaving when Callava added
that if a list of the papers were presented to him in writing he
would give them up. Brackenridge procured a list, whereupon
Callava with Innerarity beside him, invented pretexts for repudi-
ating his promise. As the Americans withdrew, Innerarity remarked significantly: "The die is cast."[9]

Jackson took these words as a call to battle. "Sir," he directed
Callava's late host, Colonel Brooke, "you will furnish an
officer, sergeant, corporal, and twenty men, and direct the officer
to call on me by half past eight o'clock for orders. They will have
their arms and . . . twelve rounds of ammunition."[10]

Butler, Brackenridge and Bronaugh accompanied the soldiers
to the residence of Colonel Callava. A small light burned in one
room, but no one answered the knocks of the Americans. Butler
entered the hall with two or three soldiers and guided their steps
toward the lighted room. Callava was in bed, though fully clothed
except for his military blouse. He demanded the reason for a
visit "at that time of night."[11] The request for the papers was repeated, and refused. Butler said in that case he had no alternative
but to ask the Colonel to appear before the Governor. The Spanish officer exclaimed that he might be murdered but that he would
not quit his house alive. With as much delicacy as the situation
permitted, Robert Butler stated that he had received his orders
and would obey them. He motioned a file of soldiers into the
room. Deliberately Callava put on his coat, and, taking up his
sword, made a formal tender of it to Lieutenant Mountz commanding the guard. The token of surrender was declined and
at ten o'clock Don José was escorted before Governor Jackson
sitting in his capacity as chief magistrate, or judge, of the Floridas
in the audience chamber of the Government House.

4

The Governor had not left his office since early in the morning.
The yellow rays of the lamps overhead etched more deeply the
lines on his alert but thin and weary face. He politely waved

Callava to a seat at the table facing him. Beside the prisoner sat Cruzat, his secretary. Brackenridge took a chair at one end of the table to act as interpreter. Every other seat in the dim chamber was occupied. Tall Innerarity's lean countenance was intent. Andrew Jackson had not abandoned his habit of looking people in the eyes when he addressed them. Without useless preliminaries he began the interrogation of Callava.

"Were or were not the papers mentioned in a schedule handed to you by H. M. Brackenridge, Alcalde of the city of Pensacola, delivered by Domingo Sousa at your house this day?"[12]

Colonel Callava stood up, looked at his watch and at the audience. He asked permission to write his answer. After writing a few words, he complained that his eyes were weak and asked if he could dictate to his secretary. He began to dictate in a low tone, and some one whispered to the Governor that instead of replying to the question Callava was illuminating the record with a protest against his arrest. The sharp voice of the Governor stopped Cruzat's pen in the middle of a word. An answer to the question was demanded, yes or no.

Colonel Callava replied that he was before the Governor in his capacity as Commissioner of Spain and declined to answer except as he saw fit. Jackson interposed that he was before him "as a private individual, charged with refusing to surrender papers" belonging to the archives and with being a party to an attempt to remove them from the territory.[13] The question was repeated. Callava refused to answer and Antoine Fullarat, his butler, was called before the interrogator. He corroborated the story of Sousa on the delivery of the papers to Callava's house and said that they were still there.

Jackson crisply demanded that Callava surrender the documents. The Colonel replied by objecting to the testimony of a servant and began to harangue the spectators on the indignities done the person of a Spanish Commissioner. Jackson cut him short. He did not wish to hear the word commissioner again. Callava was here as an "individual," amenable to the laws of the territory, charged with complicity in the theft of public documents

The exchange became too rapid for Brackenridge's translating. He asked Cruzat, then Innerarity, to help him and as Callava's friends to remove any impression of a mistaken rendering of his words. They refused.

Jackson tried persuasion. He urged Callava to surrender the papers and to avoid the consequences his refusal must entail. He urged Innerarity and others of the Callava retinue to employ their influence. It was futile. Callava began another speech. The chamber was in a babble. The Governor yelled to Callava to stop and to Brackenridge to stop him, but the confusion went on. The yellow lamplight gleamed on the high cheek-bones. The blue eyes were afire. Quivering with wrath Andrew Jackson seized a paper from the pile before him and splashed his angular autograph at the bottom. So be it with those who opposed the strong waters of his will.[14]

General Jackson had convened his court armed against all contingencies. The paper he had signed was a commitment remanding José Callava to the city jail. Had it stipulated the military dungeon of Fort Barrancas, the case would have been grave enough, though at least the dignity of prisoner of state would have been preserved to Colonel Callava. But the dingy little calabozo, reserved for offenders of the meanest kind—Callava's band was speechless. At the moment its sole occupants were Domingo Sousa and a homeless youth from New Jersey charged with shooting snipes on the communal lands, contrary to municipal regulation.

It was after midnight when the Colonel and his servant, Fullerat, escorted by a crowd of Spanish officers and sympathizers, reached the lockup. By degrees their normal faculties returned. The spirit of Callava rose above the tormenting malady his flesh was heir to. Food and champagne were brought. Corks were drawn and the prisoners went on a bender.

5

Next morning Governor Jackson issued the requisite warrant

of search, and the testamentary papers in the cases of Nicolas Maria Vidal and of three other decedents were taken from the Colonel's files. Jackson had what he wanted and so he signed an order for the release of the prisoners, a kingly instrument, including in the broad sweep of its magnanimity the liberation of the snipe shooter. But stay. Before this act of amnesty could be executed, Judge Fromentin issued and caused to be served on the Officer of the Day a writ of habeas corpus in favor of Callava. Immediately Jackson cited the Judge to appear "and show cause why he has attempted to interfere with my authority." The prisoners were released in obedience to the order of the Governor and not the writ of the Judge.

Fromentin replied that a delicate state of health precluded him from leaving his home, where he remained in expectation of arrest. Jackson failed to gratify this wish, however, and on the following day Eligius Fromentin appeared at the Government House. To this meeting he had traversed a long road. Born in France and ordained as a priest of the Society of Jesus, this gentleman had been left without occupation by the shopping of the clergy during the Revolution. Turning up in Maryland as a college professor, he married into an influential family there, drifted to New Orleans, and in 1812 was elected to the United States Senate. The end of his term found the Bourbons and the Jesuits in clover in France. Fromentin reappeared in Paris with a petition for restoration to his priestly office. The discovery of the American marriage proving an obstacle to the realization of this devout desire, the ex-Senator returned to New Orleans and reembraced his wife. Through the exertions of her family, James Monroe had named him to the Federal bench in Florida in place of the eminent though less widely traveled John Haywood, of Tennessee, who was Jackson's choice.

In the Vidal case Governor Jackson had taken a few short-cuts to justice, as he perceived it.[15] But his procedure had been by no means as irregular as that of Fromentin, not to mention Callava. Fromentin was without jurisdiction except in litigation pertaining to the revenue laws or the importation of slaves. He had issued his writ at the request of John Innerarity and others without asking to see the warrant of commitment, and had it served by a private citizen. Jackson's citation halted him in the act of preparing bail for Callava, the legality of whose confinement he had yet to determine. "The lecture I gave the Judge," wrote Jackson in another contribution to John Quincy Adams's mail bag, "will, I trust, for the future cause him to obey the spirit of his commission, ... instead of attempting to oppose me."[16]

In a mauve cloud of indignation Don José soared off to Washington and plumped his protests before the Spanish Minister. A long and fantastic account from the Colonel's pen of his scandalous treatment in Florida was published by the *National Intelligencer*.[17] As in the past John Quincy Adams supported Jackson. The bold declarations of the Secretary of State provoked a curious echo within the white walls on Pennsylvania Avenue. "The *momentary* gov^t. of Florida," James Monroe described it to a friend, "for *temporary* is too strong a term. ..." This was boldness with a degree of safety, Mr. Monroe being quite aware that Andrew Jackson was moving mountains to be out of Pensacola at the first moment possible. Yet to be altogether secure, the presidential confidant was warned against divulging "[this] sentiment, ... in consideration of the high temper of the general."[18]

On October 5, 1821, the high-tempered General informed Mr. Monroe that "having organised the Government, ... and it being in full operation,"[19] he was going home. The President asked him to remain, but, long before his letter reached Florida, the handsome carriage, drawn by four white horses, had emerged from the Government House gate and crossed the flowering Plaza. A sentry presented arms, and the Gargantuan quit the land of Lilliput.

When he was well on his way, Colonel Brooke distributed invitations to a ball. "A great constellation of Spanish beauties," John Innerarity and Judge Fromentin were there, but Jackson partizans heard the cadenced thrum of guitars from afar. "It is impossible," one lamented, "to describe the vacuum in the society of this place occasioned by the departure of yourself."[20]

6

How peaceful the Hermitage. "Our place looks like it had been abandoned for a season, But we have a cheirful fire for our friends, and a prospect of living at it for the . . . ballance of our lives. I have sent on my resignation by Doctor Brunaugh."[21]

It was over, this uncertain adventure into which Andrew Jackson had been drawn by an unreciprocated sense of loyalty to the President and a wish to help his young friends. Rachel again felt a release from the alien and unassimilable world against which she had striven for thirty years. She and Andrew undertook to make their home comfortable for the decline of their days. In the great hall stood seven cases of furniture and table silver purchased at New Orleans. The freight bill was two hundred and seventy-three dollars and seventy-five cents. However Rachel might deplore the wicked luxury of the complaisant Creole town there was no denying the comfort of good French beds. "1 Bedstead, of Mahogony, fluted, $100" was for her own and Andrew's tall south chamber; likewise "1 Matress of fine ticking, $45, 1 moschetto Bar of muslin, $16, 1 Counterpane knotted, Marseilles, $24."[22] There was also a new sideboard and something to fill its decanters: "18 Gallons Best Brandy $45, 1 half pipe Old Madeira, $275; 1 Bll Old Whiskey $29.75. 6 Boxes Claret $72, 2 do $26, 1 Cask Porter $28, 3 bottles Bitters $3, 6 Boxes Cigars $24, 2 Boxes Brandy fruits $16."[23] In all sufficient to impart a mellow cast to conversation beside the cheerful fire for many a winter's evening. And to prove that no human experience is wholly barren, Rachel had brought away from Florida a preference for Spanish cigars.

These domestic preparations promised to afford an answer to a letter of inquiry from an old friend of the General, Seth Lewis, who wrote: "Since we saw each other both of us have passed through a variety of Scenes, and we are now approaching the evening of our lives. Your career has been brilliant but stormy—

mine more humble but more peaceful. . . . We have both had time and opportunity to make a full trial of the gifts of fortune, as they are usually called, and to form a correct Judgment of their real value. We have both pursued them with the same object in view— We have pursued them as a means of happiness. Have they yielded us that happiness? For myself I must answer . . . in the negative, . . . and I presume your answer . . . must be the same."[24]

Seth Lewis presumed too much. His friend was content and the measure of his contentment was in proportion to the sincerity of his resolution to exchange a brilliant career for a quiet one. General Jackson was fifty-five and looked ten years older. His hair bristled up like the crest of a hussar's helmet, but it was almost white. His remaining strength he meant to dedicate to the service of his family. Besides the Hermitage he had the affairs of two other plantations to direct—his own place at Florence and the Hutchings boy's legacy at Huntsville.

The cotton yield of 1821 was satisfactory, and, after two years of depression, men looked to spring for signs of the rainbow. The General's crop was ginned by New Year's and he planned to send it to New Orleans on his own account rather than accept the prices of Nashville and Alabama commission merchants. Waiting for the winter rains to fill the rivers that were to float his produce to market, he boxed up his public papers and declined an invitation to tour the North and the East. Other concerns, he said, engaged him. "I have my little sons including Lincoyer, at school, and their education has been greatly neglected in my absence."[25]

He subscribed for twenty newspapers from all parts of the country. They littered the floor of his study whose walls were a reliquary of his military past. With a faculty which, as always, was half discernment and half leaping instinct, he surveyed the nest of new national problems irresistibly centering about slavery—and remained inert before them. "The Missouri [Compromise] question . . . will be the entering wedge to separate the union. . . . I hope I may not live to see the evils that must grow out of this wicked design of demagogues, who talk about humanity, but whose sole object is self agrandisement."²⁶

7

Already there was a theater in Nashville, with a brick sidewalk in front, and they were speaking of street lamps to light the steps of the new era. The town claimed thirty-three hundred inhabitants, counting eight hundred slaves. Fifty municipally owned negroes kept the clay thoroughfares tidy in dry weather and passable in wet. Busier shops and stores and statelier homes were not to be seen elsewhere between Lexington and Natchez. The Nashville Inn had adorned its front with a three-story gallery and its barroom with a billiard table. While still well patronized the cockpit on the vacant lot next door was losing its refined social tone. Davidson Academy had become Cumberland College, General Jackson contributing one thousand dollars toward the erection of the new buildings. The two Andrews, as he called his adopted son and the Hutchings boy, attended its elementary classes. Nieces and grandnieces of Rachel pursued the genteel arts at the Nashville Female Academy.

The tradition of the sword was fading from the Hermitage family. Colonel Robert Butler and Lieutenant Andrew Jackson Donelson followed the head of their clan into retirement, Butler to restore his plantation, Donelson to study law at Transylvania University in Kentucky. "Amuse yourself occasionally, with history," counseled his uncle, "amongst which if to be had, I would recommend to you the history of the scottish chiefs. I have always thought that sir William Wallauce . . . was the best model for a young man. In him we find a stubborn virtue, . . . too pure for corruption, . . . allways ready to brave any danger for the relief of his country or his friend."²⁷

Young Mr. Donelson did not have to seek so far afield for a model. Striding the level acres of Hermitage farm was another Celtic chieftain, a man of fire and tenderness, of strong and sincere, if sometimes rash, emotions—a product of the vibrant forces

that had swept him, thirty-four springs before, across the gusty
Blue Ridge into the Western wilderness. He had helped to beat
back that wilderness from the Mountains to the Mississippi and to
raise the frontier to an almost equal partner with the seaboard in
the management of public affairs. By virility, experience and,
since the war, the prestige of victory, pioneers compensated for
the disparity of their numbers. They lived close to the machinery
of government. They had seen it made: "offices" for the registra-
tion of land titles housed in immigrant wagons, courts in log
cabins; Indian wars, Indian treaties; every man a soldier and a
servant of the law. Thus county governments had taken shape,
and over them territorial and state régimes from which it was
an easy step for the frontiersman with all the aplomb in the
world to shoulder into the councils of the nation.

Yet, in 1816, the greatest of the race had drawn back from the
presidency. Nor did five more years on the plinth of popularity
alter his resolution. A New York editor took sly cognizance of
the lingering ambition of a few of the General's friends. Jackson
thrust the sheet from him. "Do they think I am such a damned
fool! No sir; I know what I am fit for. I can command a body
of men in a rough way; but I am not fit to be President."[28]

So the old border captain: heart-beat of a throbbing era, turning his face toward the shadows enclosing the epoch that had
made him, a national hero high above the ignoble rivalries of
politics.

He wrote young Captain Richard Call not to despair. Despite
all that Jackson could do, this demobilized officer had been left at
Pensacola without employment. "Believe me when I first met you
in the field . . . my opinion was formed of you. . . . Your soldier
like conduct when deserted by your company . . . drew my particular attention to you to see a gallant youth of Eighteen abandoned
by his captain and company all retiring from the field of Honour,
and you left alone, determined to die rather than tarnish your
military fame. . . . I regret our separation but still more I regret
that injustice and inattention of the executive in not having provided for you agreeable to his promise and my expectation. But

my dear Call I have been Tossed upon the waves of fortune from youthood, I have experienced prosperity and adversity. . . . It was this that forced into action all the energies of my mind. . . . Pe[r]mit me to say to you that long experience has made me well acquainted with human nature. It is well to study it as you progress through life—you will find many . . . who by their openness of conduct . . . obtain your confidence that it may be betrayed. Guard against such impositions."[29]

8

Andrew Jackson deemed that he had guarded against them well. To Mr. Monroe's affectation of regret at Jackson's determination to close his public career, the General responded with smooth civility. Before him lay a letter dated from Augusta, Georgia, and signed "FRIEND." Jackson was not a man ordinarily to lay great store by anonymous communications, but he could not deny that this one was exceptional. Six months later found him still speculating on the identity of the author.[30]

"I have long known the President of the U. States and understood his character, . . . dull and stupid—cold & selfish, . . . under the dominion of a pride so inordinate that nothing short of universal homage can satisfy. . . . Upon this pride you inflicted a wound when you consented to attend him . . . through part of his Southern & western Tour— In that journey M^r. President intended to play the great man, but . . . Genl. Jackson . . . attracted all eyes. . . . Hence the intrigue to get you from the Army, hence the submissiveness to a dictation from Genl Brown, Genl Scott & M^r. Crawford— hence all your measures are traversed, your recommendations neglected. . . . When you were appointed Governor of Florida they told your friends it was a compliment to you—amongst themselves they said it was *to get rid of you.* at the head of the army you were still formidible, . . . as a Govr. of a Territory, a mere colonial prefect, soon forgotten." The letter closed by saying that Crawford would be the next President "unless someone other than Adams is taken up." Jackson was

urged to "rouse the western Country" to an appreciation of this
posture of affairs.[31]

This was a seductive invitation for support for the cause of Calhoun, and not the last of its kind. Faithful Doctor Bronaugh,
who carried his chief's resignation to Washington, wrote from
the capital. "The course which M^r. Adams has pursued in relation to Callava & Fromentin does him much credit," Don José
having been rebuffed and the Judge rebuked. "He is an honest
and independent politician. . . . This is also [true of] M^r. Calhoun, . . . but M^r. Monroe in my opinion never acts without a
view to his popularity. M^r. Adams & M^r. Calhoun on every occasion speak in the most decided approbation of all your acts in
Florida."[32]

The General's withdrawal from public life had caused a vacuum
not alone at Pensacola. The Eastern press continued to conjure
up implications touching the presidential contest. They remembered the toast to DeWitt Clinton. Was it the mark of a covert
alliance? inquired the New York *Advocate*. This was more than
the retired soldier could permit to pass unchallenged, and the
result was Andrew Jackson's first expression on the looming campaign of 1824. "I have an opinion of my own on all subjects, and
when that opinion is formed I persue it *publickly,* regardless of
who goes with me. . . . You are at liberty to say in my name to both
my friends and enemies, that I will as far as my influence extends
support Mr. Adams unless Mr. Calhoun should be brought forward. . . . As to Wm. H. Crawford you know my opinion I would
support the Devil first."[33]

Now would they leave him to the contemplation of his fire?

NOTES

CHAPTER I

[1]Previous biographies of Jackson, including that of Reid and Eaton, prepared under the General's eye, say that Jackson's parents landed at Charleston and reached the Waxhaws by the southern route. The same statement appears in a document, not in Jackson's hand, found in the Library of Congress collection of Jackson Manuscripts (CXVIII, 33). This gives an account of Jackson's father in Ireland and of his father's three brothers. After he became famous General Jackson from time to time was in receipt of genealogical information from persons claiming kinship. All such material examined by this writer seems warped to meet the aspirations of the authors. For example, *The Genealogy of the Jackson Family*, by Reverend Hugh Parks Jackson and others (1890), 6-11; also an engaging letter dated County of Down, Ireland, September 21, 1821, William M. McCully to "General Jackson near New Orleans, North America." (Library of Congress.)

Had the Jacksons landed at Charleston at any time between 1761 and 1775 their debarkation would have been noted in the records of His Majesty's Council for South Carolina, which are intact in the original manuscript in the office of the Historical Commission of South Carolina at Columbia. These list all immigrants passing through that port. The only member of the Waxhaw clan to which General Jackson was connected by blood or marriage thus shown is James Crow who disembarked a single man, was granted land in the Waxhaws in 1768, when Jackson was one year old, and married Grace Hutchinson, Jackson's aunt. Grace was the sixth Hutchinson sister to turn up in the Waxhaws. When she came is not known, though it is barely possible that she accompanied Jackson's parents in 1765.

This is negative evidence that the Jacksons came by the northern route, but it is practically conclusive and moreover reenforced by other circumstances. The Crawfords who, the widely copied Parton (I, 49) says, accompanied the Jacksons from Ireland, were born in Scotch-Irish dominated southeastern Pennsylvania, the sons of Colonel John Crawford, a native of Ayrshire, Scotland. (*Daughters of the American Revolution Magazine*, November, 1920, p. 640. The unnamed Crawford brother of this article is James who married General Jackson's aunt, Jennet Hutchinson in Pennsylvania.) Most of the Waxhaws was settled by Scotch-Irish who came the Pennsylvania route, many of them second generation Americans. After the Revolution when counties were organized in that part of South Carolina, the three in the Waxhaw region were named Lancaster, York and Chester after counties in Pennsylvania. See also: a letter, J. G. Wardlaw, York, South Carolina, to A. S. Salley, junior,

May 20, 1922, private collection of Mr. Salley, Columbia, South Carolina; James D. Craig memoir, dated September 24, 1858, in Walter Clark Manuscripts, III, 332, North Carolina Historical Commission, Raleigh.

In view of the inaccuracies of the latter document, to which the writer adverts in Note No. 17 *post*, anything in it must be considered with caution. Yet it contains material worthy of belief as, for instance, the landing in Pennsylvania of the Jackson emigrants. Although the writer has refrained from using several details of the landing which are patently the result of poor memory on the part of old Mr. Craig or his informant, others which appear credible are incorporated as the best evidence on the subject extant.

The Craig Memoir states that the Jacksons "Landed at Caninigigo Pennsylvania & Jackson came Straight to the Carolinas." Mr. Craig's "Caninigigo" rather clearly refers to the Scotch-Irish settlements along Conowingo Creek, a tributary of the Susquehanna. The place of actual debarkation was probably Philadelphia, but possibly Port Deposit, Maryland, at the head of navigation of the shallow Susquehanna, a few miles below the mouth of Conowingo Creek. The place of embarkation— Larne, County Antrim—is "Learn" in the Craig manuscript.

²Craig Memoir, Walter Clark Manuscripts, III., 332, North Carolina Historical Commission, Raleigh.

³Reminiscence of William Allen, member of Congress from Ohio during the Jackson Administration, reporting a conversation with Jackson, from Augustus C. Buell, *A History of Andrew Jackson* (1904), I, 20.

⁴Craig Memoir, Walter Clark Manuscripts, III, 332, North Carolina Historical Commission, Raleigh.

⁵Thus she signed herself (June 1, 1774. See Deed Book H., p. 100, Lancaster County, South Carolina, records, Lancaster), but survives in the Waxhaw tradition and in print as Jane, although in several contemporary records the spelling is Jean. (S. H. Walkup, reprinted in *North Carolina University Magazine*, X, 225, and *Congressional Record*, June 18, 1926, p. 11582.)

⁶*The Daughters of the American Revolution Magazine*, November, 1920, p. 640, gives date of arrival of the three Crawford brothers in the Waxhaws as "about 1760." In 1763 Robert and Joseph Crawford bought the Crawford lands in the Waxhaws. (Deed Book 5, p. 215, Mecklenburg County records, Charlotte.) Joseph died shortly thereafter and James occupied the portion of the land on which General Jackson said he was born; at any rate, was reared, though James did not get a title to this land until September 12, 1768. Such delay in executing titles after possession was not unusual. The grant stated that he was then resident on the land and had "improved" it.

⁷Walkup, who correctly cites the land records.

⁸"Lessley" is their own spelling. John Lessley's land was ordered surveyed October 7, 1766, by the South Carolina authorities. (Manuscript, Journal of Council, Historical Commission of South Carolina, Columbia.)

Settlers often occupied lands before they were surveyed. No record of land owned by Samuel Lessley has been found.

[9]The declaration of entry, by which Ewing initiated his claim to his land, is missing from the records, but he had made such declaration prior to April 20, 1766, when it was surveyed. (Land Grant Records, Office of Secretary of State, Raleigh.)

[10]*Ibid.*

[11]George Howe, D.D., *History of the Presbyterian Church in South Carolina* (1870), I, 289.

[12]Walter Clark Manuscripts, III, 331, North Carolina Historical Commission, Raleigh.

[13]Reminiscence of H. E. Coffey, Rock Hill (South Carolina) *Record*, August 19, 1920.

[14]The story of the temporary loss of the body of Andrew Jackson, senior, is unsupported by any contemporary documentary evidence that the writer has been able to discover, but it is supported by the uncontradicted and unanimous tradition of the locality. I have had it from collateral descendants of General Jackson, many of whom still reside in the Waxhaws. On October 8, 1931, the Fort Mill (South Carolina) *Times*, published a few miles from where the burial took place, reprinted an account of T. D. Faulkner, a third cousin of General Jackson, who died in 1916. Mr. Faulkner was born in 1825 and his grandparents may have attended the funeral. Mrs. Anne Hutchison Bigger, of Rock Hill, South Carolina, and others assure me of the existence of an account of the funeral written in the 1840's by Reece Massey from the recollections of persons who were present. Reece Massey was a distinguished local figure. His father, uncles and aunts went to school with General Jackson, and his grandparents, whose farm adjoined the Crawfords', attended the funeral. Though unable to find Mr. Massey's narrative, I feel that some day it will be publicly available.

[15]The location of the grave of Andrew Jackson, senior, is not known with assurance, but generations of old residents pointed to a brown stone, weather-worn to a knob about a foot high, as marking the burial place. In 1931 an inscribed boulder was ceremoniously dedicated to mark this spot definitely as Jackson's resting-place. According to published accounts of local origin (see Yorkville *Enquirer*, York, South Carolina, April 14, 1931), this ceremony originated with the visit in 1931 of an "unidentified stranger" carrying a broken piece of stone in a motor-car. He said he had brought it from Tennessee. Digging into the supposed grave another stone was found. The broken edge of the two fitted together. The conclusion is that some one, presumably General Jackson, had transported to Tennessee half of his father's gravestone. Some old residents of the Waxhaws with whom the writer has corresponded are skeptical of this form of "proof." Others whose veracity is unassailable have given me affidavits as to the visit of the stranger and the fitting of the stones together. In Tennessee the existence of such a stone is unknown to history.

[16]Andrew Jackson to James H. Witherspoon, August 11, 1824. *Correspondence of Andrew Jackson*, edited by John Spencer Bassett, III, 265. Circumstances surrounding this letter are mentioned in Note 17 following.

[17]Andrew Jackson has been accredited with eight birthplaces or one more than Homer. The controversy began in 1815, a few weeks after the Battle of New Orleans made him famous.

I shall dismiss without discussion the claims advanced in favor of Ireland, England, the high seas, York County, Pennsylvania; Augusta County, Virginia; Berkeley County, Virginia (now West Virginia); also the narratives, respectably sponsored, making, on one hand, his father a mulatto and his mother an army camp follower; and on the other hand his mother "the only child of John Vance (a corruption of de Valebus) who . . . claimed royal descent."

There remains the seasoned controversy as to whether Andrew Jackson was born in South Carolina or in North Carolina. He was born in South Carolina, a fact established by Crown authority fixing the limits of the North and South provinces which made the thirty-fifth parallel of latitude the boundary in the Waxhaws. To reach this parallel it was necessary first to run the boundary up in a northwesterly direction from the coast to it. This line was properly started in 1735. In 1737 a surveyor in the service of the provinces set out to complete it and thought he had done so. But he miscalculated and instead of driving his stake at the thirty-fifth parallel, where actually the boundary turned west, he drove his stake in a meadow about eleven miles south of the thirty-fifth parallel.

As the country filled up a guessed-at westward projection of a line from the stake was mistakenly thought to be the boundary. The brothers-in-law, James Crawford and George McKemey, got lands by North Carolina authority in the eleven-mile strip. In 1764 commissioners representing the two provinces came to the Waxhaws with surveyors to finish running the boundary. From a stake in the meadow they started the line westward. When they got to the Charleston-Salisbury post road, a mile south of James Crawford's house, they discovered the error and went no farther, but set a stake beside the road in the shade of a hickory tree and reported to the authorities. The matter was referred to London, and things became lively in the Waxhaws where the sovereignty of the eleven-mile strip was in contest between North Carolina and South Carolina. Law was on South Carolina's side. The land was legally hers. But possession was largely on North Carolina's side. Owing to the surveyor's blunder, North Carolina had made grants to settlers within the strip and taken other measures to establish her authority there.

In 1771 the King approved a compromise. South Carolina surrendered to North Carolina the eleven-mile strip in the Waxhaws, in exchange for which North Carolina surrendered to South Carolina about an equal amount of land west of the Catawba River. In 1772 this decision was carried into effect on the ground. The line of 1764, from the stake in the meadow to the stake under the hickory beside the road, was legalized, but not extended. At the stone the line turned north, following the windings of the highway north for about eight miles, to where this road cut across a corner of the Catawba Indian reservation.

As the McKemey house was on the east side of the road, this arrangement put it in North Carolina. The Crawford house, being on the west side of the road, landed in South Carolina. Thus both houses stood within shouting distance of the border for more than forty years when again the line was changed slightly. The shifting highway had proved an unsatisfactory boundary, and two states collaborated to fix the line without reference to the vagaries of the road. The conferences were long-drawn-out. Whether the Governor of South Carolina's quotable amenity to the Governor of North Carolina about its being a long time between refreshments hastened a conclusion is not known, but in 1813 the line, as it stands to-day, was determined. This left the McKemey house four hundred and seven yards over the border in North Carolina and the Crawford house a good half-mile in South Carolina. (For original documents on the boundary controversy see A. S. Salley, junior, *The Boundary Line between North Carolina and South Carolina* (1929), and William L. Saunders [Editor], *Colonial Records of North Carolina* (1887), V, xxxv *et seq.*)

North Carolina's claim to being the state of Andrew Jackson's nativity rests on the assumption that he was born in the McKemey house, although this house was not on North Carolina soil until Jackson was four years old. A North Carolina Chapter of the Daughters of the American Revolution has erected of the stones from a cabin that stood on Mc-Kemey's land a monument on that site which records that Jackson was born there. Two and a half miles away a South Carolina Chapter of the Daughters of the American Revolution has put up a conspicuous marker on the site of the James Crawford homestead. Between the merits of these opposed claims the historian must choose, though the choice does not affect the fact that both houses were in South Carolina at the time of Andrew Jackson's birth. My choice is in favor of the Crawford place because Jackson said he was born there, and I think it more likely than not that he knew.

Nevertheless, the McKemey house claim is worthy of examination in some detail. As promulgated in 1858 by Samuel H. Walkup, a lawyer of Union County, North Carolina, in which the McKemey lands lie, it convinced James Parton when he visited the Waxhaws the year following in quest of material for his biography. If not the most accurate work of its kind, Parton's three volumes remain after seventy-five years the most readable and the most copiously copied of the many lives of General Jackson. The acceptance without investigation of Parton's conclusion has done much to give the McKemey claim the authority of fact.

Contrary to a wide-spread belief, which one finds even among some who have studied the subject, the McKemey claim did not originate with the labors of Mr. Walkup. He merely consolidated, in the form of a very respectable case, a body of hearsay that had been current in the Waxhaws for more than a generation. Two months after the Battle of New Orleans had made him famous there was a discussion in Charleston as to Jackson's birthplace. Colonel William Richardson Davie, who had known Jackson from childhood, being appealed to, affirmed a statement that "he is a native of Lancaster [District, now County] in this state." (Charleston *City Gazette and Commercial Daily Advertiser*, March 27, 1815.) This *may* mean that Davie believed him to have been born in the Crawford rather than the McKemey house which was then in North Carolina, and, in 1815, seems generally thought to have always been there.

In the autumn of 1815 the South Carolina Assembly formally acknowledged Jackson as a native son in a resolution of thanks for the victory at New Orleans. On February 9, 1816, Jackson expressed his appreciation in a letter to Governor Williams in which he said his pleasure was enhanced by the fact that the resolution came from "that state which gave me birth." (*Correspondence*, II, 229.) This is the earliest of a long series of statements in Jackson's own hand fixing his birthplace in South Carolina, though mindful that North Carolina had its claimants owing to the McKemey house tradition.

In 1817 Reid and Eaton's life of Jackson appeared. The writer has examined the opening chapters in the original manuscript. Jackson supervised the production of this pioneer biography and let stand the loose statement that he was born "about forty-five miles above Camden." This vagueness was one of the things that stimulated Mr. Walkup to his researches under the mistaken idea that Jackson was uncertain in his own mind as to his exact birthplace. In 1819 S. Putnam Waldo's *Memoirs of Andrew Jackson* came out, making the General a native of South Carolina. The statement prompted Thomas Watson of Baltimore to write Jackson asking if the statement were true, and Jackson replied under date of March 4, 1820, that it was. (For his letter see New York *Times*, November 4, 1922.)

In 1820 South Carolina began the compilation of a state map under the direction of Robert Mills, one of the eminent cartographers and engineers of the day. The contract for Lancaster District was sublet to J. Boykin, a native of the region. Present-day surveyors in the Waxhaws testify as to the fidelity of Mr. Boykin's lines, and tactical historians have found him fairly exact in locating Revolutionary battles and skirmishes. Boykin placed a star on his map to denote the James Crawford homestead as "Gen¹ A. Jackson's Birth Place." The map was published in 1825 and Mills, who had fought under Jackson at New Orleans, sent him a copy at the Hermitage. The reminiscent glow its perusal afforded is reflected in a warm letter of acknowledgment. "A view of the map pointing to the spot that gave me birth brings fresh to my memory many associations dear to my heart, many days pleasure with my juvenile companions; but alas most of them are gone to that bourne from which no one returns. . . . Most of the names of the places [plantations] are changed; all the old generation appears to have passed away. . . . The crossing of Waxhaw creek within one mile of which I was born, is still, however, I see, possessed by Mr. John Crawford, son of the owner (Robert) who lived there when I was growing up and at school. . . . From the accuracy with which this spot is marked on the map I conclude the whole must be correct." (Dated July 8, 1827. Private collection of Thompson D. Dimitry of New Orleans, a descendant of Mr. Mills.)

In 1824, in response to an inquiry from James H. Witherspoon, a prominent resident of Lancaster District, Jackson wrote: "I was born in So Carolina, as I have been told at the plantation whereon James Crawford lived about one mile from the Carolina road [crossing] of the Waxhaw Creek." (*Correspondence*, III, 265.)

None of these assertions by the General was published, however, and the Eaton biography, with the vague statement as to his place of birth, remained the account generally accepted and read. For this or some other reason the McKemey tradition quietly persisted. The first reference to it in print known to this writer appeared in 1824 in a brief note, signed "K," to the editor of the Columbia (South Carolina) *Telescope*, copied on November 24, 1824, by the Charleston *Courier:* "There has been much uncertainty in regard to General Jackson's birthplace; some asserting that he was born in North Carolina, others . . . that he was born in South Carolina, and others that he is a native of Ireland. I am glad that I have it in my power to settle this question. . . . After the death of his father, his mother . . . went to live with her brother-in-law, a Mr. McAmey. . . . General Jackson was born at the house of Mr. McAmey, and therefore in the State of North Carolina. When he was about six weeks old his mother removed with him to the house of Mr. James Crawford, another brother-in-law, on the South Carolina side of the road."

The death of General Jackson in 1845 revived interest in the question, and in a Fourth-of-July oration that year Mr. Walkup obtained the signed statements of two aged and respectable residents of the Waxhaws to support his position. Benjamin Massey declared that "about the year 1822" he had heard Mrs. Sarah Lathan say that Jackson was born at the McKemey house and that, as a child of seven, she was present at the birth. Sarah Lathan was a first cousin of General Jackson, her mother, Sarah Hutchinson Lessley, being Jackson's aunt. The other statement was by John Carnes who said he had often heard Mrs. Sarah Hutchinson Lessley say that Jackson was born at McKemey's.

Thirteen years later, in 1858, a Virginia claim to the nativity of Jackson, brought forth the now celebrated "Walkup evidence," to which, despite voluminous subsequent controversy and extravagant claims pro and con, nothing material has been added. It was published originally in a weekly newspaper, the *North Carolina Argus* (Wadesboro), September 23, 1858. Later it appeared as a pamphlet. The most available reprints appear in the *North Carolina University Magazine*, X, 225-44, and the *Congressional Record* for June 18, 1926, pp. 11535-40. From the ambiguities of Reid and Eaton's and other biographies Mr. Walkup concluded that "there was no settled opinion by General Jackson himself of the place of his birth. . . . He just supposed that he was born at Crawford's place . . . because his earliest associations were connected with it. . . . I think it can be as clearly demonstrated as any such thing can be at this distance of time that Gen. Jackson . . . was born at the house of George Mc-Kemey or McCamie." In the light of evidence then publicly known, this was a reasonable assumption, and not a reckless claim for the testimony Mr. Walkup had to offer.

This testimony consisted of written statements by six persons (including the Massey and Carnes statements of 1845) that they had heard Sarah Lessley, or her daughter Sarah Lathan, say that they knew Jackson was born at McKemey's because they were present. One of Mrs. Lathan's sons and two of her nephews, second cousins therefore of General Jackson, were among those so testifying. All had to remember rather a long way back for Mrs Lathan had then been dead thirty years and Mrs. Lessley fifty years. The composite story of the six statements is this: After the death of Andrew Jackson, senior, the widow started from the Twelve Mile Creek place to James Crawford's to make her home, but at the McKemey house, two and a half miles short of her destination, was taken with pains of labor. In the nighttime Sarah Lessley, Mrs. Jackson's sister and a midwife, was sent for. She went, taking her seven-year-old daughter along, and assisted at the birth.

Additionally there were seven written statements of old persons who had heard it said on no named authority that Jackson was born at Mc-Kemey's, and one statement to the effect that the birthplace "has always been disputed" by partizans of the Crawford and McKemey sites.

I am unable to dismiss this evidence as cavalierly as some modern proponents of the Crawford claim are inclined to do, but this is true: it presents one side of the case, argued in professional fashion by a lawyer. If the McKemey claim had "always" been disputed, as one of Mr. Walkup's witnesses admits, there must have been some basis in local evidence for the Crawford pretensions. But unfortunately no one reduced this to writing, or rounded it out in the form of a case. Whereas the McKemey claim had the benefit of an energetic and skilled advocate who traveled about gathering depositions, prompting witnesses, and, in at least one instance, amplifying and correcting testimony when it presented demonstrable errors in detail which, if given to the public, might have impaired belief in the whole.

I do not challenge the sincerity of Mr. Walkup's research, notwithstanding a perusal of his papers in the original manuscript (Walter Clark Manuscripts, III, North Carolina Historical Commission, Raleigh) suggests that at times his method was that of a barrister rather than a historian. The affidavit of James Faulkner, Jackson's cousin, was one of the most important offered. The published affidavit is one of three made by Mr. Faulkner that are preserved in the manuscripts. All appear in the hand of Mr. Walkup, though signed by Mr. Faulkner and sworn to. The first deposition. dated August 26, 1858, contains several small errors, due no doubt to slips of memory, and corrected with a different pen and ink by Mr. Walkup. The deposition published also bears the date of August 26, 1858, but as a matter of fact could not have been written earlier than September sixth, because it appears on the same four-page folio with two other depositions bearing date of September sixth, and was unmistakably written *after* these depositions were. The published Faulkner declaration is a recasting of the original with corrections. A third Faulkner declaration, dated September fifteenth, is more positive on some points than the published statement.

Another thing one hears much about is the "Craig evidence" in favor of the McKemey contention. This was first mentioned by Parton (I, 55) who says Mr. Craig "remembers hearing old James Faulkner [father of James Faulkner of the preceding paragraph] say that, while sleeping with Andrew Jackson in the McKemey house, Andrew told him that he was born in that house." What old Mr. Craig really said in the letter which Parton perused was that Faulkner "Slept with Andrew. . . . A Lad about 14 years old & understood"—not understood Jackson to say—"he was Born in that house." (Walter Clark Manuscripts, III, 332. North Carolina Historical Commission, Raleigh.)

The origin of the Craig evidence is this. When Mr. Walkup was gathering his data he wrote to James D. Craig who had moved to Mississippi twenty years before. Mr. Craig's reply came too late for inclusion in the publication in the *North Carolina Argus*, but Walkup showed it to Parton whose misquotation gave it an importance that has grown with the years until it has been represented as settling the question absolutely by supplying what the Walkup evidence lacks to make out a prima-facie case. "The weakness in the [Walkup] case," writes Dr. Archibald Henderson of the University of North Carolina (Raleigh *News and Observer*, October 3, 1926), "inhered in the fact that the affidavits set forth not the statements of eye-witnesses . . . of Jackson's birth but statements of neighbors who heard the narrations of alleged eye-witnesses." The Craig evidence, continues Doctor Henderson, supplies this deficiency in a manner "unimpeachable." During the campaign of 1828 when the born-in-Ireland, the negro-father and other stories were being circulated against the General, Mr. Craig, at the request of a Jackson manager in Ohio, gathered certain affidavits as to Jackson's parentage and place of birth, which was designated as the McKemey house. The affidavits were lost and no one has been found who ever saw any scrap of them. Thirty years later Mr. Craig undertook to repeat to Mr. Walkup the substance of the lost affidavits and succeeded, according to Doctor Henderson, in recalling "an exact summary" of the originals.

If this is true, the originals were almost worthless because the 1858 summary contains so many grotesque, if entirely unintentional, misstatements of known facts. James Faulkner, who is reported to have slept with Andrew, is made to say that Jackson's father arrived in the Waxhaws with "2 Daughters & Settld in No Caroling 12 Mile Creek Afterwards his 2 Daughters Married A Lassely & James Crawford." Another affidavit gives an account of the military service of Andrew Jackson and his two brothers in the Revolutionary War that is inaccurate in almost every particular. In a third affidavit "Mrs. Mary Cowsar An Aged Lady I believe Daughter of Magor [Robert] Crawford" [incorrect] says she called at the McKemey house the morning Andrew was born and "Before . . . [he] was Dressed." This is the eye-witness testimony that is supposed to clinch everything. Such is the Craig evidence, often alluded to but never published, except such excerpts as support the particular contention under review.

Between 1922 and 1928 the subject of Jackson's birthplace was periodically discussed in the House of Representatives in connection with the compilation of the *Biographical Dictionary of the American Congress*. Representative William F. Stevenson, of South Carolina, leaning heavily upon the researches of A. S. Salley, junior, for twenty-seven years secretary of the Historical Commission of South Carolina, and the late Representative William C. Hammer, of North Carolina, were the opposing champions. While rather declamatory their speeches are repositories of valuable evidence on both sides. (*Congressional Record,* February 23, 1922, p. 3395; June 18, 1926, p. 11534; May 24, 1928, p. 10116; July 2, 1928, p. 11312.)

My opinion is that neither party has proved its case, but that the Crawford house has a little the better of it on Jackson's own testimony. Jackson became a conscious performer before the glass of history. After the Battle of New Orleans he began filing away papers endorsed "for the historian." He knew of this dispute. The boundary question agitating the Waxhaws during his childhood, I think, should have tended to fix in his mind his exact birthplace. When he wrote that he had been told that he was born at Crawford's, I think that statement clearly represented his own belief in the matter, attained after weighing the evidence. Mr. Walkup has a case—for which he claimed less than his modern followers—but I do not think that this case, resting as it does on the distant recollection of conversations with two aged women, one of them a child of seven when the event took place, is sufficient to refute Jackson himself.

[18]Deed Book XX, 21, Mecklenburg County records, Charlotte. Jackson owned this property until after his marriage in Tennessee, selling it in 1793. (Deeds, Book D, old, p. 227, Lancaster County records, Lancaster.)

[19]Some particulars of this boundary dispute, as it concerns the controversy over the state of Jackson's nativity given in Note No. 17 *ante.*

[20]Reminiscences of Susan Smart Alexander, *National Intelligencer,* August 1, 1845.

[21]Howe, I, 416.

[22]Buell, I, 37.

[23]John Reid Manuscript, p. 1, Tennessee Historical Society, Nashville. John Reid, Jackson's aide-de-camp in the War of 1812, began a life of his chief immediately thereafter. With about a third of the work com-

pleted, Reid died and John Henry Eaton finished the book which was published under their joint authorship in 1817. In 1823 Eaton brought the work to date and Reid's name was dropped. Two manuscript copies of Reid's effort exist. One is in the Tennessee Historical Society at Nashville and one in the Library of Congress. The Nashville copy seems to be the first draft. I presume that Jackson influenced several changes that appear in the printed text in the interest of accuracy and policy.

[24]Charles C. Royce and Cyrus Thomas, "Indian Land Cessions in the United States," *Eighteenth Annual Report*, Bureau of American Ethnology (1899), II, 632.

[25]Sydney George Fisher, *Men, Women & Manners in Colonial Times* (1898), II, 327.

[26]Revolutionary Accounts, Audited, No. 1592, South Carolina archives, Historical Commission of South Carolina, Columbia.

[27]Buell, I, 37, 38.

[28]No autograph of James Crawford can be found. The name is spelled Crawford in these pages to avoid confusion, inasmuch as his brother and nephews invariably, and his sons usually, used that form. In those days it was not a mark of illiteracy, as now understood, for one to vary the orthography of one's name. In this book the writer has endeavored to spell the name of persons as the individuals themselves usually wrote them, which explains numerous departures from other printed texts. Concerning persons who, like George McKemey, could not write, I have made arbitrary decisions, in his case taking the spelling that appears on his tombstone in the Waxhaw churchyard.

[29]Buell, I, 38. William Allen's reminiscence, quoted by Buell, is corroborated by local tradition.

CHAPTER II

[1]Walter Clark Manuscripts, III, 318, North Carolina Historical Commission, Raleigh.

[2]Parton, I, 64.

[3]*Ibid.*

[4]*Correspondence* I, 2. The original in the Library of Congress has been called the earliest known example of Jackson's handwriting. It is not in Jackson's hand.

[5]Reid and Eaton, *The Life of Andrew Jackson* (1817), 11.

[6]Unpublished researches among Revolutionary manuscripts by A. S. Salley, junior, secretary of the Historical Commission of South Carolina.

[7]Reid and Eaton, *The Life of Andrew Jackson* (1817), 11.

[8]David Ramsay, M. D., *The History of South Carolina* (1809), I, 367.

[9]Revolutionary Accounts, Audited, No. 1592, South Carolina archives, Historical Commission of South Carolina, Columbia.

[10]Buell, I, 52.

[11]Revolutionary Accounts, Audited, No. 1592, South Carolina archives, Historical Commission of South Carolina, Columbia.

[12]*Ibid.*, Nos. 1587, 1589 and 1594; and Jackson to James H. Witherspoon, August 11, 1824, *Correspondence*, III, 265.

[13]Parton, I, 73. See also reminiscences of Susan Smart Alexander in *National Intelligencer*, August 1 and 29, 1845. Parton is in error calling her Mrs. Smart. Smart was her maiden name. I am unable to reconcile Mrs. Alexander's statement in the *Intelligencer* that Mrs. Jackson and her two sons were at her home in August, when it is known that the boys were in the field with Davie most of that month, and Jackson's own statement is that the flight into North Carolina took place in September. I, therefore, accept Parton's version of her story which places her meeting with Jackson in September.

[14]Banastre Tarleton, *Campaigns of 1780-1781 in the Southern Provinces* (1787), 186.

[15]Amos Kendall, *Life of Andrew Jackson* (1843), 19.

[16]Every published reference to this action that the writer has seen calls it Wahab skirmish and similarly misspells the name of Captain Wauchope who, incidentally, was the paternal grandfather of S. H. Walkup of "Walkup evidence" renown (Note No. 17, Chapter I). See S. H. Walkup to David L. Swain, September 25, 1857, Swain Manuscripts, North Carolina Historical Commission, Raleigh, and Deed Book XI, 112-13, Mecklenburg County records, Charlotte.

[17]An old but undated clipping from the Charlotte (North Carolina) *Observer*, in the collection of Waxhaw memorabilia of Mrs. Anne Hutchison Bigger of Rock Hill, South Carolina.

[18]Revolutionary Accounts, Audited, No. 1592, South Carolina archives, Historical Commission of South Carolina, Columbia.

[19]A manuscript account among the Jackson Papers, Library of Congress, apparently prepared by Amos Kendall for his biography from conversations with Jackson. See also: Kendall, 45; Buell, I, 52; Parton, I, 86.

[20]Reid Manuscript, 5, Tennessee Historical Society, Nashville; Parton, I, 87; Reid and Eaton, 12.

[21]Jackson to Amos Kendall, May 15, 1843, collection of Thomas F. Madigan, New York City; Parton, I, 89.

[22]*Correspondence*, I, 2. The original in Jackson's hand (Library of Congress) is dated "April 1781," but apparently was written in 1843, for Kendall's uncompleted biography.

[23]W. H. Sparks, *The Memories of Fifty Years* (1870), 147. I prefer this version of Elizabeth Jackson's last words to her son because they sound more natural than in the better known account of Jackson's godson, Thomas Butler (Buell I, 56). Colonel Sparks knew Jackson well and had no ax to grind. His book is filled with the solecisms of sincerity and an unrefreshed memory, but is no less valuable on that account. He has Jackson parting from his mother after the war when he left to practise law. But the substance of her words is identical with that of Butler, who allocates them correctly and improves their literary quality.

[24]Jackson to James H. Witherspoon, August 11, 1824, *Correspondence*, III, 265. Governor's Gate was probably the gate to the avenue of Belve-

dere plantation, which one time had been the home of the governors of South Carolina. Forty-three years after his mother's death, Jackson made an unsuccessful attempt to locate her grave.

[25]Buell, I, 56.

CHAPTER III

[1]Revolutionary Accounts, Audited, No. 1594, South Carolina Historical Commission, Columbia. The official record of this appraisal represents the earliest known example of the handwriting of Andrew Jackson, then fifteen years old.

[2]*Ibid.*

[3]Unpublished researches from Revolutionary Manuscripts of A. S. Salley, junior, secretary of South Carolina Historical Commission.

[4]Revolutionary Accounts, Audited, South Carolina Historical Commission, Columbia.

[5]Buell, I, 63; Parton, I, 96. The report mentioned by Parton and disputed by Buell, that Jackson challenged Galbraith to a duel, is supported by local tradition.

[6]Buell, I, 56.

[7]I fix the time of year by the fact that Jackson was there for the racing; the year itself by the fact that in the spring of 1782 and 1784 Jackson appears otherwise engaged at home.

[8]Kendall, 68, whose account of Jackson's early life is based on conversations with the subject of his memoir. A. S. Salley, junior, secretary of the Historical Commission of South Carolina, whose opinions I respect, says no Charleston refugees went to the Waxhaws.

[9]Johann David Schoepf, *Travels in the Confederation* (1785), English translation (1911), 167-68.

[10]John B. Irving, *The South Carolina Jockey Club* (1857), 11.

[11]*Ibid.*, 20, 42.

[12]*Ibid.*, 45.

[13]*Cabinet and Talisman* (1829), 4. Quoted from Parton, I, 98.

[14]Reminiscences of Susan Smart Alexander, *National Intelligencer*, August 1, 1845.

[15]Anne Hutchison Bigger of Rock Hill, South Carolina, to the writer, communicating a local tradition. The Massey farm adjoined Major Crawford's.

[16]Revolutionary Accounts, Audited, No. 1594, South Carolina Historical Commission, Columbia. The date of the appraisal, December 4, 1784, fixes Jackson's departure at a date later than has been given hitherto.

[17]An old clipping in the scrap-book of Dr. William A. Pressly of Rock Hill, South Carolina, quotes a letter written by Stephen Decatur Miller, former United States Senator, Governor of South Carolina, and a friend of Jackson, as authority for the romance with Major Crawford's daughter who later married Dr. Samuel Dunlap.

[18]Parton. I, 104.

[19]Mrs. Anne (Nancy) Jarret Rutherford, from Augustus C. Buell, *A History of Andrew Jackson* (1904), I, 68.

[20]Rowan County Court Minute Book 1785-86.

[21]Parton, I, 107, whose authorities, withheld at their request, were Misses Christine and Maria Howard and their mother, the latter being present. For this and certain other information in this chapter, I am indebted to Mr. Walter Murphy, of Salisbury, a nephew, three generations removed, of Jackson's preceptor, Colonel John Stokes.

[22]Anson County (North Carolina) Records, Wadesborough, from S. G. Heiskell, *Andrew Jackson and Early Tennessee History*, I, 428.

[23]Buell, I, 68.

[24]Walter Murphy, of Salisbury, North Carolina, and Miss Katherine Hoskins, Summerfield, North Carolina, to the writer; Bassett, I, 13; Dr. Archibald Henderson in Raleigh *News and Observer*, October 17, 1926.

[25]Miss Katherine Hoskins, of Summerfield, North Carolina, a student of local history, to the writer, September 23, 1931.

[26]*Ibid*. Miss Hoskins's researches have made her familiar with the character of McNairy whom she admires. She believes Jackson to have been the inspiration of their decision to go West.

[27]*State Records of North Carolina*, XX, 270.

[28]The regular course would have been for the Legislature to have named the attorney-general, as Parton implies that it did by naming Jackson before he crossed the mountains. Jackson received his first legislative appointment to that office in 1789 (*State Records*, XXI, 403), which has led some to assume that he did not reach Nashville until then. But McNairy first appointed him to the office in November, 1788, a few days after their arrival in Nashville (*Ibid.*, XXI, 637).

CHAPTER IV

[1]Dr. Archibald Henderson, "Jackson's Loose Living Common Sin of the Period," Raleigh (North Carolina) *News and Observer*, October 17, 1926.

[2]*Correspondence*, I, 5.

[3]Henderson, *op. cit.*

[4]John Allison, *Dropped Stitches in Tennessee History* (1897), 8.

[5]Minute Book No. 1 in the Davidson County archives supports the generally accepted statement that Judge McNairy's first court was held there in January, 1789. *State Records of North Carolina*, XXI, 637, disclose that court was held in November, 1788, and that Jackson was paid for his services as prosecutor. *The American Historical Magazine* VIII, 294, reproduces the indictment in November, 1788, of George Gibson who, according to evidence presented by Jackson, "feloniously and Burglarously did Break and enter" William Barr's house and "steal take and carry away one Bever Skin."

[6]Parton, I, 135.

[7]Ancestry of John and Rachel Stockley Donelson derived mainly from

unpublished studies of Miss Butler Chancellor, of Washington, D. C., a great-niece of Rachel Donelson Jackson. Her work is based on original documents in Maryland and Virginia county archives.

[8]Spelled Caffrey by some of his present-day descendants in Louisiana.

[9]The circumstances of Colonel Donelson's decision to go to the Cumberland, his short stay there and later removal to Kentucky, are derived from unpublished studies from original documents by Dr. William A. Provine, secretary of the Tennessee Historical Society. These researches, generously placed at the author's disposal, correct practically everything previously written on the subject, notably A. W. Putnam's widely copied *History of Middle Tennessee* (1859). Putnam's book is very valuable, but too eulogistic of the Robertson and Donelson families. The author disregarded fact to make Donelson a permanent settler in 1780.

[10]From a copy of Donelson's journal, contemporary or nearly so, Tennessee Historical Society, Nashville. This copy has generally been mistaken for the original, only four pages of which exist. These are in the private collection of John Donelson, of Nashville.

[11]Mary Donelson Wilcox in *Leslie's Weekly*, quoted from Heiskell, III, 279.

[12]See Note 9 *ante*.

[13]Jackson Manuscripts, Library of Congress. The entry was made April 6, 1784.

[14]Statement of John Overton, *United States Telegraph*, June 22, 1827. The *Telegraph* article, referred to frequently in the documentation of this chapter and the next, was compiled by a committee of Jackson's friends in answer to attacks on Mrs. Jackson's character by partizans of John Quincy Adams in the presidential campaign of 1828. It was widely copied and later issued as a pamphlet. Although a campaign document, and susceptible of refutation in some of its details (for one thing the contributors wrote from memory after a lapse of thirty-seven years), it is much more worthy of belief on the whole than the literature to which it is a reply. Some of the contributors, such as Judge McNairy, were then opposed to Jackson, but had the grace to speak in defense of his wife.

[15]Statement of Elizabeth Craighead, *ibid.*

[16]Mary Donelson Wilcox, *op. cit.*

[17]Statement of John McGinnis, *United States Telegraph*, June 22, 1827.

[18]Statement of Elizabeth Craighead, *ibid.*

[19]Statement of George L. Davidson, Parton, I, 168.

[20]Dr. W. A. Provine, secretary of the Tennessee Historical Society, to the writer.

[21]Statement of John Overton, *op. cit.*

[22]*Ibid.* "*At length* I communicated to Mr. Jackson the unpleasant situation." Overton's words thus indicate that it was not done *at once.* His actual apprizal of Jackson of the lay of the land will be reached in the logical course of the narrative.

[23]John W. Monette, *History of the Discovery and Settlement of the Valley of the Mississippi* (1846), II, 16.

[24]Kendall, 90.

[25]February 13, 1789, *Correspondence*, I, 7.

[26]John Haywood, *Civil and Political History of the State of Tennessee* (1823), reprint of 1915, p. 251.

[27]Smith to Miró, March 11, 1789, Papeles de Cuba, Legajo 196. Photostatic copy in Lawson McGhee Library, Knoxville, Tennessee. Original in Spanish archives, Seville, Spain.

[28]Robertson to Miró, February 18, 1789, *ibid.*, 41.

[29]Dispatch dated April 23, 1789, quoted from Charles E. Gayarré, *History of Louisiana*, II, 262.

[30]Miró to Smith, April 20, 1789, Draper Manuscripts, State Historical Society of Wisconsin, Madison.

[31]Haywood, 256.

[32]*Ibid.*, 257.

[33]*Ibid.*, 258.

[34]Jackson apparently started for Natchez shortly after the close of the October, 1789, term of court, which Minute Book No. 1, pp. 318-32, shows he attended at Nashville. A marginal note on page 8 of the Reid Manuscript (Tennessee Historical Society copy) reading, "1789 went to Natz," suggests that the author may have intended to expand the theme. No mention of the journey, or for that matter any journey of Jackson to Natchez, prior to 1813, appears in Reid and Eaton's biography, however.

[35]Dated March 14, 1790, *Correspondence*, I, 8.

[36]W. H. Sparks, *Memories of Fifty Years* (1870), 151.

[37]*Ibid.*, 149.

[38]Dated November 8, 1790, *Correspondence*, I, 9.

[39]Dated February 26, 1791, private collection of Andrew Jackson IV.

[40]Robertson to Gayoso, May 17, 1790, Papeles de Cuba, Legajo 203. Photostatic copy in Lawson McGhee Library, Knoxville. Original in Spanish archives, Seville.

[41]In the Jackson Manuscripts, Library of Congress, is a bill from Melling Woolley, a Natchez merchant, to Jackson, chiefly for liquor, totaling two hundred and thirty-four dollars and one cent, dated "July 1790." These purchases may have been made during the earlier visit, or may have been ordered by letter. The rapidity of Jackson's movements constantly astonishes the researcher, but I do not believe he could have left Nashville as late as May 17, 1790, and returned in time to have "eloped" with Mrs. Robards from Mercer County, Kentucky, on July first. In 1793 this "elopement" was proved in court. It took place some time in July, though possibly not on July first. Jackson's presence in Nashville on July fourteenth, however, is established by Minute Book No. 1 of the Davidson County Court, p. 373.

[42]Statement of John Overton, *op. cit.*

[43]Mary Donelson Wilcox, *op. cit.*

[44]Statement of Thomas Crutcher. *United States Telegraph*, March 28, 1828.

[45]The whereabouts of the original of the court record of the Robards divorce is unknown. Some time since 1891 it has been abstracted from the court-house files at Harrodsburg (modern spelling), and C. E. Rankin, a local attorney, informs the writer that "I think some historical crank is responsible." In 1891 it was there, however, and was copied by a correspondent of the St. Louis *Post-Dispatch*. From this transcription the excerpt quoted in the text is taken. The *Dispatch* article is reproduced in Thomas E. Watson's *Life of Andrew Jackson* (1912), a work of low values, so hostile to Jackson as to impair confidence in almost anything it contains. I have been able, however, to corroborate the essential particulars of the *Dispatch* copy by other testimony, practically all from sources friendly to Jackson, and entertain no doubt but that the *Dispatch* copy is a faithful reproduction of the originals, possibly the only one in existence. Suffice to note in this place that Mary Donelson Wilcox (*op. cit.*) mentions Jackson's presence in Kentucky at this time, and also Robards's formal allegation that his wife "had eloped and was cohabiting adulterously with one A. Jackson." Mrs. Wilcox is mistaken in her suggestion that Jackson's name appeared in the documentary record, however.

CHAPTER V

[1]Robertson to Miró, September 2, 1789, *Mississippi Valley Historical Review*, XII, 171.

[2]Jackson Manuscripts, Library of Congress.

[3]*Ibid.*, January 15, 1791.

[4]Jo C. Guild, *Old Times in Tennessee* (1878), 61.

[5]Haywood, 340.

[6]Statement of John Overton, *United States Telegraph*, June 22, 1827. Overton, who omits a great deal, does not mention the Kentucky trip, but he gives Rachel's residence during the summer of 1790 as at the Hays house.

[7]The universal assumption, that Rachel's journey under Jackson's protection to Natchez in 1791 constituted the grounds upon which Robards obtained his divorce, is untenable because this journey did not take place until after the passage by the Virginia Legislature of the enabling act under which the action for divorce was instituted.

[8]Parton, I, 168.

[9]James L. Armstrong, *General Jackson's Juvenile Indiscretions* (1832), 4.

[10]Statements of Thomas Crutcher and John Overton, *United States Telegraph*, June 22, 1827.

[11]Statement of Overton, *op. cit.*

[12]*Ibid.*

[13]*Ibid.*, Thomas Crutcher (*op. cit.*) fixes the start in December, 1790, or January, 1791. Mary Donelson Wilcox (*op. cit.*) says December. Overton is more nearly right. From a check of evidence of Jackson's known presence in Nashville, it appears that the journey could only have

been made between January twentieth and April twelfth, or April eighteenth and July twelfth, 1791. (*Correspondence*, I, 9; Davidson County Court Minute Book No. 1, p. 415; *Correspondence*, I, 11; Minute Book No. 1, p. 432.)   My opinion is that they departed in January.

¹⁴Virginia *House Journal* (1790), 123, 127, 147; *Senate Journal*, 53, 62, 72.   In 1827 James Breckenridge, a member of the Legislature in 1790, declared he had voted for the bill under the impression that Mrs. Robards would establish her innocence in court. (*United States Telegraph*, June 22, 1827.)

¹⁵*Acts Passed at a General Assembly of the Commonwealth of Virginia* (1790), 155.

¹⁶Robards to Hays, January 10, 1791.   Jackson Manuscripts, Library of Congress.

¹⁷Robards wrote from Mercer County, Kentucky, twenty-one days after the Virginia Assembly had passed the enabling act, but owing to the state of the roads in winter may not have received news of it.   But as the Legislature was to adjourn on December thirty-first, he knew his petition had been acted on one way or another, and apparently was confident that action had been favorable.

¹⁸Mary Donelson Wilcox (*op. cit.*).

¹⁹*Ibid.*

²⁰*Ibid.*

²¹In 1922 James Payne Green, eighty-six years old, a graduate of Yale in 1857 and a great-grandson of Thomas M. Green, junior, gave the late S. G. Heiskell, of Knoxville, Tennessee, a written statement of what had come down to him about Jackson's marriage.   He said that T. M. Green, junior, performed the ceremony (Knoxville *Sentinel*, November 26, 1922).   James Payne Green then lived at Gayoso, the house built by Gayoso de Lemos and owned by Abner Green during Rachel's stay in the Natchez district before her marriage.   No documentary record of the marriage has ever been found though in 1827 when it became an issue in the presidential campaign Jackson's confidant, W. B. Lewis, went to Natchez presumably for that purpose.

Another tradition of the Green family is that before the marriage, Rachel obtained a divorce from the Spanish authorities.   (Sparks, 151. Mr. Sparks married the youngest daughter of Abner Green.)   This seems impossible for two reasons: the extreme difficulty of obtaining divorces under Spanish law and that, if true, there would have been no need two years later for a second ceremony.   When Robards finally decided to complete his divorce transaction, Rachel could have exhibited her Spanish papers in proof of the fact that she had not been Robards's wife for two years.

In 1785 the Greens had espoused the cause of Georgia, which claimed the Natchez territory and attempted to exercise sovereignty there by forming the district into a county called Bourbon and appointing magistrates and a register of probates.   Abner Green accepted the latter office and both T. M. Green, senior, and junior, were magistrates.   The elder

Green got in jail for his zeal and was obliged to transfer his property to his sons. In 1788 Georgia abandoned the conquest which terminated the official powers of the Greens. Therefore, when Jackson was married in 1791, Green was not a magistrate, but, as the frontier viewed such matters, that fact alone would not have placed the ceremony outside the pale. It sometimes happened that in frontier communities there was no one authorized by the letter of the law to perform marriages. In such cases a ceremony before any person of T. M. Green's standing would have been recognized by a court of review, in case no legal impediment to the union existed. Springfield, the house in which the marriage took place, is still standing.

²²*Op. cit.* Mrs. Wilcox is in all probability mistaken, as I can not imagine that the fruitless quest made in 1827 for documentary evidence of the ceremony failed to include an examination of church records.

²³George Cockran to Jackson, with an enclosure to Mrs. Jackson; undated, but filled with papers for 1796 in Jackson Papers, Library of Congress.

²⁴Kendall, 94.

²⁵Jackson Papers, January 1, 1792, Library of Congress.

²⁶On February 23, 1792, the two hundred acres on Twelve Mile Creek in the Waxhaws, where Andrew Jackson's father had established the family on his arrival from Ireland in 1765, were sold possibly to help meet the expenses of establishing Rachel at Poplar Grove.

²⁷Now called Hadley's Bend.

²⁸Parton, I, 136.

²⁹*Ibid.*, I, 138.

³⁰Dated November 6, 1893, private collection of Andrew Jackson IV.

³¹Jackson to Jesse Wilkinson, January 6, 1797, refers to the sale of land in Sumner County which he had never seen. Private collection of S. P. Hessel, Woodmere, Long Island, New York.

³²January 30, 1793, *Correspondence*, I, 12.

³³*American State Papers, Indian Affairs*, I, 44; Charles C. Royce, "The Cherokee Nation of Indians," in *Fifth Annual Report*, Bureau of American Ethnology (1887), 148-71.

³⁴Haywood, 380.

³⁵Knoxville *Gazette*, September 14, 1793. From Mary French Cald-well, "Massacres in this Section," Nashville *Tennessean*, August 30, 1931.

³⁶Parton, I. 146; Watson, 74; Blount's draft, dated June 11, 1796, Jackson Papers, Library of Congress.

³⁷Statement of John Overton, *United States Telegraph*, June 22, 1827.

³⁸*Ibid.*

³⁹Statements of John Overton, Sally Smith, Thomas Crutcher, Judge John McNairy, Elizabeth Craighead, the latter a sister of Senator Brown, Robards's attorney, *ibid.*

⁴⁰*United States Telegraph*, June 27, 1827. This defense of Jackson, filling ten columns, consisted of the statements of a number of persons, several of which have been referred to in foregoing notes, with

explanatory remarks by a committee of eighteen of the most prominent men in the Nashville district—not all of them blind followers of Jackson—who deplored the level to which some of Mr. Adams's protagonists had brought the campaign. The quotation referred to is from the committee's remarks.

[41]Court record, from Watson, 73. Why did Robards wait two years before taking action under the Legislature's enabling act? Why did he, by his silence if nothing more, countenance the false report of a divorce in 1791? No one knows, though the suppositions are not creditable to Robards. The accepted theory, however, that the consequences of the false report provided Robards with grounds to obtain his divorce—grounds he may have lacked when he appealed to the Legislature—is unsupportable. The acts established in court as cause for the divorce antedated, as was necessary under the law, the enabling act of December 20, 1790. The fact that Robards remarried shortly after the divorce may be the key to the riddle, supposing that he instituted the court action with that in view. His second marriage was happy and he had no part in the politically inspired attacks on Mrs. Jackson's name in 1827.

[42]Court record, ibid., 73.

[43]Committee report, United States Telegraph, June 22, 1827.

[44]Tennessee State Library, Nashville. It is an interesting, though probably not significant, fact that during this trying period when Overton and Jackson were so closely associated, Robards was a client of Overton. Robards's apprehensions of a division of his Cumberland property in 1791 had been without basis. But on February 19, 1794, less than a month after Jackson's remarriage, Robards gave Overton power of attorney to dispose of his Cumberland holdings. Acting under this authority, Overton sold the farm to John Shannon on March seventeenth (Deed Book D, 42; Deed Book C, 277, Davidson County records). Two years later Jackson bought the place of Shannon. It adjoined the property later known as the Hermitage.

[45]Marriage Records, 1789-94, Davidson County records, Nashville. Thomas Crutcher (United States Telegraph, June 22, 1827) says the ceremony was performed January seventeenth. According to a local tradition Reverend Thomas B. Craighead officiated, but his widow does not mention this in her statement published in 1827 (United States Telegraph, June 22).

[46]March 8, 1795, Correspondence, I, 13.

[47]Jackson to Overton, June 19, 1795, ibid., I, 14.

[48]Jackson-Allison "Indenture," June 11, 1796, ibid., I, 21; Jackson to Overton June 9, 1795, ibid., I, 14; Parton, I, 242.

[49]Jackson to James Jackson, August 25, 1819, Correspondence, II, 427.

[50]Jackson's "Account of Expences May and August 1795," ibid., I, 15.

[51]Jackson to Overton, June 9, 1795, ibid., I, 14.

[52]James Grant to Jackson, August 13, 1795, private collection of Andrew Jackson IV.

[53]Jackson to Nathaniel Macon, October 4, 1795, Correspondence, I, 17.

[54]Mark Mitchell to Jackson, November 21. 1795, Library of Congress.

[55]J. G. M. Ramsey, *Annals of Tennessee* (1853); 655.

[56]Jackson to James Jackson, August 25, 1819, *Correspondence,* II, 427.

CHAPTER VI

[1]Parton, I, 196.

[2]Andrew Jackson to Hays, December 6, 1796, collection of Thomas Madigan, New York City.

[3]Jackson to Hays, December 16, 1796, Library of Congress.

[4]Parton, I, 214.

[5]Jackson to John Sevier, January 18, 1797, *Correspondence*, I, 27.

[6]January 8, 1797, *ibid.*, I, 24.

[7]Jackson to his wife, May 9, 1796, private collection of Andrew Jackson IV.

[8]Jackson to Sevier, May 8, 1797; to McNairy, May 9, 1797; Sevier to Jackson, May 11, 1797; McNairy to Jackson, May 12, 1797, *Correspondence*, I, 31 *et seq.*

[9]November 2, 1797, *ibid.*, I, 38.

[10]Jackson to James Robertson, January 11, 1798, *ibid.*, I, 41.

[11]Jackson to Robert Hays, January 25, 1798, *ibid.*, I, 44.

[12]Jackson to Cocke, June 24 and 25, 1798; Cocke to Jackson, June 25, 1798, *ibid.*, I, 48-50.

[13]Private collection of Andrew Jackson IV.

[14]August 16, 1799, *Correspondence*, I, 56.

[15]An affidavit dated June 15, 1800, *ibid.*, I, 57.

[16]Memoir of Mary Donelson Wilcox, Heiskell, III, 280.

[17]Narrative of Isaac T. Avery, Parton, I, 167.

[18]A warrant for the arrest of Russell Bean, dated February 12, 1802 is preserved in the Washington County records, Jonesboro (modern spelling). This discloses that Bean had been at large for more than a month when the fire lured him from hiding.

[19]James A. McLoughlin to Amos Kendall, January 3, 1843, *Correspondence*, I, 65.

[20]One purchase of books Jackson made in Philadelphia, January 7, 1797, as listed by the seller: "Vattel, Law of Nations, Powell on Contracts, Espinasse Nisiprius, Gilbert's Law of Evidence, Butler's Nisiprius, Comyn's Digest 6 Vols, Vessey's Reports, Brown Reports, Vernon's Chancery, William's Report 3 Vols, Hawkin's Pleas of the Crown, Laws of the United States, Impey's Practice 2 Vols, Equity Cases Abridged, Hinde's Practice, Gilbert on Equity, Atkyns' Reports, Coke upon Littleton 5 Vols, Wilson's Reports 3 Vols, Raymond Reports, Burns Law Dictionary, Sheridan's Dictionary, Barnes Notes." Jackson Manuscripts, Library of Congress.

[21]Thomas Perkins Abernethy, *From Frontier to Plantation in Tennessee* (1932), 171 *et seq.*

[22]Knoxville *Gazette*, July 27, 1803.

[23] Narrative of Isaac T. Avery, Parton, I, 164.

[24] W. W. Clayton, *History of Davidson County Tennessee* (1886), 142.

[25] October 3, 1803, *Correspondence*, I, 71.

[26] Clayton, 142.

[27] Petitions dated October 5 and 7, 1803, *Correspondence*, I, 72-73.

[28] Superior Court record book No. 3, Knoxville.

[29] October 9, 1803, *Correspondence*, I, 73.

[30] Superior Court record book No. 3, Knoxville.

[31] Sevier to Jackson, October 10, 1803, Clayton.

[32] Affidavit of Andrew Greer, October 23, 1803, *American Historical Magazine*, V, 208. See also Thomas J. Van Dyke to Jackson, November 5, 1803; William Dickson to Jackson, November 20, 1803, Library of Congress. The tree that Sevier interposed between himself and Jackson's pistol was long pointed out by Jackson's friends.

[33] John H. DeWitt, editor, "Journal of John Sevier," *Tennessee Historical Magazine*, VI, 36.

CHAPTER VII

[1] August 7, 1803, *Correspondence*, I, 67.

[2] Division Order, August 7, 1803, *ibid.*, I, 68.

[3] Concerning these transactions: Jackson to Coffee, January 7 and February 28, 1804, and one undated letter, *ibid.*, I, 80, 82, 83; to Hutchings, March 17, 1804, *ibid.*, I, 84.

[4] April 6, 1804, *ibid.*, I, 87.

[5] Jackson to George W. Campbell, April 28, 1804, *ibid.*, I, 90.

[6] "Account of Expence," dated "Spring 1804," *ibid.*, I, 94.

[7] July 24, 1804.

[8] Jackson to Edward Ward, May 7, 1805, private collection of Andrew Jackson IV.

[9] Parton, I, 253.

[10] The date of Jackson's removal to the Hermitage has been a subject of speculation. It was between August 25, and September 21, 1804. On the former date Jackson dated a letter to N. Davidson, "Hunter's Hill" (*Correspondence*, I, 106), and on the latter date William Preston Anderson addressed a note to Jackson at the Hermitage (Library of Congress). In "August 1804" Deaderick & Littler of Nashville billed Jackson for a 125-gallon still (Library of Congress), it would seem, for the new farm.

[11] Jackson & Hutchings to Boggs, Davidson & Co., Philadelphia, July 31, 1804, *Correspondence*, I, 101.

[12] To Jackson, Library of Congress.

[13] "Patton" is his own spelling.

[14] Dr. Felix Robertson, son of James Robertson, founder of Nashville; from Parton, I, 249.

[15] Jackson to John Coffee, June 21, 1804, *Correspondence*, I, 95.

[16] Jackson & Hutchings to Boggs, Davidson & Co., July 31, 1804, *ibid.*, I, 101.

[17]August 25, 1804, *ibid.*, I, 106.

[18]To Theodosia Alston, May 29, 1805. From Matthew L. Davis, *Memoirs of Aaron Burr* (1837), II, 370.

[19]"If Burr has any treasonable intentions in view he is the bases[t] of all human beings. I will tell you why. he always held out the idea of settling the Washita unless a war with Spain [should take place]. in that event, he held out the idea that from his intimacy with the Secretary of War, he would obtain an appointment, and if he did he would revolutionize Mexico." Jackson to George W. Campbell, January 15, 1807 (*Correspondence*, I, 168). This was written when Jackson suspected Burr and was searching for him with twelve companies of militia.

[20]James B. Ranck, "Andrew Jackson and the Burr Conspiracy," *Tennessee Historical Magazine*, October, 1930.

[21]See Note No. 19 *ante.*

[22]Burr to Theodosia Alston, August 13, 1805. From Davis, II, 372.

[23]Jackson to Ward, June 10, 1805, private collection of Andrew Jackson IV.

[24]From John Morrell & Son, January 8, 1805, Library of Congress.

[25]From John Smith & Son, June 5, 1805, *ibid.*

[26]Memorandum of purchase, May 11, 1805, *Correspondence*, I, 113.

[27]Balie Peyton, "Sumner County Races 1804-05," *The Rural Sun*, 1873. From James Douglas Anderson, *Making the American Thoroughbred* (1916), 242.

[28]*Ibid.*

[29]Balie Peyton, "President Jackson's Orders and Reminiscences," *The Rural Sun*, 1873; from Anderson, 246.

[30]Balie Peyton, "Sumner County Races 1804-05," *The Rural Sun*, 1873; from Anderson, 242.

[31]Parton, I, 269; Guild, 219.

[32]Statements of Jackson and John Hutchings dated February 10 and 5, 1806, *Correspondence*, I, 127, 128.

[33]Jackson to Swann, January 7, 1806, *ibid.*, I, 124.

[34]Swann to Jackson, January 12, 1806, *ibid.*, I, 139.

[35]Statement of John Coffee, February 5, 1806, *ibid.*, I, 130.

[36]*Ibid.*

[37]*Ibid.*, I, 122. The original, in the Tennessee Historical Society, Nashville, was found where General Coffee had preserved it among his papers.

[38]*Ibid.*, I, 138.

[39]February 1, 1806, Library of Congress.

[40]March 15, 1806.

[41]Jackson to Hutchings, April 7, 1806. Jackson misdated this letter 1805," under which date it appears in *Correspondence*, I, 111. The original is in the Library of Congress.

[42]*Ibid.*

[43]March 24, 1806. From Parton, I, 313.

[44]Hutchings to Jackson, April 24, 1806, *Correspondence*, I, 141.

[45]Parton, I, 291.

[46]*Correspondence*, I, 142.
[47]May 23, 1806, *ibid.*, I, 144.

CHAPTER VIII

[1]This account of the duel is drawn from the documents concerning the same and from the files of the *Impartial Review* (Nashville) as reproduced in Bassett's *Correspondence*, I, 144-49; from a memorandum of Catlett and Thomas Overton dated May 25, 1806, and a letter, John Overton to Jackson, "June, 1806," private collection of Andrew Jackson IV; from Parton, I, 289-301, who consulted most of the foregoing and in 1857 interviewed residents of Nashville who had had their accounts from witnesses; from Buell, I, 167-82, whose partizanship of Jackson nowhere is more marked, but who discovered one useful source that escaped Parton— the gist of Jackson's conversation en route to the field, as related by Thomas Hart Benton; from Mary Donelson Wilcox's memoir, Heiskell, III, 293; and from Major Ben Truman's *Field of Honor* (1884), 280-84. Additional material on the duel is extensive, but nothing of which I am aware adds to the facts.

[2]Joseph Erwin in the *Impartial Review* (Nashville), June 21, 1806, in which the writer admitted the agreement that a half-cock should not constitute a fire, but held that this article was not in force because it had not been committed to writing. This drew from Overton and Catlett, the second, the public rejoinder that the duel had been fought in accordance with stipulations agreed upon by all parties.

[3]Overton to Jackson, dated "Nashville June, 1806," private collection of Andrew Jackson IV.

[4]Parton, I, 302.

[5]Jackson to an unnamed correspondent, September 25, 1806, *Correspondence*, I, 149.

[6]Parton, I, 316.

[7]Jackson to Daniel Smith, November 12, 1806, *Correspondence*, I, 154. Jackson fails to name Fort in this letter, but does so in his letter to Campbell. See Note No. 10 *post*.

[8]Henry Lee Manuscript, p. 55, Library of Congress. This is my designation of this manuscript, and may be incorrect, but will be used in these pages for purposes of identification. The manuscript appears to be a fragment of an unpublished biography of Jackson, and was written during his lifetime. It consists of twenty-two pages, numbered from 53 to 75, and is preserved in Volume III of the Library of Congress collection of Jackson papers. Comparison has been made with the handwriting of Coffee, Benton, Kendall, Lee and others and it seems to resemble that of Lee who, while Jackson's secretary and a resident of the Hermitage, is known to have begun a life of his patron. Whoever the author was, he drew from sources close to Jackson.

[9]Jackson to Daniel Smith, November 12, 1806, *Correspondence*, I, 154.

[10]Jackson to George W. Campbell, January 15, 1807. The original

of this letter, owned by Mrs. Susan P. Brown, of Franklin, Tennessee, is
reproduced in *Correspondence*, I, 167.   It gives the name of Jackson's
caller concerning whom historians have been curious for more than a century.   The Henry Lee Manuscript, p. 55, mentioned in Note No. 8 *ante*,
describes Fort, without naming him, as "a natural son of Burr . . . on his
way from N. York to join him."   Burr had such a son, but his name was
not Fort, nor is there any other testimony as to his connection with his
father's Western schemes.   A Fort family was prominent in New Jersey
where Burr had numerous adherents, but there is no direct evidence to
connect Jackson's caller with it.   In 1828 when Jackson's political enemies
were accusing him of collusion with Burr, Campbell published Jackson's
letter, deleting the name of Fort and making other small changes.   Parton
(I, 330) had access to the original letter, but he also made textual changes
and omitted the names of Fort and Swartwout.

[11]Jackson to Smith, November 12, 1806, *Correspondence*, I, 153.
[12]Jackson to Campbell, *ibid.*, I, 167.
[13]*Ibid.*
[14]November 12, 1806, *ibid.*, I, 152.
[15]Jackson to Jefferson, November 12, 1806, Parton, I, 319.
[16]November 12, 1806, *Correspondence*, I, 152.
[17]Jackson to Campbell, *ibid.*, I, 167.
[18]*Impartial Review* (Nashville), December 20, 1806.
[19]Henry Lee Manuscript, p. 54, Library of Congress.   The author
mistakenly ascribes the incident to Burr's summer visit, however.
[20]Albert J. Beveridge, *Life of John Marshall* (1916-19), III, 327;
Henry Adams, *History of the United States* (1889-1911), III, 228,
and Parton, I, 321, are among those who mistakenly cite Stockley
Hays's journey as proof of Jackson's full confidence in Burr.   The
letters Stockley carried can not be found, but Jackson's letter to Claiborne of January 8, 1807 (*Correspondence*, I, 163), states what his
suspicions were at the time.
[21]Statements of J. B. McMaster (*History of the People of the United
States*, III, 72), of Beveridge (*Marshall*, III, 326), and of others that
the President's proclamation for the apprehension of Aaron Burr arrived
in Nashville on December nineteenth, before Burr's departure, are incorrect.   Parton (I, 322) and Bassett (I, 46) say it arrived a few days
after Burr's departure, and the effigy burning followed at once.   This
puts Jackson in little better light.   Buell (I, 198) says the proclamation came late on December twenty-second, or early on the twenty-third,
when it was published.   None cites an authority.

I can not discover exactly when the proclamation arrived, but it was
several days after Burr had gone—too long to overtake him, as General
James Robertson makes clear in his letter to Senator Daniel Smith, dated
February 2, 1807 (*Correspondence*, I, 164).   The *Impartial Review* does
not mention the proclamation until its issue of January third.   The issue
of December twenty-seventh contains a brief mention of Burr's departure.
In 1828 a committee, friendly to Jackson (*Correspondence*, I, 167), held

that the proclamation arrived on December twenty-seventh. All the evidence that I can find tends to support this. No evidence supports the implications of McMaster and Beveridge that Jackson conspired in the escape of Burr from Nashville. The extraordinary sluggishness with which the proclamation traveled in the West calls for explanation, but the explanation probably lies in what Jackson had already heard about the arrangements for delaying news inimical to Burr.

[22] Jackson to Patton Anderson, January 4, 1804, Parton, I, 328; to Claiborne, January 8, 1807, Correspondence, I, 183.

[23] From the private collection of Emil Edward Hurja, New York City.

[24] January 8, 1807, Correspondence, I, 163.

[25] George Smith to Daniel Smith, January 15, 1807, Jackson papers, Library of Congress.

[26] Undated draft, Correspondence, I, 177.

[27] March 17, 1807, ibid., I, 172.

[28] Buell, I, 206.

[29] June 16, 1807, Correspondence, I, 181.

[30] Josiah Meigs to Return J. Meigs, August 29, 1807, Lawson McGhee Library, Knoxville.

[31] Excerpt from a version published in 1824 by Thomas Ritchie, the distinguished Richmond editor. Once asked concerning its accuracy, Jackson said it was not strong enough.

[32] Jackson to J. Stephenson, March 11, 1804, Library of Congress.

[33] Their mother was Polly Smith, daughter of General Daniel Smith. On March 24, 1807, William Ballard sent Jackson a timid reminder that seventeen dollars, due for the boys' schooling, would be very acceptable (ibid.).

[34] Ben Smith to Jackson, May 10, 1810, ibid.

[35] Statement of November, 1808, Correspondence, I, 190. An ininteresting analysis of the statement appears in Douglas Anderson's "Andrew Jackson, Frontier Merchant," Nashville Tennessean, April 13, 1928.

[36] Jackson to Daniel Smith, November 28, 1807, Correspondence, I, 183.

[37] Jackson to an unnamed correspondent, ibid., I, 198.

[38] Jackson to James Jackson, August 25, 1819, ibid., II, 427.

[39] Abernethy, From Frontier to Plantation in Tennessee, 263.

[40] Guild, 59.

[41] Parton, I, 349-60.

[42] Ibid., I, 344. Parton probably had the story from W. B. Lewis or some one else close to Jackson. Jackson's great interest in this trial is attested by the fact that after his death between fifty and sixty pages of manuscript bearing on it were found among his papers. They are now in the Jackson Papers, Library of Congress, in a folder marked, "Doubtful and Undated." They are not in Jackson's handwriting. They give attorneys' arguments and the substance of the testimony of witnesses. On the point above one reads that "Genl Jackson deposed

generally to A.³ character. A heart humane, honest and generous; the natural enemy of villains and scoundrels."

⁴³Thomas Hart Benton, *Thirty Years' View* (1854), I, 737.
⁴⁴Jackson to Whiteside, February 10, 1810, *Correspondence*, I, 199.
⁴⁵Donelson Caffery to Jackson, December 5, 1810, *ibid.*, I, 201.
⁴⁶Deaderick to Jackson, June 4, 1810, Library of Congress.
⁴⁷Deaderick to Jackson, April 25, 1807, *ibid.*
⁴⁸Deaderick to Jackson, March 5, 1809, *ibid.*
⁴⁹Certificates of George Blakemore, Benjamin Rawlings, Robert Williamson and Shadrach Nye, dated March 22, 1808; of Robert Purdy, February 15, and — Boyd, March 12, Jackson Papers, Library of Congress.
⁵⁰Donelson Caffery to Jackson, July 10, 1810, *ibid.*
⁵¹Lem Hutchings to Jackson, May 31, 1811, *ibid.*
⁵²Isabella Vinson to Jackson, September 10, 1810, *ibid.*
⁵³Jackson to Whiteside, February 10, 1810, *Correspondence,* I, 199.
⁵⁴*Ibid.*
⁵⁵A letter to Jackson, June 4, 1811, from which the sheet containing the writer's signature is missing, Library of Congress.
⁵⁶Hampton to Jackson, December 9, 1810, *Correspondence,* I, 205.
⁵⁷February 10, 1810, *ibid.*, I, 199.

CHAPTER IX

¹To "Arbitrators" (in a business dispute), February 29, 1812, *Correspondence*, I, 217. An interesting letter, showing Jackson in a conciliatory frame of mind and also still interested with the Green family in the slave trade at Natchez which he began twenty-three years before. Jackson was now related to this family, two of Abner Green's sons having married nieces of Rachel.
²Division Orders, *ibid.*, I, 220.
³Pronounced Wylie Blunt. He was a half-brother of Territorial Governor and ex-Senator Blount.
⁴Donelson Caffery to Jackson, December 5, 1810, *Correspondence,* I, 201.
⁵Buell (I, 247-51) rescued from oblivion the ride of Billy Phillips. He quotes a receipt of Governor Blount for Phillips's dispatches, dated Nashville, June 21, 1821. This must be an error. Blount's letters in the Jackson Papers, Library of Congress, show that the Governor was in Knoxville on June twenty-third. Thus he would have had to travel almost as fast as Billy to have been in Nashville two days before.
⁶P. Perkins to Jackson, July 5, 1812, Library of Congress.
⁷Blount to Secretary of War, June 25, 1812, Library of Congress.
⁸Parton, I, 361.
⁹The Club's premises were the old Clover Bottom track purchased from Jackson and his associates.
¹⁰Secretary of War to Blount, October 21 and 23, 1812, Library of Congress.

[11]November 11, 1812, *Correspondence*, I, 238.

[12]To Coffee, September 15, 1812, Library of Congress.

[13]Parton, I, 368.

[14]Promissory note, dated December 30, 1812, Library of Congress.

[15]To George W. Campbell, November 29, 1812, *Correspondence*, I, 244.

[16]January 18, 1813, *ibid.*, I, 271.

[17]January, 1813, *ibid.*, 272.

[18]January 25, 1813, *ibid.*, I, 274.

[19]*Ibid.*, I, 273.

[20]To W. B. Lewis, March 4, 1813, private collection of Oliver R. Barrett, Chicago.

[21]April 5, 1813, Chamberlain Manuscripts, Boston Public Library.

[22]February 6, 1813, *Correspondence*, I, 275. The copy of the letter Jackson received from Secretary Armstrong was misdated January 5, 1813, giving rise to the confusion in the mind of Jackson and of historical commentators. In a subsequent letter March 22, 1813 (*ibid.*, I, 300), the Secretary reveals when the order was written.

[23]March 8 and 16, 1813, *Correspondence*, I, 290, 296.

[24]To John P. Hickman, December 26, 1837, private collection of William M. Hall, Memphis.

[25]March 15, 1813, *Correspondence*, I, 296.

[26]To W. B. Lewis, April 9, 1813, *ibid.*, I, 304.

[27]Parton, I, 382.

[28]"Carrol . . . is I think the best Brigade Major in the armies of the United States—he ought and must be at the head of a regiment." (Jackson to W. B. Lewis, March 4, 1813, private collection of Oliver R. Barrett, Chicago.) This is one of several examples of Jackson's ability to recognize a military leader in the embryo.

[29]The Carroll-Benton duel: Carroll's statement, October 4, 1824, *Correspondence*, I, 311; a statement by the opposing parties' seconds, Andrew Jackson and John M. Armstrong, August 23, 1813, Jackson Papers, Library of Congress; Jackson to Armstrong with marginal notations by the latter, August 9, 1813, *ibid.*; statement of Felix Robertson, August 5, 1813, *ibid.*; Parton, I, 387; Bassett, I, 67.

[30]The fight with the Benton brothers: Andrew Hynes to Jackson, July 16, 1813; T. H. Benton to Jackson, July 25; Benton's statement, September 10; Jackson to Benton, July 19 and July 28 (?); James W. Sitler's statement, September 5, *Correspondence*, I, 309-18; Parton, I, 390.

[31]George S. Gaines's account, Pickett Manuscripts, Alabama State Library, Montgomery.

[32]General Order, September 24, 1813, Library of Congress.

CHAPTER X

[1]Jackson to Blount, October 13, 1813, *Correspondence*, I, 332.

[2]John Strother to Jackson, October 9, 1813, *ibid.*, I, 329.

[3]J. Lyon to Jackson, October 27, 1813, Library of Congress; Jackson to Leroy Pope, October 31, 1813, *Correspondence*, I, 339.

[4]To Pope and others, October 23, 1813, *ibid.*, I, 335.

[5]To W. B. Lewis, October 24, 1813, *ibid.*, I, 336.

[6]Order dated Fort Deposit, October 24, 1813, *ibid.*, I, 337.

[7]Reid to W. B. Lewis, October 24, 1814, Parton, I, 432.

[8]Reid Manuscript, 38, Tennessee Historical Society, Nashville.

[9]Reid to W. B. Lewis, October 24, 1813, Parton, I, 432.

[10]October 27, 1813, Library of Congress. James Jackson, a Nashville merchant, held the note.

[11]David Crockett, *Life of David Crockett* (1865), 75.

[12]To Blount, November 4, 1813, *Correspondence*, I, 341.

[13]Parton, I, 439.

[14]Crockett, 78.

[15]Reid and Eaton, 56-58.

[16]John Henry Eaton, *Life of Andrew Jackson* (1824), 66.

[17]Reid and Eaton, 60.

[18]General Orders, November 13, 1814, *Correspondence*, I, 344.

[19]Reid and Eaton, 70; Kendall, 217; Parton, I, 464.

[20]Library of Congress. James Jackson held the note.

[21]Jackson to Blount, November 19, 1813, *Correspondence*, I, 362.

[22]To Jackson, December 9, 1813, Library of Congress.

[23]December 9, 1813, *Correspondence*, I, 378.

[24]Reid and Eaton, 84.

[25]Jackson to his wife, December 14, 1813, *Correspondence*, I, 391.

[26]December 12, 1813, *ibid.*, I, 387.

[27]To Coffee, December 22, 1813, *ibid.*, I, 404.

[28]December 29, 1813, *ibid.*, 416. Original in Library of Congress. Reid and Eaton (110) contains a refined version of this letter that has been widely copied.

[29]Morning reports, or returns, showing the strength at Fort Strother are available only periodically, but on January fourteenth the last of the militia departed. The 800 new troops came up the same day and on the seventeenth the march began. In his report to Pinckney, dated January 29, 1814 (*Correspondence*, I, 447), Jackson gives the "remainder of my force," exclusive of the 800 recruits, on January seventeenth as 130.

[30]Jackson to Pinckney, *ibid.*; to his wife January 28, 1814, *ibid.*, I, 444; Reid and Eaton, 128.

[31]To Pinckney, *op cit.*, 451.

[32]Reid and Eaton, 136.

[33]February 10, 1814, *Correspondence*, I, 459.

[34]To Lewis, February 21, 1814, Parton I, 502.

[35]To Lewis, February 25, 1814, New York Public Library.

[36]Parton, I, 508.

[37]*Ibid.*, 509-12.

[38]Reid Manuscript, 131, Tennessee Historical Society, Nashville.

[39]Jackson to Blount without date. Buell, I, 325. This letter contradicts

the substance of the letter to Pinckney referred to in the note immediately following. Jackson wrote Blount that as the hour of execution drew near he mounted his horse and rode out of ear-shot.

[40]To Pinckney, March 14, 1814, *Correspondence*, I, 481.

[41]Two notes of $1,000 each, payable to James Jackson, dated February 9 and March 2, 1814, Library of Congress.

[42]General Orders, March 24 (?), 1814, *Correspondence*, I, 488.

[43]Charles Edwards Lester [and Sam Houston], *Life of Sam Houston* (1855), 33.

[44]Jackson to his wife, April 1, 1814, *Correspondence*, I, 493.

[45]*Ibid.*

[46]To Blount, March 31, 1814. A report entitled "Battle of Tehopisko or the Horse Shoe," Tennessee Historical Society, Nashville.

[47]W. G. Orr, in *Publications of Alabama Historical Society*, II, 57. Mr. Orr writes from memories of conversations with his father who saw the surrender.

[48]Albert James Pickett, *History of Alabama* (Reprint of 1896), 594. I favor Pickett's version which was derived from witnesses.

[49]The quotation thus far is taken from an undated fragment of a letter in the hand of John Reid (Tennessee Historical Society, Nashville). At this point Reid's letter ends. I have finished the quotation from Reid and Eaton, 166. Pickett calls Reid and Eaton's version of Weatherford's speech camp gossip. I do not think so. That part of their book was written by Eaton, but the Weatherford incident follows, almost literally, Reid's private letter.

CHAPTER XI

[1]May 8, 1814, *Correspondence*, II, 1.

[2]To Josiah Nichols, June 9, 1814, *ibid.*, II, 5.

[3]John Overton to Jackson, May 8, 1814, *ibid.*, II, 1.

[4]G. W. Campbell to Jackson, May 29, 1814, Library of Congress. Jackson's first appointment, on May twenty-second, was as a brigadier-general, vice Wade Hampton resigned, following his failure in Canada. Six days later the retirement of Harrison, virtually driven from the service, resulted in the proffer of the higher rank. Jackson accepted both appointments, the former, June 8, the latter, June 20, 1814.

[5]Armstrong to Jackson, June 25, 1814, *Correspondence*, II, 11.

[6]June 27, 1814, *ibid.*, II, 12.

[7]To Benjamin Hawkins, July 11, 1814, *ibid.*, II, 14.

[8]August 10, 1814, private collection of Oliver R. Barrett, Chicago.

[9]Kendall, 89.

[10]August, 1814, Library of Congress.

[11]Eaton, 205.

[12]*American State Papers, Indian Affairs*, I, 837; see also Hayne to Jackson, March 27, 1816, and statement of Benjamin Hawkins, April 16, 1816, *Correspondence*, II, 237.

[13]The Creek Nation has kept alive a claim against the United States for the compensation for the lands taken from the friendly tribes by Andrew Jackson. In 1853 the Commissioner of Indian Affairs was Luke Lea, of Tennessee, an old follower of Jackson. He informed a committee of the House of Representatives: "The . . . claim is eminently just. . . . The case is simply this, that a great Government, at the close of a war . . . forces . . . her allies, who fought bravely in every battle . . . to make a treaty. . . . In the history of our country it does not appear that any such [similar] case has ever occurred; nor has the Government ever desired to take lands from friendly Indians except . . . for a satisfactory compensation." The most recent opinion of the Indian Bureau, under the signature of Commissioner C. S. Rhoads, May 27, 1930, takes an opposite view of the justice of the Creek claim (Senate Report 1527, 71st Congress, 3rd session).

[14]August 10, 1814, private collection of Oliver R. Barrett, Chicago.

[15]Jackson to Manrique, July 12, 1814, Correspondence, II, 15.

[16]John Gordon to Jackson, July 30 (original misdated July 20), 1814, ibid., II, 17.

[17]July 17, 1814, ibid., II, 16.

[18]July 24, 1814, ibid., II, 19.

[19]Eaton, 212; Bassett, I, 128.

[20]August 10, 1814, private collection of Oliver R. Barrett, Chicago.

[21]Jackson to Blount, August 5, 1814, American State Papers, Military Affairs, III, 792.

[22]Charles Warren, Jacobin and Junto (1931), 269.

[23]Parton, I, 567.

[24]Jackson to Monroe, January 6, 1817, Correspondence, II, 272.

[25]To Robert Butler, August 27, 1814, ibid., II, 31.

[26]August 28, 1814, ibid., II, 35.

[27]Major Howell Tatum, "Topographical Notes and Observations on the Alabama River, August 1814," Publications of the Alabama Historical Society, II, 173; Jackson to Manrique, September 9, 1814, Correspondence, II, 44.

[28]To the Secretary of War, August 25, 1814, Library of Congress.

[29]Major A. Lacarrière Latour, Historical Memoir of the War in the West (1816), xxiv.

[30]Bibliotheca Parsoniana, New Orleans.

[31]Dated August 21, 1814, writer and addressee undisclosed, Jackson Papers, Library of Congress.

[32]Fragment of a letter dated Havana, August 13, 1814, apparently addressed to Jackson or intended for him, Jackson Papers, Library of Congress.

[33]August 24, 1814, Correspondence, II, 29.

[34]Marquis James, "Napoleon, Junior," The American Legion Monthly, III, No. 4. An account of Jean Laffite's rôle in the New Orleans campaign. In this article the author spelled the name Laffitte, as the individual in question sometimes spelled it. A more extensive study of

Laffite manuscripts in Bibliotheca Parsoniana, which is the notable private collection of Edward A. Parsons, of New Orleans, and in the Rosenberg Library, Galveston, prompts the use, in this volume, of the form, Laffite, because Laffite himself seems to have preferred it.

[35]*Ibid.*
[36]*Ibid.*
[37]*Ibid.*
[38]August 31, 1814, Bibliotheca Parsoniana, New Orleans.
[39]September 1, 1814, *ibid.*
[40]Jean Laffite to Lockyer, September 4, 1814 (" . . . *Je serai tout à vous.*"), *ibid.*
[41]Percy to Lockyer, August 30, 1814, *ibid.*
[42]Tatum, 174.

CHAPTER XII

[1]Tatum, 175.
[2]September 14, 1814, *Correspondence*, II, 48.
[3]Tatum, 176.
[4]Jackson to Robert Butler, September 17, 1814, *Correspondence*, II, 49.
[5]McKinley to Stewart, September 9, 1814, Jackson Papers, Library of Congress.
[6]Tatum, 177.
[7]To Robert Butler, September 17, 1814, *Correspondence*, II, 49.
[8]Lawrence's loss was 4 killed, 5 wounded; the British, 32 killed, 40 wounded. The size of the British landing force and of Lawrence's force has been variously stated. Jackson's report to the Secretary of War, September 17, 1814 (*Correspondence*, II, 50) gives the latter as 158 "fit for duty," and the former as 110 marines, 20 artillerymen and 200 Indians. The British figures, 60 marines and 120 Indians, are probably more accurate. The crews of the ships numbered 600.
[9]Jackson to John Rhea, October 11, 1814, private collection of Mrs. Charles R. Hyde, Chattanooga, Tennessee.
[10]September 4, 1814, Bibliotheca Parsoniana, New Orleans. Blanque is generally supposed to have been a close friend of Laffite. This letter, however, is couched in formal terms and in a note to Claiborne (*ibid.*), Blanque declared himself unacquainted with Laffite.
[11]Bibliotheca Parsoniana, New Orleans. The original is without date. Laffite's letters to Lockyer, Blanque and Claiborne appear in Latour whose versions of them have been accepted by all subsequent writers. Latour wrote in French. His manuscript was translated for publication by H. P. Nugent whose polished rendering of Laffite's language effaces much of the flavor and simplicity of the original. Laffite was a man of quiet force and personal charm, but no scholar. His orthography and grammar are Jacksonian and his penmanship worse than Monroe's. In an effort to approximate the true expression of the man, the translation is rather literal. In the French of Laffite the excerpts quoted read:

"*Dans la ferme persuasion que le choix qui éte fait devous pour . . .
d'Emploi de premier Magistrait . . . a eté par L'Estime & accorde au
Merite, Je M'addresse avous avec confiance pour un objet dont peut
dependre la Salut de l'Etat. Je vous offre Rendres á cette Etat plusiers
Citoyeńs, Qui peut-Etre 'ont perdu a vos yeux catitre sacré. Jevous
offre . . . Leurs Efforts pour La Défense delapatrie.*

"*Cepoint dela Louisienne que j'occupe est d'une Grand Importance
dans la situation présente. Je m'offre ala déffendre. . . . Je suis la Brebie
Égarrié qui désire rentrit au l'un dutroupeau . . . vous penitre de mes
fauts tille quelles sonts. . . .*

"*Au cas, Monsieur Le Gouverneur, que votre Response, Ne soit
favorable a mes desires ardents, je vous déclare que je part desuite pour
N'étre pas tenu, d'avoir Co-opéré à une invasion. . . . Ce qui ne peut
Manquer d'avoir lieu, et me son mettre entièrment au jugement de ma
consience.*

"*Jai L'honneur d'étre, M. Le gouverneur*

"LAFFITE"

[12]To Jackson, September, 1814, Library of Congress.

[13]October 3, 1814, *Correspondence*, II, 66. After the war Colonel
Ross and Commandant Patterson went to court with a dispute over their
personal shares of the booty.

[14]Jackson to Livingston, October 23, 1814, *ibid.*, II, 81.

[15]September 30, 1814, *ibid.*, II, 63.

[16]*Ibid.*, II, 57.

[17]Claiborne to Jackson, October 24, 1814, *ibid.*, II, 81.

[18]Gayarré, IV, 354.

[19]Claiborne to Jackson, September 19 and 20, 1814, *Correspondence*,
II, 54 and 55.

[20]Committee on Defense to Jackson, September 18, 1814, *ibid.*, II,
51. Although sent in the name of the committee, the document is
Livingston's work.

[21]Jackson to Livingston, April, 1804, Buell, I, 148.

[22]September 30, 1814, *Correspondence*, II, 63.

[23]September 30, 1814, *ibid.*, II, 65.

[24]To Monroe, February 18, 1815, *ibid.*, II, 174.

[25]On September 25, 1814, Monroe wrote Governor Blount of British
intentions to attack "thro' the mobile" (*ibid.*, II, 62). A copy of this
letter was forwarded to Jackson who received it probably late in October.
Not until after Jackson had departed for New Orleans in November did
Monroe begin his oft-cited requests for the General to hasten to the
defense of the city.

[26]Thomas L. Butler to Holmes, September 30, 1814, *ibid.*, II, 64.

[27]October 21, 1814, *ibid.*, II, 78.

[28]*Columbian Centinel* (Boston), September 10, 1814.

[29]Monroe to Jackson, September 27 and October 10, 1814, *ibid.*, II,
60 and 71.

[30]From Charles Cassidy, October 15, 1814, Library of Congress.

[31]To John Rhea, October 10, 1814, private collection of Mrs. Charles R. Hyde, Chattanooga, Tennessee.

[32]Robert Butler to Robert Hays, October 21, 1814, Jackson Papers, Library of Congress.

[33]To his wife, October 21, 1814, *Correspondence*, II, 78.

[34]John Coffee to his wife, without date, Buell, I, 358.

[35]To Monroe, October 26, 1814, *Correspondence*, II, 82.

[36]Charles Cassidy to Jackson, September 23, 1814, Library of Congress.

[37]Reid and Eaton, 226.

[38]Jackson left Pensacola November 9, 1814, the day after the flight of the British, arriving on the Tensas, November thirteenth. Casualties at Pensacola: American, 7 killed, 11 wounded; Spanish, 4 killed, 6 wounded. (Richard L. Campbell, *Historical Sketches of Colonial Florida* [1892], 233.)

[39]Reid and Eaton, 235.

[40]November 22, 1814, Library of Congress.

[41]Jackson to Blount, November 14, 1814, *ibid*.

[42]November 5, 1814, *Correspondence*, II, 90.

[43]Claiborne to Jackson, November 16, 1814, *ibid*., II, 100.

[44]To Winchester, November 22, 1814, *ibid*., II, 106

[45]October 10, 1814, *ibid*., II, 70.

[46]General Order, November 16, 1814, *ibid*., II, 100.

[47]To Winchester, November 22, 1815, *ibid*., II, 106.

[48]*Ibid*.

[49]November 20, 1814, *ibid*., II, 101.

[50]James Jackson to Jackson, December 14, 1814, Library of Congress.

CHAPTER XIII

[1]Louisiana usage of the term Creole ofttimes is imperfectly understood in other parts of the United States. In 1814, as now, it had a meaning different from that in the French and Spanish West Indies where it designates a native of part negro blood. Louisiana Creoles are white persons of French or Spanish extraction. "Creole negroes" in Louisiana are negroes reared among the French-speaking inhabitants.

[2]Alexander Walker, *Jackson and New Orleans* (1856), 14.

[3]Jackson to Coffee, December 11, 1814, *Correspondence*, II, 112; Claiborne to Monroe, December 9, 1814, Gayarré, IV, 379.

[4]Jackson to Winchester, November 22, 1814, *Correspondence*, II, 106; to Monroe, December 10, 1814, *ibid*., II, 111.

[5]Walker, 13.

[6]*Ibid*., 16.

[7]*Ibid*., 15.

[8]*Louisiana Historical Quarterly*, VI, 82. This article is a translation by Grace King of Marigny's pamphlet, *Reflexions sur la Cam-*

pagne   du   Général   André   Jackson   en   Louisiane   (1848).
[9]Walker, 17.
[10]Grace King, *Creole Families of New Orleans* (1922), 33.
[11]Walker, 17.
[12]*Ibid.*, 18.
[13]Marginal note in Jackson's hand on Monroe's letter to Jackson, December 10, 1814, *Correspondence*, II, 110.
[14]Vincent Nolte, *Fifty Years in Two Hemispheres* (1854), 207.
[15]Livingston's statement, Buell, I, 366.
[16]*Louisiana Historical Quarterly*, VI, 82.
[17]To James Brown, February 4, 1815, Library of Congress.
[18]Jackson's address to the New Orleans volunteers, December 18, 1814, *Correspondence*, II, 118.
[19]Jackson to James Brown, February 4, 1815, Library of Congress.
[20]Captain Alexander White to Jackson, December 14, 1814; Lieutenant B. M. Stokes to Brigadier-General Morgan, December 21, 1814, Jackson Papers, Library of Congress.
[21]December 10, 1814, *Correspondence*, II, 111.
[22]December 11, 1814, *ibid.*, II, 112.
[23]January 21, 1815, Louisiana State Museum, New Orleans.
[24]*Correspondence*, II, 114.
[25]Parton, II, 57.
[26]*Ibid.*, 55.
[27]Latour, 72.
[28]Report of Lieutenant Colonel McRea to Jackson, December 12, 1814, *Correspondence*, II, 120.
[29]Latour, 64.
[30]Parton, II, 56.
[31]*Ibid.*
[32]December 16, 1814, *Correspondence*, II, 116.
[33]Parton, II, 56.
[34]December 16, 1814, *Correspondence*, II, 116.
[35]Proclamation of martial law, December 16, 1814, Parton, II, 60.
[36]Latour, 72.
[37]Sister Superior Marie Olivier to Jackson, December 20, 1814, Library of Congress.
[38]*Friend of the Laws*, January 16, 1815.
[39]Nolte, 208.
[40]*Louisiana Historical Quarterly*, VI, 65.
[41]*Ibid.*
[42]*Ibid.*
[43]Latour, 71. Latour's assertion that it was Jackson who interceded with Judge Hall to obtain the safe conduct is at variance with Marigny's account, which is undoubtedly correct. Marigny wrote in 1848 after differences with Jackson during the campaign were long forgotten and he had become a belligerent supporter of Jackson's policies in national affairs.

⁴⁴December 22, 1814, Bibliotheca Parsoniana, New Orleans.

⁴⁵Walker, 143.

⁴⁶*Ibid.*, 154.

⁴⁷Nolte, 203.

⁴⁸An incomplete manuscript narrative, in Carroll's hand, describing incidents of the river journey and the subsequent engagements near New Orleans, including that of January eighth, gives December twentieth as the date of his arrival (private collection of Albert Lieutaud, New Orleans). Other authorities give the dates of December twenty-first and twenty-second. Jackson was mistaken in his assertion (*Correspondence*, II, 110) that Carroll arrived without arms.

⁴⁹Carroll's Manuscript Narrative, *op. cit.*

⁵⁰*Ibid.*

⁵¹*Correspondence*, II, 123.

⁵²His own spelling. The name is usually written Delaronde.

⁵³Latour, 87.

⁵⁴Walker, 151.

⁵⁵I follow tradition in preserving for Gabriel Villeré the conspicuous rôle in bringing word of the British landing because research seems to justify it. Walker (151), who gives a detailed account of Villeré's arrival, is trustworthy. Although he did not record the incident until thirty-three years later, he was in New Orleans at the time and knew all the persons concerned. Moreover he is supported by contemporary evidence. The next morning—December 24, 1814—the Eastern mail left the city at daybreak when the results of Jackson's night battle were still in doubt. This mail carried a private letter written by a soldier who mentions Villeré, and no one else, as the bearer of the news of the British coup. "Without this providential warning," says the writer, "we should probably have been taken by entire surprise" (*Columbian Centinel* [Boston], January 28, 1815).

The prior visit of Rousseau, however, is apparently authenticated by Walker (151). Reid and Eaton (284) give the credit solely to Tatum whom Jackson had known for thirty years. Eaton may have relied on an undated memorandum of Colonel Arthur P. Hayne, now among the Jackson Papers at the Library of Congress, which merely says that Jackson was informed at two P.M. of the British landing by Howell Tatum. In view of Tatum's own statement, it is impossible to believe that this officer reached headquarters in advance of Villeré ("Major Howell Tatum's Journal," *Smith College Studies in History*, VII, 107). The modest Tatum does not even mention his own name, merely saying that "this day the Commanding General received information, by Maj. Latour, that the enemy had effected a landing."

CHAPTER XIV

¹Losses: American, 45 killed and wounded; British, 95 killed and wounded, Bassett, I, 169.

[2][George Robert Gleig] *A Narrative of the British Campaigns against Washington, Baltimore and New Orleans* (1821), 264. He calls it Pine Island. Jackson's men would have lived on ducks which Gleig found "so timorous that it was impossible to approach within musket shot."

[3]Gleig, 266. The British writer calls his informants "American deserters." Latour (93) gives the names of three Louisianians in the Spanish service who, he says, had joined the British at Pensacola. Walker (118) identifies them as "ex-officials of the Spanish government in Louisiana" who had never acquiesced to the transfer of the country to the United States.

[4]Called by British writers Bayou Catalin or Cataline. On old maps of Louisiana it appears as River St. Francis.

[5]To Holmes, December 25, 1814, *Correspondence*, II, 124; to Blount, February 6, 1815, Library of Congress.

[6]Lest my remarks in the main text should be taken as innuendo reflecting on the patriotism of General Villeré, which is unimpeachable, I shall say exactly what is in my mind. The route of Bayou Mazant and Bayou Bienvenue was the commonly used way from the Villeré plantation to the lake. Had it been blocked as Jackson ordered, it would only have had to be cleared again after the campaign at the cost of much labor. As did most Louisianians, and Jackson himself, Villeré thought the British would attempt the Bayou Chef Menteur. Under these circumstances did the General seek to avoid what he deemed a useless inconvenience to his property by casually overlooking this one bayou during his obstructing operations? The question may be very unjust to General Villeré, but history shows many examples wherein small personal interests have swayed the official conduct of perfectly upright persons.

Major Villeré's negligence, however brilliantly atoned for, is clear. Jackson's "astonishment" at the discovery that Bayou Bienvenue had not been obstructed, bordered on suspicion. (Jackson to Holmes, December 25, 1814, *Correspondence*, II, 124.) Young Villeré participated in the battle of December twenty-third (Jackson to Monroe, December 27, 1814, *Correspondence*, II, 127), but later Jackson deprived him of his sword and placed him under arrest. After the news of peace he was tried for "harboring and protecting the enemy" and "neglect of duty." Major Hinds of the Mississippi Dragoons was president of the court. It was alleged that on the night of December twenty-second one of the Spanish fishermen informed Villeré of the British landing, and Villeré denounced him as a spreader of false alarms. Villeré entered no defense and was acquitted. Of the first charge he was innocent. Of the second, the war being over, the court took a lenient view. (General Orders, Headquarters Seventh Military District, March 3, 1815. Louisiana State Museum, New Orleans; Latour, cxxxi.)

[7]Latour, 104. Bassett (I, 172) says 1,688 "rank and file" which is practically the same thing.

[8]Gleig, 278.

[9]I am unable to account for this coincidence. Walker (124) states

that Ducros and his comrades deceived the British by prearrangement. I think Latour (86), who probably had the story from Ducros himself, more plausible in his suggestion that the men had honestly fallen into one of the most common of errors among untrained soldiers, that of over-estimating the magnitude of any force.

[10]Nolte, 209.

[11]Walker, 157.

[12]*Ibid.*; Parton, II, 73.

[13]Reid and Eaton, 503, from a statement of Colonel Robert Butler, Jackson's adjutant-general. Latour (105) enumerated 2,131, not count-ing staff: the *Louisiana Gazette*, June 10, 1815, 2,325. In a letter to Monroe, December 27, 1814 (*Correspondence*, II, 127), Jackson gave his force as "not exceeding in all fifteen hundred." The Commander's preoccupation with more important matters may account for this under-estimate.

[14]These trees which to-day conduct one to the ruins of Versailles form the most magnificent double row of oaks in Louisiana. They are now erroneously known as the Pakenham Oaks. See Note No. 39, Chapter XV.

[15]Hayne Manuscript, Jackson Papers, Library of Congress.

[16]A manuscript account in the handwriting of Jackson, hereinafter referred to as Jackson's Manuscript Narrative, Library of Congress. This account, which Jackson wrote sometime in 1815, gives a succinct run-ning story of events from December 23, 1814, to January 19, 1815, with the exception of happenings between December twenty-eighth and about ten A.M. on January eighth. These sheets are missing.

[17]Jackson to Laffite, undated, Bibliotheca Parsoniana, New Orleans.

[18]Hayne Manuscript, Jackson Papers, Library of Congress.

[19]Jackson's Manuscript Narrative, *ibid*.

[20]Latour, 112.

[21]Walker, 171.

[22]Jackson to Monroe, December 27, 1814 (*Correspondence*, II, 128), does not mention his participation in this affair, but gives the credit to Colonels Butler and Piatt and Major Chotard, who rushed into the scene of confusion beside the General.

[23]Latour, 97.

[24]*Ibid.*, 240.

[25]The brigade had dismounted before going into action and the horses let run loose. Latour's map of the battle is in error where it indicates two companies detached to hold the horses. Eventually most of the mounts were retaken by the Tennesseans, but the British caught a good many of them. Colonel Henry R. Richmond, U. S. A., who has made a careful study of the campaign from British sources, believes that six months later some of these captured Tennessee horses were ridden on the field of Waterloo.

[26]Gleig, 294.

[27]To his father, undated, Parton, II, 101.

[28]Jackson's Manuscript Narrative, Library of Congress.

[29]Latour, 102, clx.

[30]Jackson's Manuscript Narrative, Library of Congress.

[31]To Jackson, December 25, 1814, *Correspondence*, II, 125.

[32]December 27, 1814, *ibid.*, II, 128.

[33]December 24, 1814, *ibid.*, II, 124.

[34]Anderson, 97.

[35]Walker, 212.

[36]Livingston to Jackson, December 25, 1814, *Correspondence*, II, 125.

[37]Parton, II, 102.

[38]François-Xavier Martin, *The History of Louisiana* (1882), 376.

[39]Nolte, 214.

[40]Latour, 114.

[41]Martin, 376.

[42]Jackson to John McLean, March 22, 1824, *Correspondence*, III, 239; affidavit of T. L. Butler, May 23, 1815, *ibid.*, II, 210; Gayarré, IV, 562.

[43]This is the most innocuous construction that can be placed on Declouet's understanding of Guichard's remarks, and the one admitted by Marigny (*Louisiana Historical Quarterly*, VI, 68). Abner Duncan and Auguste Davézac said under oath that Declouet told them Guichard tried to obtain his adhesion to a scheme of capitulation in event the Rodriquez Canal line was taken. This is a grave charge. The whole subject of "treasonable" intentions on the part of Guichard and other members of the Legislature was investigated by a committee of that body after the battle of January eighth. The result was exoneration. Gayarré (IV, 534-77) analyzes the testimony with his usual conservatism and care. That of Guichard is remarkable and, as Gayarré broadly hints, difficult of belief. The body of evidence leaves this writer with the impression that an influential coterie in the Legislature did hope to contravene the plans of Jackson and save the city should matters come to that extremity.

[44]Gleig, 309.

[45]Walker, 226.

[46]To a committee of the Legislature, December 31, 1814, Gayarré, IV, 540; Plauché to Phillips, January 17, 1843, Jackson Papers, Library of Congress; Parton, II, 145; *Louisiana Historical Quarterly*, VI, 68; Reid and Eaton, 320.

CHAPTER XV

[1]Patterson to Secretary of Navy, December 29, 1814, Latour, xlix.

[2]*Louisiana Historical Quarterly*, VI, 68.

[3]To John McLean, March 22, 1824, *Correspondence*, III, 240. Marigny's version (*Louisiana Historical Quarterly*, VI, 68) is that Jackson accepted his assurances of the patriotic intentions of the Legislature and merely said to "Return to the City. Reassure your colleagues." After the campaign Jackson defined his meaning of a warm session. "I

should have . . . fired . . . the city . . . and fought the enemy amidst the surrounding flames. . . . Nothing for the comfortable maintenance of the enemy would have been left. . . . I would have . . . occupied a position above the river, cut off all supplies, and in this way compelled them to depart from the country" (Parton, II, 143).

⁴*Ibid.*, II, 140. During this engagement Jackson had 3,282 men on his line, though only the artillerymen and a small body of infantry under Carroll were engaged. The British strength was about 5,500. American losses were 9 killed, and 9 wounded, including one seaman wounded on board the *Louisiana*. The British made no separate return of casualties for December twenty-eighth, but for the period of December 25-31 reported 16 killed, 42 wounded, 2 missing (Latour, clxxi).

⁵Contemporaries barely mention the use of cotton bales of which so much subsequently has been made (Latour, 134; Nolte, 216 and 232). The latter, who owned two hundred and fifty bales seized by Jackson, says no others were used in the works. Isaac Edward Morse, a member of Congress from Louisiana whose father served under Jackson, wrote to his sons in 1853: "The story of the cotton bales was greatly exaggerated, only a few hundred were used . . . mostly as platforms to place cannon on (private collection of Miss Ethel Morse, Tampa, Florida)."

⁶Latour, preface, xvii.

⁷Walker, 257-58.

⁸Nolte, 218.

⁹Losses: American, 11 killed, 23 wounded. The British reported 32 killed, 42 wounded and 2 missing between January first and fifth (Latour, clxxii).

¹⁰John F—— (illegible) to Jackson, January 2, 1815, Library of Congress.

¹¹Library of Congress.

¹²January 3, 1815, *Correspondence*, II, 130.

¹³Jackson's Manuscript Narrative, Library of Congress.

¹⁴January 3, 1815, *Correspondence*, II, 132.

¹⁵Buell, I, 423.

¹⁶January 7, 1815, *Correspondence*, II, 132.

¹⁷Walker, 319.

¹⁸*Ibid.*

¹⁹Jackson Manuscript Narrative, Library of Congress.

²⁰Buell, II, 8.

²¹*Ibid.*, II, 10.

²²Statements of Jackson's strength vary considerably. Bassett (I, 192) places it at 3,989, adding that the estimate is based on Latour and is not far from the figures Jackson cited in his controversy with Adair in 1817. The *Louisiana Gazette*, June 15, 1815, listed 4,698. My figure is based on the consolidated morning reports for January eighth of the commands stationed behind the Rodriquez line (Jackson Papers, Military, Library of Congress). It includes only officers and men marked present for duty. It is perhaps doubtful if all these actually were on the line during the

fighting and certainly the figure includes some troops who had no arms.

[23]Buell, II, 12.

[24]*Ibid.*

[25]*Ibid.*

[26]Jackson to Monroe, January 9 and 13, 1815, *Correspondence*, II, 136 and 142.

[27]Buell, II, 20.

[28]To Monroe, January 13, 1814, *Correspondence*, II, 143.

[29]Parton, II, 208.

[30]The action on the west bank brought the total of American casualties to 13 killed, 39 wounded, and 19 missing. The British losses as reported to the home government on January tenth were 291 killed, 1,262 wounded and 484 missing in the actions on both sides of the river (William James, *Military Occurrences of the Late War between Great Britain and the United States* [1818], II, 554). Of the wounded many did not live to reach the fleet. Combat casualties since December twenty-third had been 2,694 or about half of the number actually engaged.

[31]To Robert Hays, January 26, 1815, *Correspondence*, II, 156.

[32]Parton, II, 212.

[33]Bassett, I, 203.

[34]January 9, 1815, *Correspondence*, II, 137.

[35]Morgan to Claiborne, January 25, 1815, Louisiana State Museum, New Orleans.

[36]General Orders, February 25, 1815, *ibid.*

[37]Nolte, 224.

[38]Jackson's Manuscript Narrative, Library of Congress.

[39]Pierre Favrot to his wife, January 21, 1815, Louisiana State Museum, New Orleans. The avenue of oaks leading from the ruins of Versailles, the de La Ronde plantation château, are known as the Pakenham Oaks from a tradition that the British commander died under their branches. Stanley Clisby Arthur of New Orleans has rediscovered the fact that Pakenham died under a group of four oaks on the Colomb plantation. These trees are still standing.

[40]G. M. Ogden to Jackson, February 3, 1815, *Correspondence*, II, 156.

[41]Jackson to Hays, February 4, 1815, *ibid.*, II, 157.

[42]February 4, 1815, Library of Congress.

CHAPTER XVI

[1]McMaster, IV, 249.

[2]National *Intelligencer*, Washington, January 20, 1815.

[3]To his wife, February 9, 1815, from Samuel Eliot Morison, *Life and Letters of Harrison Gray Otis* (1913), II, 163.

[4]*Ibid.*, February 12, 1815.

[5]*Ibid.*

[6]*Correspondence*, II, 150.

[7]January 21, 1815, Louisiana State Museum, New Orleans.

[8]Latour, 199.

[9]To Robert Hays, February 9, 1815, Library of Congress.

[10]Jackson to Winchester, January 19, 1815, *Correspondence*, II, 150.

[11]January 21, 1815, Louisiana State Museum, New Orleans.

[12]Parton, II, 288.

[13]To Hays, February 17, 1815, Collection of Thomas F. Madigan, New York City.

[14]February 14, 1815, Library of Congress.

[15]February 13, 1815, *ibid.*

[16]February 19, 1815, Latour, xc.

[17]Jackson to Holmes, February 21, 1815, *Correspondence*, II, 178.

[18]February 13, 1815, *Correspondence*, II, 177.

[19]Nolte, 227.

[20]Nolte, 227; Jackson to Godwin B. Cotten, editor of the *Gazette*, February 21, 1815, *Correspondence*, II, 179. The latter is a rough draft differing slightly from the version of Nolte which evidently was taken from the newspaper.

[21]Rachel Jackson to Robert Hays, March 5, 1815, Library of Congress.

[22]James Jackson to Jackson, January 26, 1815, *ibid.*

[23]Nolte, 238.

[24]Parton, 323.

[25]Rachel Jackson to Robert Hays, *op. cit.*

[26]*Ibid.*

[27]Nolte, 238.

[28]To Robert Hays, *op. cit.*

[29]Order dated February 28, 1815, *Correspondence*, II, 181.

[30]Jackson to Arbuckle, March 5, 1815, *ibid.*, II, 183.

[31]Jackson to Monroe, March 6, 1815, *ibid.*, II, 184.

[32]March 6, 1815, *ibid.*, II, 184.

[33]Gayarré, IV, 611.

[34]Latour, cxiv.

[35]*Ibid.*, cxiv.

[36]Buell, I, 56.

[37]General Order, January 21, 1815, Latour, clxxv; Jackson to [Pierre] Laffite, without date, Bibliotheca Parsoniana, New Orleans. On Jackson's representations Madison pardoned the Laffites and their followers, thus ending the proceedings against them suspended by Judge Hall in order that they might bear arms in the defense of the city.

[38]Jackson Papers, XXXIV, Library of Congress.

[39]*Ibid.*

[40]Gayarré, IV, 625.

CHAPTER XVII

[1]Dated April 15, 1815, Library of Congress.

[2]Jackson to Coffee, April 24, 1815, Library of Congress.

[3]Jackson to Dallas, July 11, 1815, *Correspondence*, II, 213.

[4]James Kearns to Jackson, February 22, 1815, Library of Congress.

[5]Stephen Kingston to John Rhea, February 24, 1815, private collection of Mrs. Charles R. Hyde, Chattanooga, Tennessee.

[6]Balie Peyton, "Haynie's Maria Against the World," the *Rural Sun* (1873), Anderson, 259.

[7]*Ibid.*, 260.

[8]Guild, 249.

[9]Abernethy, *From Frontier to Plantation in Tennessee*, 263 *et seq.* It will be remembered that in 1811, Jackson had averted possible ruin by a bold and astonishingly successful bargain which put him in a position to demand a settlement from the sellers of eighty thousand acres, in order to clear their warranted titles. All met his terms except Andrew Erwin who precipitated a long court and legislative contest. Finally, in 1823, Jackson let Erwin off on a plea of his wife that an enforcement of the claim would impoverish the family.

[10]Library of Congress. Jackson's deposit book for this period is filed with papers for June, 1815.

[11]September 20, 1815, *Correspondence*, II, 215.

[12]October 4, 1815, *ibid.*, II, 217.

[13]Andrew Hynes to Jackson, October 24, 1815, *ibid.*, II, 218.

[14]November 7, 1815, *ibid.*, II, 220.

[15]November 15, 1815, Chamberlain Manuscripts, Boston Public Library.

[16]Parton, II, 334.

[17]Reid to an unidentified correspondent, November 21, 1815, Tennessee Historical Society, Nashville.

[18]Monroe to Jackson, July 3, 1816, Library of Congress; Bassett, I, 224.

[19]Coffee to Jackson, January 21 and February 8, 1816, *Correspondence*, II, 225 and 228; Jackson to Coffee, February 13, 1816 (two letters), *ibid.*, II, 230 and 231; Jackson to Colbert, a Cherokee chieftain, February 13, 1816, *ibid.*, II, 233.

[20]January 2, 1816, collection of Thomas F. Madigan, New York City.

[21]Jackson to James Brown, September 6, 1816, *Correspondence*, II, 259.

[22]April 8, 1816, *ibid.*, II, 238.

[23]April 22, 1816, *ibid.*, II, 241.

[24]Jackson to Monroe, October 23, 1816, *ibid.*, II, 261.

[25]July 27, 1816. The actual operation was conducted by Colonel Clinch of the Army and Sailing Master Loomis of the Navy.

[26]March 1, 1817, *Correspondence*, II, 276.

[27]Jackson to Monroe, March 18, 1817, collection of Thomas F. Madigan, New York City.

[28]Abernethy, *op. cit.*, 271.

[29]March 17, 1817, *American Historical Magazine*, V, 235.

[30]Parton, I, 105.

[31] February 24, 1817, *Correspondence*, II, 275.

[32] Division Order, April 22, 1817, *ibid.*, II, 291.

[33] Parton, II, 376.

[34] September 8, 1817, *Correspondence*, II, 325.

[35] October 4, 1817, *ibid.*, II, 327. Parton's estimate of Scott's letter (II, 377) as "every thing that . . . it should have been" has found general acceptance among historians, but Parton apparently saw only such excerpts of the letter as appears in Mansfield's *Life of Scott*, 171.

[36] December 3, 1817, *Correspondence*, II, 338.

[37] January 2, 1818, *ibid.*, II, 344.

[38] Carroll to Jackson, September 11, 1817, Library of Congress. Parton (II, 383-91) covers this controversy rather thoroughly, drawing from the pamphlet, *Letters of General Adair and General Jackson*, published at Lexington, Kentucky, in 1817.

[39] August 4, 1817, *Correspondence*, II, 320.

[40] Monroe to Jackson, July 3, 1816, Library of Congress.

[41] December 14, 1816, *Correspondence*, II, 266.

[42] Bassett, I, 242.

[43] Captain Ferdinand Amelung to Jackson, June 4, 1816, *Correspondence*, II, 243.

[44] Livingston to Jackson, February 2, 1816, Library of Congress.

[45] October 4, 1817, *Correspondence*, II, 329.

[46] Rhea to Jackson, November 27 and December 24, 1817, *Correspondence*, II, 335 and 341.

[47] Jackson to Monroe, October 22, 1817, *ibid.*, II, 332; Monroe to Jackson, December 29, 1817, collection of Thomas F. Madigan, New York City; Calhoun to Jackson, December 29, 1817, *Correspondence*, III, 343.

[48] *Ibid.*, 342.

[49] January 6, 1818, *ibid.*, II, 345.

[50] Monroe to Jackson, December 28, 1817, collection of Thomas F. Madigan, New York City.

CHAPTER XVIII

[1] Jackson to his wife, January 27, 1818, Heiskell, III, 289.

[2] The Rhea letter controversy broke in 1830 during the political warfare between Jackson and Calhoun, breeding a question which nonpartisan historians have been unable to settle to their satisfaction. The contentions of Monroe and Jackson are diametrically opposed, and, on the face of existing evidence, Monroe has the better of the case. Dr. Bassett (I, 247) calls it an issue of veracity and of memory between the two men, equally truthful. But, being obliged to choose, Bassett thinks Monroe, possessing the more trained and orderly mind, would be the more reliable as to memory. On the point of memory I follow with some misgivings my distinguished predecessor, but as to comparative veracity, or "honesty" to use Bassett's broader term, I submit that the record of

Mr. Monroe's dealings with Andrew Jackson leaves room for a dissenting opinion.

At an early date Mr. Monroe sought to disassociate himself from the "say Mr. J. Rhea" suggestion. On December 18, 1818, when the Administration was arduously striving to throw responsibility for the Florida campaign on Jackson—Monroe going so far as to propose a "correction" of Jackson's dispatches—the President wrote the General: "Your letter of January 6th was received while I was seriously indisposed. Observing it was from you, I handed it to Mr. Calhoun to read. . . . He remarked after perusing the letter that it was a confidential one relating to Florida, which I must answer" (Benton, I, 170).

Later Crawford happened in and read it but made no comment.

The original of the letter in question is now in the Monroe Papers in the New York Public Library. It bears this endorsement in Monroe's hand: "I was sick when I recd. it, and did not read it, till after . . . [the campaign]. Hearing afterwards that an understanding was imputed to me. I asked Mr Rhea, if anything had ever pass'd between him and me. He declard that he had never heard of the subject before. I knew the suggestion to be false, but . . . it being possible that Mr Rhea might have spoken to me by distant allusion, . . . to which I might have innocently given, from a desire to acquire Florida, a reply, from which he might have inferred a sanction not contemplated, I was glad to find that nothing of the kind had occurred."

Two weeks before his death, Mr. Monroe repeated the substance of the above. The striking feature about the whole thing seems to me to be this. Florida was the dominating issue before the Administration at that moment. Jackson was the dominating personality of that issue. He writes the President a confidential letter on this topic which had been the subject of many confidences. The Secretary of War says it is something the President must attend to personally. Yet, the President lays the letter aside and forgets about it until after the war when the prickly question of responsibility arises. The incident does not speak well for Mr. Monroe's memory, or for his judgment.

With Mr. Monroe's version, Jackson's story is irreconcilable. His account of the delivery of Rhea's reply at Big Creek is contained in an "Exposition," written or dictated by him at the White House in 1831 during the quarrel with Calhoun. It was not given to the newspapers, as intended, and was first published by Benton (I, 169-80) in 1854. Though he does not say so, Jackson received Monroe's disclaimer of December 18, 1818, either while in Washington or on his way there in January, 1819. This was during the Congressional investigation of the Florida campaign. While in Washington, Jackson apparently took up the Rhea matter with the President, and, if his Exposition sets forth the facts correctly, he did it in such a way as to refresh Monroe's memory. In any event, Jackson says that Monroe asked him to burn Rhea's letter when he got home, which Jackson says he did, making an entry in his letter-book opposite the copy of his confidential letter of January sixth;

"Mr. Rhea's letter in answer is burnt this 12th April, 1819" (*ibid.*, **179**; Jackson to Rhea, June 2, 1831, *Correspondence*, IV, 288).

Jackson's official letter book for this period is missing, but the General's private copy of his letter of January 6, 1818, is available in the Jackson Papers in the Library of Congress. It bears the notation: "Mr. J. Rhea's letter in answer is burnt this 12th April 1818," which was obviously a slip of the pen for 1819.

Thus far we have a good deal of corroboration of Jackson's account, unless one would assume him guilty of faking the endorsement just quoted. Such an assumption is not in character with Jackson. Mr. Monroe is the only party to this controversy who has proposed the amendment of public documents in an effort to prove something by them which they did not prove when written.

Other facts and circumstances, however, tend to weaken Jackson's case. With the exception of John Overton, no one has been found who claims to have seen the Rhea letter in question, and Overton's statement is indefinite (Overton to Jackson, June 2, 1831, *Correspondence*, IV, 287). It might have referred to some other Rhea letter.

Moreover during the passage of confidential letters between Jackson and Monroe in 1818 over the question of responsibility, Jackson makes no allusion to the indirect permission to seize Florida that he claims was given (Jackson to Monroe, August 19, 1818, *Correspondence*, III, 389; to Monroe, November 15, 1818, Parton, II, 525). And most significant, Rhea himself appears to have had no recollection of having sent any such letter as Jackson says he received. This is shown by his letter of December 18, 1818, to Jackson (*Correspondence*, II, 403), and by his behavior in 1831 when Jackson appealed to him for support. Rhea was then seventy-nine years old and his faculties were weak; but surely, if he had been the secret link between Monroe and Jackson in a matter such as the Florida campaign, he would not have forgotten it.

He was willing to help his old friend, however, and wrote three times to find out exactly what Jackson wanted him to say (Rhea to Jackson, January 4, 1831, *ibid.*, III, 221; March 30 and April 2, 1831, *ibid.*, III, 254). When he finally got the matter straight in his mind, he wrote Monroe (Rhea to Monroe, June 3, 1831, *ibid.*, IV, 288) repeating Jackson's whole story and asking the ex-President's corroboration. Monroe was dying when he received the letter, but in the presence of witnesses he dictated a denial, and signed it two weeks before the end came. Rhea died less than a year later and relatives questioned his competence to make a will (Margaret B. Hamer, "John Rhea of Tennessee," *East Tennessee Historical Society's Publications*, January, 1932).

Only one of Jackson's letters to Rhea has been found. Judging from Rhea's answers the others seem to have been filled with promptings. Mrs. Charles R. Hyde, of Chattanooga, a niece of John Rhea, has several of her uncle's papers, among which is a fragment which resembles the handwriting of Andrew Jackson. It is undated and reads:

"I wish to See the Letters That Gen'l Jackson addressed to John Rhea respecting a Letter that Should have been written by John Rhea to him to authorise him to go to pensacola and also secure a Coppy of the Letter in my hand write to John Rhea directed to me dated——"

This may explain the absence of Jackson's other letters to Rhea.

Certainly Jackson would not have gone to all the trouble he did had he not honestly believed that he received some kind of letter from Rhea at Big Creek which he interpreted as containing Monroe's assent to the Florida adventure. Rhea was writing Jackson often during those days, and had acted as mediator in the dispute arising from Jackson's General Order of April 22, 1817. On January 12, 1818, Rhea wrote Jackson a letter (*Correspondence*, II, 348) which quite possibly was delivered at Big Creek, and which, by a wide stretch of the imagination, Jackson may have misconstrued. Another guess is that Rhea may have written Jackson on his own responsibility and dared not confess it.

[3]To Isaac McKeever, March, 1818, Parton, II, 447. See also Colonel George Gibson to Jackson, February 12, 1818, *Correspondence*, II, 354.

[4]*Ibid.*, II, 357.

[5]To John Arbuthnot, April 2, 1818, *American State Papers, Military Affairs*, I, 722.

[6]*Ibid.*, I, 721-28.

[7]*Ibid.*, I, 731.

[8]*Ibid.*, I, 734.

[9]*Ibid.*, I, 734.

[10]Memoir of Lieutenant J. B. Rodgers, who was present, Parton, II, 477.

[11]Jackson to Monroe, June 2, 1818, *Correspondence*, II, 378.

[12]Proclamation, May 29, 1818, *ibid.*, II, 374.

[13]*American State Papers, Foreign Relations*, IV, 496.

[14]Charles Francis Adams (editor), *Memoirs of John Quincy Adams* (1875), IV, 107 *et seq.*

[15]July 19, 1818, Library of Congress.

[16]August 19, 1818, *Correspondence*, II, 389.

[17]To Thomas Cooper, August 24, 1818, Library of Congress.

[18]James Gadsden to Jackson, September 18, 1818, Library of Congress. For other light on the Secretary's change of heart see Calhoun to Charles Tait, July 20, 1818, *Gulf States Historical Magazine*, I, 92, and Calhoun to a friend, September 5, 1818, *ibid.*, I, 94.

[19]Monroe to Jackson, October 20, 1818, and Jackson to Monroe, November 15, 1818, *Correspondence*, II, 398.

[20]*American State Papers, Foreign Relations*, IV, 539 *et seq.*

[21]October 5, 1818, *Correspondence*, II, 398.

[22]Heiskell, II, 443.

[23]January 2, 1819, Library of Congress.

[24]Jackson to Andrew Jackson Donelson, January 31, 1819, *Correspondence*, II, 408.

[25]Jackson to James Gadsden, August 1, 1819, *Correspondence*, II, 241; Gadsden to Jackson, February 6, 1820, Library of Congress.
[26]Bassett, I, 283; Parton, II, 536.
[27]Parton, II, 569.
[28]This story was published by Mr. Lacock in 1828. Decatur was killed in a duel the following year and apparently left no record of the incident. In a campaign letter in 1827 Jackson made a guarded allusion to his conduct in Washington on this occasion, which is not, however, sufficiently explicit to form a basis for contradicting the Lacock story (Parton, II, 569-71).
[29]Adams, IV, 243.

CHAPTER XIX

[1]Jackson to Robert Butler, December 31, 1815, *Correspondence*, II, 223.
[2]Jackson to Andrew Jackson, junior, October 23, 1834, *ibid.*, V, 302.
[3]Parton, II, 644.
[4]The house here described is not to be confused with the Hermitage of to-day, which was built in 1834 and '35. The first house was begun in 1818 and occupied in that year or early in 1819. In 1831 it was extensively remodeled, along the lines of the present structure, erected three years later when a fire had left little except the walls of the original standing.
[5]John Jackson to Andrew Jackson, April 30, 1819, Library of Congress.
[6]John H. DeWitt, "Andrew Jackson and his Ward Andrew Jackson Hutchings," *Tennessee Historical Magazine*, series II, Vol. I, No. 2.
[7]February 27, 1821, Library of Congress.
[8]March 4, 1821, *ibid.*
[9]March 23, 1821, *ibid.*
[10]Rachel Jackson to R. E. W. Earle, February 23, 1819, *ibid.*
[11]*Ibid.*
[12]July 3, 1819, Library of Congress.
[13]Jackson vs. Kerzee, *et al.* Section A, Bin 9, State Supreme Court Records, 1819, Nashville.
[14]It appears from one paper bearing Jackson's money accounts that in the twelve months ending March 31, 1819, his Alabama investments absorbed more than six thousand dollars (*Correspondence*, II, 412).
[15]Thomas Perkins Abernethy, "Andrew Jackson and Southwestern Democracy," *American Historical Review*, XXXIII, p. 67.
[16]Jackson to James Gadsden, August 1, 1819, *Correspondence*, II, 421.
[17]November 6, 1819, *ibid.*, II, 439.
[18]James Houston to Jackson, September 24 and November 17, 1819, *ibid.*, II, 430 and 440.
[19]November 21, 1819, *ibid.*, II, 440.
[20]December 10, 1819, *ibid.*, II, 447.
[21]To Calhoun, January 10, 1820, *ibid.*, III, 2.
[22]To Jackson, January 23, 1820, *ibid.*, III, 12. Jackson's letter to Calhoun is not available, but the Secretary's reply reveals its substance.

[23]Jackson to James C. Bronaugh, February 12, 1820, *ibid.*, III, 14.
[24]Adams, IV, 76.
[25]Eaton to Jackson, March 9, 1821, Library of Congress.
[26]Jackson to Coffee, March 1, 1821, *Correspondence*, III, 39.
[27]Jackson to James C. Bronaugh, February 11, 1821, *ibid.*, III, 39.
[28]To Monroe, February 11, 1821, *ibid.*, III, 38.
[29]Jackson to Coffee, *op. cit.*
[30]Andrew Jackson in account with S. W. Stout & Company of Nashville, April 14, 1821, *Correspondence*, III, 48.
[31]Rachel Jackson to Eliza Kingsley, April 27, 1821, Parton, II, 595. I have not encountered the original of this letter, the orthography and grammar of which is here reproduced as rectified by Mr. Parton or some other copyist. The same applies to the other letters of Mrs. Jackson to Mrs. Kingsley quoted in this chapter.
[32]To Eliza Kingsley, June 21, 1821, *ibid.*, II, 597.
[33]Jackson to Andrew Jackson Donelson, March 31, 1821, *Correspondence*, III, 46.
[34]To Coffee, May 11, 1821, *ibid.*, III, 55.
[35]*Ibid.*
[36]*Ibid.*
[37]To Calhoun, May 22, 1821, *ibid.*, III, 59.
[38]Order and postscript as they appear in Jackson's Letter Book are in *Correspondence*, III, 62. The copy in Parton, II, 590, has been extensively altered.
[39]To Eliza Kingsley, July 23, 1821, Parton, II, 603.
[40]*Ibid.*
[41]*Ibid.*
[42]To Andrew Jackson Donelson, July 3, 1821, *Correspondence*, III, 87.
[43]To Calhoun, May 22, 1821, *ibid.*, III, 58.
[44]June 9, 1821, *ibid.*, III, 65.
[45]June 19, 1821, *ibid.*, III, 71.
[46]July 15, 1821, *ibid.*, III, 104.
[47]June 20, 1821, *ibid.*, III, 72.
[48]July 14, 1821, *ibid.*, III, 89.
[49]To Eliza Kingsley, July 21, 1821, Parton, II, 603.
[50]July 16, 1821, *Correspondence*, III, 104.
[51]Rachel Jackson to Eliza Kingsley, *op. cit.*

CHAPTER XX

[1]*American State Papers, Foreign Relations*, IV, 751.
[2]To Eliza Kingsley, July 23, 1821, Parton, II, 606.
[3]*Ibid.*
[4]Narrative of H. M. Brackenridge, Alcalde of Pensacola, Parton, II, 614.
[5]August 3, 1821, *Correspondence*, III, 111.
[6]The firm name was then Panton, Leslie & Company. McGillivray was buried on Panton's estate.

[7]H. M. Brackenridge to Jackson, August 24, 1821, *American State Papers, Miscellaneous*, II, 811; affidavit of Brackenridge, October 21, 1821, *ibid.*, 829.

[8]James C. Bronaugh to Jackson, August 23, 1821, *Correspondence*, III, 112; affidavit of Brackenridge, October 21, 1821, *American State Papers, Miscellaneous*, II, 829.

[9]*Ibid.*

[10]Dated August 22, 1821, *ibid.*, 805.

[11]Affidavit of Brackenridge, *op. cit.*

[12]Minutes of Callava's examination, *Correspondence*, III, 113.

[13]*Ibid.*

[14]Affidavit of J. C. Connor, September 22, 1821, *American State Papers, Miscellaneous*, II, 825; affidavit of Brackenridge, October 21, 1821, *ibid.*, 830.

[15]The Vidal case was thrown into the courts where it had a long career. What, if anything, the heirs ultimately received from Innerarity does not appear in such records as are included in the *State Papers*. Court records at Mobile or Pensacola should show this, however. Parton's assertion (II, 639) that the estate was found to owe Forbes & Company one hundred and fifty-seven dollars seems incorrect. This was the decision of a court at Mobile which did not, however, mark the end of the litigation. See Bassett, I, 309.

[16]August 26, 1821, *Correspondence*, III, 115. Apparently in an effort to improve the appearance of the record, Fromentin on October third wrote Jackson two letters in which he gave his own version of the interview. Jackson flung back challenging answers (*American State Papers, Miscellaneous*, II, 820). A question of veracity between these men should not be difficult to decide.

[17]*American State Papers, Foreign Relations*, IV, 768. My characterization of Callava's account is based on a comparison with the reports of Jackson and his subordinates covering the same incidents. Parton pays considerable attention to Callava's story, and through him it has colored several subsequent accounts.

[18]To an unidentified correspondent, September 24, 1821, Chamberlain Manuscripts, Boston Public Library.

[19]*Correspondence*, III, 122.

[20]From John C. Mitchell, October 24, 1821, Library of Congress.

[21]To Richard K. Call, November 15, 1821, *Correspondence*, III, 131.

[22]Bill of S. Seignouret, May 16, 1821, Jackson Papers, Library of Congress.

[23]Bill of A. H. Inskeep & Company, New Orleans, May 16, 1821, *ibid.*

[24]February 9, 1821, *ibid.*

[25]To James Gadsden, May 2, 1822, *Correspondence*, III, 161.

[26]To Andrew Jackson Donelson, April 16, 1820, *ibid.*, III, 21.

[27]March 21, 1822, *ibid.*, III, 156.

[28]Parton, II, 354.

[29]November 15, 1821, *Correspondence*, III, 130.

[30] Jackson to James Gadsden, May 2, 1822, *ibid.*, III, 160.
[31] To Jackson, October 29, 1821, Library of Congress.
[32] December 11, 1821, *ibid.*
[33] To James Gadsden, December 6, 1821, *Correspondence*, III, 140.

BIBLIOGRAPHY

BIBLIOGRAPHY

[In the following lists appear the full title of sources and authorities referred to in the text and notes of this volume. It is not a complete roster of sources read or consulted, and omits a few works which, though not directly cited or quoted, were extremely helpful These, with other light on sources, appear in the remarks entitled "Personal Acknowledgments."]

MANUSCRIPT SOURCES

PUBLIC COLLECTIONS

Alabama State Library, Montgomery, Pickett Manuscripts.

Boston Public Library, Chamberlain Manuscripts.

Davidson County (Tennessee) court, marriage and land records.

Harvard University, Museum of Comparative Zoology, Journal of J. J. Audubon.

Knox County (Tennessee) court records.

Lancaster County (South Carolina) land records and wills.

Lawson-McGhee Library, Knoxville, miscellaneous manuscripts.

Library of Congress, Washington, Jackson Papers. This is the largest and most notable collection of Jackson manuscripts in existence, numbering approximately forty thousand items of which about twenty thousand pertain to the period covered by this volume.

Louisiana State Museum, New Orleans, miscellaneous manuscripts.

Mecklenburg County (North Carolina) land records and wills.

Mercer County (Kentucky) court and marriage records.

New York Public Library, Lewis Manuscripts, a collection of more than two hundred items, only a few of which, however, bear on the period treated by this book.

North Carolina Historical Commission, Raleigh, Walter Clark and Swain Manuscripts.

North Carolina, office of Secretary of State, colonial land grant records.

Rosenberg Library, Galveston, Texas, Laffite Manuscript.

Rowan County (North Carolina) court records.

South Carolina, Historical Commission of, Columbia, Revolutionary Accounts and the Journal of His Majesty's Council for South Carolin and miscellaneous manuscripts. These papers are indispensable to an understanding of the environment of Jackson's youth.

Tennessee Historical Society, Nashville. This society's collection of Jackson papers and those of his contemporaries contains perhaps six hundred manuscripts and is second in importance to that in the Library of Congress.

Tennessee State Library, Nashville, miscellaneous manuscripts.

Tennessee State Supreme Court records, Nashville.

United States District Court records, New Orleans.

Washington County (Tennessee) records, Jonesboro.

Wisconsin, State Historical Society of, Madison, Draper Manuscripts.

PRIVATE COLLECTIONS

Oliver R. Barrett, Chicago.

Bibliotheca Parsoniana (collection of Edward A. Parsons), New Orleans.

Thompson D. Dimitry, New Orleans.

William M. Hall, Memphis.

S. P. Hessel, Woodmere, New York.

Emil Edward Hurja, New York City.

Mrs. Charles R. Hyde, Chattanooga.

Andrew Jackson IV, Los Angeles.

Albert Lieutaud, New Orleans.

Thomas F. Madigan, New York City.

Miss Ethel Morse, Tampa, Florida.

Alexander S. Salley, junior, Columbia, South Carolina.

PRINTED SOURCES

Thomas Perkins Abernethy, "Andrew Jackson and Southwestern Democracy," *American Historical Review*, XXXIII.

——, *From Frontier to Plantation in Tennessee* (1932).

Acts Passed at a General Assembly of Virginia (1790). *Re* Robards divorce.

Henry Adams, *History of the United States* (1889-1911).

Susan Smart Alexander, reminiscences of Andrew Jackson, *National Intelligencer*, August 1 and August 29, 1845.

John Allison, *Dropped Stitches in Tennessee History* (1897).

American Historical Magazine, V, contains affidavit of Andrew Greer, *re* Jackson-Sevier encounter; VIII, indictment in case with which Jackson was connected in November, 1788.

American State Papers, Foreign Relations.

American State Papers, Indian Affairs.

American State Papers, Military Affairs.

American State Papers, Miscellaneous.

Douglas Anderson, "Andrew Jackson, Frontier Merchant," Nashville *Tennessean,* April 13, 1929.

James Douglas Anderson, *Making of the American Thoroughbred* (1916).

James L. Armstrong, *General Jackson's Juvenile Indiscretions* (1832).

John Spencer Bassett, editor, *Correspondence of Andrew Jackson* (1926–33).

——, *Life of Andrew Jackson* (1911).

Thomas Hart Benton, *Thirty Years' View* (1854).

Albert J. Beveridge, *Life of John Marshall* (1916–19).

Biographical Dictionary of the American Congress.

Augustus C. Buell, *A History of Andrew Jackson* (1904).

Mary French Caldwell, "Massacres in this Section," Nashville *Tennessean,* August 30, 1931.

Richard L. Campbell, *Historical Sketches of Colonial Florida* (1892).

Charleston (South Carolina) *City Gazette and Commercial Daily Advertiser,* March 27, 1815. Colonel William Richardson Davie's statement about Jackson's birthplace.

Charleston (South Carolina) *Courier,* November 24, 1814. Letter signed "K" about Jackson's birthplace.

W. W. Clayton, *History of Davidson County, Tennessee* (1886).

H. E. Coffey, reminiscences of the Waxhaws, Rock Hill (South Carolina) *Record,* August 19, 1920.

Columbian Centinel (Boston), September 10, 1814. Attitude of the East toward the war with England; January 28, 1815, news of the December 24 attack on New Orleans reaches New England.

Congressional Record, discussions about Jackson's birthplace, February 23, 1922; June 18, 1926; May 24, 1928; July 2, 1928.

David Crockett, *Life of David Crockett* (reprint of 1865).

Daughters of the American Revolution Magazine, November, 1920. Arrival of the Crawford brothers in the Waxhaws.

Matthew L. Davis, *Memoirs of Aaron Burr* (1837).

John H. DeWitt, "Andrew Jackson and His Ward Andrew Jackson Hutchings," *Tennessee Historical Magazine,* Series II, Vol. I, No. 2.

——, editor, "Journal of John Sevier," *Tennessee Historical Magazine,* VI.

East Tennessee Historical Society's Publications.

John Henry Eaton, *Life of Andrew Jackson* (1824).

——and John Reid, *Life of Andrew Jackson* (1817).

T. D. Faulkner, reminiscence of Jackson's father, reprinted in the Fort Mill (South Carolina) *Times*, October 8, 1931.

Sidney George Fisher, *Men, Women & Manners in Colonial Times* (1898).

Friend of the Laws (New Orleans).

Charles E. Gayarré, *History of Louisiana* (1866).

[George Robert Gleig] *A Narrative of the British Campaigns against Washington, Baltimore and New Orleans* (1821).

Jo C. Guild, *Old Times in Tennessee* (1878).

Gulf States Historical Magazine.

Margaret B. Hamer, "John Rhea of Tennessee," *East Tennessee Historical Society's Publications*, January 3, 1932.

John Haywood, *Civil and Political History of the State of Tennessee* [1823] (reprint of 1915).

S. G. Heiskell, *Andrew Jackson and Early Tennessee History* (1920–21).

Archibald Henderson, article about Jackson's birthplace, Raleigh (North Carolina) *News and Observer*, October 3, 1926; "Jackson's Loose Living Common Sin of the Period," *News and Observer*, October 17, 1926.

George Howe, D.D., *History of the Presbyterian Church in South Carolina* (1870).

Impartial Review and Cumberland Repository (Nashville), files for 1806 and 1807 consulted re Burr conspiracy, Dickinson duel and other matters.

John B. Irving, *The South Carolina Jockey Club* (1857).

Reverend Hugh Parks Jackson, *Genealogy of the Jackson Family* (1890).

Marquis James, "Napoleon, Junior," *The American Legion Monthly*, III, No. 4. Account of Laffite's rôle in New Orleans campaign.

William James, *Military Occurrences of the Late War between Great Britain and the United States* (1818).

Amos Kendall, *Life of Andrew Jackson* (1843).

Kentucky *Gazette* (Lexington), 1790 to 1793, re Robards divorce.

Grace King, *Creole Families of New Orleans* (1922).

Knoxville *Gazette*, September 14, 1793. An article on Indian warfare in vicinity of Knoxville; July 27, 1803, Jackson's exposé of Sevier's North Carolina land fraud.

Knoxville *Sentinel*, November 26, 1922. Statement of James Payne Green on Jackson's marriage in Natchez.

Major A. Lacarrière Latour, *Historical Memoir of the War in the West* (1816).

La Courrière de la Louisiane (New Orleans).

Charles Edward Lester [and Sam Houston], *Life of Sam Houston* (1855).

Letters of General Adair and General Jackson, published at Lexington, Kentucky, in 1817.

Louisiana *Gazette*, various dates in 1814 and 1815.

Louisiana Historical Quarterly, VI. Grace King's translation of Bernard Marigny's pamphlet on the New Orleans campaign.

Edward Deering Mansfield, *Life of General Winfield Scott* (1848).

François-Xavier Martin, *History of Louisiana* (reprint of 1882).

John Bach McMaster, *History of the People of the United States* (1883–1906).

Mississippi Valley Historical Review.

John W. Monette, *History of the Discovery and Settlement of the Valley of the Mississippi* (1846).

Samuel Eliot Morison, *Life and Letters of Harrison Gray Otis* (1913).

Niles's *Weekly Register.*

Vincent Nolte, *Fifty Years in Two Hemispheres* (1854).

North Carolina Argus (Wadesboro), September 23, 1858. First publication of the famous "Walkup evidence," relating to Jackson's birthplace. Reprints appear in the *North Carolina University Magazine*, X, and the *Congressional Record*, June 18, 1926, pp. 11535–40.

W. G. Orr, memoir of Wetherford's surrender, *Publication of Alabama Historical Society*, II, 57.

James Parton, *A Life of Andrew Jackson* (1859–60).

Albert James Pickett, *History of Alabama* (reprint of 1896).

Publications of Alabama Historical Society.

A. W. Putnam, *History of Middle Tennessee* (1859).

David Ramsey, M.D., *History of South Carolina* (1809).

J. G. M. Ramsay, *Annals of Tennessee* (1853).

James B. Ranck, "Andrew Jackson and the Burr Conspiracy," *Tennessee Historical Society Magazine*, October, 1930.

John Reid and John Henry Eaton, *Life of Andrew Jackson* (1817).

Charles C. Royce, "The Cherokee Nation of Indians," *Fifth Annual Report*, Bureau of American Ethnology (1887).

Charles C. Royce and Cyrus Thomas, "Indian Land Cessions," *Eighteenth Annual Report*, Bureau of American Ethnology.

A. S. Sailey, junior, *The Boundary Line between North Carolina and South Carolina* (1929).

William L. Saunders, editor, *Colonial Records of North Carolina* (1887).

Johann David Schoepf, *Travels in the Confederation* (1785, English translation 1911).

Senate Report 1527, 71st Congress, 3rd Session.

W. H. Sparks, *The Memories of Fifty Years* (1870).

State Records of North Carolina.

Lieutenant-Colonel [Banastre] Tarleton, *Campaign of 1780–1781 in the Southern Provinces* (1787).

Major Howell Tatum, "Topographical Notes and Observations on the Alabama River, August, 1814," *Publications of the Alabama Historical Society*, II.

——"Major Howell Tatum's Journal," *Smith College Studies in History*, VII.

Cyrus Thomas and Charles C. Royce, "Indian Land Cessions," *Eighteenth Annual Report*, Bureau of American Ethnology.

Major Ben Truman, *Field of Honor* (1884).

United States Telegraph (Washington, D. C.), June 22, 1827, article answering attack on character of Mrs. Jackson; March 28, 1828, statement of Thomas Crutcher.

Virginia House Journal (1790). Re Robards divorce.

Virginia Senate Journal (1790). Re Robards divorce.

S. Putnam Waldo, *Memoirs of Andrew Jackson* (1819).

Alexander Walker, *Jackson and New Orleans* (1856).

S. H. Walkup, *North Carolina University Magazine*, X, 225. An article on Jackson's birthplace. Reprinted in *Congressional Record*, June 18, 1926. Originally appeared in *North Carolina Argus* (Wadesboro), September 23, 1858.

Charles Warren, *Jacobin and Junto* (1931).

Thomas E. Watson, *Life of Andrew Jackson* (1912).

Yorkville Enquirer (York, South Carolina), April 14, 1931. An article about grave of Jackson's father.

PERSONAL ACKNOWLEDGMENTS

PERSONAL ACKNOWLEDGMENTS

CARLYLE observed of biography that a well written life is almost as rare as a well spent one. If this narrative shall be received as a partial exception to the first case the circumstance is due in considerable measure to the good companions, casual and constant, who have attended the biographer during his years of labor.

This book would not be finished now, possibly would not have been finished at all, and in any event would have been more deficient in merit than it is, had it not been for the unfailing collaboration of my wife, Bessie Rowland James. To assist me she laid aside important and engaging researches of her own, for a life of Anne Royall. In connection with this book of mine much of her work has integrated itself with the whole so as to leave no distinctive impress, though if it were absent the finished product would be measurably poorer. But much of her work is of the positive kind that bears its own banner.

David Laurance Chambers of Indianapolis is another who has traveled the long road which had its beginning when a few stray discoveries in the course of research for *The Raven* determined the undertaking of this study. Though Laurance Chambers is the head of the Trade Department of the publishing house whose mark this volume bears I have fallen into the habit of regarding him more particularly as a keen, critical and useful student of Americana, who, very fortunately for me, appreciates the material problems arising from a task of historical inquiry of this stamp.

The present volume is derived from contemporary sources almost entirely and benefits by the scrutiny of a large body of manuscript not previously consulted by a biographer of General Jackson, or, indeed, for any historical purpose. Some of these papers have turned up in strange places, as one cache aggregating more than twelve hundred letters and documents, especially culled for their biographical value, that was found in Massachusetts, not more than a three hours' journey from Northampton where the late John Spencer Bassett labored the greater part of a lifetime to perfect his knowledge of Andrew Jackson.

While occupied chiefly with manuscripts the author has paid careful attention to published sources and has profited by the learning of those who have been over the ground before him. They comprise a numerous company, for of the presidents only the names of Washington and Lincoln appear more often on the printed page. From the bulk of this material the task of weeding the important from the unimportant is not, however, as serious as one might suppose. As those who have read the preceding pages may remember, the first biography of Jackson was begun by John Reid, completed by John Henry Eaton and published in 1817. As a contemporary account it is valuable and no subsequent biographer of Jackson has been able to ignore it. The present writer has obtained a little deeper insight into the historical method of Reid than appears on the printed page from a perusal of two copies of his manuscript, one at the Tennessee Historical Society in Nashville and the other, which is a later draft, among the "find" of twelve hundred Jackson papers above referred to, which within the past year have been acquired by the Library of Congress.

The next biography of significance is the unfinished one by Amos Kendall, a Kentucky editor who became an auditor in the Treasury Department and a member of the "Kitchen Cabinet" during the Jackson Administrations. In 1842 Jackson turned over to Kendall a great many of his papers. The following year seven parts of a projected fifteen-part life were published. The financial returns were not what the author had expected, Kendall became associated with Morse in the sale of stock in his telegraph company and the biography was neglected.

Jackson was not very well satisfied with what Kendall had written, and before his death in 1845 Old Hickory directed Kendall to turn over the papers to Francis Preston Blair, who had been editor of the *Globe*, the Jackson organ at Washington. Blair wished George Bancroft to write a life of Jackson. Kendall relinquished a few of the Jackson papers, but kept the more vital ones, and relations between him and Blair became strained. In 1857 James Parton appeared on the scene and began his energetic researches. Blair gave him some assistance and Kendall gave him some, but without disclosing the contents of the most important part of the General's papers which he still retained. Parton was a man of too independent mind to gain the complete confidence of either of these uncritical Jackson partizans. Parton's first volume appeared in 1859, his other two in 1860. Their success with the public was instantaneous, and despite the flood of Jacksoniana that has appeared since, this popular attachment continues. At the time many of the General's old friends and admirers, including Blair, were not so well pleased, however.

The mantle of this displeasure has descended to several authoritative and precise historians of the present day who are at pains to point out that Mr. Parton was an indifferent and superficial historian with a faulty comprehension of the underlying historical forces of the period. Therefore the background before which he causes Jackson to move is defective, sometimes to an extreme degree, and the likeness of the central character thus contrived, however entertaining, is not always an accurate or properly proportioned portrait.

These criticisms are true and they are important, but not all-important. The fact remains that *a man* walks through the numerous pages of Mr Parton, and that man, in the main, is Andrew Jackson, whom the reader comes to know as he knows a friend or neighbor. Such is James Parton's contribution to our knowledge of Jackson and to the art of American biography; and it is the secret of his enduring popularity. Biography is not history in the general sense. It is a more personal and individual thing, and more difficult to do well. Yet in this country biography has been regarded as a sort of bi-product of history, rather than the cellular life of the same. The spotlight must ever be on the central character. Background must remain background and by selection and emphasis be kept from swamping the man we are trying to tell about. This is the salient contribution that "moderns," for all their general lack of scholarship and disinclination toward serious or laborious research, have brought to this branch of letters—and I am unable to except some of the "debunking" brethren, their keyhole views of creation and original ideas of taste notwithstanding.

Parton ever dogged the man, Jackson. He is the only biographer of the General (excepting the one who now bores you) to visit practically every place that Jackson visited, absorb something of its local flavor and dig for his materials on the spot. Parton began these travels only twelve years after his subject had been laid to rest in the Hermitage garden. Persons who had known Andrew Jackson as a boy were still living. Everywhere he talked to those who had been Jackson's friends, foes and acquaintances and thus preserved a body of reminiscence and anecdote which but for him must have perished. Parton was superficial, he was hasty, undiscriminating, needlessly voluminous and often carried away merely by the picturesque—but he did preserve. It is easy to understand why written documents were a secondary consideration to this agile gatherer who had so many priceless living sources at his command. Instead of wishing too ardently that some one might have done this better than Parton we should be grateful that it was done at all.

The success of Parton's lively books was the death of Blair's ambition to induce Bancroft to immortalize his patron. Kendall's half-hearted determination to finish his work also faded, and when the ex-auditor died the Jackson papers in his possession passed to a daughter who stored them in a warehouse in Washington. Shortly thereafter this building burned and the papers were assumed to have been lost.

In 1882 Professor William G. Sumner of Yale published his *Andrew Jackson*, thus marking the singularly belated entry of scholarship into the populous field of Jacksonian biography. As a study of administrations of the seventh president this book is valuable. As a proportioned biography it lacks distinction. The first chapter carries Jackson to the age of forty-five, when the forces that formed his character had completed their work. It is impossible to understand the man and difficult to understand some of his official conduct without a more intimate view of the origin and play of those forces.

Dr. John Spencer Bassett of Smith College understood the shortcomings of his predecessors and, as the preface to his first edition indicates, sought to correct them by associating a human and personable Jackson, such as Parton recreated, with the proper historical environment. For the latter task he seemed eminently qualified. A scholar who derived his materials from original sources, he had an all-round knowledge of the Jackson period which no one to date has surpassed, though amplifications and corrections are possible. His two volumes appeared in 1911. Although the most valuable work on Jackson in existence, Dr. Bassett's books are rarely seen in the hands of the general reader, because, alas, as reading they are saltless fare. The author failed to impart the savor of life to his man. If Parton, in his researches, emphasized field work to the neglect of library work, Bassett reversed the order.

But in the cloister he was supreme and when the Carnegie Institution decided to publish six volumes of Jackson's correspondence there was no question but that the most competent hand for the task was John Spencer Bassett. The first of these volumes appeared in 1926. Dr. Bassett died in 1928 but the text, annotation and arrangement of the fourth, fifth and sixth volumes had been completed by him. The remaining work of preparing them for publication fell to Dr. J. Franklin Jameson, chief of the Division of Manuscripts of the Library of Congress. A seventh volume will be issued of selections from the twelve hundred manuscripts whose acquisition the Library announced in December, 1932. These comprise the bulk of the so-called "Kendall Papers" which, after all, had survived the Washington warehouse fire. By a fortunate turn of events the writer had been able to begin his study of them before their existence was known to the Library. After the purchase, and before they were made publicly available, Dr. Herbert Putnam, Librarian of Congress, and Dr. Jameson generously permitted me to complete my examination of them in Washington, so as not to delay the appearance of this volume.

Throughout my researches the valuable volumes of Bassett's *Correspondence of Andrew Jackson* have never been far from my side, but in justice to my own endeavors I will say that, within and somewhat beyond the scope of the present work, I have examined in the original manuscript nearly every document reproduced therein. In my "Notes" credit is given to the *Correspondence*, not only because it is owing to the labors of Dr. Bassett, but for the convenience of those who may wish to consult the full text of a given document. Space limitations prevented Dr. Bassett from publishing more than a selected part of the Jackson manuscripts available to him. He used his judgment in eliminating what seemed to him unessential. A desire to make decisions on this head for myself induced me to go over collections in the wake of the editor. It has not been altogether unprofitable work. Nothing I can say would liquidate my debt to this scholar, yet I have found many documents omitted or condensed by him that seem to me to be useful in an interpretation of Andrew Jackson.

And I suppose that I might as well confess a certain predilection for work among manuscripts. They convey something, some essence, that is lost in the transition to type. For the same reason I like to visit places that one time or another have been the environment of my man. The opportunities that were Parton's of course are not mine. But it is possible by the study of old maps, deeds, wills, court records and general accumulated memorabilia fairly to reconstruct the past. Concerning the military operations about New Orleans, for example, I first wrote or sketched out, largely from contemporary sources, a full story of the campaign, and then pared it down to the requirements of biography, which I repeat are not synonymous with those of history. Incidentally a general is often one of the hardest men in an army to follow through a battle, and I think this was especially true of Jackson.

After more than a year of library work a sense of duty took Mrs. James and myself to the Carolinas. Really I did not expect to find much that would be new or of value, and was prepared to remain only a few days. I remained six weeks, and had not so many kindly and competent assistants sprung up in my path my stay would have been longer. The result is a rather fresh picture of the youthful Andrew. I am especially indebted to Alexander S. Salley, junior, of Columbia, for twenty-seven years secretary of the Historical Commission of South Carolina, and to A. R. Newsome, of Raleigh, secretary of the North Carolina Historical Commission. In my opinion these gentlemen know the source materials and the histories of their native commonwealths as well as any one knows them. After pointing the way to invaluable data they were good enough to read the manuscript of the first three chapters of this book. Inasmuch as that is still a controversial subject in those parts, and some others, I may say that neither expressed dissatisfaction with the accuracy of my conclusions as to the birthplace of the subject of this memoir. For other assistance in these early stages of the work I am indebted to A. E. Hutchison, Mrs. Anne Hutchison Bigger and Dr. William A. Pressly of Rock Hill, and to William R. Bradford of Fort Mill, South Carolina; to Miss Katherine Hoskins of Summerfield, Walter Murphy of Salisbury and Mrs. Lindsay Patterson of Winston-Salem, North Carolina; to G. Walter Barr of Keokuk, Iowa, and to Miss Queena Pollack, of Philadelphia.

Moving across the Blue Ridge the canvas enlarges. The young solicitor becomes a chip on the eddy of big events, and I find in the recapitulation which I have passed off as a "Bibliography" of this volume no mention of Frederick J. Turner's *Rise of the New West* and *Frontier in American History.* These books formed the framework of my understanding of the frontier, though devotees will perceive the extent of some of my departures from the doctrine of the essential democracy of the border. I discover that Edward Channing's *History of the United States* is not acknowledged. On this work I relied for the general pattern of national affairs for the period covered by this narrative, irrespective of certain departures, especially with respect to the attitude of New England during the War of 1812. I also profited by my readings of Schouler and Von Holst, likewise unmentioned elsewhere.

Judge John H. DeWitt, of Nashville, president of the Tennessee Historical Society and himself a fine critical historian was an unfailing friend and counselor during the long and pleasant course of my work in Tennessee, and in the end he read in manuscript Chapters IV to VIII of this book. I am also particularly obligated to Miss Mary U. Rothrock and her amiable colleagues of the Lawson-McGhee Library at Knoxville, which was my headquarters for two months. When I think back on places like this and like Dr. Paul DeWitt's lodge on the Cumberland and the Pflanze's hotel at Montvale Springs in the Big Smokies I do not regret that I still have a volume on Jackson to write.

I am indebted to Mrs. Samuel G. Heiskell of Knoxville, widow of the author of *Andrew Jackson and Early Tennessee History,* which is a veritable mine of material not to be found elsewhere. Mrs. Heiskell gave me the freedom of her husband's papers. I am indebted to Mrs. John Trotwood Moore of Nashville, State Librarian and Archivist of Tennessee, and to my friend George Fort Milton of Chattanooga, who interrupted his labors on a life of Stephen A. Douglas to lend a helping hand. I also express my gratitude to P. E. Cox, Mrs. Elsie W. Stokes, Miss Alice Stockell, Reau E. Folk, Mrs. Mary French Caldwell and William Henry Morgan of Nashville; to James Douglas Anderson of Madison, Tennessee; to John Jennings, junior, Knoxville, and Professor P. M. Hamer of the University of Tennessee, Knoxville; to Mrs. L. W. McCown of Johnson City, to Hugh L. Taylor of Elizabethton, and to the owners of privately owned manuscripts, in Tennessee and elsewhere, whose names are recorded under "Bibliography." Later it will be a pleasure to acknowledge the donors of material which does not fall within the compass of this book.

Andrew Jackson IV of Los Angeles is the grandson of Andrew Jackson, junior, nephew and adopted son of General Jackson. Several years ago he placed in my hands copies of a hundred or more manuscripts for use in this book. My account of the ancestry of Rachel Jackson is based on researches among Maryland and Virginia archives by a grand-niece, Miss Butler Chancellor of Washington. My narrative of the early years of the Donelson family in Kentucky and Tennessee is derived largely from the unpublished researches of Dr. William A. Provine, of Nashville, secretary of the Tennessee Historical Society. Miss Elizabeth Pickett of Montgomery, a granddaughter of Albert James Pickett, the Alabama historian, examined for me the Pickett Papers in the Alabama State Library. I have also profited by the assistance of Captain Samuel A. Greenwell of the office of the Chief of Staff of the Army, Judge E. J. Van Court of Eufaula, Oklahoma, Edward Caffery of San José, Costa Rica, Mrs. Julia Welder of Liberty, Texas, William MacLean of Larchmont, New York, and Emil Edward Hurja, Frank L. Jones and David Kirchenbaum of New York City. I call myself fortunate for having been able to induce Lowell L. Balcom of Norwalk, Connecticut, to execute the maps that appear in these pages.

New Orleans has been a pleasant place as long as I have known it, that is to say since 1913 when James Evans Crown tried to teach me something about the profession of letters as practiced by his reporters on the *Item*. There were few journeymen journalists in my day who had not learned something from Jim Crown. To contemporaries of that spacious era I would report that Mr. Crown liked New Orleans too well to leave for long. In the same case is Stanley Clisby Arthur who, in the fulness of time, has become an authority on such matters as may be found in his book *Old Families of Louisiana*. Colonel Henry R. Richmond of the Regular service has been stationed in New Orleans for four years. Jackson's Louisiana campaign is his hobby. I am in the debt of Colonel Richmond for giving me the benefit of his tactical studies, to Mr. Arthur for leads on sources and to both for reading Chapters XII to XV. I wish to thank Miss Josie Cerf of the Louisiana State Museum for her courtesies and Edward A. Parsons for the use of his notable private library.

At the Library of Congress I have been much helped by the scholarship, counsel and general interest in my method and subject manifest by Dr. Thomas P. Martin, assistant chief of the Division of Manuscripts. I have also to thank Martin Arnold Roberts of the circulating division and nis assistant David C. Mearns for the investigations in my behalf they caused to be made at the Public Record Office in London. I am grateful to the memory of the late William A. Taylor of the American History Room of the New York Public Library, to the New York State Library at Albany and to my neighbor Mrs. Evelyn H. Allen and her assistant of the Free Library of Pleasantville, New York, who by their contacts with other institutions have demonstrated how greatly a small library can shorten the hours of labor involved in an undertaking of this nature.

Every student of American history owes a debt to William O. Lynch of Indiana University for his *Fifty Years of Party Warfare*. My obligations are somewhat greater. Professor Lynch read the whole of this book before publication, and his suggestions have added materially to its soundness.

M. J.

Pleasantville, New York,
January 12, 1933.

INDEX

INDEX

Barry, Dr. Redmond Dillon, 246.

Baton Rouge, Louisiana, 196, 213, 221, 224, 227, 281.

Bayou Pierre, Mississippi, 63; Jackson spends honeymoon at, 71; 146.

Beale, Captain, of Louisiana, 241, 261.

Bean, Russell, arrested by Jackson, 92; 97; marshal of Memphis, 331; 385.

Beasley, Major Daniel, 166.

Bell, Caroline S., 329.

Bell, Hugh F., 61.

Belluché, Captain, 229.

Benton, Jesse, 160, 161; pistol fight with Jackson, 162.

Benton, Thomas Hart, 159, 160, 161; pistol fight with Jackson, 162; 332.

Betty, mulatto maid, 341.

Bibbs, Governor, of Alabama, 309.

Big Warrior, Creek chief, 189.

Bissell, Captain, 134, 135.

Blackburn, John, 62.

Blakemore, George, 144.

Blanque, Jean, 204.

Bledsoe, Anthony, 66.

Blennerhasset, Harman, 132.

Blount, William, Governor of Territory south of River Ohio, 65; 73; Senator from Tennessee, 81; 82, 85; expelled from Senate, 87; 93, 95.

Blount, Willie, Governor of Tennessee, 151; recommends Jackson to War Department, 152; 153; commissions Jackson a major general, 154; 156; recommends retreat to Jackson in Creek campaign, 175; 180, 186, 192, 231.

Boggs, Davidson, & Company, of Philadelphia, 107.

Boleck, Creek chief, 311, 312, 313.

Bonaparte, Napoleon, 88, 102, 150. 192, 193, 199, 235, 247, 262, 313, 318.

Bordeaux, France, 198.

Bosley, Captain John, 60.

Boston, Massachusetts, 16, 193, 272.

Boundary dispute between North and South Carolina, 11, 12, 368.

Boyd, Mrs., friend of Elizabeth Jackson, 30.

Boyd, "King," Nashville tavern keeper, 50.

Boyd, William, 13.

Boykin, J., 370.

Brackenridge, Henry M., 349, 350, 352, 353.

Bradley, Ed, 153.

Breckenridge, James, 382.

British, in Waxhaws and South during Revolutionary War, 17, 18, 19, 20, 21, 22, 24, 25, 26, 29, 43; contemplate reconquest, 59; 73, 87, 109, 138; in Florida, 165, 187, 190, 191, 192; at Mobile, 194, 196; seek Laffite for ally. 197, 204; fail to take Fort Bowyer, 203; fleet advances on New Orleans, 208; defeated by Jackson at Pensacola, 211; advance on New Orleans, 213, 215, 217, 219, 223, 225, 226, 227, 232, 233; land below New Orleans, 235; first battle for New Orleans, 241; second battle, 250; battle of January 8, 1815, 260; 271, 272, 273, 277, 287, 289, 296, 298, 312, 348. See England.

Bronaugh, Dr. James, C., 328, 341, 343, 348, 350, 351, 356, 361.

Brooke, Colonel, 350, 351, 355.

Brown, Major General Jacob, 336, 339, 360.

Florida—*Continued*
chase offer by United States, 325;
Spain hesitates to sell, 332; Jackson's program for new invasion
of, 335; 336; Monroe names
Jackson governor of, 337; 341;
formally transferred to United
States, 344; 347, 349; Jackson
departs from, 355: 356.

Forbes & Co., Pensacola, 310, 312,
348; influence in Florida, 349.

Forbes, Colonel, 341.

Fort Barrancas, Florida, 195, 197,
211, 315, 334, 335, 353.

Fort Bowyer, Alabama, 194, 195,
200; besieged by British, 202;
208, 211, 213, 224, 227, 236;
captured by British, 276; 282.

Fort, Captain, 128, 129, 134.

Fort Deposit, Mississippi Territory,
167.

Fort Gadsden, Florida, 314.

Fort Jackson, Mississippi Territory,
182, 187.

Fort Massac, Ohio, 134.

Fort Mims, Mississippi Territory,
163, 164, 168, 182, 183.

Fort Patrick Henry, North Carolina, 52.

Fort Scott, Georgia, 309.

Fort St. Jean, Louisiana, 216, 217,
241.

Fort St. Michael, Florida, 210, 211.

Fort St. Philip, Louisiana, 224, 227.

Fort St. Rose, Florida, 210.

Fort Strother, Mississippi Territory,
168, 169, 171, 173, 176, 177,
180.

Fort Toulouse, 164, 182. See Fort
Jackson.

Foster, J., 62.

Fowltown, Georgia, 305.

Fraize, John, 38.

France, 60, 61, 84, 88, 89, 164, 165,
198, 199, 293.

Francis, Creek leader, 309, 310,
311.

Frankfort, Kentucky, 109, 131.

Franklin, Tennessee, 143, 159, 161,
297.

Friend of the Laws, 228.

Fromentin, Judge Eligius, 348, 350;
trouble with Jackson, 354, 355,
414; 361.

Frontier, in Pennsylvania, 3; in
North and South Carolina, 6, 7;
passing of Waxhaws, 15; 93, 94,
146, 300, 359.

Frost, William, 328.

Fullarat, Antoine, 352, 353.

Fulton, Robert, 206.

Gadsby's Hotel, Baltimore, 273.

Gadsden, Captain James, 319.

Gaines, Brigadier-General Edmund
P., president of Louaillier court
martial, 283; 288, 298, 299, 305,
306, 307; presides at court martial of Arbuthnot and Ambrister,
312; 316, 318.

Galbraith, Captain, 33.

Gallatin, Albert, 83.

Gallatin, Tennessee, 57.

Garçon, slave leader, 298.

Gates, General Horatio, 22, 23, 29.

George III, 35.

Georgetown, District of Columbia,
273.

Georgia, 19, 20, 41, 97, 108, 142,
151, 167, 189, 209, 289, 293,
298, 304, 307, 308, 309, 316,
322, 329, 360.

Ghent, Belgium, 209, 213, 232, 275,
278, 287, 298, 299, 322.

Gibbs, General, British Army, 263,
264, 265, 266.

Miró, Don Estéban—*Continued*
Spanish alliance with Cumberland settlers, 59, 60, 65; 87, 102, 165, 217.
Mississippi, 146, 227, 237, 240, 283, 323.
Mississippi Territory, 163, 167, 186.
Missouri Compromise, 357.
Mitchell, Major, British Army, 243.
Mitchell, Mark, 80, 283.
Mobile, Alabama, 109, 157, 167, 176, 189; Jackson defends, 194, 201; 207, 208, 209, 210, 211, 212, 213, 216, 221, 227, 275, 276, 289.
Monkey Simon, a jockey, 290.
Monroe, James, 141; Secretary of State, 151; Secretary of War, September, 1814, 208; 209; supports Jackson's expedition against Florida, 210; 211, 212, 213, 224; difficulty in financing War of 1812, 232; 245, 259, 268, 293; Aaron Burr's opinion of, 294; 296, 297; elected President. 1816, 299; 300, 302, 303, 304, 305, 306; Jackson's plan for seizure of Florida sent to, 307; "approval" of seizure, 208; 309; ready to disavow Jackson's acts in Florida, 315; suggests Jackson "correct" his Florida dispatches, 317; rebuffed, 319; 322, 323, 326; welcomed to Tennessee by Jackson, 330; 332; his insincerity toward Jackson, 336, 341, 355, 360; 336, 339, 346, 348, 354, 355; version of Rhea letter controversy, 409.
Montpelier, Alabama, 338, 339.
Moore, Colonel William, 40.
Morales, Don Juan Ventura, 217.
Morgan, Brigadier-General David, 260, 263; Jackson's anger over defeat at New Orleans, 267.

Morganton, North Carolina, 43, 44, 47.
Morrell, Jack, 134, 135.
Mountz, Lieutenant, at Pensacola, 351.
Murfreesborough, Tennessee, 187.

Nashville, 47; description of, in 1788 when Jackson arrived, 50; 57, 58, 60, 62, 63, 66, 69, 72, 73, 74, 78, 79, 94; described in 1804, 104; 109, 113, 114, 116, 117, 120, 122, 124, 127, 132, 133, 145, 152, 154, 156; Benton brothers fight with Jackson in, 160; after Creek campaign, Jackson's reception at, 185; 191, 231, 279; description of, in 1815, 287; 289, 292, 297, 307, 320, 328, 329, 330, 335, 337, 357; improvements in 1821, 358.
Nashville Bank, 143, 292, 301, 331.
Nashville Female Academy, 358.
Nashville *Gazette*, 224.
Nashville Inn, 105, 162, 358.
Nashville Jockey Club, 140, 153, 289.
Nassau, Bahamas, 310, 312, 313.
Natchez, Mississippi, 62, 63, 64, 67, 68, 69; Jackson escorts Rachel to, 70; 75, 77, 104, 151; encamps at, in 1813, 156, 157, 158; 159, 160, 173, 289, 358.
Natchez Trace, 67, 155.
Natchitoches, Louisiana, 131, 146.
National Intelligencer, Washington, D. C., 341, 355.
Neely, Alexander, 66.
Negro Fort, Florida, 298; blown up by General Gaines, 299, 309, 314. See Fort Gadsden.
Nesbit, Captain, Revolutionary soldier, 27.